CASES IN LABOR RELATIONS

CASES IN LABOR RELATIONS

Thomas Kennedy
Visiting Professor of Industrial Relations, Babson College
Professor Emeritus, Harvard Business School

John H. Stamm
Professor of Industrial Relations, Babson College
Lecturer, Harvard Trade Union Program

SHERBORN-EXETER
PUBLISHING COMPANY
PO Box 79, Wellesley, Massachusetts 02157

Case material is made possible by the cooperation of individuals and organizations who may wish to remain anonymous by having names, quantities, and other identifying details disguised while maintaining basic relationships. Cases are prepared as the basis for class discussion rather than to illustrate either effective or ineffective handling of administrative situations.

Library of Congress Catalog Card Number: 81-52246

International Standard Book Number: 0-940980-00-2

Printed in the United States of America

To Walter H. Carpenter
Teacher, Scholar, Colleague
and most importantly, Friend

PROFESSOR JOHN STAMM
BABSON COLLEGE
WELLESLEY, MASS. 02157

PREFACE

We have been designing, developing and teaching courses in labor relations for a combined total of over forty years. Time and again our experiences have convinced us that the most effective and sustained learning results from the rigorous use of cases and simulations drawn from actual situations. An effective real-world focus infuses the study of labor relations with the vitality, excitement and challenge which practioners find so appealing about the field. But cases and simulations do more than simply heighten student interest.

The challenge of confronting labor-management situations, of ferreting out the problems, some of which are not so obvious, and of making decisions regarding those problems engenders an improved student attitude toward acquiring knowledge. Learning has a purpose; knowledge is acquired actively rather than passively. Knowledge thus gained is more readily internalized and, as part of the students' experience, is retained far beyond the conclusion of a formal course of study. Students also develop skills in analyzing labor-management situations and they develop judgement in deciding upon purposeful courses of preventive as well as remedial action. With such pedagogical objectives in mind, it is our purpose in authoring this book to encourage the use of cases and simulations in the teaching of labor relations.

This case book represents our efforts to provide students and professors with the best contemporary collection of cases and simulations in the field of labor relations. We believe strongly that such material must be drawn from real life, from actual experiences, in order to be meaningful. In the majority of the cases students are placed in the role of the executive decision maker who confronted the actual situation as it evolved. Other cases require students to assume the perspective of the union leader involved or the arbitrator selected to decide an issue in dispute between the parties. Regardless of role or perspective, these cases emphasize decision making in actual labor relations situations.

In most instances the case material was developed with the active assistance and cooperation of an individual or individuals who actually participated in the labor dispute. In a few instances some or all of the material came directly from a court decision, an arbitration decision and/or other public sources. All but a few of the cases have been disguised; the names of the company, the union and individuals have been changed. However, we have been careful that these changes and any other alterations required to assure a disguise have not deminished the significance of the problems and issues inherent in the particular case. Nor have the changes interfered with the approaches which can be taken to find solutions to these problems. We have maintained the controversy of the issues and the need for rigorous analysis.

The cases included in this book were selected from among the many cases we have taught in classes at the Harvard Business School, The University of Michigan, Babson College and in executive development programs and seminars conducted in the United

States, Europe and Latin America. They have been used successfully in labor relations courses for both graduate students and upper-level undergraduate students; for executives (generalists as well as specialists in labor relations); and for trade union leaders. We have chosen those cases which have proven to be most valuable to these groups in the development of labor relations knowledge and decision-making skills. We have used these cases in conjunction with a variety of textbooks in the field and with selected readings in labor relations.

This book is comprised of seven sections. The major portion of the book involves disputes between management and labor in the private sector of the economy in the United States. We have devoted the first three sections to cases in all three phases of labor relations: organizing, contract negotiation and contract administration. Section I - Organization and Recognition, includes cases involving the unionization of professional and white collar employees as well as traditional blue collar unionization. In addition to representation cases we have also included a decertification election case in this section. In Section II - Contract Negotiation, we have included cases on negotiation strategy, tactics, legal requirements and two of the major negotiations in the U. S. economy. Section III - Contract Administration, contains twenty cases and deals with both the procedural and substantive aspects involvied with living under a collective bargaining agreement. Issues covered include: grievance procedures, arbitration, discipline, theft, wildcat strikes, bargaining unit work, promotion, layoffs, discrimination, wage levels, wage structures, job evaluation and pensions. A number of the cases in this section may be used for simulating a grievance hearing and/or for a mock arbitration.

Labor unions are among the least understood institutions in our economy. The significance of their internal problems, especially since the passage of the Landrum-Griffin Act in 1959, has had an impact upon labor relations. Section IV - Intra-Union Relationships, contains cases which deal with some of the internal problems faced by two of the largest unions in the United States.

Even though the major thrust of this book is concerned with problems between management and labor in the private sector, we decided it was important not to limit our selection to that sector of the economy. Because of the differences between the private and public sectors and the growing importance of collective bargaining in the public sector in the United States, we have included cases in that area in Section V - Public Sector Relationships. The cases cover collective bargaining by policemen, by firefighters and by federal employees at a military base.

Finally, because many U. S. firms now have operations in Europe and because it is frequently stated that we in the U. S. can learn much from examining the practice of labor relations in Europe, we have included cases from that area. Section VI - Foreign Labor Relations, contains cases situated in three European countries and a fourth case concerning a multinational corporation with headquarters in Europe.

Section VII - Negotiation Simulations, concludes the book with two current negotiating situations. These cases enable students to assume management and union roles and renegotiate the terms of an actual collective bargaining agreement. Additional information is available to professors regarding the design and conduct of the simulations.

Our thanks are extended to the many representatives of labor, management and the government who, by sharing their experiences and their time, have provided the substance of these cases and have made learning more meaningful.

We wish to thank the President and Fellows of Harvard College for permission to use cases under their copyright and to thank Audrey Barrett for her assistance in obtaining this permission.

The great majority of the cases were written or supervised by one or the other of the two authors. However, the following cases were written by other individuals: 1979 Automobile Negotiations by Richard O. von Wessowetz; Food Mart, Inc. by Charles Biderman and George C. Lodge; Gordon Paper Products Company by Robert McKersie and revised by William Fulmer; Hopedale Mining Company by C. C. Ellsworth; Southwestern Bell Telephone Company by David Keuchle and John S. Bartlett; The Washington Post by William Fulmer and Philip Lawrence; Wilmington Bureau of Fire by David Keuchle and David Condliffe; and Wilson Cement Block by David Keuchle. We are greatly indebted to the above persons for permitting us to reproduce their cases in this book.

We wish to thank three individuals, each of whom granted permission to use their original case as the basis for a new or revised case; Darcey Coyle for Adelphi Company; Harry T. Edwards for Johnson Chemical Company and Donald White for Jones Company.

A number of the cases, although produced under the supervision of Professor Kennedy, were written by others. These include: Border State Bus Company, UAW Public Review Board and Wilson Distributors written by Michael J. Jedel; Bouclier Copper written by Yaakov Keren; Norwell Air Force Base written by Major Earl Pontius and revised by Captain Doris R. Vail; Pickardt-Rhine International A.G. written by Leroy B. Fraser III; and Suburban Transit (A) and (C) and Tarbo Lumber Company written by Kimball Kehoe. We are indebted to each of these writers for their contributions.

We acknowledge the excellent work of Mary Jane Drinkwater in preparing the bulk of the manuscript for publication. Our book has benefited greatly from Sue Wetherill's good advice and her fine design and graphics work. The cooperation of the members of Babson's Word Processing Center, especially Jan Manter, Connie Stumph, Vickie Delbono and Carol Mc Carron, was greatly appreciated.

Lastly, we wish to thank the members of our families whose encouragement, aid and support was so essential to our successful completion of this work.

July 1981

Thomas Kennedy
John H. Stamm

CONTENTS

SECTION I

Organization and Recognition

VOLPE METAL PRODUCTS

Following graduation with a degree in metalurgical engineering from one of the country's leading engineering schools 20 years ago, Peter Volpe took a job as a customer service representative in the research department of a major steel company. Peter progressed very rapidly and came to be highly regarded by the steel company and many of its customers to whom he proved very helpful in solving difficult material and production problems. However, Peter was eager to have his own company and after 10 years, when the owner of a small machine company (50 employees) he had been servicing became seriously ill and had to retire, Peter saw his opportunity. His father-in-law, a successful general contractor, arranged the necessary bank financing and thus was born Volpe Metal Products.

Peter decided to spend most of his time and effort on the research and development area of the business. Eric Berg, who had been superintendent of production under the previous owner, was highly regarded by Peter and eventually promoted to Vice President of Manufacturing. The two of them made an excellent team. The company became known as a dependable supplier of special metal parts. In 10 years it grew from 50 to over 500 employees, including 40 in research and development.

One morning when Peter was driving to work he noticed several men and a woman at the plant gate passing out fliers. Peter took one as he drove in. He was surprised to find that it was an invitation to his employees to join a union, the International Metal Workers Union (IMWU). When he got to his office Eric was waiting for him.

Volpe: Eric what do you make of this? (holding up the flier)

Berg: First thing I knew about it was 15 minutes ago when I drove in. I've talked to the foremen. Bill Evans says he thinks its the work of the men in the forge room. You know they haven't been happy about the new incentive rates. Bill thinks a new man, Paul Berry, whom we hired down there may actually be an inside organizer.

Volpe: Isn't this the same union that organized Paul Brown's company a couple of years ago?

Berg: Yes, I think it is and they've had a lot of trouble.

Volpe: Well I guess we're babes in the woods when it comes to this business Eric. I'll call Paul and see if he has any advice for us.

Peter talked with his secretary and asked her to get Brown on the telephone. In a few minutes he was talking with him.

Brown: Pete, I'm glad you called. You know we're having a hell of a lot of trouble with that X-42 part you make for us. It just won't take the stress.

Volpe: Oh, I'm sure we got that licked, Paul. We're putting more alloy in it. It's really tough now. Jerry will bring some samples down in a few days. But I've got my own problem here, Paul, I need your advice. The IMWU is trying to organize us. Isn't that the outfit that organized your plant?

Brown: Yeah, that's our union. I've been wondering how long before they'd hit you guys.

Volpe: Well Eric and I don't know anything about this union business. They're out there now handing out literature and talking to our people as they come in. What can we do about it?

Brown: The most important advice I can give you Pete is to get a damn good labor lawyer. The biggest mistake we made here was relying on our regular law firm for advice and help in the beginning. You need an attorney who specializes in labor law. We use Joan Gould now, and if we had used her from the beginning we'd be a lot better off today. I'd recommend Joan, but there are several other good labor lawyers in town. The best thing you can do is hire one of them and follow their good advice. This labor law is a complicated and changing business. You can get burned plenty if you don't have good advice. The IMWU has expert lawyers and you'd better have one too. Why don't you call Joan Gould?

Peter took Brown's advice and called Joan Gould. They talked briefly on the phone and Gould agreed to meet with Peter and Eric at the plant the following morning.

Volpe: Well I guess you got one of their invitations to join on the way in. Some of the men told Eric they've also received letters at their homes and that the union is trying to get them to sign membership cards. We think they have an inside organizer by the name of Berry down in the forge room. Eric and I think we should get rid of him right away just to be sure. Can we do that under our New Jersey laws or do they have everything stacked against us? But we're here to listen so why don't you talk.

Gould: Actually the state law isn't involved here. There is a New Jersey Labor Relations Act, but that applies only to small companies involved only in intrastate business. I assume you do business with companies in other states and have gross sales of over $50,000.

Volpe: Oh yes, we do a lot more than $50,000 and we sell all over the country and in a number of foreign countries.

Gould: Then your labor relations comes under a federal law, the National Labor Relations Act (NLRA), which was passed in 1935 and was modified by the Taft Hartley Act in 1947, and the Landrum Griffin Act in 1959 plus a number of minor modifications.[1]

The NLRA is administered by the National Labor Relations Board (NLRB) which is an independent agency of the federal government. The agency has two separate parts - The Board and The General Counsel. The Board consists of five members who are appointed by the President with the consent of the Senate for staggered five-year terms. The Board functions like a court and hears unfair labor practice charges against employers and union. The General Counsel is also appointed by the President with the consent of the Senate but for a four year term. The General Counsel's office carries on all the investigatory and prosecutory activities of the agency and also supervises the 32 regional offices, each of which is headed by a Regional Director.

The agency's main functions are to deal with unfair labor practices (ULP) and hold elections to determine if employees desire to be represented by unions. Any person or group can file an unfair labor practice charge at any one of the regonal offices.[2] A board agent then investigates the charge and recommends either dismissal of the charge or the issuance of a ULP complaint. The Regional Director then reviews the recommendation and either dismisses the charge or issues a complaint. If a complaint is issued a formal hearing is held before an administrative law judge. A lawyer who represents the General Counsel presents the case against the party charged with the ULP. The administrative law judge renders a written decision including a remedy. Either side may appeal this decision to the Board in Washinton, and if either party is not satisfied with the Board's decision it can appeal to a federal court of appeals. In election cases the full Board in

[1]The National Labor Relations Act applies only to businesses whose labor problems may affect interstate commerce, but the term "interstate commerce" has been so broadly interpreted by the federal courts that many enterprises which think of themselves as "local business" are covered by the Act. However, the NLRB has set certain minimum size limitations below which it will not assert jursidiction: 1. Non-retail enterprises-$50,000 per year gross inflow or outflow of revenue; 2. Retail establishments-$500,000 per year gross business volume. (There are special limitations for office buildings, shopping centers, public utilities, newspapers, radio and T.V. stations, telephone companies, hotels and motels, transit systems, health care facilities and educational institutions.)

Since 1935 at least 17 states have passed state labor relations acts patterned after the NLRA, but applicable to enterprises which affect only intrastate commerce. Since 1959 the state labor relations boards may assume jurisdiction also over any labor dispute which the NLRB refuses to take under its minimum size rules.

[2]In fiscal 1979 a total of 41,259 unfair labor practice charges were filed with the Board. Of this total 29,028 charges were filed against employers, 12,218 charges were filed against unions and 13 charges were filed against employers and unions jointly.

Volpe: What do we do now?

Gould: Well, this is an entirely new ball game. Evidently they have more support then we suspected, but it doesn't mean we have to bargain. They may not have a majority signed up and even if they do they might not win an election. However, if you think they represent a majority of your employees and you want to bargain with them, you are legally free to voluntarily recognize the union and com mence bargaining.

Volpe: Well, I don't want to bargain with them unless I have to.

Gould: OK, then I'll prepare a letter for you to send to them in which you will say that you sincerely doubt they represent a majority. If the union believes it does represent a majority it can then ask the NLRB for an election. We'll have at least 30 days to carry on a campaign to convince the employees to vote for "no union". In the meantime if one of the union men should bring the cards to you don't look at them. If you check over them and find they do have a majority you may be required to bargain without an election.

The next day Volpe signed the letter which Gould had prepared and sent it to the union. Four days later he received a letter from the Regional Director of the NLRB informing him that the IMWU had filed a petition for representation accompanied by signed membership cards for what it claimed to be more than 30% of the company's employees. He stated the union had requested an election for the purpose of certification as the bargaining agent for all the production and maintenance employees, including the assistant foreman.

The next day Gould met again with Volpe and Berg.

Gould: In representation cases the Board requires a "showing of interest" by a union that it has cards signed by at least 30% of the employees in the proposed bargaining unit before it will consider an election. The purpose of this 30% rule is to prevent elections which the unions have no chance of winning. They must convince the Board that a sizeable group, at least 30%, want an election. Actually I know of no union that would ask for an election unless it had well over 50% of the employees signed up. One of the IMWU representatives once told me that they never ask unless they have at least 70%. But don't let that scare you. Despite the sign ups, unions lose over one-half of the elections.[4] A worker often signs a card to get the union off his back, then votes against it in the secret election.

[4]In fiscal year 1979 the NLRB conducted 8,043 conclusive representation elections in cases closed that year. 506,040 employees or 88% of those eligible voted. The average number of voters in an election was 63. Unions won 3,623 or 45% of the elections.

VOLPE METAL PRODUCTS

Volpe: Well, Eric and I are not convinced that a majority of our people want a union.

Gould: I'm not either, sometimes a union may be bluffing.

Volpe: Well what do we do about it?

Gould: Now you must be even more careful than before that none of your management or supervisory people promise or threaten the employees or take any other action that the NLRB could interpret as preventing a fair and free election. The filing of an election petition marks the beginning of what the NLRB considers to be the election process during which it insists that "laboratory conditions", that is, "conditions as nearly ideal as possible to determine the unihibited desires of the employees" be maintained. One of the first things to do is determine if we can reach agreement with the union on the bargaining unit.

Volpe: Joan, I don't want to sound stupid but what's a <u>bargaining unit.</u>

Gould: It's a legal term and consists of an identifiable and distinguishable group of employees that have the legal right as a group to determine in an election if they wish to be represented by a union. All employees in the bargaining unit are eligible to vote in the election, and if the union wins all employees in the bargaining unit will be represented by the union for collective bargaining purposes. Usually it consists of all the production and maintenance workers in a plant, in other words, an industrial unit. But it can consist of a smaller craft group such as your forge room employees or your electricians. There can also be multi-plant units, but we needn't be concerned about that, because you have only one plant.

Volpe: From what Eric tells me we'd probably lose an election in the forge room. Does that mean we'd have to bargain with the union for the forge workers even though the rest of the employees don't want a union?

Gould: It could, if the forge room employees were set up as a separate unit, but I don't think we'll have to worry about that. The IMWU is an industrial union, and they are likely to seek a plant-wide P&M unit.

Volpe: Who determines the bargaining unit?

Gould: If we can reach an agreement with the union, the Board will usually accept our wishes. However, if we can't agree with the union then the Board will make a decision after holding a unit determination hearing.

Volpe: Do they have some kind of a formula?

Gould: No, its done on a case by case basis and the Board has found it to be an elusive concept, but it has stated that in determining the appropriate bargaining unit it will be guided by such things as history, organization, interest of employees, and interchangeability of employees. A term frequently used by the Board in this respect is "community of interest." However, as I said before, I don't think we'll have any trouble agreeing on an industrial unit, that is, one which will include all the production and maintenance workers. That's what the union asked for both in their letter to you and in their petition to the Board. I suggest that I call up Ed Grannery, their International Representative, and tell him we're agreed on that.

Volpe: What about the chemists and other professionals out in the Lab? My guess is they'd all vote against the union. It would help our chances to win the election if we could get them into the unit.

Gould: Under Section 9(b)(1) of the NLRA if the Board establishes a unit in which both professionals and non-professionals are involved there would have to be an election among the professionals to determine if they wanted to be in the same unit as the other employees or have a separate unit. But, before we take action to try to get them in the unit, I think you'd better be sure you want them in. It's true that their votes might be enough to swing the election against the union. On the other hand if we were successful in getting them in the unit and the union won anyhow, would you be happy to have to bargain about wages, hours and other terms and conditions of employment for your chemists and engineers?

Volpe: I guess we better think that one over. Maybe we better not try to get the Lab in the unit.

Gould: We'll probably have some difficulties agreeing with the union regarding whether some of your foremen or assistant foreman should be in the unit, and also your guards.

Volpe: What do you mean, Joan? I just assumed the guards and foremen would not be in the union. Who is going to represent our interests around here if they all belong to the union? I want you to keep all of them out.

Gould: It isn't that simple. If the guards meet the NLRB's definition of a guard they won't be included in the unit and will not be allowed to vote in the election. But if they are really just watchmen and the union wants them in, the NLRB will put them in.[5]

Volpe: I think you'll find our guards are not just watchmen. They are all sworn in as deputy sheriffs and they all carry guns. How about our foremen?

Gould: With respect to the foremen, the NLRA draws a distinction between employees and supervisors. Employees are protected from discrimination for union activities and have the right to vote in an election. Supervisors are not protected and do not have the right to vote. However, just because you call a person a supervisor or a foreman doesn't make him or her one under the NLRA. Section 2(11) of the law contains the following definition of a supervisor. Reading from the Act:

> The term "supervisor" means any individual having authority, in the interest of the employer, to hire, transfer, suspend, lay off, recall, promote, discharge, assign, reward, or discipline other employees, or responsibly to direct them, or to adjust their grievances, or to effectively recommend such action, if in connection with the foregoing the exercise of such authority is not of a merely routine or clerical nature, but requires the use of independent judgement.

You notice that it says or. He doesn't have to have all those authorities, but he must have one of them. How about your supervisors and foremen?

Volpe: I think there's no doubt about our supervisors and foremen. They have the authority. I have some doubts about the assistant foremen.

Gould: Do you think we should try to keep them all out of the unit?

Volpe: I'd like to have the assistant foremen vote but not have them represented if the union wins the election.

Gould: You can't have it both ways.

Volpe: Then I guess we'd better play it safe and try to keep them out.

---

[5]The 1947 Taft-Hartly Amendments to the NLRA provided that "the Board shall not...decide that any unit is appropriate...if it includes, together with other employees, any individual employed as a guard to enforce against employees and other persons rules to protect property of the employer or to protect the safety of persons on the employer's premises." However, unionization of guards is permitted and protected under the Act, but a union will not be certified for guards by the NLRB if it admits other employees into membership or is affiliated with a union which admits other employees.

Gould: With your authority then I'd like to call Grannery and see what he wants in the way of a unit. We'll probably be able to agree on most of it. If we can't agree the Regional Director of the NLRB will decide for us. I'll give Grannery a call tomorrow. I guess that's about as far as we can go today. Give me a call if you have any questions.

The next day Gould called Volpe to tell him that she had talked with Grannery and that they had been able to agree that the unit would consist of all production and maintenance employees in the manufacturing plant and would not include the Lab employees. They agreed also that the supervisors and foremen would not be in the unit. However, Grannery had insisted that the assistant foremen had no real authority and, therefore, should be in the unit.

Gould: We'll have to let the NLRB decide on the assistant foremen. If we could have reached an agreement on that and could have agreed on the time and place of the election we could have had a consent election. However, since we are in disagreement on the assistant foremen issue, we'll have to have a formal hearing. The union and the company will be given a chance to argue the assistant foremen matter before a hearing officer and we can present a written brief later if we want to.[6] This will all take more time, but that may well be to our advantage.

Volpe: OK, Joan, we'll be guided by your advice. We do have one other question. What about part-time employees, temporary employees and employees on layoff?

Gould: Regular part-time employees and employees on layoff who have a reasonable expectation of being recalled can vote. Temporary employees cannot.

Several days later Volpe received a notice of a formal hearing from the NLRB. The date and time of the hearing had been arranged to suit the calendars of the two parties and the hearing officer.

At the hearing Gould presented evidence and argued that the assistant foremen did possess authority to make decisions and, therefore, should not be permitted to vote. The lawyer for the IMWU took the opposite position. It was agreed that the parties could file written briefs within two weeks following the hearing. One week after the briefs had been filed, Volpe received a decision from the Regional Director of the NLRB. It supported the union's position that the assistant foremen were not "supervisors" as defined by the Act and,

---

[6] The hearing is a non-adversary procedure conducted by a field agent of the NLRB. At the close of the hearing the transcript and exhibits are turned over to a Board attorney for preparation of a decision which is never written by the same person who conducted the hearing. The decision is then reviewed by and sent out over the signature of the Regional Director.

therefore, were eligible to vote. The decision stated also that the election would be held within 30 days.

That afternoon Gould met again with Volpe and Berg.

Gould: I was afraid the Regional Director would decide against us on the assistant foremen. They really don't have much authority. The decision of the Regional Director on an issue like this is practically final. The Board in Washington would probably not accept an appeal on it.[7] Anyhow there may be an advantage to us in having them in the unit. They may vote against the union.

Volpe: Eric, how do you think the assistant foremen will vote?

Berg: My guess is they're all strongly opposed to the union.

Gould: From now on until the election date the IMWU will probably carry on a very active campaign to convince the employees to vote for them. They'll promise to try to negotiate a big increase in wages and benefits. You may disagree strongly with some of the things they say.

Volpe: What can we do about it? Are they allowed to lie to the employees? Can we correct any false statements?

Gould: The Board doesn't try to edit the statements made by either side. However, you can reply and correct any statements made by the union. But remember what I said earlier, you can't promise the employees anything for not voting for the union or threaten them with anything if they do. And that applies not just to you two but to all the foremen and supervisors or anyone else who is your agent.

Berg: We know that the boys down in the forge room are sore about the rates down there. Some of them have told Evans that if they got 10% we could forget about the union.

Gould: Would you have raised the forge room rates at this time if the union hadn't come along?

---

[7]The Board delegates to Regional Directors the determination on matters concerning elections. Upon request of an interested party the Board may review the actions of a Regional Director, but such review does not stop the election process unless the Board so orders. It is possible for a company to circumvent the apparent bar to review of a unit determination by refusing to bargain with the newly-designated union. Then if the union files an unfair labor practice charge, the employer can raise the question of the appropriateness of the bargaining unit as a defense. The Board would have to address the unit question and its decision is appealable to the federal court of appeals.

Berg: Oh no. Those rates will be OK as soon as the bugs are out of the new equipment.

Gould: Then you can't change them now just to try to influence some votes. That would be an unfair labor practice.

Volpe: What about our hospital and life insurance plans. We usually review them this time of the year and make new benefits, if any, effective July 1. That might help us a lot coming just before the election, especially if we give a sizeable boost. On the other hand maybe we ought to hold back and see if the union wins. If they do we'd be in a better bargaining position if we hadn't made the changes.

Gould: The law is that you should act exactly the same as you would have acted if we had no election pending. You can't raise the forge room rates, but you should increase the hospital and life insurance plans on July 1 by whatever amounts you intended to increase them before you knew about the union. By withholding such benefit improvements you could be guilty of an unfair labor practice.

Volpe: You mentioned unfair labor practices. What's the penalty if we are found guilty?

Gould: The usual penalty for granting an unlawful wage increase is that the Board will issue a cease and desist order which you would have to post in the plant.

Volpe: That doesn't sound like much.

Gould: It isn't. However, if you should violate the cease and desist order the Board would secure a court order and if you should violate that you would be in contempt of court which can carry very heavy penalties. Another penalty, even for a first offense, can be a reelection if the union loses. In extreme cases the Board could order you to recognize and bargain with the union even if the union lost the election. The Board may issue such a bargaining order when it finds that a fair election could not be held because of ULPs committed by the employer. Aside from these penalties you must remember that I am sworn, as a lawyer, to uphold the law and that I knowingly would not advise you to break the law even though the penalty may be pretty light.

Volpe: I agree with that Joan. How do you suggest we beat the union and stay within the law? Some of the things the union has been saying and writing are just not right. Can we tell the people the truth?

Gould: Yes, you can call the employees together all at once or in small groups and talk with them. You can even talk to them individually, but it would probably be better to have a management witness present. And remember you can't promise or threaten. But before you talk to the employees I think we ought to get all the supervisors and foremen together. They ought to know your position and be ready to answer any questions which the employees raise. You should emphasize with the foremen that if the union gets in the foremen's authority in the plant and their flexibility to accomplish things may be greatly curtailed.

Volpe: If I speak to the workers in the cafeteria do I have to give the union the same opportunity?

Gould: No, the Board doesn't require you to do so.

A meeting was arranged for the supervisors and foremen. Gould briefed them on the NLRA with special reference to what they could and could not say to the employees. She emphasized that they should not threaten or promise but were free to point out the disadvantages of a union as they saw them. She encouraged them to report to Eric any information that they received, but warned them against spying. Volpe gave them data to answer charges made by the union that the company's wages and benefits were below those of unionized firms.

It was decided also that Volpe would write a letter to the home of each of the employees in which he would answer the union's charges. In the letter Volpe pointed out that the company's wages and benefits were as good as those in union plants, using specific examples. He also encouraged any employee who had a question to take it up with his foreman and if he didn't get satisfaction, to bring it directly to Berg or to Volpe himself. The following week meetings of all the employees in groups of 20 to 25 employees were arranged in the cafeteria during work hours.

The next week Volpe received a notice from the NLRB stating that a second union, the Amalgamated Electrical Workers, had filed a petition to be included on the ballot. Volpe called Gould.

Volpe: I got a letter from the NLRB saying another union, the AEW, will also be on the ballot.

Gould: That's not unusual. Once one union has shown that 30% or more of the employees want an election the Board will allow another union on the ballot even if less than 10% of the employees have signed cards or a petition for it. Actually that may help us. The AEW may take some votes away from the IMWU.

The two unions carried on vigorous campaigns during the days remaining before the election. The organizers appeared at the gate each day passing out literature and urging employees to vote for their unions. Each week the employees received letters from the unions. Volpe replied to the charges in each of these. The unions also held a number of meetings of Volpe employees at their headquarters. Volpe received information about what happened in these meetings from foremen who were told by their employees.

During the last week in June the Company announced an increase in Hospital-Medical Benefits and a $2,000, boost in life insurance. In letters to the employees the unions branded these changes as an unfair labor practice, but took credit for them. A flier from the IMWU read:

> If we can get these kinds of increases for you while we're on the outside - just imagine what we can do for you when we're in. Vote IMWU and get what's really coming to you!

As the time of the election approached Gould called Volpe to advise him that all meetings and speeches during working hours had to cease 24 hours before the election.

Volpe: How about getting out the vote? Can we send a car out for someone who is sick?

Gould: Yes, that's OK so long as you don't discriminate. You've got to offer the same service to all employees. You should indeed make every effort to have all the employees vote. The election is won by a majority who vote. There are 329 in the unit, but if only 50 vote and 26 vote for the union it becomes the bargaining agent for the entire 329. You can be sure the union will get out those who favor it, so you should encourage everyone to vote.

The election was held in the plant cafeteria on July 10 from 9:00 to 12:00 and 1:00 to 4:00. A table was placed in the front of the cafeteria with the ballot box on it. The NLRB field agent , two representatives of the company and one representative from each of the unions sat at the table. As each employee entered, his name was checked off the eligibility list. The union or the company representatives or the NLRB election officer could challenge any employee's right to vote. The union representatives did challenge two employees whom they claimed were really foremen rather than assistant foremen. Their votes were placed in special sealed envelopes and placed in the ballot box. A decision whether or not to include the challenged ballots would be made by the NLRB if the number of challenged ballots could affect the outcome of the election. Each employee was given a ballot which had a place to vote for:

IMWU
AEW
NO UNION

Each employee took his ballot to one of the private voting booths and marked his preference. He then folded it, brought it back to the table and placed it in the ballot box in front of the NLRB field agent, the company representatives and the union represenatatives.

At 4:00 p.m. the polls were closed. The NLRB officer then opened the ballot box and counted the votes in front of the four representatives. Of the 329 employees on the list 312 voted.

The results were as follows:

For the IMWU	177
For the AEW	53
For No Union	77
Void Ballots	3
Challenged Ballots	2
	312[8]

The next day Gould met with Volpe and Berg.

Volpe: The election results shocked me. I never thought our people would vote for a union. What do we do now?

Gould: Unless we file an objection to the election or an unfair labor practice charge against the union the NLRB will now certify the IMWU as the bargaining agent for all the employees in the bargaining unit.

Volpe: What about the two voters whom the union challenged. Will they be in the unit?

Gould: We'll try to work that out with the union, and if we can't agree the Board will decide. What's your preference?

Volpe: Now that the election is over we'd rather have them out of the unit. They are really foremen, but we knew they'd vote against the union so we told them to try to vote.

Gould: Since the union challenged them, I imagine Grannery will agree they should be out. I'll call him about it.

Volpe: Are we stuck with this union forever?

Gould: Probably but not necessarily. Once an election is held the Board won't hold another election in that bargaining unit for a year. If the union had lost you would have been free from dealing with any union for a full year. But the IMWU won and they will be certified by the Board as the representative of your production and maintenance employees. You'll have to recognize the IMWU as the representative of your employees for a full year even if during the year a majority of the employees should decide they no longer want IMWU to represent them. It's known as an election bar (a valid election serves as a bar to election for one year from the first election) and it lasts as I said for one year.

[8]In this election IMWU received a majority of the votes. However, if no choice on the ballot had received a majority of all the valid votes cast, the NLRB would have conducted a runoff election between the two with the highest number of votes. For example, if the result had been IMWU-142, AEW-53, and No Union-116, a runoff election would have been held with only "IMWU" and "No Union" on the ballot.

There is also what is known as a contract bar. If you sign a labor contract with the IMWU, it will serve as a bar to another NLRB election for up to 3 years depending on the length of the contract. If the contract is 2 years long, it will bar another election for 2 years, if 3 years for 3 years, but if over three years an election could still be held at the end of three years if a petition is filed during the window period between 90 and 60 days prior to the end of the third year.

Volpe: So there is a possibility we can get rid of the union sometime?

Gould: Yes, the employees could vote it out just as they have voted it in. It's called a decertification election. If 30% of the employees sign a petition asking for a decertification election the Board will hold one, assuming there is no election bar or contract bar in effect. If a majority of those voting should not vote for the union then the IMWU would be decertified and you no longer would have to bargain with it.[9] A second union could also get on this ballot and could possibly win representation rights.

Volpe: What happens to the AEW? It got 53 votes. Do I have to bargain with it too?

Gould: No. Under our law we have exclusive representation. Management has to bargain and must bargain only with the union which wins the election, in this case the IMWU. Even though 53 of your employees voted for the AEW you do not have to bargain with that union and indeed you must not do so. At the same time the IMWU must represent in good faith not just its own members and those who voted for it, but also those who opposed it, including some who may have joined and may still be members of the AEW.

Volpe: Will everyone have to join the IMWU now?

Gould: Oh no. No one has to join the IMWU or pay dues at this point even though the IMWU has to represent them. Membership is a matter for bargaining between the company and the union. If you and the IMWU should negotiate a union shop then everyone in the union would have to pay dues to the IMWU, but that's something we'll bargain with them later. None of your employees will have to join a union unless you agree to it.

---

[9] In the fiscal year 1979 the NLRB conducted 770 decertification elections. Unions won in 194 elections (25%) involving representation of 17,450 employees and lost in 583 elections involving representation of 22,088 employees.

CONTRACT NEGOTIATIONS

One week after the election Volpe received a notice from the NLRB certifying the IMWU as the bargaining agent for all employees in the bargaining unit. Later that same week he received a letter from Grannery requesting a time and place for beginning contract negotiations, together with a copy of the union's proposed contract.[10] Volpe called Gould and they met that afternoon.

Volpe: We can't agree to that contract. It would put us right out of business!

Gould: Grannary doesn't expect you to agree to it as it is. He'd be very much surprised and upset if you did. Those just represent his initial demands. We'll give him some counter offers which are lower than we expect to settle for and then we can begin to bargain. Don't take these original demands too seriously. But we do have to meet and bargain with him. The NLRA in Section 8(a)(5) makes it an unfair labor practice for an employer to refuse to bargain with the certified representative of his employees. We have to meet with him and make a serious effort to reach an agreement and he does too. If either one of us fails to do so, we would be guilty of an unfair labor practice. We both are required to bargain in good faith.

Volpe: What does bargaining in good faith mean? There are some things in the union's list of proposals that are unacceptable. Does bargaining in good faith mean I've got to give in on them?

Gould: No. Just because you or the union engage in tough bargaining doesn't mean you are not bargaining in good faith. I don't foresee any problem because I assume you honestly want to reach a fair and reasonable agreement with the union. The Board considers what it calls the "totality of conduct" of the parties, and I'm sure we'll be well within the boundaries.

Volpe: Do we have to bargain about any issue that the union raises? For example, they are asking for a 20% increase for employees who are already retired.

Gould: Section 8(d) of the NLRA provides that the parties must bargain with respect to "wages, hours, and other terms and conditions of employment." "Conditions of employment" is a broad phrase, but there are a lot of things it doesn't cover. Since retired employees are no longer members of the bargaining unit the union cannot insist on bargaining for them.

---

[10]Frequently the negotiation of the contract is done by a union official who has not been in charge of the organization drive. In this case, however, Grannery assumed both roles.

The Board has divided issues into three types with respect to bargaining: 1. prohibited or illegal items, 2. permissive items, and 3. mandatory items. There are some things such as a closed shop or a "hot cargo" agreement[11] which you and the union are not permitted to negotiate even though you both may agree to do so. Then there are items which you can bargain about if both of you agree to do so, but not if one of you objects. Pensions for already retired employees is one of the permissive items. You can bargain about it if you want to, but you don't have to, and it is illegal for the union to strike over the company's refusal to bargain on a prohibited or a permissive item. Finally, there are those items which you must bargain about if the other side so desires. These are the mandatory items and are those which the Board and the Courts have decided are included in the phrase "wages, hours and other terms and conditions of employment." It's a long list which over the years has grown and grown.[12]

Volpe: One of their demands is that every employee must join the union 30 days after he is hired. Is that legal?

Gould: Yes, its legal and a mandatory bargaining item in this state. Remember I told you right after the election that no one had to join the union because it won the election, but that that was a matter about which the union and you could bargain. There are a number of different union security or compulsory membership clauses which you can bargain about and one, the closed shop, which is prohibited. A closed shop is one in which all employees must join the union before they can be hired. A closed shop is illegal. You couldn't bargain that even if you wanted to. However, Section 8(a)(3) of the NLRA provides that an employer and a union may bargain a union shop. A union shop is where the employer is free to hire union or non-union employees, but they must join the union after they are hired. The law provides that they cannot be required to join until at least 30 days after being hired.

---

[11]Gould provides a definition of closed shop below. A "hot cargo" contract clause is one in which the employer agrees not to do business with unorganized employers or with organized employers with whom the union had a strike in process, i.e., an employer designated by the union as "unfair."

[12]Included among the growing list of mandatory bargaining items are: hours of work, overtime, hourly pay rates, piece rates, incentives, merit pay, overtime rates, shift differentials, bonuses, profit sharing, stock purchase plans, vacations, holidays, sick leaves, pensions, health and welfare plans, life insurance, severance pay, rest periods, lunch breaks, safety, work environment, work loads, seniority, promotions, demotions, transfers, layoffs, discipline and discharge, subcontracting, plant rules, grievance procedures, arbitration, no-strike clause, management rights, check off and union security.

Many contracts extend that to 60 or 90 days. Other compulsory membership clauses such as maintenance of membership, modified union shop or agency shop [13] are also legal in this state. I emphasize this state because Secion 14(b) of the NLRA provides that a state may adopt legislation which prohibits any type of compulsory union membership, and 19 states have such laws which are known as Right-To-Work Laws.

Volpe: I notice the union is demanding that we collect their dues for them. Is that legal?

Gould: Yes, it's called a checkoff and is a mandatory bargaining item. You don't have to agree to a checkoff, but many companies do so to avoid collection of dues in the plant. Before you can check off the dues from any worker's pay check you must get his voluntary written consent to do so and such authorization and cannot be revoked for at least one year.

Volpe: Who will do the bargaining for the union and the company?

Gould: The union has the right to choose its negotiators. IMWU usually follows the pattern of having one of its International Representatives, in this case Grannery, do the bargaining aided by the president of the local union and half a dozen or so representatives from the bargaining unit.

---

[13] In addition to the closed shop which requires the employer to hire only union members and which is illegal there are a number of different types of union security clauses which are permitted by the NLRA. Among these are: union shops in which as a condition of employment an employee must join the union, but not until after he has been employed for at least 30 days; modified union shop in which all new employees must join the union, but workers who were employees of the company before the clause was negotiated do not have to join; maintenance of membership in which no employee has to join the union, but if he does join must maintain memebership in good standing for the duration of the contract; (under all of the above clauses the employee may not be discharged for not being a union member if he has been denied membership for any reason other than failure to pay the dues and initiation fees uniformly required by the union); agency shop in which an employee does not have to join the union, but must contribute to the support of the union, usually in an amount equal to the regular dues. Section 9(e) of the NLRA provides that if 30% of the employees in a bargaining unit petition for an election to eliminate a union security clause, the Board will hold such an election. If the majority of unit employees vote against the clause, it shall no longer be enforced by thc cmploycr. In 1979 the NLRB held 134 of these deauthorization elections. The unions lost in 69% of the elections covering 3,025 employees and won in 31% covering 2,677 employees.

I imagin that's what they will do here, but they could decide to have some others do it and we'd have to bargain with them. The same is true on your side of the table. You can do the bargaining aided by whomever you wish, or you can have someone else do it for you.

Volpe: I don't think I should do the bargaining. I'm afraid I'd need someone with more patience and a lot more knowledge about labor relations. What about you, could you take care of it?

Gould: I think it would be wise for you not to be at the bargaining table, but for another reason. You can make final decisions for the company. It's better to keep you in reserve. I do the bargaining for a number of companies and I'd be happy to do it for you. Of course, I'd like Eric and some of the other company executives to sit in with me. If I'm to be your negotiator you have to give me the free authority to negotiate effectively. Of course, you can set the ranges within which I can operate, but I must have authority to reach an agreement which can be subject to your ratification if you want to reserve that right.

Volpe: I want you to do the negotiating and you'll have authority to reach an agreement.[14]

Gould: OK. Then we should develop our counter offers and also get together a lot of data prior to the first meeting. We'll need to know what our wage rates and benefits are and how they compare with the wage rates and benefits at other plants in the industry and in the area. We'll need to know also what each cent per hour increase will cost the company and many, many other things if we are to be able to bargain effectively. Do you have someone who can work with me to develop such material?

Volpe: Yes, Art Brown in payroll would probably be the best.

Gould: OK. I'll start working with him later this week. In the meantime the union will probably be asking you for wage and other information. Under the law you must supply them with wage and employee benefit information. Any other information they ask for check with me. Unless we decide to plead "inability to pay" we don't have to give them financial data.

---

[14]Many employers prefer not to have a lawyer as negotiator. If the company uses a lawyer as negotiator the union may feel that it should have a lawyer, too. Frequently the negotiator for the company is the Director of Industrial Relations and does not have a law degree.

AN IMPASSE AND STRIKE THREAT

A few weeks later the company and union representatives opened negotiations. Gould kept Volpe informed after each meeting and also held a number of meetings with the foremen and supervisors to get their opinions on various items. At the end of three weeks everything except the general wage increase had been agreed upon. Gould had insisted that the wage issue be kept open until everything else was settled. After several days of bargaining on the wage issue an impasse was reached. The union refused to come down below 12% the first year, 10% for the second year and 10% for the third year plus a cost-of-living adjustment every three months. The company refused to increase its offer beyond 8%, 6%, and 6% with no cost-of-living adjustment. The union then informed Gould that unless a contract was achieved by a ceratain day it intended to strike. That night Gould met with Volpe.

Gould: I think the union is serious about striking unless we up the wage offer.

Volpe: Then I guess we'll have to take a strike. I don't see how we can offer more. Isn't there some way the government can make them settle for a reasonable amount?

Gould: No. Under the NLRA the union is free to strike a private employer if it isn't satisfied with the wage offer or other mandatory bargaining items. Incidentally you are also free to lock out, that is, close down the plant when an impasse is reched until the union agrees to a settlement satisfactory to you even if the union would prefer to continue to work at the old rates.[15]

Volpe: What about our people who don't want to strike?

Gould: Under Section 8(b)(1)(A) of the law they have a right to come into work, but the IMWU will put up a picket line and probably most of the workers will honor it.

Volpe: Can I hire new employees to replace them?

---

[15]Under the NLRA a union is free to strike the employer when there is no contract in effect except when: 1. the purpose of the strike is to force bargaining on a non-mandatory issue; or 2. there has been a contract in effect and the union has not given the employer and FMCS 60 days notice of its intent to terminate it; or 3. the President had determined that the strike would imperil national health and safety in which case he can secure a court injunction postponing the strike for 80 days. (At the end of the 80 days, however, the union is then free to strike.) With respect to lockouts by an employer it is necessary to distinguish between a lockout which is used to avoid collective bargaining entirely and one which is used as an economic weapon after an impasse has been reached. The former is illegal, the latter is legal.

Gould: Yes, you can hire new employees and when the strike is over you don't have to replace them with striking employees. You have to take the striking employes back only if their jobs are unfilled after the strike is over.

Volpe: What about violence?

Gould: Section 8(b)(1)(A) outlaws violence or coercion on the picket line. Moreover after the strike you can refuse to reinstate any employee who engages in violence.

Volpe: Isn't there anything we can do to head off this strike?

Gould: Yes, we can ask the Federal Mediation and Conciliation Service to help us by sending in a mediator. I haven't called them because I imagine Grannery has done so and we'll be getting a call from them. The FMCS is an independent agency of the Government. The mediators who work for it have as their job trying to help the parties resolve impasses such as we have here. They have no power to force an agreement, but many times they are successful in breaking a deadlock such as we have.

The following day Joseph Sweeney, a federal mediator, arranged a meeting with the bargaining group. Both Grannery and Gould had worked with Sweeney in other negotiations and had confidence in him. After several days of bargaining under Sweeney's supervision and with his help the parties reached accord on a new three-year agreement.

LIVING UNDER AN AGREEMENT

The day after the collective bargaining Agreement was signed, Volpe asked Gould to come to his office.

Volpe: Now that we have an Agreement what does it mean?

Gould: First, since it's a three-year contract, there can't be another certification election here for 3 years so the IMWU is in for that long as least. Second, since we have an exhaustive no-strike clause in the agreement the union can't strike until the end of the Agreement and then only after giving 60 days notice before termination. Third, under Section 301 of the NLRA the union or the company can be sued in federal court for violating the Agreement. Moreover, under the Boys Market Doctrine the federal courts will quickly issue an injunction ordering the employees back to work if they strike in violation of the no-strike clause and the arbitration provision of the Agreement.[16]

Volpe: Speaking of arbitration I notice that the grievance procedure ends in (reading) "final and binding arbitration." What if I strongly disagree with an arbitrator's award? Can I get a court to change it?

Gould: Generally speaking, no. The courts will enforce an arbitrator's award even though they may disagree with it. Only if you can prove that the arbitrator had a conflict of interests, was bribed, exceeded his jurisdiction, was insane or rendered a decision which violates the law will the courts alter an award.

Volpe: Some time back you said the union had to represent all the employees in good faith. Does that mean it has to carry a non-member's grievance to arbitration? And suppose one of our old non-union employees brings a grievance directly to me or Eric as he has in the past, can we still work it out with him?

Gould: The union has to represent every bargaining unit member fairly; it has the duty of fair representation. But that doesn't mean it has to take up a grievance if it honestly believes it doesn't have merit. Any employee can bring a grievance directly to management rather than through the union grievance procedure. However, the IMWU has a right to have a representative present and any settlement you make with an individual employee cannot violate the Agreement.

Volpe: It's nice to have everything settled for three years.

Gould: That's not completely true. There are some mandatory items we didn't bargain about during these negotiations. Under the Jacobs Manufacturing Company Doctrine, the union (or the company) can insist on bargaining during the life of the agreement on any mandatory bargaining item which is not

---

[16] The Norris-LaGuardia Act passed by Congress in 1933 placed severe limitations on the issuance of court injunctions in labor disputes. Prior to 1970 the Supreme Court interpreted the Norris-LaGuardia provisions as preventing it from enforcing the no-strike provisions of labor contracts. (See Sinclair Refining v. Atkinson,(50 LRRM 2420), issued in 1962.) However, in 1970 in Boys Markets, Inc. v. Retail Clerks, Local 770, (77 LRRM 2257), the Supreme Court reversed its position and ruled that a federal court can issue an injunction to halt a strike where "a collective bargaining contract contains a mandatory grievance adjustment or arbitration procedure."

covered in the agreement and was not bargained to an impasse.[17]

Volpe: Then we don't really have a closed contract. Couldn't you have bargained a clause which would have closed it up.

Gould: We could have tried to get a so called "zipper clause" in which the parties would have agreed that they had considered all possible mandatory items and the contract represented a complete expression of agreement. However, in the New York Mirror case in 1965 the Board ruled that such a clause does not by itself constitue a sufficiently clear waiver of a specific mandatory bargaining item. However, I don't think you have to worry too much about the fact that the contract isn't completely closed. The union isn't likely to insist on bargaining again until the contract terminates three years from now and even if it does, it can't strike to force us to give in on anything. Our no-strike clause protects us from such action.

Volpe: It's a relief to have it all over. Now Eric and I can forget about this union stuff and put our minds to running the business again.

Gould: Well the contract negotiations are finished, but that's only one part of dealing with a union. Now you'll have the problem of living with it. I think we negotiated a good contract, but during the next three years there probably will be many grievances and perhaps a few arbitrations as you and the union try to interpret and apply it to specific situations. If I can be of help anytime give me a call.

---

[17]In 1951 in NLRB v. Jacobs Manufacturing Company,(30 LRRM 2098), a federal court ruled that an employer has a continuing duty to bargain during the term of a labor agreement "as to subjects which were neither discussed nor embodied in any of the terms and conditions of the contract."

FIRST NATIONAL BANK OF LAKE CITY (A)

On a Monday afternoon Wynn Evans, President of the First National Bank of Lake City, received a formal notice from the National Labor Relations Board (NLRB) that an election would be held at the bank's offices 30 days hence to determine if the employees wished to be represented by the International Metalworkers Union (IMU). Evans arranged for a meeting to be held the following afternoon with the bank's labor attorney, Francis Grant, and a group of its executives including Paul Blanton, Vice President of Personnel. Evans indicated that at the meeting the action taken so far by the bank and the union would be reviewed and he would welcome recommendations concerning what further action, if any, management should take during the 30 days remaining before the election.

Lake City, which was located in a northcentral state, had a population of approximately 70,000 which had remained relatively stable during the past ten years. The economy of the community was completely dependent upon one large plant, an automotive parts plant, which was owned by one of the big three of the auto industry. When auto production was high the Lake City economy was high and vice versa.

During the mid-thirties Lake City had had some turbulent labor strife as representatives from the national headquarters of the International Metalworkers Union (IMU) tried to organize the workers in the local plant. In the late thirties, however, the automobile company had signed a national agreement with the IMU which included the Lake City plant. Moreover, since 1956 the agreement had included a union shop clause which required all workers at the plant to be members of the union. The IMU had been successful also in organizing a number of machine shops and other types of small plants in the area. The IMU was very active in local politics. Lake City was sometimes described as "a union town."

Most of the employees of the bank had relatives who worked at the auto plant and were members of the IMU. In fact some of the bank's employees were closely related to the local IMU leaders. The IMU had made several unsuccessful attempts to organize the white collar workers at the auto plant. Four years ago it had been successful in organizing the maintenance workers at one of the smaller banks. However, unionization at that bank had not spread to the tellers and the other white collar employees and none of the employees in the other banks of the community were organized.

One group of professional employees in the community were represented by a union - the school teachers. Most of the grade school and high school teachers in Lake City had been members of the National Education Association (NEA) for many years. However, until the sixties the NEA had been a purely professional society which opposed collective bargaining. In the late sixties the NEA, pressed by the success of a rival organization the American Federation of Teachers which was an affiliate of the AFL-CIO and which had negotiated sizeable wage increases for teachers in some of the major cities, decided to support collective bargaining by its local groups.

FIRST NATIONAL BANK OF LAKE CITY (A)

The business community of Lake City was surprised and disturbed when some of the local teachers who were members of NEA began to organize for bargaining purposes under the protection of the State Public Employees Relations Act. They were even more surprised when in an election the teachers voted to have NEA serve as their bargaining agent.

Following the election the school board and representatives of NEA entered into collective bargaining. It was six months before agreement was reached on the first labor contract. It was generally agreed that the teachers had secured sizeable economic gains as a result of unionization and bargaining.

The First National was the oldest and largest commercial bank in the Lake City community. It had assets of approximately 300 million dollars which was twice the size of the next largest of the other six commercial banks in the area. Founded in 1892 First National had remained a single unit bank until about ten years ago when it had begun an expansion program by merger with and acquisition of a number of smaller banks in nearby communities. As a result by now it had 18 offices including two which had been opened recently in newly developed suburban shopping areas.

Although the First National was the largest financial institution in the area it was not the salary pacesetter in the community or even in the banking sector. First National salaries were generally 10 to 20 percent below those for comparable jobs at the auto plant and one or two of the smaller banks had somewhat higher salary scales than the First. However, the First seldom lost employees to other banks although recently there had been some movement of younger employees to the auto plant. This had been especially true of men and women that the First had trained in data processing.

Everyone at the bank except the maintenance employees was on salary. The bank had a formal salary evaluation program in which there were 10 classifications, each with a maximum and a minimum rate. The maximum of the range varied from 13% above the minimum for the lowest level classification to 30% above for the highest level classification. Within the ranges increases were granted each year entirely on merit. All increases, whether as a result of a change of job or merit evaluaton, became effective January 1 of each year. If an employee was promoted during the year he received the new job title immediately, but his salary frequently was not changed until January 1. Management was of the opinion that its somewhat lower salary scale was more than made up by its excellent working conditions, its job security, and its liberal profit sharing plan.

The First National was looked upon by the employees as a prestigous place to work. The offices were clean and pleasant and the atmosphere was congenial and unhurried. Most of the employees were proud to say that they worked at the First National. The established work week was 38 hours during a five day period. However, most employees averaged only 35 hours. For work between 38 and 40 hours employees received additional compensation at straight time rates. Beyond 40 hours per week a rate of time and one-half was paid.

The bank was also viewed as a place where employees without college education, especially men, could rise to important positions. Practically all of the bank's employees, including all but two of its top officers, had terminated their formal education upon graduation from the local high schools. After entering the First, many of them had attended American Institute of Banking courses at night which the bank encouraged and financed. A job at the First represented an avenue for dependable young men without college educations to become eventually important leaders in the community.

Jobs at the First were valued also because of their security. Employees were never laid off and discharge for poor work or offensive conduct was extremely rare. Once a person was hired he or she could count on a regular pay check for the rest of life. In the past this job security had been very important in a community where the major industry was known for heavy overtime one year and heavy layoff the next. However, in recent years the advantage of working at the bank in this respect compared to working at the auto plant had largely disappeared as the union in the fifties and early sixties negotiated supplementary unemployment benefits (SUB) and in 1967 topped off its drive for income security by negotiating a Guaranteed Annual Income (GAI) which replaced the SUB. Under the GAI employees at the auto plant with seven years of service were guaranteed 95 percent of their take home pay for a period of 52 weeks. (Employees with less then seven years of service received the 95% guarantee, but for a lesser number of weeks.) Moreover, employees who were discharged at the auto plant could usually count on strong support from the union, including carrying the issue to the last step of the grievance machinery which was arbitration by a neutral third party. One of the union leaders was quoted as saying: "Discharge is the capital punishment of labor relations so we almost always walk the last mile with them."

The management was of the opinion that its profit-sharing plan was highly valued and appreciated especially by its older employees. All employees became eligible for profit sharing after two years of employment and percentage-of-salary participation was equal for everyone including officers. Under the plan the bank contributed an amount each year which was equal to 7½% of its net operating income after customary reserves and dividends. The amount was then divided by the combined yearly salaries of the plan participants and that percentage was applied to each employee's base annual salary to determine his or her amount. During the 20 years that the plan had been in effect it had never paid less than 10% of salaries and in recent years it had approached the 15% limit set on such plans by the Internal Revenue Service. However, the payments from the profit-sharing plan were not immediately available to a participant, but instead were held in a trust fund which earned income until the employee left the employment of the bank either as a result of quitting or as a result of retirement at age 65. At retirement at 65 the employee received 100% of the balance in his account. Employees who left the bank before 65 received less than the full amount depending upon the number of years they had been in the plan. It became 50% vested after 5 years and then increased 10% each year becoming fully vested at the end of 10 years. The plan did permit employees to withdraw any amount in their balance which exceeded two and one-half times their annual salary. Likewise, if an employee died the entire amount in his account was paid to his estate. The First National was the only bank in the Lake City area which had a profit-sharing plan in effect. The International Metalworkers Union had tried to negotiate a profit-sharing plan with the auto company, but had not been successful. None of the other smaller industrial and commercial firms in the area had profit-sharing plans.

In addition to the profit-sharing plan the bank had also a death benefit plan, a pension plan and a salary continuation plan. The death benefit plan was intended to supplement the amount which the employee's family or estate would received at his death from the profit-sharing plan. It paid $3,000 to employees whose salary was $5,000 or less and dropped down in $500 units for each $200 increase in salary so that it paid nothing for salaries over $6,200.

The bank's pension plan required an employee to have 15 years of service to be eligible for benefits. Retirement was mandatory at age 65. Early retirement was possible at age 55. However, in the case of early retirement benefit payments were decreased on an actuarial basis unless the employee opted to have his payments begin at age 65. The plan provided also for payments at any age after 15 years of service in case of total and permanent disability.

Determining one's pension benefit under the plan was a complicated matter. It involved three separate calculations. Most of the employees had difficulty understanding it although the bank had prepared and published a booklet which explained it with examples.

Benefits under the pension plan were not as liberal as those provided under the union contract at the auto plant, especially for the lower-paid employees and for those who wished to retire early. However, they were as good or better than those paid by any of the other banks in the area. In fact two of the other banks had no pension plans. Management was of the opinion that the pension plan and the profit-sharing plan had to be considered as a package and that when this was done the retirement benefits compared well even with those of the auto company.

The bank's salary continuance program, which became effective for employees immediately following the 90 day probationary period, provided one full week of sick pay during the first year and six full weeks of sick pay per calendar year thereafter. The six weeks were not cumulative. The weekly pay check was decreased for any day of absence other than those covered by the salary continuance program.

The bank's vacation plan provided two weeks of paid vacation after 1 year of service, and three weeks after 15 years of service. It was identical with the vacation plans of the other banks in the area, but not as good as the vacation plan at the auto plant. The bank also paid for six holidays which was the same as the number of paid holidays at the other banks in the area, but only about half the number at the auto plant.

The bank also permitted employees to borrow at reduced interest rates on mortgages, car loans and personal loans. On mortgage loans, for example, the rate was reduced by $\frac{1}{4}$%, thus enabling an employee to save a considerable amount of interest cost over the purchase period of his property.

The bank also enrolled all of its employees in the American Institute of Banking (AIB). The AIB conducted night courses in Lake City in bank accounting and numerous other subjects. The employees of the First National could attend without cost. Approximately 25% of the employees took one or more courses each year.

Conspicuous by its absence in the bank's benefit package was an employer-paid hospital and medical care program. Such a program had been discussed by the management with Blue Cross-Blue Shield and several insurance companies and on several occasions proposals had been presented to the board of directors. However, each time they had been turned down because of the vigorous opposition of Mr. Fred Savage. Savage, who was in his late seventies and controlled the largest block of stock in the bank, felt very strongly on the issue. It was his sincere belief that the good of the country would be served best if each person paid his own medical and hospital bills. He was able to bring enough pressure to bear on the president and the other members of the board to prevent adoption of any employer-paid hospital and medical plan.

The bank did work out a group plan with Blue Cross-Blue Shield to be paid for entirely by the employees. Individual rates varied from $25 to $48 per month depending on the type of coverage. The bank agreed to deduct the amounts from the paychecks if employees so desired. The great majority of the employees participated in the group coverage and many of those who did not were covered elsewhere because their husbands or wives worked in other firms which provided free family coverage.

The First National was the only bank in the area which did not have a hospital-medical plan which was entirely or partially paid by the employer. At the auto plant the union had negotiated a very liberal hospital-medical plan, the cost of which was born entirely by the company. Many of the other industrial and retail firms in the area also had plans in which the employer paid all or part of the costs.

The first indication of union activity at the bank occurred one Sunday morning. John Mason, a guard at the main office discovered that IMU membership cards had been distributed to the various teller stations on the first floor, the desks in the bookkeeping department on the second floor, at the switchboard and in the ladies lounge. Mason reported the matter to his superior who in turn reported it to Paul Blanton, Vice President of Personnel. Blanton discussed the matter with the bank's attorney, Francis Grant, and upon his advice it was decided to collect and hold the cards.

On Monday morning Wynn S. Evans, president of the bank, called Blanton to his office. Evans, who was scheduled to retire in less than a year, had been President for 15 years. He had spent his entire working career with the bank. Starting out as a clerk, immediately after graduation from Lake City High School, he had worked his way up through the ranks to his present position. He had good reason to be proud of the progress that had been made at the bank during his presidency. From a single office it had expanded to the point where it now had 17 branch offices. Total assets and profits had increased far more rapidly than any other bank in the area.

Blanton showed the cards to Evans and told him where they had been found. Blanton said that he and the other members of management with whom he had talked had no idea who might have been responsible for distributing them. Evans did not appear to be disturbed. Blanton was surprised when he said "Paul, I don't think we should get too excited about this. After all, in a place like Lake City, I suppose its inevitable that we will eventually have to deal with a union. Let's keep it all low key."

Management never was able to determine who was responsible for the distribution of the cards and the only action which was taken was to tighten security. Four months passed by without any outward indication of further union activity and management came to feel that the card distribution incident could be dismissed as the act of a single disgruntled employee. Supervisors who were in close touch with the employees who worked for them reported no evidence of any organizing activity. Then one Monday morning a number of employees reported to their supervisors that they had received a letter from the IMU addressed to their homes. It was soon learned that the letter had been sent to all of the employees. Evidently one of the employees had provided the union with a runoff of the names and addresses from the computer. The letter is reproduced as Exhibit 1.

One of the employees gave Blanton his copy of the letter which Blanton took to the president's office. Evans read it and discussed it by phone with attorney Grant. Evans then scheduled a 1:00 p.m. meeting of the top management people and attorney Grant to discuss the matter. At the meeting Grant explained that the union would have to get 30% of the employees to sign membership cards before the NLRB would hold an election. He said, however, that it was his experience that the IMU would not ask for an election unless it had at least 60 or 70% of the employees signed up. Among those present at the meeting surprise was expressed that the union felt it had enough interest among the employees to warrant sending out the letter. On the other hand there was a belief that only a very small number of the employees were involved and that the union had no chance of getting 30% to sign cards. It was agreed that for the time being management would take no special action except to gather as much information as possible. Blanton was appointed by the president to serve as clearing house for any facts or rumors which become known to any of them.

Approximately one month after the union's first letter it addressed a second letter to the employees which read in part as follows:

> Your response to our first letter was very encouraging. As a result an informative meeting will be held next Thursday evening at the Lake City Hotel at 8:00 p.m.
>
> We will tell you what we believe we can gain through collective bargainng and will answer any questions you may have.

The meeting was held as scheduled and management learned that between 75 and 100 of the bank's 350 employees had attended. The group was made up largely of employees from Bookkeeping, Personal Loan, and Main Office Tellers although there were some from other departments and from some of the branch offices. It was reported that not all those who attended appeared to be in sympathy with unionization.

Although salaries, individual grievances and other matters were talked about at the meeting the discussion centered around two major topics: (1) the pension and profit-sharing plans and (2) the lack of an employer-paid hospital-medical plan. Several of the older employees spoke favorably about the pension and profit-sharing plan and indicated that they were fearful that the bank might decrease the pension benefits and eliminate profit-sharing if it had to bargain with the union. The union representatives assured the employees that the union would never agree to changes in the pension and profit-sharing plans which would be to the detriment of the employees. Instead they said that the union would insist that the employees receive even better pensions and a larger share of the profits, too much of which, they declared, now went to the owners and the management.

The issue which seemed to be of most concern to the majority of the employees at the meeting was the lack of an employer-paid hospitalization-medical plan. The union leaders played up this issue. They said they found it hard to believe that in this day and age a major bank like First National could be so little interested in its employees' welfare as to refuse to cover them with hospital-medical insurance. They showed the employees a copy of the employer-paid plans which the union had negotiated for the employees at the auto plant. They also referred to a number of other contracts which the union had negotiated with other companies in the Lake City area all of which contained employer-paid plans and it assured the employees that if they chose the IMU as their bargaining agent the union would insist that the bank foot the entire bill for a good hospital-medical insurance plan. One of the union representatives stated that the value of this benefit alone would more than make up the cost of the union dues.

As the reports of the union meeting filtered in to Blanton he became convinced that the bank was facing a serious unionization threat. Blanton had been appointed as Vice President of Personnel about 10 months earlier. Prior to that time the personnel function had been handled by an officer of the bank who had other major functions. Blanton had had no prior training or experience in personnel work. Among the bank officers he was relatively young both in age and service having been hired only five years earlier. Prior to coming with the First he had worked with one of the big Chicago banks. At the First he had served as Vice President of Mortgages and Manager of a Branch before becoming Vice President of Personnel.

Blanton proposed to Evans and the other officers that the bank should engage in an active campaign to convince employees not to join the union. Attorney Grant urged a very aggressive campaign including a series of letters by President Evans and a meeting of all the employees. It was decided that Blanton should work out a series of questions and answers with the attorney and that Blanton should read these to the employees whom he would meet in small groups and then invite discussion. (See Exhibit 2). Attorney Grant cautioned Blanton to be careful not to promise the employees anything as a result of not becomng unionized or to threaten them with anything if they did. "If you promise them anything or threaten them with anything the NLRB could find us guilty of an unfair labor practice and might even order us to bargain with them on the basis of their signed cards without ordering an election - assuming they have a majority of the employees signed up," Grant warned.

Blanton discovered that after he had read the questions and answers the employees were primarily interested in discussing the bank's wage and benefit policies, which to his surprise most of them had very little knowledge and appreciation. (The bank had never developed an employees handbook or a pamphlet explaining the various benefit plans.) The newer employees seemed to be better informed than many of the older employees because at the employment interview the policies and plans were explained. Blanton believed that the meetings were helpful, but came away from some of them with a conviction that there was a sizeable group that really wanted the union.

In several areas Blanton felt that he got a very cool reception. One of these was the data processing center. The center had been set up in the bank's main office building six years earlier. In addition to the bank's work it did some outside work for customers. Although a few of the bank's former employees had moved into jobs in the data center the great majority of the thirty workers there were new employees. It was the only area in the bank which was on shift work. The 12 key punch operators were on two fixed shifts and the computer operators were on three rotating shifts. Blanton had the impression that the employees here looked upon themselves as a group apart with very little loyalty to the bank. "Their loyalty", he said, "is first to the equipment, then to the system, and only after that to the bank. They are a lot closer to the data processing people at the auto company and other companies and banks in the area than they are to employees in the other departments here at the First." During the six years of its operation there had been a considerably higher turnover of employees in this division than elsewhere in the bank except in the Personal Loan Department. Blanton felt that the bank to a considerable extent served as a training school for employees in data processing who once trained moved to the auto company or in some cases even to out-of-town companies and banks.

Blanton divided the data-processing employees into four meeting groups. At each of these meetings the question of wage rates for similar jobs at the auto company was raised by the employees. They seemed to be very well informed. Blanton admitted that the bank's rates were not as high as those paid by the auto company, but said that in some cases this was due to the fact that there was a difference in the skill requirements of the jobs. Moreover, he said that if they took into account the whole pay package including the profit-sharing plan he believed the pay was as good or better at the bank. However, Blanton left the meeting with the feeling that the employes were unconvinced. He was of the opinion that all of the data-processing employees were interested in the union and many of them were strongly interested.

Another area where the reception was quite cool was the Consumer Loans Department in the main office. This division of the bank had been unusually successful compared with similar divisions in the other banks in the community, primarily because of the ability and drive of Frank Lockard who had become Vice President of Consumer Loans ten years earlier. Blanton was aware that although Lockard's performance in terms of profit to the bank was outstanding that he lacked skill and understanding in dealing with employees. In the short time that Blanton had been Vice President of Personnel several of the 35 employees from consumer loans had discussed with him actions by Lockard which they believed to be very unfair and autocratic. On one occasion a female employee complained that she had been demoted from an interviewer to a loan teller without any explanation or warning. Lockard had simply attached a note to her time card which said, "As of today you will work as a teller instead of an interviewer." Turnover in this department was higher than anywhere else in the bank including the data center. In the past year 35% of the employees had quit or transferred to jobs elsewhere in the bank. Blanton had discussed the problem with President Evans and had recommended that some action be taken. Evans had replied, "I know Frank has problems with people, but with his performance on loans I think we'll just have to live with his people problems." Blanton came away from the meetings with the consumer loan groups convinced that 100% of them favored the union.

When Blanton returned to his office from one of the question and answer meetings, Harold Newton, Vice President of Branch Operations, was waiting for him. Newton reported to him that a number of the branch office employees had informed him that the three assistant auditors were engaging in union organizing activities in the branch offices. At the time the bank was in the process of converting its savings accounts to the computer. As part of the conversion program meetings were scheduled at all branch offices during which the "internal auditors" as they were called explained the new system. According to Newton's informants the auditors spent only about 15 minutes explaining the computer printouts and the remainder of the two-hour session talking about the advantages of having a union. At the end of the meetings they had passed out union membership cards. By the time Newton received the information meetings had already been held by the auditors at about half of the branches. Newton called off the other meetings.

The news that the assistant auditors were engaging in union organizing activities came as a surpirise and a shock to the officers of the bank who had always considered them as part of the management team. It was agreed that Newton and the cashier should meet with the auditor and three assistant auditors. At the meeting the assistants admitted that they favored a union and had been trying to get other employees to join. Following the meeting Newton discussed the matter with attorney Grant who said it was his opinion that the assistant auditors were a part of management and, therefore, that union activity by them was not protected under the National Labor Relations Act. Newton then recommended to President Evans that the three assistant auditors be discharged. However, Evans was of the opinion that the discharge of all three of the internal auditors would raise serious questions in the community regarding the integrity and soundness of the bank. As a result no disciplinary act on was taken. The meeting at the other branch offices were rescheduled at times when Newton could be in attendance and the assistant auditors limited their discussions to an explanation and discussion of the printouts.

Two weeks following the union meeting at Lake City Hotel, Robert Marple, the International Representative of the IMU, called on attorney Grant and informed him that 80% of all the bank's employees had signed up with the union. He offered to produce the signed cards for signature comparison. Grant informed him that he would prefer not to see the cards, but had "an honest doubt" that the union really represented the majority of the employees. Marple then informed Grant that the union would petition the National Labor Relations Board (NLRB) to hold a representation election.

One week after informing the bank's counsel that it had a majority of its employees signed up and wished to bargain for a contract the union sent another letter to the employees which is reproduced as

Exhibit 3.

Copies of the letter were given to management by several of the employees. A meeting of management representatives was then called to discuss it by the president and it was decided that the president should reply. Evans' letter, which was the first written communication from anyone in management to the employees on the union matter, is reproduced as Exhibit 4.

Two weeks after sending out its first letter to its employees regarding the union organizing drive the bank filed with the Internal Revenue Service a request to institute a hospital-medical plan, the costs of which would be paid entirely by the bank. (Mr. Fred Savage, a major stockholder and influential director of the bank, who had successfully opposed such plans in the past had died eight months earlier.) Following the filing, announcements were sent to all department heads, supervisors and branch managers informing them that the bank was instituting a free hospital-medical plan subject to approval by the necessary government agencies. No letter was sent directly to the employees on the hospital-medical plan at this time, but they were informed about it by their supervisors.

Two weeks after the bank announced its intention to assume the cost of a hospital-medical insurance plan the union filed a petition with the NLRB requesting a representation election. At the same time the union filed an Unfair Labor Practices (ULP) charge against the bank claiming that the promise to institute a hospital-medical plan paid by the employer was for the purpose of avoiding unionization. The charge as filed by the union with the NLRB read as follows:

> The above-named employer, by its officers, agents and representatives, has, by establishing a hospitalization plan for employees and their dependents and other acts and conduct, interfered with, restrained and coerced its employees in the exercise of the rights guaranteed in Section 7 of the Act.

As a result of the filing of the ULP charge the NLRB held in abeyance the union's request for a representation election.

Four weeks following the filing by the union a hearing on the ULP charge was held before an officer of the NLRB. The company produced witnesses and correspondence to show that work on the hospital-medical plan had been undertaken before the bank was aware that the union was attempting to organize its employees. Attorney Grant argued that if the bank had not proceeded to develop the plan and try to place it into effect according to its original schedule, then indeed the bank would have been guilty of unfair labor practices. He requested that the hearing officer find that the union's charge was without merit.

One month later the bank received a notice from the NLRB that the union had withdrawn the ULP charges. The president then addressed a letter to all the employees informing them that the new hospital-medical plan would become effective in two months. See Exhibit 5.

At about this same time three employees at the bank's main office were observed by a supervisor in a part of the bank other than where they worked, handing out union membership cards to other employees during working hours. The officers of the bank were surprised when they learned that one of the employees was Esther Douglas, who had an excellent record of employment with the bank for the past 29 years. A review of her personnel record showed the following facts:

> unmarried and supports her mother; hired 29 years ago as a clerk upon recommendation of Wynn Evans who attended same church; excellent attendance record; very good ratings by her supervisors; interested in advancement, took AIB courses at night and worked hard; advanced over time to better and better jobs; eight years ago placed in charge of General Ledger Bookkeeping which required her to bring together all the data from the main office and the branches and deliver it to the President by noon each day; two years ago bank computerized the General Ledger and Esther was moved to the Savings Department where she maintained controls over vaious matters; Savings Department job was important and bank maintained her prior salary; President still called upon her for data from time to time, but not every day; two months ago as a result of computerization of the Savings Department Esther was moved to the job of Collection Clerk with no decrease in salary; works with two other Collection Clerks who receive considerably less pay; still has desk at back of main floor but no reason for President to see or talk to her now.

Two of the vice presidents discussed the incident with Esther. She admitted that she had passed out the cards and urged employees to join the union. She agreed with the officers that it was not fair to the bank for her to do this during working time and assured them that she would not do it again. Attorney Grant recommended that Esther and the other two employees who were observed passing out the cards be discharged. However, President Evans decided that it was better not to take any disciplinary action other than a warning. Esther continued to be interested in the union, but limited her activities to non-working time.

Two weeks following the withdrawal by the union of the ULP charge the NLRB informed the bank that it was proceeding with the union's request for a respresentation election. The bank refused to follow the informal procedure, but instead requested a formal hearing.

At the hearing, which was held a month later, the matter of the employees who should be included in the bargaining unit and therefore would be eligible to vote was discussed. Much to the surprise of management the union did not ask to have the watchman and the other building and maintenance employees included in the unit. Management was happy to go along with their exclusion. Management argued also for the exclusion of the secretaries of the President and the Personnel Vice President on the grounds that they had access to confidential material. The union agreed to their exclusion. The greatest difference of opinion developed regarding supervisory employees. The National Labor Relation Act defines the term "supervisor" and provides that supervisors, as defined, shall be excluded from the bargaining unit. (See Exhibit 6.) Some of the employees whom the bank had given the title of supervisor did not meet the requirements as set forth in the Act. The bank argued that most of the branch managers, the assistant branch managers and the purchasing agent should be included in the unit, but that the auditor and the assistant auditors should not be included. After discussing the content of the above jobs it was agreed that three of the branch managers, three of the assistant branch managers, the three assistant auditors and the purchasing agent should be included and the others excluded. However, the election was delayed because the bank challenged the validity of the union's signature cards and moved that the election petition be dismissed.

Following the hearing the union sent another letter to the employees explaining the delay and assuring the employees regarding the profit-sharing plan (see Exhibit 7). Two weeks later the hearing officer denied the bank's motion to dismiss and his decision was approved by the Regional Director of the NLRB. The bank then filed a petition for review with the NLRB which was denied two weeks later. The Regional Director of the NLRB then set a date for the election and sent formal notices to the bank and the union. The date was approximately one month later, and almost exactly five months after the union had filed for an election. It was also a few days after the new hospital-medical plan became effective.

On the Monday afternoon on which the bank received the notice of the election date Paul Blanton, Vice President of Personnel, discussed the matter briefly with Wynn Evans, President. They agreed it would by wise to have a meeting the next afternoon with their labor lawyer, Francis Grant, and the other executives of the Bank in order to plan management's strategy and tactics during the 30 days which remained before the election. Evans informed Blanton that he would expect him to present a tentative plan of action which could form the basis for discussion and final decision.

Exhibit 1

INTERNATIONAL METALWORKERS UNION
LOCAL 76

TO THE EMPLOYEES OF FIRST NATIONAL BANK OF LAKE CITY

A considerable number of your co-workers have shown an extreme interest in the desire to unite for the good of all the First National Bank employees in Lake City and area branches.

You have the right by law from the National Labor Relations Act to self organize, to form, join or assist labor organizations for the purpose of collective bargaining.

In order to petition the National Labor Relations Board (NLRB) for an election, we must have a sufficient number of the enclosed cards - signed! These signed cards are held in strict confidence and no one but a staff member of IMU or a field representative of the NLRB will see these cards.

No initiation fees or monthly dues are payable until an NLRB election is won. This is accomplished by each of you voting by secret ballot to accept IMU as your collective bargaining representative along with a committee of employees of your own choosing.

The professional employees of banking institutions are long overdue in exercising their right to self organize. You must realize that you are way behind professional employees pertaining to wages, vacations, pensions, paid hospitalization and accident and sickness insurance.

In just a few short years of self organization, professional teachers of America have made substantial gains in all of the aforementioned benefits. You have that same privilege guaranteed by federal law. For your own benefit, take the first step as your fellow co-workers have and sign the enclosed card, which is held in strict confidence, and return it to IMU, Box 72, Lake City.

An extra card is enclosed for any of your fellow employees who wish to sign cards but did not receive a copy of this letter.

IMU ORGANIZING COMMITTEE

Exhibit 2

QUESTIONS AND ANSWERS

A number of questions have been asked about what would happen if a union were to get in. Here are the answers:

1. Question: Is there any real reason why you need a union to speak for you and to pay dues to a union?

   Answer: No. You are always free to speak to any officer of the bank about wages, working conditions, or other conditions of employment without paying dues to a union.

2. Question: If the union wins, would there automatically be a contract with the union?

   Answer: No. The Bank doesn't have to sign any contract that is not in the best interests of the Bank. There is no law to force the Bank to agree to anything the union asks and there can be no contract until we agree.

3. Question: Under a union, would you automatically get the things that the union promises?

   Answer: No. The Bank doesn't have to grant any request which the union makes. Our Bank would agree only to those things that it is willing and able to grant which are in the Bank's opinion in its best interests.

4. Question: With a union, would the employees go out on a strike?

   Answer: We don't know; but if the Bank cannot agree to grant the things that the union has been promising or that the union wants for its own interests, the only way the union can try to force the Bank to do these things is to get the employees to go out on a strike. It is easy for the union to make all kinds of big promises to you, but these are not always easy to fulfill.

5. Question: If the union calls a strike, can I be replaced?

   Answer: Yes. If the union makes you strike to try to force the Bank to agree to the union's demands, under the law an employer is free to continue to operate and to replace the strikers. In addition, if our customers do not wish to be bothered with a strike, they can decide to end their relationship with us. Without customers where are we?

6. Question: Will I have to join the union if it gets in here?

   Answer: It is hard to tell what may happen if the union gets "in". Most unions try to force a company to sign a contract which requires all the employees to become union members or pay dues. Many strikes have been called to get just this kind of contract.

Exhibit 2 (continued)

7. Question: If the union calls us out on strike, will we get paid while the strike is going on?

Answer: No. If you don't work, you won't get paid. An employer won't pay your wages and neither will the union.

8. Question: Why is it so often said that the employees lose by a strike even though they get a wage increase?

Answer: An employee who earned $100 a week loses $500 pay during a strike of only 5 weeks. If at the end of the strike he got a 5 cent an hour wage increase, how long do you think it would take to make up that kind of loss?

9. Question: If you did vote the union in and try it, and find that you don't like it, can you get rid of the union?

Answer: Not easily. It is a lot harder to get a union out than it is getting one in. If you vote the union in, you will probably be stuck with it as long as you work here.

10. Question: Would the union get us higher wages, additional benefits, and more job security, or is it possible that we could lose something we now have?

Answer: The union has probably told you that you have everything to gain and nothing to lose by voting it in. This is not true. The union can't guarantee you any new and additional benefits.

11. Question: Can a union do anything or punish an employee because he opposes it, speaks out against the union, or refuses to let them in his home?

Answer: No. It is a violation of the Federal Law for a union to even attempt to discriminate against an individual in his job or pay, or to attempt in any way to punish an employee because he opposed the union. The right of the employee to oppose a union is guaranteed by law. It is the employee's right and duty to make his own decision and make that decision known if he should so determine.

12. Question: If I signed a union card, can I vote against the union in an election?

Answer: Yes. If there is an election you can vote against the union. It doesn't make any difference whether you signed a union card or went to the union meetings or even paid the union money. What you have signed or have told anyone would not count in an election. You would have an opportunity to vote freely and secretly under government supervision. It is illegal for a union to threaten or force an employee to vote its way.

Exhibit 3

INTERNATIONAL METALWORKERS UNION
LOCAL 76

TO THE EMPOLOYEES OF FIRST NATIONAL BANK OF LAKE CITY

For the benefit of the employees who were unable to attend our last meeting, I would like to point out the major question that arose during the meeting and that is of the current profit-sharing pension program

There is absolutely no way that you can jeopardize this benefit or any other benefits that you presently enjoy by self organizing. Your pension program is currently available to all employees of the bank including some twenty (20) or so officers who are not eligible by law to join with you in a collective bargaining agreement.

The monies in this program have been set aside for pension benefits and your employer has already received a tax exemption by meeting Internal Revenue Service requirements. The pension money which has been set aside cannot be used for anything else but pension benefits. Furthermore, the federal law forbids your employer from reducing any of your present benefits for the reason you chose to self organize.

Organization can impove on benefits in two ways. First, eliminate those not in the bargaining unit who take a lion's share from the fund, and second, negotiate higher benefits for those in the bargaining unit.

Unfortunately, a few employees at the First National honestly believe they can gain more on their own. Take a good look at these individuals and see where this has led them. What have they gained? Even your employer is distrustful of them. However, he would use them to his advantage. What happens when they are no longer useful to him? In unity there is strength and in strength and unity there are rewards at the bargaining table with the employer.

Exhibit 4

FIRST NATIONAL BANK OF LAKE CITY

TO: ALL EMPLOYEES

I understand each of you received a letter signed by a stenographer in the name of an international representative of the IMU, which stated the following:

"Unfortunately, a few employees at the First National Bank honestly believe they can gain more on their own. Take a good look at these individuals and see where this has led them. What have they gained? Even your employer is distrustful of them. However, he would use them to his advantage. What happens when they are no longer useful to him? In unity there is strength and in strength and unity there are rewards at the bargaining table with the employer."

The statement that we are distrustful of any of our employees is absolutely false and untrue. If we were distrustful of an employee, he or she would not be working for us.

You have the right to deal with us directly without the intervention of a union on any matter, both with respect to either present benefits of the consideration of any new or additional benefits.

It certainly has not been necessary in the past to have a union intervening on your behalf and we hope that our past record would indicate that a union is neither needed nor necessary in considering future benefits.

The letter states that we would use employees so long as they are advantageous to us and asks what happens when they are no longer useful to us. We do not use any of you in the manner suggested in the letter.

In fact these statements are outrageous and show what lengths the union will go to get you to sign cards.

We wish to make it perfectly clear, however, that you have the right to join a union. You have just as much right not to join. No union can guarantee you economic benefits. If a union wins an election, the bank is not required to sign any contract that it feels is not in its best interests.

In their letter the union refers to our profit sharing plan. Both your pension and profit sharing plans are purely voluntary an the part of the bank and, as you know, both are totally paid for by the bank. We hope to continue them, but there is nothing in the law to require us to do so if we feel economic considerations warrant a change. If you vote in favor of a union, all of these items are subject to negotiation.

I trust that each of you will give all these mattters your serious consideration.

Wynn S. Evans,President

Exhibit 5

FIRST NATIONAL BANK OF LAKE CITY

TO: ALL EMPLOYEES

We are writing this letter in order to report upon the progress to date of our efforts to install a fully paid hospital and major medical plan for all of our employees.

You will recall that you were advised of the bank having to obtain clearance from the Internal Revenue Service prior to the introduction of such a plan

After consultations with appropriate Internal Revenue Service officials, it has been determined that the earliest date when such installation would be permissible is January 1, of next year. This year's salary increases already granted and the increases in profit sharing and pension allocations prevented any earlier implementation of the new hopital and major medical plan.

We are pleased, therefore, to inform you that we will be instituting a fully paid hospital-major medical plan covering both you and your dependents and under which you as an employee make no contribution, approximately two months from date of this letter.

Various proposals from insurance companies and Blue Cross-Blue Shield have been under study. As soon as complete details have been worked out, we will be sending them to you.

We are pleased that we are able to offer this protection to you because we recognize the pressures which unforseen medical expenses can place upon family budgets.

Wynn S. Evans, President

Exhibit 6

Provisions of the
NATIONAL LABOR RELATIONS ACT
(relating to Supervisors and Professionals)

Section 2(3)

The term "employee" shall include any employee, and shall not be limited to the employees of a particular employer, unless the Act explicitly states otherwise, and shall include any individual whose work has ceased as a consequence of, or in connection with, any current labor dispute or because of any unfair labor practice, and has not obtained any other regular or substantially equivalent employment, but shall not include any individual employed as an agricultural laborer, or in domestic service of any family or person at his home, or any individual employed by his parent or spouse, or any individual having the status of an independent contractor, or any individual employed as a supervisor, or any individual employed by an employer subject to the Railway Labor Act, as amended from time to time,or by any other person who is not an employer as herein defined.

Section 2(11)

The term "supervisor" means any individual having authority, in the interests of the employer, to hire, transfer, suspend, layoff, recall, promote, discharge, assign, reward, or discipline other employees, or responsibly to direct them, or to adjust their grievances, or effectively to recommend such action, if in connection with the foregoing the exercise of such authority is not of a merely routine or clerical nature, but requires the use of independent judgement.

Section 14(a)

Nothing herein shall prohibit any individual employed as a supervisor from becoming or remaining a member of a labor organization, but no employer subject to this Act shall be compelled to deem individuals defined herein as supervisors as employees for the purpose of any law, either national or local, relating to collective bargaining.

Section 9(b)

The Board shall decide in each case whether, in order to assure to employees the fullest freedom in exercising the rights guaranteed by the Act, the unit appropriate for the purposes of collective bargaining shall be the employer unit, craft unit, plant unit, or subdivision thereof: Provided, That the Board shall not decide that any unit is appropriate for such purposes if such unit includes both professional employees and employees who are not professional employees unless a majority of such professional employees vote for inclusion in such unit.

Exhibit 7

INTERNATIOANL METALWORKERS UNION
LOCAL 76

TO: EMPLOYEES OF FIRST NATIONAL BANK OF LAKE CITY

This letter will explain the delay in our organizing campaign and is also intended to let you know that the IMU is still very much interested in you as a member of our Union and as an employee of The First National Bank of Lake City.

I am sure the delay concerns you as much as it concerns me. I want you to know there is little the Union can do about the delay but I do want to explain the reason for it.

Recently a hearing was held before a Hearing Officer of the NLRB. Following the hearing, attorneys for the Company and the Union were given twelve days to file post-hearing briefs. After the twelve days, the entire record is turned over the the Regional Director of the Labor Board. When he has completed his study he will then decide what jobs wlll be included in the bargaining unit, and will set the date of the election.

During the course of every union orgainizing campaign, many rumors, usually untrue, are circulated. These rumors are circulated in most instances, by some supervisors or company propagandist who is taken in by the company's opposition to the Union.

Your company is no different. Our orgnaizing committee has informed me that most of the present crop of rumors are so ridiculous that the men are laughing at them. However, there is one persistent rumor that the Committee has asked me to put to sleep once and for all!

These rumor mongers are saying you will lose your profit sharing and pension benefits because you joined the IMU. Nothing could be further from the truth!

We challenge the company, its propaganda artists or anyone else to put in writing that you will lose benefits if the IMU wins!

Don't be taken in by these rumors that are intended to fool and confuse you.

Stick together and be part of the victory parade of the Union.

BLUE JAY RESEARCH COMPANY (C)

Blue Jay Oil Inc. was a major producer, refiner, and marketer of petroleum products with a number of refineries in eastern United States. To carry on its research and development on petroleum and chemical products and processes Blue Jay had established a separate corporation, Blue Jay Research Company, with headquarters and a research lab at Quaker Landing on the Delaware River near Philadelphia.

About twenty years ago some of the Research Company's technicians and office workers at the lab organized an independent association, which they called Blue Jay Technicians and Office Workers Association (BJTOA). Several years after the organization was formed the BJTOA officers indicated to management that they wished to be recognized as the bargaining agent for all the technicians and office workers at the Quaker Landing Lab. Management refused to grant recognition whereupon BJTOA requested the National Labor Relations Board to hold a certification election. (BJTOA had been able to show the NLRB that it had signed cards from more than 30% of the technicians and office workers.) The management and the BJTOA officers were able to agree on the employees to be included in the bargaining unit so that a consent election could be held. Management was of the opinion that a large majority of the employees were opposed to BJTOA and would vote against it. It decided to play a neutral role in the election campaign. Much to its surprise the election results were as follows:

Total eligible voters	355
Total voters	283
BJTOA	148
No Union	135

Following the election management carefully reviewed the situation to determine why the employees had voted for the union and why this had come as a surprise to management.
The conclusions of the review were:

1. The desire for representation came primarily from the technicians rather than from the office workers. If a separate election had been held for the office workers alone, management was convinced the majority would have voted for "no union."

2. Seventy-two employees (which was equal to 20% of those in the bargaining unit) did not vote. Most of these were office employees who did not favor representation. If management had been more active in encouraging employees to vote, enough of these employees might have participated to have altered the results.

3. Wages and benefits were not a significant cause for the desire for representation. The earnings of the technicians and the office workers were better than the earnings of

similar employees in other research labs in the industry and area. The union had not emphasized wages and benefits in asking employees to vote for it.

4. Many of the technicians were unhappy because of the nature of the job. They believed they had little opportunity for advancement beyond the technician classification. With few exceptions, the product manager jobs were held by engineers and chemists with college degrees, mostly Ph.D's A few technicians had been advanced to foremen in pilot plants, but in general the technician job was a dead end.

5. The relationship between a number of the project managers and the technicians was not good. Many of the managers were not people-oriented and lacked skill in dealing with employees. A number of incidents came to light which indicated that company personnel policies were not being properly implemented at the technician level.

6. Communications between management and the employees left much to be desired. One advantage of having a bargaining representative was that the grievance procedure provided an avenue of communications which had been lacking when there was no union.

Among the first demands of BJTOA were the union shop and the check-off. The company agreed to check-off, but turned down the demand for the union shop. However, it did agree to a maintenance of membership clause with a yearly escape provision. Although 42% of the office workers and technicians had voted for the BJTOA in the election, less than 25% signed check-off authorization cards. BJTOA made repeated attempts to increase its membership during later years, but the check-off authorizations never exceeded 25%.

There was nothing spectacular or unusual in the contract negotiations in the first year or in the ten years which followed. Negotiations were amicable. There were no strikes or boycotts or even threats of same. The settlements were comparable to those given by the company to its union and non-union employees at other operations.

A number of grievances did arise each year, but with few exceptions they were settled by the parties themselves without use of the "ad hoc" arbitration procedure provided in the labor contracts. Most of the arbitration awards were favorable to the company.

In 1958 management decided to adopt a merit pay plan throughout the company for its technical and clerical employees. Ranges were established for each job classification and actual pay of each individual within the range was supposed to reflect performance. In order to make the plan effective for the technicians and office workers at the Lab, the company had to negotiate it with BJTOA. As a result the company included the plan among its proposals in the 1958 contract negotiations.

The union leaders were very suspicious of the new plan. In the early negotiating meetings they argued strongly for single job rates. However, as the negotiations proceeded it became clear that a majority of the employees favored the merit pay plan. The union bargaining committee raised many questions about it and the negotiations consumed much more time than any of the prior negotiations, but in the end the plan as proposed by the company, with only minor modifications, became part of the new 1958 labor agreement.

There was always a sizeable group of the office workers and technicians who were opposed to BJTOA. In 1962 a number of them decided to take action. They developed and circulated a decertification petition and were able to get more than the 30% signatures required by the NLRB for an election. After receipt of the petition, the NLRB set an election date for approximately 30 days later. During the 30 days the BJTOA and its opposition campaigned vigorously for and against representation.

Management played no role in the development and circulation of the decertification petition. Once the election date had been set, some representatives of management were of the opinion that the company should actively support the non-union position. After careful consideration, however, the company decided to play a neutral role. No meetings were held with the employees and no letters or statements were sent to them by management. In a statement distributed to the management and supervisory groups the company stated its position as follows:

> The company believes that the best position in this decertification case will be to remain strictly neutral and let the employees decide the issue for themselves, in order to avoid any charges of "maneuvering" by management.

However, the company did urge all employees to vote, pointing out that a majority of those who voted would determine if BJTOA would be retained as the bargaining agent.

In the election, which was held at the Lab during working time, 573 or 74% of the 776 eligible voters cast ballots. The election results as certified by the NLRB were as follows:

BJTOA	417	(73%)
No Union	156	(27%)

Thus, BJTOA continued to represent all the employees in the unit, although its membership as indicated by check-off authorizations was less than 25% of the employees in the unit.

Soon after the election, the President of BJTOA wrote a letter to the company in which he expressed appreciation for the neutral position taken by the management. The letter read:

> We wish to take this opportunity to comment on the position taken by the company during the recent decertification proceedings and subsequent election.
>
> It was noted with appreciation the company maintained a neutral position throughout the entire matter thereby allowing represented employees complete freedom in exercising their individual determination.

BLUE JAY RESEARCH COMPANY (C)

Following the decertification election, BJTOA leadership had a series of meetings in which it attempted to reevaluate the status of the organization. The election had shown that, although 73% of those who voted favored BJTOA, a sizeable group, 27%, were opposed to it. In addition, 203 members of the bargaining unit or 26% failed to vote, indicating lack of interest in BJTOA. Thus, only 54% of the employees in the unit had supported the union by voting for it. The union was even more concerned by the fact that only 25% of the employees (less than half of those who voted for it) were dues-paying members.

As a result of the meetings, the union leadership was convinced that many employees viewed BJTOA as a "company union" with no real power to enforce the demands of the employees. They decided that BJTOA needed more "muscle," more knowledgeable and stronger leadership, and more financial support. As a result, the leadership recommended to the membership that BJTOA seek affiliation with one of the big strong unions in the Philadelphia area. Some thought was given to joining up with the Teamsters. An arrangement was finally worked out and approved by the membership whereby BJTOA would be affiliated with one of the maritime unions, but would retain considerable autonomy. The maritime union was one which did not represent any of the other employees of the company, including the men on its tanker fleet.

Following the affiliation, one of the officers was given a leave from the company and devoted full-time to the union. The number of grievances increased and more were carried to arbitration, although the great majority continued to be decided in favor of the company. The union leaders became more militant and assumed an increasingly adversary attitude in the company-union relationship. The Treasurer of the union, who was not a full-time officer, became especially aggressive and eventually filed a grievance, in which he accused the company of actively discriminating against him. The union carried the grievance to arbitraion, but the arbitrator decided that the company was not guilty of discrimination. The union also carried on an actve campaign to increase it membership, but was not successful in pushing it above the 25% mark.

With the support of the maritime union behind it, BJTOA assumed a much more aggressive position in negotiations in the late 1960s and early 1970s. However, the company and the union were able to reach agreement without resorting to strikes or lockouts, although the help of federal mediators was frequently employed. On July 1, 1972 following several months of difficult negotiations, the parties signed a new two-year agreement which became effective June 1, 1972, and terminated June 1, 1974. The 1972-74 agreement provided, among other things, for an 8.5% increase in wages rates and ranges retroactive to March 1, 1972, and another increase of 7.5% effective as of March 1, 1973.

The rate ranges for Reasearch Technician Jobs after March 1, 1973 were:

MONTHLY RATE RANGE (40 hour basis)		
Classification	Minimum	Maximum
Senior Reasearch Technician (SRT)	$862	$1,178
Research Technician (RT)	775	1,058
Associate Research Technician (ART)	694	947
Laboratory Assistant (LA)	641	842

The Contract contained the following language regarding merit rating:

> Wages shall be administered within the above ranges in accordance with the following policy:
>
> 1. Employees with minimum or starting performance shall be paid at least the range minimum, but not significantly higher.
>
> 2. Employees with excellent and outstanding performance after thorough seasoning in their jobs or classifications shall be paid the range maximum.
>
> 3. Employees whose performance is intermediate between the above ranges shall be paid appropriate intermediate wages.

By 1972 the company had become convinced that the merit pay plan, which was applicable not only at the Lab, but also elswhere throughout the company, needed major revisions. A committee was appointed to make a companywide study and to come up with recommendations. The committee found that the plan was not truly serving its original purpose of rewarding employees in relation to their performance, but instead had degenerated to the point where it was primarily a time progression plan. The senior employees were all at or near the top of the rate ranges, whereas the junior employees were at or near the bottom. The ranges were quite broad, and it frequently happened that some employees in a low job classification received a higher rate than employees in a job classification several grades higher. Additionally, performance differences between the highest and lowest paid employees in a classification didn't justify the wide disparity in pay. However, administration of the merit pay plan had not resulted in serious difficulties between the company and the union, perhaps because it had become largely a time progression plan. Although there had been some grievances involving it, not one of them had resulted in arbitration.

In May 1974, the company and the union were starting negotiations to replace the 1972-74 agreement, which terminated on June 1. At that time the company's Merit Pay Plan Committee had not yet completed its study and recommendations. The company proposed, therefore, a general wage increase for the first year of the contract retroactive to March 1, 1974, but instead of a wage increase the second year (as had been customary in earlier contracts) a wage reopener so that the merit pay plan could be negotiated when it became available.

The BJTOA negotiating committee strongly opposed the wage reopener in lieu of a second year wage increase. It pointed out that the other unions which represented the hourly-paid employees at the refineries had already negotiated a general wage increase for 1975. The company assured the committee that when the new merit pay plan became available, it would see to it that the average increase would be equal to that which the hourly-paid employees would receive in 1975. However, it was clear that some employees would receive more and some employees would receive less than the average. The committee argued that all of the employees should receive a general increase, and that any changes in the merit plan should be in addition to a general increase.

No agreement on the terms of a new contract had been reached on June 1, 1974 when the 1972-74 contract terminated. However, the union did not strike, but instead continued to work under the terms of the old contract. Negotiations continued into June without success. The company then indicated that, although it had been willing originally to make the pay increase retroacive to March 1, 1974, if agreement had been reached on June 1, it would insist on moving the date forward one month for each month that signing of a new agreement was delayed.

As the negotiations continued into July, considerable discontent developed among the employees over the possible loss of the retroactive pay. Finally, the union leadership agreed to take the company's proposal to the membership without recommendation. The majority of the membership approved the company's proposal, which provided for a 6% wage rate and wage range increases retroactive to April 1, 1974 (the employees lost one month of retroactive pay), and a wage reopener effective as of November 1, 1974. The wage ranges for Research Laboratory Jobs in the new contract were:

MONTHLY RATE RANGE
(40 hour basis)

Classification	Minimum	Maximum
Senior Research Technician (SRT)	$914	$1,249
Research Technician (RT)	821	1,122
Associate Research Technician (ART)	735	1,003
Laboratory Assistant (LA)	679	892

BLUE JAY RESEARCH COMPANY (C)

Article XXV, Paragraph J, of the new 1974-76 Agreement read:

> It is recognized by the parties that it may become desirable to negotiate on the basis for salary administration for classified office and technician employees during the term of this Agreement, and for this purpose only, each party may once only, on or after November 1, 1974, by written notice to the other, request a conference to consider revision in the light of existing conditions. If agreement is not reached during the sixty (60) days following date of delivery of such notice by registered United States mail, either party at any time thereafter may give sixty (60) days written notice of desire to terminate the Agreement in which case the Agreement shall terminate as of the end of such sixty (60) day period following receipt of such notice unless by mutual consent the parties agree to extend the Agreement for a specific period for the continuation of negotiations.

By October 1974 the company's Merit Pay Plan Committee had completed its study and recommendations. It proposed that the old merit pay plan should be replaced by a new "pay for performance" plan. Under the proposed plan new, narrower rate ranges would be established; and the position of an employee within the range would be determined solely by performance without reference to the time spent within the grade. Recognizing that negotiating such a plan with the union would be difficult, the company decided to propose that it be put into effect gradually over a period of time with full implementation in about two years. The company informed the union then that it wished to open the contract on November 1, 1974 as permitted under Paragraph J of Article XXV for the purpose of negotiating the new "pay for performance" plan.

The company proposed that effective March 1, 1975 every employee would receive an increase of at least $25 per month; that increases beyond that level would be solely on the basis of performance, but would average $50 per month; that higher, but narrower, ranges would be established as follows:

	Minimum	Maximum
SRT	$1,070	$1,300
RT	950	1,125
ART	835	985
LA	745	870

The company indicated that the average percentage increase for the technicians would be the same as that to be effective March 1, 1975, in the contracts negotiated with other unions for the refinery workers. The company's proposal provided, however, that disputes over individual merit ratings would <u>not</u> be subject to arbitration.

At first the union refused to negotiate regarding the "pay for performance" plan, claiming that under Paragraph J the parties could negotiate only with respect to a general wage increase. The union also filed an unfair labor practice charge against the company claiming that some of the foremen had violated the law by talking with employees concerning possible increases under the company's proposed plan. Later the union withdrew the unfair labor practice charge and entered into negotiations by filing a long list of demands, including many non-wage items.

As the negotitations proceeded, most of the union's demands were settled, but no progess was made on the company's "pay for performance" proposal. Although the union opposed the "pay for performance" plan in general, it was especially strong in the opposition to two aspects: 1. that the plan would be in lieu of the March 1, 1975, general wage increase; 2. that individual merit ratings under the plan would not be subject to arbitration. The company tried to meet the first objection by agreeing that every employee would receive some increase, and that the average increase would be equal to the March 1, 1975, general increase granted to the refinery workers. The union insisted, however, that any increases resulting from the new "pay for performance" plan should be in addition to the general increase, which should be shared equally by all employees. With respect to arbitration, the company believed it was necessary to deny it if the new plan was to be effective. It pointed out to the union that although arbitration had been possible under the old plan, the union had never made use of it. The union was not convinced. It contended that without arbitration, mangement's decision in merit cases would be final and the union's ability to protect the employees against injustices in this important area would be lost. Finally, it argued that if management intended its decisions on merit to be fair and just, it should have no fear of defending them before an impartial arbitratior.

On January 1, 1975, the 60-day deadline for negotiations provided in paragraph J of Article XXV was reached. The union was then free to give notice that it was terminating the contract in 60 days, which would have left it free to strike on March 1, 1975. However, the union decided to keep the contract in effect and to continue to bargain. It did not strike or threaten to strike, although it did engage in sporadic informational picketing at the Lab and at one of the company's nearby service stations.

On January 11, 1975, the company took the initiative by officially notifying the union that it intended to terminate the contract in 60 days as provided under Article XXV, Paragraph J. January and February passed without any real progress toward a settlement, and as the March 11, 1975, termination date approached, the union called in federal mediators. A meeting was held with the mediators on March 6, and again on March 11, but they were not successful in achieving agreement. After the contract ran out on March 11, 1975, the company continued to operate under the old terms except that it refused to check off union dues and refused to arbitrate grievances.

In March 1975 the company made the "pay for performance" plan effective for its technician and office employees elsewhere throughout the company. Those employees received the higher rates retroactive to March 1, 1975

As the stalemate continued into April, the company notified the union and the employees that it would not agree to retroactivity to March 1, 1975, for employees represented by BJTOA unless an agreement was reached by May 1. On April 18, the union offered and the company rejected a proposal that all outstanding issues be put to binding arbitration.

As the May 1 date approached, it became apparent that many of the employees were not in sympathy with the union's position. They had lost a month's retroactive pay in 1974, and did not want this to happen again. About this time the foremen in one of the Lab departments informed the company that some of the employees were circulating a petition which requested the NLRB to hold a decertification election. Despite the developing opposition among the employees, the BJTOA bargaining committee held to its position, and the May 1 date passed without an agreement. By May 22, more than 30% of the employees in the department where the decertification petition was being circulated had signed it, and it was presented by its sponsors to NRLB regional office. However, the NLRB turned down the petition, ruling that the department was not an appropriate unit in which to hold an election.

Late in May another petition for a decertification election, this time covering the entire bargaining unit, began to be circulated. By August 13, 1975, more than 30% of the employees in the entire bargaining unit had signed the petition, and on that date the sponsors filed it with the NLRB. However, the action by the NLRB was delayed by the filing of an unfair labor practice charge by BJTOA, in which it claimed that the company had violated the law by permitting certain employees to prepare, on company time, letters which urged decertification. About this time the company offered a general 6% wage increase (which constituted the industry pattern) to the unions which represented the employees in its other operations. The 6% increase was accepted quickly by the other unions, and became effective retroactively to August 1, 1975. The company considered giving the 6% increase unilaterally to the employees represented by BJTOA, but took no immediate action.

On September 4, 1975, the union withdrew the unfair labor practice charge and the NLRB set October 24 as the date for the election. An independent union group, Blue Jay Employees Association (BJEA), which had been organized during the past several months, then petitioned for and was granted a place on the ballot by the NLRB. Thus, the ballot would give the employees the opportunity to choose between:

BJTOA
BJEA
NO Union

Following the annoucement by the NLRB of the election date, BJTOA and BJEA began aggressive campaigns to win the election. BJTOA held numerous meetings with the employees; sent letters to the employees explaining its position and criticizing management's insistence on the "pay for performance" proposal; made use of the bulletin boards to urge employees to vote for it; and developed taped telephone messages, which it urged the employees to listen to.

The dispute between the company and the union over the "pay for performance" plan and the split among the employees concerning union representation was not without cost to the company. Much valuable time, which would have been spent on research, was being spent instead not only by technicians, but also by project managers and others, discussing various aspects of the disputes. Moreover, bitter disagreement on these matters between members of many of the research groups hindered the kind of cooperation which was essential for effective teamwork. It was in this atmosphere that David Eckman, Vice President of Personnel and Labor Relations, decided to call a meeting to consider and reevaluate the company's position. Among the items on the agenda Eckman included:

1. Should the company hold firm on the "pay for performance" plan, or would it be better to drop it at this time?

2. If it was decided to hold firm on the plan in general, should the company at least agree to arbitration of merit ratings?

3. What should the company do about the 6% increase of August 1, 1975; negotiate a separate agreement on it with BJTOA; place it into effect unilaterally; do nothing?

4. Should the company continue to take a completely neutral position with respect to decertification, or should it play a more active role?

BLUE JAY RESEARCH COMPANY (D)

At a meeting which David Eckman, Vice President of Personnel and Labor Relations, called in September 1975 to revise and reevaluate the company's position with respect to the impasse in negotiations with the union over a new "pay for performance" plan and an upcoming decertification election, it was decided that the company would:

1. Hold firm with respect to the "pay for performance" plan;

2. Not agree to the arbitration of individual ratings under the new plan;

3. Do nothing regarding the 6% increase of August 1, 1975, until after the decertification election;

4. Play a positive and active role in trying to convince employees to vote for "no union" in the election.

To implement its decision to play an active role in decertification, the company decided upon the following communications program.

1. <u>Meetings With Management People</u>

   Outline communications program
   Explanation of pay for performance
   "Do's and Don'ts for Supervisors

2. <u>Meetings With All Employees</u>

3. <u>First Line Supervisor Group</u>

   "One-On-One" communicatons
   Weekly meetings to review status

4. <u>Fact Sheets for Supervisors</u>

   Questions and answers

5. <u>Bulletins Comparing Company Policy and BJTOA Contract</u>

6. <u>Taped Telephone Messages ("Hot Line")</u>

7. <u>Letters From President</u>

8. <u>Talks By President</u>

Meetings were held with groups of management people, including meetings with first line supervisors. At these meetings it was made clear that mangement expected its representatives to play a positive role. A leaflet published by the Naional Association of Manufacturers entitled <u>Do's and Don'ts for Supervisors</u> was distributed and discussed. (See Exhibits D-2 and D-3 for reproduction of part of this leaflet.)

Fact sheets were prepared and sent to supervisors and management representatives so that they could answer fully and accurately any questions which employees might raise with them. A copy of one of the fact sheets is reproduced. (See Exhibit D-1.)

A series of letters signed by the President, R.J. Jones, was sent to the employees at their home addresses. Jones' first letter is reproduced as Exhibit D-4.

A series of Employee Bulletins in which company policy statements and union contract provisions were compared were posted on the bulletin boards throughout the Lab. Employee Bulletin No. 4 is reproduced as Exhibit D-5.

The company taped several telephone messages each week, and encouraged employees to listen to them. An example of a company message, which was placed on the line on October 17, is the following:

> The BJTOA desperately wants you to believe that only through their representation can employees be assured of fair treatment and that without representation you may be at a serious disadvantage. The BJTOA's October 17 telephone message stated that the company's grievance procedure is "a stacked deck because there is no provision for an impartial third party to arbitrate disputes." Let's examine the union's record in grievance and arbitration. Of the last 30 grievances filed, four have gone to a third party for decision. In all four cases, the impartial third party found that the company had acted properly.

As indicated earlier, the two union groups, especially the BJTOA, carried on very active campaigns making use of letters, handbills, meetings, taped telephone messages, and informational picketing. One of BJTOA handbills is reproduced as Exhibit D-6.

As the election date approached, there was guarded optimism in the management group. It was believed that the company's communication program had been effective and that although the election would be close, a majority would vote for "no union."

Exhibit D-1

FACT SHEET FOR SUPERVISORS NO. 2

The following are to be used as guidelines. As a legal requirement, supervisors must not, in conversations with employees, make statments which can be construed as promises, threats, or coercion affecting the employees' free choice in a representation election.

Q. Why was the August 1st six percent increase, which was accepted by other unions, called a temporary increase?

A. This increase was an exception in that it was offered to the union while their contracts were still in effect. For that reason it was offered only for the remaining term of those contracts. Blue Jay and the unions which represent some of its employees have historically settled on whatever wage pattern has been set by the industry. Since the 1976 industry pattern won't be set until the end of 1975, it was decided that the August 1st increase would be temporary until that time and then the Company will negotiate with the unions on the basis of whatever the 1976 pattern is. Incidentally, the August 1st increase was granted to nonrepresented employees as a permanent increase; that is, the wage and salary structures were adjusted upward by the six percent.

Q. Isn't it true that without the union we would have suffered the same layoffs which occured in the Southern Operations Producing and Transportation Departments?

A. No, this is not true. In fact, the non-ememept employees of both Southern Producing and Transportation Departments are represented by unions. The reason there were no layoffs here is that we have not had to make the large manpower reductions that have been necessary in other areas. When there are no layoffs it is because of the health of the activity and the need for its services, not because of the presence of a union. Unions cannot guarantee job security.

Q. How many employees are working without labor contracts in Blue?

A. There are approxiamtely 7,500 classified Blue Jay employees in the United States and Canada who could be represented by unions, but who have chosen to remain nonrepresented. In the Blue Jay home office complex there are approximately 900 classified employees, and only about 100 of these are represented by a union. All of these nonrepresented employees' wages, hours, and working conditions are covered by company policy and/or laws.

Exhibit D-2

SOME THINGS YOU AS A SUPERVISOR CAN DO:

1. Tell employees that if a majority of them select the union (an outside organization), the company will have to deal with it on all their daily problems involving wages, hours and other conditions of employment. Advise them that the company would prefer to continue dealing with them directly on such matters.

2. Tell employees that you and other members of management are always willing to discuss with them any subject of interest to them.

3. Tell employees about the benefits they presently enjoy, all of which may have been obtained without union representation. Avoid promises or threats, either direct or veiled.

4. Tell employees how their wages, benefits and working conditions compare favorably with other companies in the area, whether unionized or not. Information should be factual.

5. Tell employees some of the disadvantages of belonging to a union such as the expense of initiation fees, monthly dues, fines, strike assessments, and membership rules restricting their personal freedom. Quote from the specific union's constitution and by-laws granting the union power to impose punishment and discipline against its members.

6. Tell employees there is a possibility that a union will call a strike or work stoppage even though many employees may not want to strike and even though the employeer is willing to bargain or has been bargaining with the union. Inform employees that any strike can cost them money in lost wages.

7. Tell employees that in negotiating with the union the company does not have to agree to all of the union's terms, and certainly not to any terms which are not in the econimic interests of the business.

8. Tell employees about any experience you may have had with unions, especially the union seeking to represent the employees. Be very factual.

9. Tell employees anything you know about the union or its officers. Be sure your statements are truthful and relevant to the employees' selection or rejection

10. Tell employees your opinion about union policies and union leaders, even though in uncomplimentary terms. (Be factually correct in referring to those policies and leaders.)

11. Tell employees about any untrue or misleading statements made by an organizer, or in a handbill, or through any other medium of union propaganda. You may always give employees the correct facts.

12. Tell employees that in your opinion, the International Union may try to control or dominate the local union, possibly to the disadvantage of the local membership.

Exhibit D-2 (continued)

13. Tell employees about known racketeering, Communist participa-tion, or other undesirable activities in the union. Relate only established facts.

14. Distribute reprints of articles containing information about unions or facts revealed through Congressional or other public hearings. Refer only to the union seeking to represent the employees, and identify, including the date, the source of such information or facts.

15. Tell employees that they are free to join or not to join any organization without prejudice to their status with the company.

16. Tell employees that merely signing a union authorization card or application for membership does not mean that they must vote for the union in an election. If the situation warrants, advise employees that the union may use the signed authorization cards to obtain bargaining rights without an NLRB election.

17. Tell employees about the NLRB election procedures, the importance of voting, and emphasize the secrecy of the ballot.

18. Tell employees about their legal rights. However, there should not be any encouragement or financing of any employee suit or proceeding.

19. Actually campaign against a union seeking representation of your employees, stressing the advantages and the history of fair, direct dealings without intervention of outsiders.

20. Make and/or consistently enforce rules that soliciation of membership or discussion of union affairs must be outside working time so that it will not interfer with an employee's own work or impede the work of others. Remember, however, an employee can solicit and discuss unionism on his own time, even on company premises, when it does not interrupt work.

21. Make or enforce a rule restricting the distribution of all literature, whether, union or otherwise, to the non-working areas of the plant premises.

22. Enforce other plant rules impartially and in accordance with customary action, irrespective of the employee's membership or activity in a union.

23. Lay off, discipline and discharge for cause so long as such action follows customary practice and is done without regard to union membership or non-union membership.

24. Make assignments of preferred work, overtime, shift preference, so long as such is done without regard to the employee's participation or non-participation in union activities.

Exhibit D-3

SOME THINGS YOU AS A SUPERVISOR CANNOT DO:

1. Promise employees a pay increase, promotion, betterment, benefit, or special favor if they stay out of the union or vote against it.

2. Threaten loss of jobs, reduction of income, discontinuance of privileges or benefits presently enjoyed, or use intimidating language which may be designed to influence an employee in the exercise of his right to belong, or refrain from belonging to a union.

3. Threaten or actually discharge, discipline or lay-off an employee because of his activities in behalf of the union.

4. Threaten, through a third party, any of the foregoing acts of interference.

5. Threaten to close or move the plant, or to drastically reduce operations if a union is selected as a representative.

6. Spy on union meetings. (Parking across the street from a union hall to watch employees entering the hall would be suspect.)

7. Conduct yourself in a way which would indicate to the employees that you are watching them to determine whether or not they are participating in union activities.

8. Discriminate against employees actively supporting the union by intentionally assigning undesirable work to the union employee.

9. Transfer employees prejudicially because of union affiliation.

10. Engage in any partially favoring non-union employees over employees active in behalf of the union.

11. Discipline or penalize employees actively supporting union for an infraction which non-union employees are permitted to commit without being likewise diciplined.

12. Make any work assignment for the purpose of causing an employee who has been active on behalf of the union to quit his job.

13. Take any action that is intended to impair the status of, or adversely affect an employee's job or pay because of his activity in behalf of the union.

14. Intentionally assign work or transfer employees so that those active in behalf of the union are separated from those you beleive are not interested in supporting a union.

Exhibit D-3 (continued)

15. Select employees to be laid off with the intention of curbing the union's strength, or to discourage affiliation with it.

16. Ask employees for an expression of their thoughts about a union or its officers.

17. Ask employees how they intend to vote in a union election.

18. Ask employees at time of hiring or thereafter whether they belong to a union or have signed a union application or authorization card.

19. Ask employees about the internal affairs of union such as meetings, etc. (Some employees may, of their own accord, walk up and tell of such matters. It is not an unfair labor practice to listen, but you must not ask questions to obtain additional information.)

20. Make a statement that you will not deal with the union.

21. Make statements to the employees to the effect that they will be discharged or disciplined if they are active in behalf of the union.

22. Urge employees to persuade others to oppose the union or stay out of it.

23. Prevent employees from soliciting union membership during their free time on company premises so long as such does not interfere with work being performed by others.

24. Give financial support or assistance to a union, its representatives or employees.

25. Visit the homes of employees for the purpose of urging them to reject the union.

26. Make speeches to massed assemblies of employees on company time within the twenty-four hour period before the opening of polls for a representation election.

27. Speak to an employee or small group of employees in your office or the office of some other management official about the union campaign and urge him, (them) to vote against the union. (Remember-the best place to talk to employees about such matters is at their work stations or in work areas where other employees are present.)

28. Help employees to withdraw union memberships.

29. Ask employees about the identity of the instigator or leader of employees favoring the union.

(NOTE: The DON'Ts included in this section also apply to discriminating against employees who favor one union over another.)

Exhibit D-4

Blue Jay Research Company
R.J. Jones, President

I am writing to you about a subject of utmost importance to all of us at Blue Jay Research - the petition which has been filed to decertify the BJTOA as your bargaining agent. This petition has been signed by a sufficient number of people at Blue Jay Research Company to cause the NLRB to order an election to determine whether the BJTOA, or the Blue Jay Employees Association (a newly formed union) , or neither should be an intermediary between us.

So long as you are represented by any union, whether it is BJTOA, an employee association, or any bargaining agent, I and my representatives are legally restrained from fully and freely discussing all matters of wages, hours, and working conditions with you as an individual. However, there are some things I can legally comment on. Therefore, I am writing to you to make sure you are fully aware of the facts and events leading up to the filing of the decertification petition.

Here is a brief outline of what has occured during the past eleven months:

- In October 1974, the Company and BJTOA began negotiations a new pay plan for office employees and technicians. Through May 1975, ten meetings were held on this matter with no agreement.

- Effective March 1, 1975, a new pay plan was installed and all non-represented classified clerical employees and technicians in the Blue Jay family received pay increases in accordance with that plan. The unions representing employees elsewhere in Blue Jay have agreed to this new plan, and pay increases were granted to those employees.

- On March 11, 1975, the contract between the company and BJTOA terminated.

- On May 22, 1975, a group of employees filed a petition to decertify BJTOA in their department. The National Labor Relations Board ruled that it would not be appropriate to hold an election for just that group since the BJTOA contract covered people in other departments.

- On August 13, 1975, another employee petition for decertification of the BJTOA was filed with the NLRB.

Exhibit D-4 (continued)

Subsequent to August 13, Blue Jay offered a 6% wage increase to other union-represented groups. The increase was accepted and was retroactive to August 1. The net result was that all groups of classified employees throughout the corporate family who normally receive increases based on the oil industry pattern received the 6% general increase, except for the BJTOA represented employees. You may perhaps not realize that the law requires the company to bargain with the BJTOA (or other unions if certified) for as long as it takes to either reach an agreement or arrive at an impasse, before any changes can be made in your wages. At the same time, the company is restrained from bargaining with the BJTOA while there is a question of its being the representative of a majority of employees.

As I said at the beginning of this letter, this decertification election is very important to all of us at Blue Jay Resaerch. If you had not been represented by a union, there would have been no legal restraints to prevent our granting you the increases given to other non-represented employees.

I have been told that there will be three choices on the ballot for the October 24 election. They will be : BJTOA, BJEA, and third, "Neither". It is my sincere conviction that it would be in the best interest of all of us for you to cast your vote for the third choice, "Neither". I am firmly convinced this is the best course for these reasons:

- A majority vote for " Neither" will permit the quickest resolution of our current pay problem.

- We will have one year to demonstrate that union representation is not necessary to assure fair and amicable relationships between you and your supervisor and all the rest of us in management. (If you are not convinced of this, you will be free to seek union representation a year after the election.)

Betweem now and the election date, October 24, I will keep you informed on this matter. In the meantime, if you have any questions, please ask them of your supervisors. If they don't know the answers, I have asked that they get the answers for you.

Sincerely,

R. J. Jones

Exhibit D-5

Blue Jay Research Company
Employee Bulletin No. 4

TO: BJTOA REPRESENTED EMPLOYEES

This is another in a series of information bulletins which will compare BJTOA contract terms with benefits or conditions of employment that are provided for by Company policy or law.

Provisions in the union contract and Company policy covering termination of employment are shown below.

UNION CONTRACT
Article IX
Termination of Employment

DISCHARGE: Discharge for just cause may be accomplished by the employee's management supervisor without review or approval except that such employee shall have the right to submit the matter under the established grievance procedure. Employees with one or more years of continuing service so discharged shall, upon their request, be given a statement in writing within seven (7) in calendar days covering reasons for the action taken. If a complaint under this section is to be made, it must be submitted in writing to the Company within fourteen (14) calendar days after the date of discharge.

The company shall notify the Union in writing , within five (5) days, after termination, the name and termination date of any employee, with one or more years of continuous service, discharged for cause.

COMPANY POLICY
Policy 380
Termination of Employment

This policy pertains to terminations of employment resulting from resignation, layoff due to lack of work, or discharge. It is desired to keep such terminations at a minimum; therefore, before any termination is concluded, all pertinent should be given thorough consideration. When a termination is necessary, however, it should be should handled a manner that will retain, as far as possible, the good will of the employee concerned.

Terminations are the responsiblility of the head of the organization concerned. However, when appropriate, authority to terminate may be delegated to local management except as provided below.

When contemplating layoff or discharge of an employee having 10 or more years of continuous service, the case shall be submitted to the head of the organization concerned before final action is taken. (When individual circumstances warrant immediate action, the employee may be suspended pending final decision on his case.) An employee shall be advised orally of the reason for his termination. In all cases of discharge for cause, this explanation should be given by his supervisor in the presence of at least one other management representative.

Exhibit D-6

WOULD YOU VOTE FOR YOURSELF?

Of course you would!

...and no one knows it better than the boss.

THAT'S WHY THE BOSS LIKES TO GET THE "**YOU**" OUT OF "**UNION**" WHEN THERE'S AN ELECTION COMING.

HE LIKES TO SEPARATE **YOU** FROM **UNION** . . . MAKE YOU THINK OF UNION AS AN "OUTSIDE" FORCE. HE WANTS YOU TO VOTE BETWEEN HIM AND THEM. HIS BEST CHANCE OF HAVING YOU VOTE HIS INTERESTS IS TO FORGET YOUR INTERESTS. THAT MEANS FORGETTING THAT ORGANIZING IS YOUR EFFORT TO DEVELOP PROGRESS AND SECURITY FOR YOURSELF AND YOUR FELLOW WORKERS THROUGH THE WORLD'S GREATEST "DO-IT-YOURSELF" PROGRAM . . . **UNIONISM.**

Only YOU can win or lose!

WIN, LOSE, OR DRAW THE UNION WILL STILL EXIST. THE COMPANY WILL STILL EXIST. BUT HOW ABOUT **YOUR** EXISTENCE? ONLY A UNION VICTORY CAN CHANGE IT AND BRIGHTED IT BY GIVING YOU A VOICE IN YOUR SECURITY **TODAY** AND YOUR PROGRESS **TOMORROW.**

EVERYONE WANTS SECURITY, PROGRESS, FAIR TREATMENT. IT BOILS DOWN TO THE BELIEF YOU AND YOUR FELLOW WORKERS HAVE IN YOUR OWN ABILITIES TO BUILD THE KIND OF UNION THAT CAN DO THE JOB. 15 MILLION AMERICANS TODAY HAVE DONE IT. YOU CAN DO IT . . . BUT NOT IF YOU FALL FOR THE COMPANY'S BAIT OF SEEING THE CAMPAIGN AS SOMETHING BETWEEN THE COMPANY AND THE "UNION." IT'S **YOUR** UNION . . . **YOUR** CAMPAIGN . . . **YOUR** ELECTION.

VOTE "YES"

KEEP YOUR FUTURE IN SIGHT

THE WASHINGTON POST (A)

On Wednesday afternoon, December 3, 1975, the strike of the pressmen's union against The Washington Post was 64 days old. To Katharine Graham, publisher of The Post, and Mark Meagher, the general manager, it was time to implement some decisions, the groundwork for which had been prepared over several weeks.

The Post management faced the pressmen's strike with the knowledge that their one rival, the Washington Star, would continue to publish. Based on precedent, if the pressmen's strike was a long one, The Post could anticipate serious short and long term losses. On December 3, The Post had beaten the odds for 6 weeeks. Against expectations The Post had succeeded in publishing a paper which had held most of its market. The Post's ability to print in the face of a craft strike, moreover, highlighted the issue which lay at the heart of the confrontation. A new technology was coming into the newspaper industry which opened to papers the possibity of operating with a substantially reduced work force. Utilizing the new technology and a small group of non-craft employees, The Post had published.

However, if The Post had so far beaten the odds, Mrs. Graham and Mr. Meagher knew that only the heroic efforts of employees who did their regular jobs by day, then produced the paper by night, had made this possible. After 9 weeks negotiations with the pressmen had shown no progress. As they evaluated their position on December 3, prominent among their thouhgts was the knowledge that the endurance of the people in the building was dwindling, that after Christmas (at a good guess), the energy and morale which had sustained them would begin to flag.

THE NEWSPAPER INDUSTRY

The American newspaper industry in the 1970s was an industry under pressure. Labor cost, as in most other industries, had steadily risen. U.S. manufacturing labor costs, on average, were 25% of production costs; in newspapers, however, labor costs were 30% to 50%. Newsprint costs, which accounted for another 25% of production costs, in turn, had risen considerably, and in 1975 were up over 40% from the beginning of 1973. Newspapers had difficulty in passing these increased costs on to their customers in the form of higher circulation prices and advertising fees.

Advertising revenue was particularly hard to increase. The advertising market structure was highly elastic. Advertising volume (measured as the number of standard column lines of advertising or "ad linage") tended to drop significantly when linage rates increased. Often increases in linage rates resulted in advertisers permanently transfering their business to radio or television. In 1974, for example, with the lifting of price controls, linage rates increase 8% while advertising revenue rose 5.3% and for the first time since 1970, newspapers' dollar share of the total advertising market declined .3%. Though less sensitive than increases in ad-linage rates, increases in circulation prices were also limited by competitive pressures. Many large American cities had two or more competing papers, and there was a growing trend for competition between neighboring cities. Increases in newsstand prices could also make readers give up newspaper buying altogether. In 1974, for example, the state of the economy and increased circulation prices were credited with a drop of 2% in overall daily circulation.

The 1974-75 recession hurt both advertising and circulation revenues. In late 1975, expectations in the newspaper industry were that with a recovering economy, ad and circulation revenues would also improve. Whether increases in revenues could keep pace with increases in costs, however, was uncertain and predictions were that for the immediate future, at least, the newspaper industry would continue in a cost-price squeeze.

THE NEWSPAPER PRODUCTION PROCESS

Until the late 1960s the process technology used at large newspapers dated from the late 19th century (see Exhibit 1). This process technology was a true industrial art. Skilled craftsmen were required for most phases. Increasingly, from the mid-1960s onward, however, technological innovations became available with the potential to significantly alter the nature of the process. While these innovations were introduced at all levels, the most radical changes occurred in the "composing room" where the newspaper pages were put together before printing.

The traditional method for preparing pages for printing was "hot-type" composition. As it was readied for processing, copy from the newspaper departments was sent to the composing room where printers (sometimes called typesetters) set the copy into type using a variety of composing machines. For the most common of these, the linotype, the printer operated a keyboard that droped brass molds and space bars into a line. Molten metal was poured into the line of molds creating a "slug" - hence "hot-type." The molds were then returned to their places in a magazine to be re-used. The slugs were collected into columns of type. Once the type columns were assembled they went to a "proof press" where proofs were printed and proofreaders checked for typographical errors (in which case the slug was recast). After proofing, the type columns, along with metal plates upon which the images of the photos to be used had been etched by photoengravers, were put together by printers into page form according to a layout specified by editors or designers. When a full page form was completed, it was sent to the stereotype department where an impression of the form was made on a soft pliable mat. The mat, in turn, became the mold from which curved lead plates were made for use on the presses.

During the latter 1960s, the marriage of photographic with computer technology resulted in a new method of preparing pages-"cold-type" composition. In the cold-type process, copy was inputted into a computer either by means of an optical scanner which "read" the copy directly or by means of the keyboard on a terminal. In the most modern cold-type plants, copy, once inputted, could be proofed, edited, and laid out in page form directly in the computer by means of video terminals. In less sophisticated plants the computer prepared printed copy in column form. The computer produced photographic reproductions of the inputs (complete pages in the most sophisticated plants, column strips and separate graphics in the less sophisticated plants). These reproductions were pasted down on cardboard page grids according to the layout design. Once completed the page grids were photographed by a photoengraving machine which produced either a plastic or metal plate which was sent to the stereotype department to be converted first into a mat and then into a lead plate.

From the composing room, finished curved lead plates went to the pressroom where they were printed on web presses. The plates were bolted to cylinders. The cylinders simultaneously printed on both sides of continuous rolls of newsprint (the "web") which was fed through the intricate series of rollers and cylinders of the press. A modern web press had the capacity to print up to 80,000 papers/hour but seldom reached capacity because of breaks in the web. These breaks occurred, on average, two or three times in the course of a normal printing run and resulted in at least a 10 minute shutdown while the web was rethreaded. At The Post, there were nine presses each with eight units. A unit could carry sixteen plates. The maximum page capacity of a press at The Post was 112 pages. The Post routinely printed papers over 100 pages in length and used six or seven presses at once, each printing the same plates. When an edition was going to be over 112 pages, on Sunday for example, supplementary sections were printed during day runs. The normal printing runs were at night.

Once printed, the sheets of newsprint from the different units of the press were combined, cut, and folded into finished papers. The finished papers went by conveyor to the mailroom where they were prepared for distribution. While technological changes on a scale with those which had occurred in the composing room had not yet taken place in the pressroom or mailroom, here too technological innovations were becoming available.

One major advantage the new technologies had over the old was that they were much faster. The major impact they were having, however, was in the area of labor. The old procedures generally called for skilled craftsmen and in fair numbers. The new procedures, on the other hand, generally called for less skill and training, and, overall, required fewer personnel. Again, the composing room supplied the most dramatic example. To operate the hot-type plant it had on line in the early 1970s, The Post had employed approximately 600 printers, each of whom had spent several years learning the trade. To operate an equivalent cold-type facility, The Post would have needed a few skilled troubleshooters and approximately 350 semi-skilled workers who had been trained for their jobs in a matter of 1 or 2 weeks. The savings in labor costs produced by such a full-scale conversion to cold-type would have paid for the cold-type facility within a year. While not so dramatic as the changes in the composing room, the changes in pressroom and mailroom technologies, in turn, had opened the possibility of reductions in the numbers and skill of the personnel employed in these areas.

THE WASHINGTON POST

In 1975, The Washington Post was the seventh largest daily paper in the United States. When Katharine Graham's father, Eugene Meyer, bought the paper in 1933, it was the weakest of three Washington morning dailies. Meyer paid $835,000 at a bankruptcy auction. He proceeded to attempt to revitalize The Post. In 1946, Meyer's son-in-law, Philip Graham, became Publisher.

The Post began its climb from a struggling daily to a successful business in 1954 when Graham and Meyer purchased The Post's only remaining morning competitor, the Times-Herald. The new Post managed to retain almost all the readers of both papers. The acquisition of the Times-Herald gave The Post the largest circulation in Washington and in so doing inaugurated an era of prosperity. From 1954 into the early 1960s, The Post grew rapidly. In 1960, it moved past the Evening Star to become the leading paper in Washingon. During this period, Philip Graham was the moving force. Under Graham, the paper remained a family owned company. His policy for the paper as a business was one of controlled growth and careful management of the impetus acquired in 1954. Graham's main interest was in building The Post's reputation for editorial excellence. He used The Post's growing revenues to hire more reporters and to establish the first foreign bureaus.

KATHERINE GRAHAM

When Katherine Graham became publisher of The Post following the death of her husband Philip in 1963, she had no business experience. Leaning heavily on company executives, she commenced to "learn from the top" as she later put it. As Mrs. Graham acquired self-confidence in her managerial abilities she became progressively a stronger and more decisive executive. One of her first decisions was that the policy of building The Post's reputation should be continued and that efforts should be expanded. Ben Bradlee was hired to run news operations. The editorial staff was increased by 20%. The number of foreign bureaus was doubled. Talented reporters and writers were sought out and hired. At a cost of $20 million, a new plant was built to house the expanded operations. As the fame and prestige of The Post increased and the number of its awards mounted, revenues also continued to rise. By September of 1975, The Post now in competition in the Washignton area with only the Star, commanded a 70% share of the ad linage and a 64% share of the paid circulation in its market area (Exhibit 2).

To improve the capital structure of her expanding operations, Mrs. Graham made the far-reaching decision to take The Post "public." As before, all Class A stock (full voting rights) would remain with the Graham-Meyer family. What would be opened to public sale was Class B stock (limited voting rights: as a block, can elect only 30% of board of directors) which previously had been only traded within the company and family. In June, 1971, The Post sold a first public issue of 1.3 million Class B shares.

By unfortunate coincidence, financial reports released at the beginning of 1971 heralded the end of the increasing prosperity The Post had enjoyed since 1954. From 1960 through 1969, The Post had achieved, on average, pre-tax profit margins of 15% on revenues. In 1969, the margin was 15% based on revenues of approxiamtely $76 million. In 1970 the gross margin dipped to 11% on revenues of approximately $79 million. From 1970 through 1974, though revenues increased by more than $45 million, The Post's profit margin continued to decline. The margin fell to 8.5% in 1974 and looked to be lower yet for the months up to October 1, 1975.

Though The Post's profits slowly fell after 1970, the decline did not threaten the overall profitability of the Washington Post Company. The Company's other activities (Newsweek magazine and radio and television holdings) continued to thrive and helped compensate for the decline in Post profits (Exhibit 3). Mrs. Graham, however, did not want The Post's operations to become underwritten with income derived from other company activities - the approach taken by the New York Times Company. It was Mrs. Graham's belief that to be successful each company activity must remain independent and that to be so each must maintain its own profitability.

Even before 1970, Mrs. Graham had come to the conclusion that in order to remain profitable, The Post needed better top management. Finding top executives who met her expectations, however, proved difficult. In 1969, following the retirement of then chief operating officer, John Sweeterman, Mrs. Graham hired Paul Ignatius as president of the newspaper. Ignatius was a veteran of the Pentagon during the Kennedy and Johnson administrations who had risen to be Secretary of the Navy. Ignatius resigned from The Post in October, 1971. He was replaced by John Prescott, Jr., an executive of the Knight Newspaper Chain. In 1974, Prescott was "promoted" to be president of the newspaper division and Mark Meagher, who had been The Post's financial V.P., became the fourth general manager in 11 years. (There were corresponding changes at other level of mangement (Exhibit 4).

If Mrs. Graham had difficulty in finding executives whom she felt could solve The Post's problems, there was no difficulty in identifying the principal source of the problems. For The Post, as with many other papers, the production process was the principal problem area. Beginning in the late 1960s, The Post came out later and later, often with a large number of typographical errors. Advertisers complained that their ads were badly set or printed. Circulation dealers, all of whom where independent and non-union entrepreneurs, complained that they had to wait for hours in the morning to pick up their papers. The newsroom complained of sloppy composing work and unreasonable restrictions on late-breaking news. The advent of new technology, however, offered the prospect of significant improvements in production if an initial set of implementation problems, mainly related to the labor situation at The Post, could first be surmounted.

LABOR AT THE WASHINGTON POST

From the time the Graham-Meyer family acquired The Post up until the mid 1950s, the relationship between management and labor was open and cordial. The Post's craft workers were largely a homogenous group drawn from the Washington area. They earned a modest living from their jobs at The Post. After the acquisition of the Times-Herald in 1954, however, things began to change. As The Post expanded, the wages paid its craft workers steadily increased to satisfy union demands for a fair share of prosperity and to attract the new craft workers required at the growing paper (Exhibit 5). (In 1967, only 75 of 590 printers were long-time Post employees.)

Newspaper craft unions had a long history of imposing strict standards on employers and of jealously guarding what they had won. During the years of prosperity, The Post management had viewed labor disputes as threats to growth to be avoided at all cost. Along with acquiring higher pay and improved benefits, The Post's 9 craft unions (Exhibit 6) had steadily expanded their jurisdiction over work practices. What this meant for The Post could be seen in the case of the printers' right to "reproduce" work: the right to reset ads brought to the paper already set in type. When the Printer's union had intially succeeded in having "reproduction" clauses added to their contracts in the 1920s, the intent had been to protect the printer's right to full employment. By the middle 1960s at The Post, with its large advertising volume, the reproduction clause had changed in its original interpretation so that the union had a right to handle reproduction backlog by allocating virtually unlimited overtime and/or by hiring new printers.

By the end of the 1960s, as more young workers joined The Post, militancy began to replace cordial cooperation as the hallmark of labor relations. Printers would curse their supervisors and had even thrown lead slugs at them. The steotypers had responded to the arrival of a new production manager, whom they considered anti-union, by imposing a $10 fine on any member who talked to him. (The ban of silence was only removed eight months later after the manager had significantly improved working conditions.) Pressmen had occasionally displayed their disapproval of certain executives by shutting down the presses when those individuals came into the pressroom. Though Mrs. Grahm and her executives made great efforts to maintain the personal relationships with union leaders which had characterized labor relations in the pre-1954 days, the ability of union leaders to go directly to the general manger or the publisher, rather than building comapny solidarity only served to frustrate circumvented managers.

During 1967, contract negotiations with the printers union had marked a major turning point. For the first time, a union conducted a slowdown during negotiations in order to pressure management to give into its demands which included, among other things, a demand for a new category of "preprints" (advertising sections inserted into the Sunday paper). Rather than threaten operations, management settled. In 1969 and again in 1971, the Newspaper Guild (representing editorial, advertising, and clerical workers) rejected "final" contract offers. Both times, management had to make "amended" final offers. Also in 1971, the printers began to negotiate a new contract. As in 1967 they staged a slowdown. This time instead of just "slowing down" they seriously disrupted operations for several weeks. Rather than risk a shutdown by taking counter measures, management settled. By the early 1970s The Post's craft unions had won great power for themselves and wage/benefit packages which were among the best in the industry.

This was particularly true for the production crafts unions (printers, sterotypers, photoengravers, pressmen, paperhandlers, and mailers). These unions' control of the production process made them the most powerful at the paper. Their strength rested on the skills of their members, the numbers in which their members were required to perform each phase of the production process and the mutual support these unions gave each other in disputes with management.[1] The production crafts also represented the most impressive case of how strong unions through control of overtime and work-practice payments could convert hourly wages, which in themselves were among the industry leaders into take-home pay which was higher still. As a general rule production operations at The Post took longer to perform or required more workers than at most non-union papers and even many union shops. (For instance, it took Post printers 32.5 man hours to set a page of type, over twice as long as the time required in an "average" union shop). In 1973, one out of every 4 hours worked in several of the production crafts was paid at an overtime rate (usually at time and one-half but up to triple time) and $1 out of every $3 earned was paid out because of special work-practice provisions.

By the early 1970s, The Post was falling behind in adopting new production technology, largely because of union resistance. Mrs. Graham had grown convinced that to the craft unions The Post had become "a Goose laying golden eggs" and that they had no intention of loosening their grip. In November 1971, she appointed John Prescott general manager. Prescott came with a mandate to improve the labor situation. His first move was to develop the capacity to print a newspaper without craft union labor - Project X!

PROJECT X - A NEW APPROACH TO LABOR

Prescott's goal in starting Project X was to give Mrs. Graham a weapon with which to counter the craft unions' ability to shut down The Post. Only if this was done, he believed, would management be in a position to bargain successfully with the unions. To Prescott the new developments in process technology looked to be a means of challenging the strength of these unions. Prescott believed that with cold-type composing as its centerpiece, Project X could be made to work. To learn how to operate the presses, small groups of management level employees were sent secretly to the best known facility for cross-training newspaper personnel in the country, the Southern Production Program, Inc. (SPPI) of Oklahoma City. SPPI offered two classes of membership: full and associate. SPPI was blatantly anti-union. Full membership carried with it a mutual-aid pledge among members (in the event of a strike manpower was loaned) and the obligation to attempt to beat a union that struck. The Post's goal was to improve its labor situation, not to turn anti-union. Consequently, The Post became an associate member of SPPI - employees, such as advertising salesmen and accountants, could be sent for the 3-week training program but there was no mutual-aid promise and no obligations. To train employees in cold-type composing, The Post established its own secret facility in Virginia.

Once Project X was well advanced, the unions were informed of its existence. This signal of a change in labor relations was further reinforced in June 1973 when Lawrence Wallace, formerly of the Detroit Free Press, became Labor Relations Director. Wallace was an

[1]Asked to compare the production crafts in terms of relative strength, one management official ranked the printers, the pressmen, and the mailers, in that order, as the three strongest.

experienced negotiator with a reputation for fairness and for toughness. His philosophy was that labor contracts were restrictions on management rights, but that management retained the initiative to test ambiguous points. Unions could respond to such tests with grievances. Wallace set about putting his philosophy into practice. A series of "tests" and grievances followed. Management looked on this process as a means to improve the labor situation. The unions came to see it as an attempt to set them up as scapegoats for indifferent management and a declining economy.

By November 1973, the new approaach to labor resulted in a confrontation with the unions. The printers were negotiating a new contract and, again, staging a slowdown. Prescott had warned that such actions could lead to firings. On Friday, November 2, a foreman fired a printer for participating in the slowdown. To protest the firing the other printers stopped work and could only be removed from the composing room by U.S. marshals. The Post missed two editions. Then, on Sunday, the decision was made to utilize the Project X capacity. By midnight Sunday, a special 40-page paper was ready to print. These preparations were watched by union engravers who had come in to work expressly to keep the other unions, who were not in the building, informed. As the presses were being readied, 100 pressmen arrived. Their local President, James Dugan, told Prescott that rather than let amateurs work the presses, the pressmen would run them. The pressmen were allowed into the pressroom where they promptly seized the room. The presses would run, Dugan stated, only after management settled with the printers by rehiring the fired employee. When Prescott protested that Dugan had given his word to run the presses, Dugan replied, "I lied!" The pressmen ripped the webs on all the presses, comitted some other minor vandalism, and waited. Some hours later The Post management agreed to reinstate the fired printer with only a reprimand. (Nothing was said about the damage.) The pressmen then ran the presses, taking care to efface the line of type stating that this edition had been prepared by non-union labor, James Dugan became the dominant union leader at The Post.

THE PRESSMEN

A pressmen's job was dirty, noisy and sometimes difficult. To produce a morning paper, the usual press run, the pressmen normally worked through the night. Saturday night was described by some as "the hardest shift of the week." Yet, many pressmen enjoyed their work. According to a post article:[2]

> The appeal of it is in the machinery, the magnificent presses.... Pressmen compare their presses.... to a beloved hot-rod; they need careful handling to run properly. Keeping them running well can be an art, and a devoted pressman thrives on it.

---

[2]Robert H. Kaiser, "The Strike at The Washington Post," The Washington Post, Sunday, February 29, 1976.

> Pressmen perform numerous tasks, some routine, some very tricky. When they come on duty, the men all work together to bolt the lead plates which carry the imprints of the next day's paper onto the rollers of the pressses. On a big paper like The Post.... this is a big job.
>
> When the press is running--creating a deafening roar and filling the air with a fine ink mist and tiny particles of newsprint-- the crew has only a few tasks to perform. The sheets of newsprint must be kept straight and running correctly... the most substantial job is to repair broken webs.

Dirty and difficult of necessity, The Post's pressmen had long complained that their work was made harder than it had to by the poor design of the pressroom (which left too little space between the presses) and by inadequate safty precautions.

THE PRESSMEN'S UNION

The pressmen's union contained the most militant element in any of The Post's craft unions. Management described them as a group of men who believed that labor should maintain a posture of complete alienation with management. Prior to the 1973 confrontation, the militants had not been a dominant force in the union and even after October 1, 1975, company officials felt that more than 100 of the pressmen were loyal, honest employees (many with decades of service). The pressmen, nevertheless, were in mangement's view among the worst exploiters of the overtime and work practice provisions in their contract. After the 1973 confrontation, the militant faction gained ground. For weeks after November 2, the pressmen slowed production both as a protest and as a show of union power--on the night of November 10, for example, there were no less than 72 web breaks during the run.

The pressmen's quest for overtime took two forms. On one hand, they took advantage of contract manning provisions which called for as many as 19 men to run a press which in non-union shops might be manned by 8 or 9. With only the unions pool of journeymen available to work, senior journeymen could work almost unlimited shifts. Weeks of 8 and 9 shifts were not uncommon, and some men had beeen known to work 11.

At the same time, managament believed the pressmen were debliberately stringing out press runs in order to earn end-of-shift overtime. Late press runs could be an aggravating problem for a morning newspaper that relied on teenaged carriers. If the papers were not dropped by a distributor in time for the carrier to make deliveries and get to school, they didn't get delivered. If late runs become chronic, they could erode circulation and posed some danger to a newspaper's basic franchise. In the months of June, July and August, 1975, 61 of 92 press runs were late (the press runs went beyond 4:30 a.m) and of these, 27 finished after 5a.m., ensuring late delivery of scores of thousands of newspapers. Managent veterans considered these three months, if anything, a bit better than usual.

The growing sense of confrontation with pressmen at The Post reflected a national trend for that union. At a number of papers mangement had replaced the union with non-union labor, after experiencing lengthy strikes. As a national union, however, the pressmen showed no inclination to improve relations with management. By 1974, The Post had among its pressmen a number of survivors from "broken" locals who vehemently argued that there could be no meaningful accommodation with management.

The increasing tempo of militancy among the pressmen after 1973 was matched by a rapid decline in militancy among the printers. In the fall of 1974, after 14 months of hard negotiations, the printers followed a national trend and accepted the inevitability of general adoption of cold-type composing. In exchange for life-time job guarantees (and a generous "buy-out" provision) the printers gave The Post a free hand in introducing new technology. The Post commenced an ordely transition to cold type, one system gradually phasing out the other, that was due for competition in 1978. By 1975 all ads were being set in cold-type, and this facility had the capacity to set all type for a full edition.

LABOR RELATIONS IN 1975

Mrs. Graham appointed Mark Meagher general manager soon after the printers ratified their 1974 contract. Meagher, formerly Vice President/Finance and Administration of The Washington Post Company, quickly started to work on improving the pressroom situation. The 1974 negotiations with Dugan were his first experience in labor relations. Though strong efforts were made during 1974 and 1975 to lessen the atmosphere of confrontation with the pressmen and reduce the heavy use of overtime and work practice provisions, little progress was made.

The pressmen's contract, along with those of all the other craft unions with the exception of the printers and the Newspaper Guild, was due to expire on September 30, 1975. When contract negotiations began in late summer of 1975, The Post demanded sweeping changes in the contract that would have greatly diminished the union's prerogatives, particularly in matters of scheduling, and would have reduced manning. The union, in turn, demanded a 4-day-week, double time for all overtime, 5 weeks vacation and retention of the status quo in every "non-economic" clause of the contract.

At each session Lawrence Wallace stressed the following basic issues:

1. The union had to work more shifts at straight time.[3]

2. The company had to regain control of the pressroom which meant exempting all salaried supervisors from union discipline.

[3]The contract said the union would make every effort to furnish straight-time coverage for 60% of employees on vcacation, ill, etc. In the past, the union made little effort to provide straight-time coverage.

3. The union had to agree that circumstances under which the "status quo" clause[4] applied would be spelled out.

4. The union had to agree to putting all "past practices"[5] in writing.

The pressmen complained about the extent of the proposed changes and refused to yield on any of the basic issues. When Dugan asked Wallace which issue was most important to him, Wallace said they were all important. When the union requested longer and more frequent negotiating sessions they were told that other contracts expired on September 30 and he could meet with the pressmen only once a week.

As September 30 approached, Mrs. Graham learned that if it came to a strike The Post could expect no support from The Star. Historically, the Washington newspapers had negotiated all craft union contracts jointly, but this year The Star had announced that it intended to make its own arrangements with individual unions. The Star was in shaky financial shape and had changed hands. The new owner, Joseph Allbritton, was in the process of negotiating a 1-year wage-hike moratorium with his unions. Allbritton feared a strike would sink The Star for sure and had no intention of risking his hard-won breathing space to face the pressmen and other craft unions in concert with The Post. Mrs. Graham was not anxious for The Post to face a strike alone and risk serious loss of market share to The Star. "If we take a strike," Mrs. Graham told Meagher, "we can't win with the other paper publishing." Rather than take a strike, Mrs. Graham would have preferred some short-term time-buying settlement. Nonetheless, she agreed that Wallace and Meagher should continue to push strongly for significant concessions from the pressmen.

On Septermber 30, negotiations had not resulted in a new contract with the pressmen or with any other of the involved unions. That evening, Dugan gave Wallace a note which said the union was terminating its contract at midnight and added, "we are willing to work under the terms and conditions of the present contract only as long as meaningful negotiations continue." He also proposed a one-week extension of the contract provided that a cost-of-living wage adjustment went into effect at once, that any eventual raises would be retroactive and that round-the-clock bargaining began at once. Wallace rejected the idea but interpreted the note to mean "no strike." When Wallae indicated a willingnewss to continue bargaining, the parties agreed to meet again on October 1 and 2 at the Federal Mediation Service. The other unions which had meetings scheduled for those days agreed to yield their time to the pressmen.

---

[4]The status quo clause provided that when disputes over the interpretation of the contract arose, the status quo would be maintained pending settlement of the dispute.

[5]On many occasions unions refused to recognize an operations change claiming the existence of a verbal agreement between management and the union on the matter.

THE STRIKE

At 4:35 a.m. the night foreman in the pressroom noticed from his office that the presses had stoped running. On opening the door to the work area he was jumped by several men. One held a screwdriver to his throat. For the next 20 minutes an unknown number of pressmen disabled all 72 units of the 9 presses. They sliced the cushions on the press cylinders, ripped out electrical wiring, removed key pieces from most presses, jammed the cylinders, cut air hoses and sabotaged other parts. The most serious damage was caused by fire, after some of the automatic fire extinguishers were disabled. Assuming spare parts were available, it was estimated that the least damaged press could be quickly repaired; it was impossible to determine immediately the extent of damage to wiring and interior parts of other presses. It was in fact more than three months before the press which suffered fire damage was back in operation. The estimated bill for repair was around $375,000.

There were 115 pressmen working the night shift, but many of them left when they saw what was happening. As the last pressmen left the building, a picket line was thrown up outside the building.

Before the pressmen left, the foreman was severely beaten. He did manage, however, to make his way to Mark Meagher's 7th floor office and confirmed the report of "a riot going on in the pressroom," that had been reported by the night production manager.

Meagher immediately telephoned Katharine Graham. According to Mrs. Graham, at first "I couldn't imagine what had happened. I didn't think. I just wanted to get down there." Rather than wake her chauffeur, Mrs. Graham drove to the office.

> The sight was unbelievable. When I got to 15th Street, I saw police cars, red lights flashing--I thought to myself, if I drive in the parking lot they'll wreck the car. I asked a policeman what to do. He said park it here, I'll keep an eye on it. I was so scared at this point. I just walked and went through (the picket line). They yelled but nothing happened. It was the most awful moment of my life.

One of Katharine Graham's first concerns, upon arriving at the office, was whether The Post could print that night. When told no, she telephoned Joe Allbritton of The Star to try to persuade him, now that a strike was at hand, to join her in facing the unions by lending The Post press time. Allbritton refused. In order to find adequate press capacity, a task-force under Post executive William Cooper canvassed small newspapers within 200 miles of Washington. Each paper was asked if they would print a small edition of The Post on its presses.

Many members of the Newspaper Guild, not having been told there was a strike, showed up for work as usual on October 1 and crossed the picket line. Top managers took them on tours of the pressroom, which was still smokey and littered with debris. According to one executive, "they were unstrung." Later that day, at a meeting of the Guild, many members expressed outrage. According to one speaker, "A group of people who call themselves a labor union tried to destroy The Washington Post...." The Post's unit of the Guild, a member of the

Washington-Baltimore local, had a history of poor relations with the production crafts. The Guild membership voted overwhelmingly to defy an honor-the-lines order from the leadership of their local and stay on the job.

Later that day, Jim Dugan told reporters that his men were "frusterated" by The Post's anti-union policies. He offered no apologies and expressed no desire to identify those responsible for the damage. Several days later he told reporters that his men "just went crazy and panicked" in a moment of "temporary insanity." The Post seized the public relations initiative by issuing press releases and having some of its top managers appear regularly on TV.

By the end of the second day of the strike, 6 papers from Pennsylvania to Virginia had agreed to print The Post. Consequently, the effort to publish was begun. Helicopters picked up paste-ups of the pages of a 24-page paper on the roof of The Post and flew them to the 6 plants. The heart of the makeshift production process used during the strike was cold-type technology.

In the first week of the strike both the mailers union and the photoengravers struck in support of the pressmen. Although the printers had a contract, they struck because of a contract clause requiring them to honor mailer lines. This meant that all unions at The Post except the Guild were honoring the pressmen's picket lines. This prompted the Guild to meet again. The decision to stay-in had been a hard one for many Guild members to whom loyalty to the organized labor movement was important on an ideological level. At the second meeting, the margin of votes keeping the Guild in dropped to a mere ten. There the tally stayed, always a near thing, always highly sensitive to union and management actions. Without a working newsroom in addition to a production-crafts strike, with only the wire services to supply copy, and an executive staff spread too thin to even prepare this material properly, The Post could not have hoped to hold its readership or advertisers in the face of a long strike. So long as the Guild stayed in, there would be as much quality copy to publish as the production process could handle.

On the night of October 6, The Post, with the help of non-union machinists brought in to make repairs, got one press running. Post employees trained in Oklahoma ran off 100,000 papers that night. After that, printing capacity began to increase.

The company's most optimistic plans were to publish 40 pages a day in the plant and add a few supplementary sections printed elsewhere. This was felt to be enough to breakeven, given the savings of $384,000 a week on craft worker salaries. Any larger paper was felt to be too difficult for the amateur crews to produce.

These plans ignored an important factor—the esprit de corps of the non-union employees. Many of the people working in production were living at The Post, sleeping on cots in their offices. They did their normal jobs during the day and worked until the early morning at production jobs. Whereas before October 1, 1,220 craft workers were employed, after October 1, a work force of 210 to 375 produced The Post. Coffee breaks and meals were served by waiters in tuxedos in the company's dining room.

Mrs. Graham herself spent almost every Saturday night in the mailroom, gluing Sunday papers in brown wrappers for mail subscribers and did regular stints during the week taking ads. Although she did not stay overnight in the building she frequently invited working employees to her home for dinner.

In a few weeks the working employees were competing with each other and were claiming they could run papers with 4 sections instead of 2, and with 56 pages instead of 40. A hand-lettered sign on one press proclaimed, "J. Press—printing its way into the hearts of thousands", seemed to sum up their attitude.

During this period, several Post executives expected Katherine Graham to give in to the pressmen's demands. The union leadership also expected the same thing. At first, merchants who had rarely or never advertised in The Star placed their ads in The Star. Also, The Star's circulation quickly increased by 30,000. Some business leaders reportedly were glad to see The Post squirm for a change. This reaction was a serious concern to Post management.

By mid-November, The Post was running a 4-seciton paper. When Jim Dugan heard of this he telephoned The Post to ask who the new pressmen were. Although he was told that the amateurs were running the presses, he continued to believe, according to newspaper reports, that professional from outside had been brought in.

On October 28, the Director of the Federal Meditation and Conciliation Service, William J. Usery, arranged for all leaders of local and international unions with members at The Post to meet with his senior deputy, Ken Moffett, and Post negotiators. The objective was to force the pressmen and The Post to prove their good faith to this audience. The plan failed when the other union leaders went out of their way to express solidarity for the pressmen. They agreed to put off their own negotiations until the pressmen reached a new contract. This occurred in spite of the fact that several of the unions were signaling The Post that they were appalled by the pressmen's violence.

Although The Post made 2 new proposals in negotiations, the pressmen did not respond substantially. They claimed that every provision in their old contract was "for sale", but they reportedly were reluctant to give any prices. Several theories were discussed among top mangement members to explain the lack of bargaining by the pressmen: (1) the pressmen leadership was involved in the violence of October 1 and could not negotiate until The Post offered amnesty; (2) Dugan did not know how to react to the new situation in which he was no longer bargaining from a position of strength; (3) the pressmen misread the entire situation and (4) Dugan's pride.

On November 5, at the request of various international officers, a secret meeting was held between Post officials and Dugan. The unions had asked Meagher to tell Dugan what the "bottom line" really was and to get away from table rhetoric. The meeting was unproductive. Moffett's suggestion for arbitration was rejected by both parties. There were informal reports that the various union leaders were assured of eventual victory. In addition, reports were circulating that The Post had exaggerated the violence of October 1 and had even caused it in order to deprive the pressmen of public support.

On Thanksgiving Day The Post was 184 pages, 104 of them having been printed in advance by the Miami Herald and trucked to Washington by a convoy of tractor-trailers. At the beginning of December, The Post was fast approaching 95% of its normal size and had substantially reduced the number of sections that were being printed outside. As The Post grew, the early advertising defectors to the Star began returning. Because of the disruption in production and in the normal size of the paper about 4.6 million lines of advertising had been lost. By the end of November, The Post had returned to a 65% market share of advertising linage and had every expectation of reclaiming more.

By mid-November several company officials were speaking openly among themselves about the possibilty of "hiring replacements" for the striking pressmen. Mrs. Graham was being pressured by numerous publishers to "bust the pressmen's union". According to the publisher of a large Southern paper, "a lot of publishers are mad at her for pussyfooting around." Mrs. Graham continued to tell them all that she still hoped for a negotiated settlement.

Mrs. Graham and her executives, however, were under no illusions that their production teams could continue to successfully put out the paper indefinitely. Though the confidence of the crews had steadily grown, though the cross-trained crews had become increasingly hostile to the striking unions (many threatening to quit if The Post gave in), Mrs. Graham had seen first hand that there was a finite limit to their strength and endurance. At the beginning of the strike Larry Wallace had pegged the time limit at about Christmas. Mrs. Graham had come to agree with Wallace's estimate. Either the strike was settled by then or production would start to fall-off from the sheer exhaustion of the producition crews. Because any decisive action The Post took would require lead time, the effective date for some sort of turning point was set at the beginning of December. When December 3 came, it was clear that it was time to take action.

DECEMBER 3, 1975

On the afternoon of December 3, Mrs. Graham and Mark Meagher once more reviewed the options as they saw them:

1. They could admit that the pressmen had outlasted them and "surrender" on the pressmen's terms.

   While this option could produce no improvement in The Post's labor situation and broke faith with the cross-trained personnel, many of whom might well quit, it would at least settle the strike before any long-term damage was done to The Post.

2. They could attempt to buy time by rounding up enough trained help from outside to releive the amateur crews. With production crews relieved, they could continue to wait and continue to try to start meaningful negotiations.

   This option would permit sending a clear signal to the pressmen that The Post was prepared to continue the strike until an equitable settlement was achieved while, at the same time, avoiding any irrevocable actions. Hopefully this signal, combined with pressure from unions which had secretly signalled that they were tired of the strike, particularly the printers with their life-time job guarantees at stake, would get Dugan and his pressmen to start to bargain seriously.

3. The Post could "go all the way." It would make the pressmen a final offer: in exchange for a substantial surrender of union prerogatives, The Post would give the pressmen substantial increases in straight-time pay and lifetime job guarantees.[6] If this offer was refused, The Post would have grounds to legally declare that a deadlock, an"impasse", had been reached. It would then begin bringing in temporary substitutes, whom SPPI had promised to supply if an impasse was called, and commence hiring new non-union pressmen.

While this third option held the promise of the greatest gain for The Post, it also entailed the greatest risks. The option, in effect, was to "bust" a union. This was something Mrs. Graham, risks notwithstanding, was loath to do. The risks, nonetheless, were very real. This sort of irrevocable action could easily cause the Guild to strike, turn what had been so far a token national labor boycott serious, adversely affect advertising and circulation, harden all the striking unions behind the pressmen, or cause any number of other reactions. Any one of these outcomes alone could turn a painful strike into a serious financial loss for The Post, and a combination of them could well do long-term damage.

On the afternoon of December 3, one of these options would have to be chosen. Once the decison was made, the manner of its announcement would have to be decided.

---

[6]It was being argued by some executives that they should seek to eliminate every disputed provision of the old contract. In return, the company should offer a package in which by the third year of the contract the average pressman would earn $22,000 to $25,000, depending on overtime, without working more than 5 shifts a week. Approximately 50 pressmen would work as "floaters" on call from the company to act as vacation reliefs and so forth.

Exhibit 1

Newspaper production process—hot versus cold type

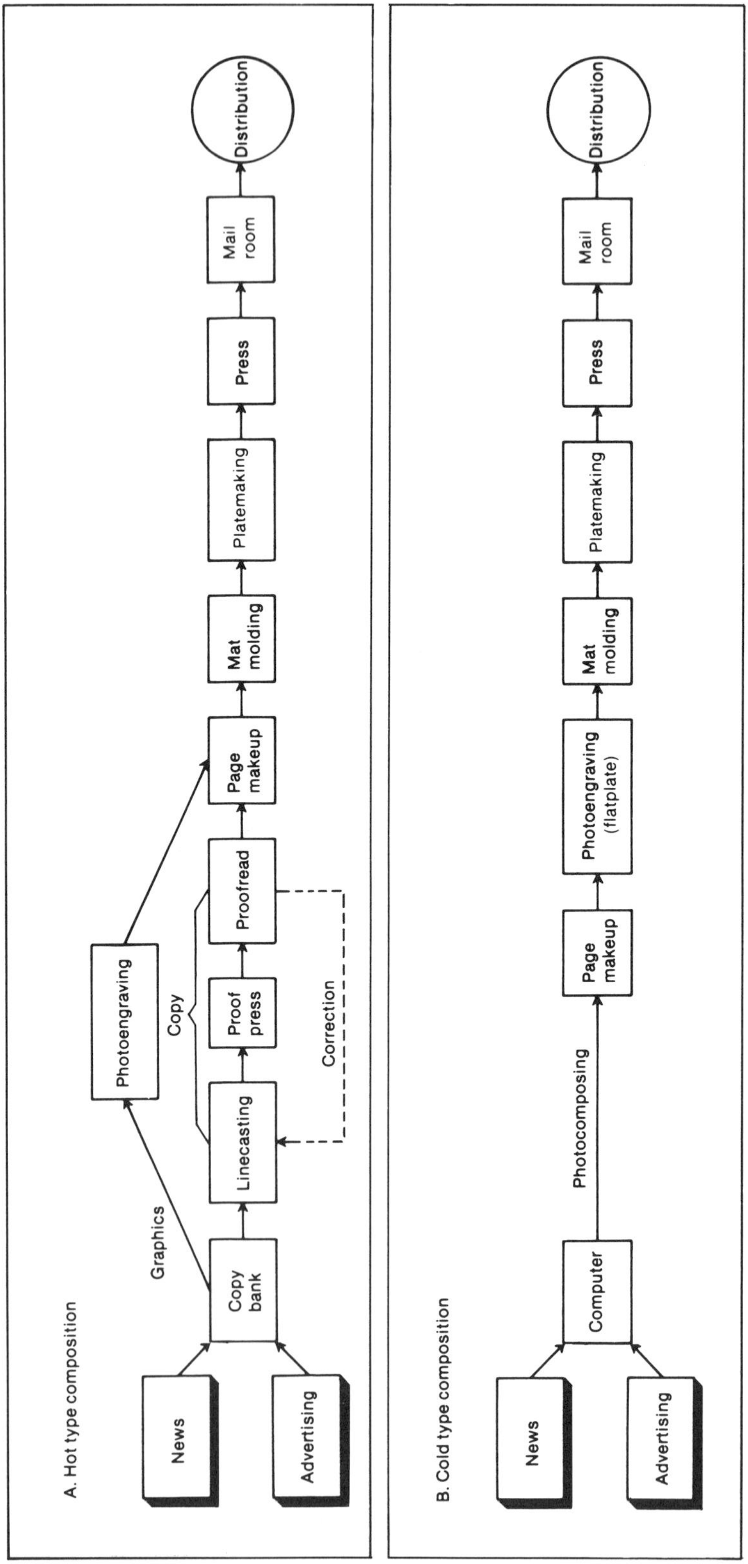

Exhibit 2

CIRCULATION AND AVERTISING REVENUES, 1963-1974

Year	Average Paid Circulation Daily	Sunday	Revenue (in 000's)	Advertising Linage (in 000's)	Revenue (in 000's)
1963	423,401	513,751	$7,598	53,055	$33,431
1964	437,810	536,376	8,054	61,166	39,566
1965	446,342	556,252	9,064	68,443	44,811
1966	457,839	576,536	9,100	73,588	50,398
1967	469,972	599,596	9,297	70,470	52,061
1968	483,497	627,914	9,961	70,442	56,278
1969	489,123	641,121	11,859	71,933	62,183
1970	505,357	665,739	13,164	69,065	64,080
1971	511,540	677,663	14,353	72,197	69,533
1972	521,565	693,370	15,528	78,768	82,032
1973	534,373	706,005	16,391	84,728	92,955
1974	532,641	712,625	18,681	83,809	101,881

Exhibit 3

REVENUE AND INCOME FROM OPERATIONS BY MAJOR DIVISIONS
1963-1974 (IN 000's)

	1963	1964	1965	1966	1967	1968
Net Operating Revenues						
Newspaper publishing & related operations	$41,139	$47,747	$54,011	$60,168	$63,404	$68,150
Magazine and book publishing & related operations	35,056	38,178	43,436	51,214	56,775	65,967
Broadcasting	9,319	10,118	10,603	11,445	11,316	12,480
Total	$85,514	$96,043	$108,050	$122,827	$131,495	$146,597
Income from Operations						
Newspaper publishing & related operations	$4,631	$6,470	$8,664	$9,604	$9,008	$10,295
Magazine and book publishing & related operations	1,525	689	2,764	3,581	2,140	4,266
Broadcasting	3,241	3,231	3,542	2,842	2,630	2,785
Total	$9,397	$10,390	$14,970	$16,027	$13,778	$17,346

Exhibit 3 (continued)

REVENUE AND INCOME FROM OPERATIONS BY MAJOR DIVISIONS
1963-1974 (IN 000's)

	1969	1970	1971	1972	1973	1974
Net Operating Revenues						
Newspaper publishing & related operations	$75,859	$79,267	$85,892	$79,796	$111,997	$125,731
Magazine and book publishing & related operations	79,280	79,985	86,044	93,790	107,617	123,121
Broadcasting	13,994	18,779	20,813	24,258	27,335	38,727
Total	$169,133	$178,031	$192,749	$217,844	$246,949	$287,579
Income from Operations						
Newspaper publishing & related operations	$11,444	$8,883	$8,706	$10,222	$10,535	$10,746
Magazine and book publishing & related operations	6,515	2,584	2,738	5,660	9,161	10,202
Broadcasting	1,695	2,458	3,750	5,924	5,996	7,192
Total	$19,654	$13,925	$15,194	$21,806	$25,692	$28,140

Exhibit 4

Commercial departments organization chart, summer 1975

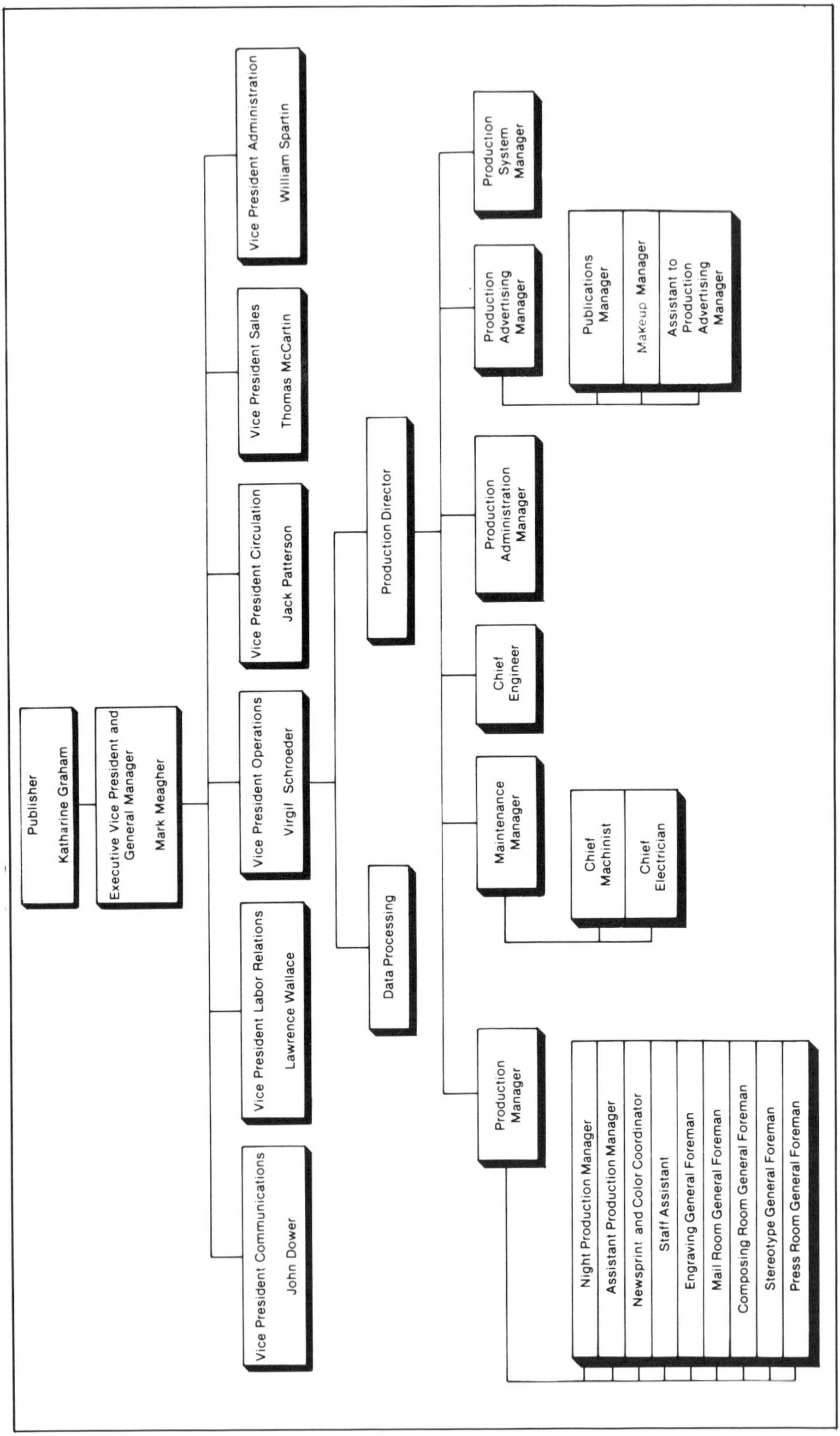

Exhibit 5

AVERAGE WEEKLY EARNINGS PAY OF PRODUCTION WORKERS IN VARIOUS INDUSTRIES IN THE WASHINGTON METROPOLITAN AREA

1964 AND 1974

	1964	1974	% Increase
Manufacturing	$108.95	$199.16	82.8
Durable Goods	107.22	184.57	72.1
Food & Kindred Products	105.81	188.84	78.5
Printing & Publishing	117.87	240.46	104.0
Washington Post*			
ALL CRAFTS	126.80	266.26	110.0
Pressmen	139.85	279.78	100.0
Sterotypers	137.00	280.65	104.9
Mailers	128.52	276.75	115.3
Photo-Engravers	155.50	301.00	93.6
Paper Handlers	95.32	218.36	129.1
Composing	148.42	290.27	95.6
Mailroom Helpers	83.68	217.07	159.4

*Weighted average weekly scale, night rate.

Source: U.S. Department of Labor, Bureau of Labor Statistics, Employment and Earnings, States and Areas, 1939-72, Washington, 1974, and current additional data from various offices, Bureau of Labor Statistics; Washington Post data from the publisher.

Exhibit 6

UNIONS and EARNINGS, 1974

Unions	Number of Members	Straight Time Scale	Average Earnings	Highest Earnings
Mailers Union-	245			
Mailers		$14,391.00	$19,054.83	$31,519.02
Newspaper and Graphic Communication Union-	220			
Pressmen		14,588.95	22,568.00	34,649.00
Sterotypers		14,628.90	22,418.78	32,838.04
Printing Specialities and Paper Products Union-	102			
Paperhandlers		11,354.85	17,932.73	26,824.23
General Workers		10,208.90	10,283.75	11,455.41
Graphic Arts International Union-	37			
Phot-Engravers		15,847.00	18,564.31	27,787.45
International Association of Machinists-	26			
Machinists		14,666.60	17,739.11	22,184.55
International Brotherhood of Electrical Workers-	24			
Electricians		15,949.70	19,159.82	23,713.27
International Union of Operating Engineers-	21			
Engineers		15,653.30	16,599.53	21,699.54
Carpenters and Painters		15,653.30	17,395.86	18,375.43
Typographical Union-	540			
Printers		NA	NA	NA
Newspaper Guild-	820	NA	NA	NA
Building Services Union-	90	NA	NA	NA

NA=Not Available

FOOD MART, INC. (A)

John Berger was Vice President of Food Mart, Inc., a nationwide supermarket chain. He was in charge of the company's northeast region, which included 200 stores with some 5,000 employees in the New York-New Jersey metropolitan area. At 35 years of age he was proud of his acheivement; he was particularly pleased by the outcome of events during the past 18 months.

Berger had been in his present position for four years. The profit margin of his stores was among the highest in the country. He had come to Food Mart after six years of experience in various administrative posts at another large supermarket chain, bringing with him a variety of new managerial techniques which he had been able to introduce successfully. Foremost among these was a decentralization scheme which followed a theory which he had been taught at business school and which left to local and district managers primary authority for handling day-to-day operating problems, including personnel and labor relations.

Food Mart's general labor policies had been laid down by Herbert P. Llewellyn III, Chairman and Cheif Executive of the company. Berger remembered well his interview with Llewellyn at the Chicago headquarters when he had been hired. Llewellyn had contended forcefully that if Food Mart's personnel men did their job properly, there was no need for a union.

"Our wages are higher than or consistent with the competition; our benefits more generous; and we are able to know and handle our workers' problems better than some crooked union leader," Llewellyn had said. "There is no reason why a union should interfere with our ability to manage and control our stores efficiently."

Berger had been somewhat concerned by Llewellyn's views, since it had been his experience that a well-run union saved management many headaches and that a bargaining relationship with workers was in general more satisfactory than one based on an individual connection between an employee and the personnel department. He was also somewhat puzzled because he knew that under his predecessor some 15% of the work force in his region - butchers and meat warehouse employees - had been organized by the United Meat Workers after a bitter strike which shut down operations for more than a month. Llewellyn explained that Food Mart had no choice in that situation. Although the union only had about 600 members, it was well organized and had been able to persuade other employees into joining the strike. "They seemed to have a lot of friends," Llewellyn said. "We finally reached agreement when the union compromised on some of its more unreasonable demands. Since then, we have had no trouble at all."

Berger remembered reading in the newspapers that the United Meat Workers was mixed up with organized crime. It had been reported that the head of the union, Leanord T. Fiedler, was in some way connected to the Borleone family of the Cosa Nostra in New Jersey. He asked Llewellyn about this.

"They're no more crooked than the rest of those guys," Llewellyn had said. "We'd be better off without any of them, but in this case we had no choice.

The interview had ended with Llewellyn's strong admonition to John to avoid getting himself into a position of having to choose between a strike or a union.

Several years later John Berger confronted his biggest challenge as a Food Mart Vice-President. It began the day that Anthony Luzo, President of local 656 of the Associated Grocery Clerks and Warehouse Employees of America (AGCWE), AFL-CIO, walked into Berger's New York office to inform him that the union was going to seek election as the bargaining representative of Food Mart's 4,000 unorganized employees, including clerks, checkers, warehouse and maintenance workers. Berger told him that another union was unnecessary; the unorganized workers were happy at Food Mart. Luzo had replied that his efforts were part of a nationwide organizing drive by the AGCWE.

Berger was impressed by Luzo's forthright sincerity; also, he was doubtful about the ability of Food Mart to withstand further organization indefinitely. It was, therefore, with considerable reluctance that he called his staff together to plan the defeat of the union in the coming election. The campaign was to be under the direction of Dana Thomas, Berger's personnel chief, who had been in his job for some 10 years. Berger ordered a public relations program aimed at informing the workers why they were better off without a union, but specifically prohibited intimidation or threats of dismissal. From time to time in the past he had heard sporadic complaints that some employees had been fired for promoting the idea of organization under the AGCWE. He had found that most of these stories were apparently untrue, but they had caused unfavorable publicity for Food Mart in the local press.

As the election drew near, Berger learned, while lunching with a friend from his old company, that the Clerks union was going to get a 40-hour week at the same pay in their new contract with that company and, indeed, that the union had succeeded in negotiating a 40-hour week in recent bargaining throughout the country. "The chances are that they'll want the same from you," his friend said.

Previously, Berger had thought that talk of a 40-hour week was union propaganda to gather worker support, but this news caused him to consider seriously the costs of such a change for his stores which were then working a 45-hour week. He estimated that the change would cost him about $4 million a year before taxes. This compared with total earnings after taxes of some $12 million a year. The high cost was due to the fact that Food Mart stores were open six days a week and the work force would have to be substantially expanded if the 40-hour work week were introduced.

With a week to go before the election, therefore, Berger told Thomas to redouble his efforts.

The election resulted in a victory for Food Mart, 1,824 votes to 1,263. Llewellyn called from Chicago with congratulations.

Several weeks later Berger picked up his newspaper at the train station on the way to work and was dumbfounded by what he saw on page one. Local 656 had requested the National Labor Relations Board to call a new election, charging the company with violations of the National Labor Relations Act during the recent elections: intimidation of pro-union employees, threats of reprisals by store managers and assistant managers if the union won the election, and illegal harassment of organizers.

Berger called a meeting of his staff and district managers as soon as he got to his office. Although there was general denial of the union's charges, some said that they had heard rumors about antiunion activity in some stores. Then Dana Thomas spoke up and said, "We had assumed that if there were such goings on, it was with your approval and Mr. Llewellyn's blessing. We know how strongly you felt about the 40-hour week business. When pressed by Berger, Thomas admitted that he had "talked with Chicago" and that they had informally approved the stronger measures.

Food Mart's lawyers told Berger that the position did not look good. The NLRB would almost certainly order a new election. With all the publicity it appeared certain that the Clerks would win.

Berger was deeply concerned. A union victory would not only bring down the wrath of Llewellyn, it would almost certainly cause pressure for a 40-hour week which would threaten Food Mart's healthy profit line. To make matters worse, at the very time that these labor problems plagued him, three stores in Newark reported sharp increases in enforcement activity by city building and traffic authorities. The stores had suddenly been charged with a number of violatons of building codes, and trucks which had generally been allowed to double park while delivering their load were being ticketed and heavily fined.

It was at this point that Berger received the following letter from Leonard Fiedler, National President of the United Meat Workers:

> Dear Mr. Berger:
>
> There is a matter which we consider of great importance as affects our organization and Food Mart which we would like to personally discuss with you.
>
> We will not bring many people and we do not feel the meeting should take much of our time. There are some things which we feel will be very advantageous to Food Mart as well as to our organizaton. It would be a good idea to talk it over, I assure you.
>
> You will let me know if you are in agreement to meet us and we can set a definite date for the conference.
>
> Very sincerely,
>
> Leonard T. Fiedler

Berger wondered why the letter was from the national head of the union and not the local secretary-treasurer with whom the company generally dealt. He was futher puzzled because as far as he knew there were no problems with the Meat Workers, although he was aware that a new two-year contract would be up for negotiation soon. He had never met Fiedler; all dealings with the union until now had been conducted by Thomas. As he thought about it, he had not wanted to meet Fiedler. In part, he supposed, his reluctance had stemmed from the reports of an underwourld tie which he had read. On several occassions he had thought of investigating further but he had decided it would just get him into trouble. There was nothing he could do about it anyway.

Pressed as he was now, however, and eager to avoid any further labor difficulties, Berger told his secretary to make an apppointment with Fiedler. For reasons of which he could not be entirely sure, he decided to meet with him and his group alone and away from the office. The meeting was set for the following week at a Holiday Inn outside of Newark.

Fiedler was a heavy-set man who looked as though he would have been more comfortable in his butcher's apron than the expensive suit he was wearing. Three men were with him, one of whom was introduced as the head of the Food Mart local. They were silent during the meeting, showing deference to their boss.

Fiedler began the conversation, reminiscing about the amicable relations which had prevailed between his unon and the company during the years of their association.

Berger replied, somewhat facetiously, "You haven't got much to complain about, getting $4 a month dues from 600 Food Mart employees, not to mention the administration of the $7 million meat workers pension fund."

Fiedler looked across the table at Berger. His large, full face was impassive; tinted glasses shaded his eyes.

"We're doing all right, Mr. Berger, but we could do better and so could you," said Fiedler. "We got problems and you got problems. My union is a big organization. Like any big organization we got big expenses. That's my problem. Your problem is the Clerks, the 40-hour week and all. And my friends in City Hall tell me you have been violating the law over there a good bit. It seems to me and my associates here that in a case like this your interests are pretty close to ours. I was thinking maybe we could help each other."

Berger said nothing as Fiedler went on to outline his plan. Prior to the new election, certain to be ordered by the NLRB, the Meat Workers would "let it be known" that a no vote - against the Clerks union - would be in effect a vote for organization by the Meat Workers. The AGCWE would thus lose the election a second time. The company would then agree to allow the Meat Workers to circulate cards as prescribed by the NLRB to the 4,000 unorganized clerks, checkers, warehouse and maintenance employees for them to sign declaring their desire to join the Meat Workers. The cards would read: "In accordance with my legal rights, guaranteed by the National and State Labor Relations Acts, I here by designate the United Meat Workers as my collective bargaining agent." The company would agree to put no obstacle in the union's way. In return the union would give the company a guarantee that all employees would continue to work a 45-hour week for the next five years. The guarantee would be included in the forthcoming bargaining agreement with the Meat Workers.

"How can you make such a guarantee when Local 656 will offer the 40-hour week immediately?" asked Berger.

"There are two reasons," said Fiedler. "Our shop stewards will make it clear to the retail and warehouse people that they will be represented by a strong, competent union which may give a little at first in order to make big gains later. And then when the word gets around that you are favorably inclined towards us, it will make a big difference. Your workers think a lot of you."

"Is that legal? It wouldn't sit well with the NLRB if we forced our people to join your union."

"No force," countered Fiedler. "Just don't hinder my men. Just keep out of the way."

Berger told Fiedler he would let him know his answer in a few days. Driving back to his New York office, he regretted not having asked Fiedler to be more explicit about the building code and traffic violation problem. He also wondered what would happen if he turned down the proposition. The AGCWE would undoubtedly be successful and there was always the chance of another strike by the Meat Workers. He knew he would have to call Llewellyn. The chairman would not like the deal but neither would he like a 40-hour week and another strike.

Berger called Chicago and found that Llewellyn was cruising off the coast of Mexico on his schooner. The executive vice president took the matter under advisement and called Berger back the following day, telling him to do what he thought best.

Berger decided to agree to Fiedler's conditions. The second election was held as ordered by the NLRB. The AGCWE was soundly defeated and the Meat Workers quickly secured the necessary majority of signed cards. Shortly thereafter a new contract was signed with the Meat Workers as Fiedler had promised, providing for the 45-hour week. Although the agreement was for five years, wages were to be renegotiable after two years.

The Clerks protested that workers had been coerced into joining the other union and that there had been collusion between the company and the Meat Workers.

After a few weeks, however, the protests subsided and all was going smoothly. Even the Newark problem had disappeared. Berger's Newark district manager reported at a regular management meeting that it had "apparently solved itself."

Berger didn't pursue the matter, glad that he was relieved of one more worry.

Thomas reported that relations with the new, expanded union were very good and that he expected no difficulties in the forthcoming negotiations.

Llewellyn's ideas are old fashioned, thought Berger. Managers must change with the times, respond to environmental pressures, act with realism.

SECTION II

Contract Negotiation

GORDON PAPER PRODUCTS COMPANY

Immediately after successful completion of 1970 contract negotiations with the union, Brian Gordon, vice president of operations for Gordon Paper Products Company, scheduled a meeting with his negotiating team. A major objective of the meeting was to review their performance during the recent round of negotiations. He also wanted to review the company's new policy toward labor relations that had been adopted prior to the 1968 negotiations and followed again in 1970. It seemed to Brian Gordon that the new approach was paying off.

COMPANY BACKGROUND

Gordon made paperboard and multicolored printed cartons for food, soap, cigarettes, and various other products. Two of Gordon's three plants were in Waukegan, Illinios, where the general office was located; the third was abut 50 miles away, in Lockport, Illinois, a suburb of Chicago. Both the Waukegan division and the Lockport division made paperboard and paper cartons. Slightly more than 2,000 employees were evenly divided between the two cities.

The company took its name from the Gordon family, whose members had closely controlled all phases of the business since its inception in 1900. The family had been known for its interest in the welfare of the employees. For instance, it had established a dispensary at Waukegan in 1918 and introduced group insurance in 1920. In general, the company had paid higher than the rates prevailing in other plants and maintained stable work even in slack times. Its concern, moreover, had not been limited to its own employees. In both communities the company sponsored Scout troops, a Junior Achievement program, a local radio program, and a college scholarship fund.

The Waukegan division had been a part of the Gordon operations since 1900; the Lockport division had been acquired in 1932-when the Gordon and Lewis companies merged. In 1946, the Gordons bought out the Lewis interests and gained complete control.

In spite of common leadership, however, the Waukegan and Lockport divisions differed because of the nature of the communities in which they were located. In Waukegan (population 50,000), Gordon with 1,000 employees was the second-largest employer; the largest, Lake City Steel Company, had 5,000 employees. Lockport, on the other hand, was a part of greater Chicago; Gordon with 1,000 employees was not a dominant factor. Furthermore, the industries of Lockport had been organized by international unions, those of Waukegan primarily by independent unions. Indeed, Lake City Steel Company was one of the few steel companies not yet organized by the United Steelworkers.

The histories of the two divisions also showed important differencs. In Waukegan, the employees and the company had jointly established in 1914 the Mutual Benefit Association--converted in the early 1940s into an independent union, the Independent Paper Workers of Waukegan which, by 1970, embraced about 85 percent of the production and maintenance employees. The only atttempt to organize Waukegan by an affliated union failed when in 1946 the Independent Paper Workers defeated the Fraternal Order of Bag and Carton Workers by a very narrow margin.

In Lockport, on the other hand, after a militant organizing campaign, the Bag and Carton Workers was certified as bargaining agent for paperboard, powerhouse, and maintenance workers in 1960. Another NLRB election in October 1962 enlarged the scope of the same union to include carton operations. The Bag and Carton Workers was then certified as bargaining agent for all production and maintenance employees. Union membership grew and by 1970 embraced 95 percent of the working force.

THE LOCKPORT STRIKE

The negotiations of the second contract at Lockport opened in November 1962. Wages and union security were the main issues. The union asked for 30 cents; the company offered 12 cents. (The company justified its position by the fact that 12 cents was within the pattern established that year by other settlements.) The union demanded a union shop; the company opposed anything more than an open shop.

Little progress was made between November 1962 and January 1963. The union lowered its demands to 20 cents and maintenance of membership, but the company remained firm with its proposals of 12 cents and an open shop. In Janury 1963, the union called upon the Federal Mediation and Conciliation Service to intervene. Four sessions were held with a member of the service during January. The offer of a check-off in place of maintenance of membership was rejected by the union; management rejected the union's offer to arbitrate the issues.

Concurrent negotiations with the Waukegan division resulted during January 1963 in a contract embodying a 12 cent wage increase. In general it had always been company policy to provide the same benefits, pay the same wage scales, and make identical offers to both unions.

Since the contract was due to expire, the parties agreed to extend it to April 1. Negotiations continued, but at the close of the final meeting on March 31, the parties were no closer to agreement. As the session broke up, the union's regional director asked, "Where does responsibility for a work stoppage lie?" The query was not academic; the next day there was a walkout which rapidly developed into a full-scale strike. On April 18, the union asked the federal conciliator to intervene once more. Only one session was held: The strike was to last two months.

On April 30, the company announced an additional increase of 9 cents in both divisions and stated that the first increase had represented a cost-of-living adjustment. The second was said to conform with recent contract settlements.

After this announcement, the union ran a number of full-page advertisements in the Lockport paper attacking the company. Simultaneously, a "Back To Work Movement" ran full-page advertisements attacking the union. The company wrote to each employee explaining that the real issue of the strike was not wages, as the union had claimed, but the union shop. A union offer to leave the issues to a group of local clergymen for decision was turned down.

On June 3, with the strike two months old, 275 employees secured an injunction against mass picketing. The limit was set at ten pickets at any one time and those restricted to the sidewalk across the street from the main gate. Shortly thereafter a Back To Work Movement began and the strike quickly ended.

With the resumption of operations, the Back To Work Movement converted itself into an independent union in opposition to the Bag and Carton Workers. The company recognized neither union from June 1963 until July 1964. The Bag and Carton Workers filed a change of unfair labor practices with the NLRB. When the company agreed to sign a six-month contract with the Bag and Carton Workers, the compaint was dismissed in July 1964. The contract provided for an open shop and a representation election by the NLRB at the end of six months.

In January 1965, Lockport employees voted two to one in favor of the Bag and Carton Workers. Two important contract changes were made during 1965. The company agreed to a modified union shop on the understanding that it would never accept a full union shop; the union agreed to a contributory pension plan.

1966 NEGOTIATIONS

The 1964 and 1965 negotiations at Lockport had been carried on by the vice president of opeations and the regional director for the union. Negotiations were resumed in July 1966 and resulted in the first of a series of two-year contracts.

The company offered an increase of 3 percent; the union asked for a flat increase of 18 cents. After some bargaining, the parties compromised on an increase of 4 percent in the first year and 2 percent in the second year.

Shortly thereafter, the chairman of the 1963 strike became president of the Lockport union. He had campaigned on the issue of a flat as against a percentage increase, directing his appeal to the lower-paid workers, who had received only 8 cents in July as compared to 14 cents for higher-paid employees.

A NEW APPROACH

Soon after the 1966 settlement, management changed its strategy. First, it developed its proposals systematically. Economic offers were based on (1) competitors' rates; (2) industry pattern set by industrywide bargaining on the West Coast, applied in the east by Container Corporation and by Gair Company; and (3) area practices. Noneconomic proposals were developed from recommendations of line and staff management.

Secondly, the whole system of communications was revised. The industrial relations department would hold prebargaining and post-bargaining meetings with all levels of line management. These meetings would provide a means of interpreting the company's bargaining positions to all managers, includeing first-line supervisors. They would also give supervision an opportunity to register employee reaction to these positions. In addition, the company would send a bulletin to all members of management after each session with the union (as well as "fact sheets" as they seemed called for) to help first-line supervisors explain the company's proposals to employees. Finally, the company would send letters to the homes of employees throughout the year, including the quarterly business and the annual safety reports. Indeed, letters had been frequently sent to employees' homes during negotiation, usually the evening following the barganing session, with interpretive comments by company officials.

The new approach was seen in the 1968 negotiations, particularly at Lockport.

1968 NEGOTIATIONS

Negotiations were started in July and completed at Waukegan on August 4 and at Lockport on August 5.

On July 11, Brian Gordon, Vice President of Operations, sent the following letter to all hourly paid employees at Lockport:

> On July 31, the labor contract between the company and the Bag and Carton Workers will expire. The union notified us on May 25 that they wanted to end the present agreement and negotiate a new contract.
>
> The first meeting to discuss the new contract will be held on Wednesday, July 16. After that, there will be other meetings for the same purpose.
>
> I know you will be interested in these meetings. As they go along, we will try to keep you informed in two ways of the progress being made.
>
> 1. Some of our management people will attend the meetings. They will tell your foreman about them. And your foreman will pass his information on to you.
>
> 2. During the negotiations, I will write you and let you know what's happening. That way you and your families will know from time to time what progess is being made. I am sure, too, that the union will make every effort to keep you informed. That is good. The more facts you have about barganing, the more able you will be to help the negotiators on both sides work out the terms and conditions of the new contract.
>
> I am hopeful we can negotiate a new contract before July 31. But it is a short time. Ordinarily, contract negotiators begin their meetings 30 to 60 days before the old contract expires. The company preferred to begin the discussions during the week of June 16, and we suggested this to the union. That would have allowed at least 40 days to complete a new contract. However, the union has said that they do not believe it should take more than two weeks to negotiate a new contract. I can assure you the company will do everything reasonable to reach a contract agreement with the union before July 31.
>
> Since we signed our contract two years ago, Gordon people have received wage increases averaging about 30 cents per hour, including job evaluation. And in only one grievance during that time has the union felt the company's decision should be reviewed by an arbitrator. In that case the company's decision was upheld.
>
> I'll let you know how things develop after the meetings start next week.

The bargaining sessions were held at a Lockport hotel. In attendance for the company: vice president of operations, vice president of labor relations and public relations, director of public relations; and for the union: the local bargaining committee, two international representataives, and the regional director. In all, seven sessions were held between July 16 and 29.

When the first session opened on July 16, the union asked to present its proposals first. To this management replied, "...(the company desires) to present its proposals first so the union could have something to compare their (the union's) proposals against. The company determines the right thing in its offer...it doesn't hold anything back." The company proceeded to present its complete offer.

The company remained firm on its proposals throughout. However, it withdrew a proposal for rotating shifts at Lockport when the foremen reported to the management committee that it was untenable because of strong opposition by senior employees. The union, on the other hand, frequently shifted or changed its position.

The following excerpt from the management bulletin of July 22 illustrates company tactics:

> To all Lockport management people:
>
> At the contract negotiations meeting yesterday, two major subjects were discussed. These were promotions and the job evaluation program.
>
> At the beginning of the meeting the company gave the union a letter outlining new language to be used in the senority clause. This letter has been distributed to all mangement people. The letter also explained that the company believed that ablility to advance should be considered for promotion if it was to manage successfully. Clauses from numerous Bag and Carton Workers contracts were cited in the letter to show that the company's proposal to make ability to advance a consideration for promotions was a common practice in our industry.
>
> After this letter was read and discussed by the two parties at the bargaining table, a recess was called. Immediately after the recess the union representatives told the company that they would accept the company proposal and recommend to the membership that ability to advance be a consideration for promotion.

At the session of July 29, management rejected a union request for a 15-day extension to present the unsettled issues to employees, on the ground that the company had made its final offer and little could be gained by additional discussion. That same evening, the following letter went to employee homes:

> We had another meeting with the union bargaining committee today. But we were not able to reach agreement with them on a new contract.
>
> The same issues are still in dispute. As I told you in my last letter, the company feels its position on these subjects is fair and reasonable. And, in additon, the employee

benefits proposed by the company are very liberal.

We understand a union membership meeting has been scheduled for this week to vote on whether or not to accept the contract proposed by the company. This will be a very important vote—for you and the company.

Naturally, we hope employees will vote to accept our proposals. They include many new and improved benefits for Gordon people. The wage increases, improved insurance plan at less cost to employees, the more liberal vacation plan, and shift differentials are all a part of this contract proposal. These are things which the union agrees Gordon people want.

The union disagrees with us on these things:

1. They want a full union shop. That would mean that a few long-service employees who do not belong would have to join the union to keep their jobs. We don't believe that is right.

2. The union doesn't want the company to pay extra money (in accordance with a merit plan) to our outstanding highly skilled people.

3. The union wants the right to arbitrate how many people should work on a job and whether we can set up a new job or discontinue an old one. These things depend in part on the needs and desires of our customers. They are also affected by the price our customers are willing to pay for our products. If the company cannot have control of these things, we would be seriously handicapped in operating our business successfully. We have the right to make these decisions under our present contract. The union does not claim we have abused it. So we see no reason for changing our contract on this subject.

4. They want some other economic benefits for a small number of people....

The people who attend the union meeting will decide whether or not we sign a new contract within the next few days. As you know, our present contract expires on July 31. Without a contract the stable and favorable working conditions which we have been enjoying can more easily be interrupted. However, the company has told the union that it will do its best to maintain the present wage rates and working condition during the short period when a contract will not be in force.

I am sure you know how important this union meeting will be. I want to urge you to attend the meeting, give your opinions, and vote for whatever you believe is fair. We hope, of course, that most Gordon people will vote to accept the company's contract proposal and continue to enjoy steady work, high wages, and good working conditions.

We hope you will think these problems over very seriously. If there is anything you do not understand about the company's position, please ask your foreman. I know he will be glad to talk to you about it.

On August 5, the membership voted (against the recommendations of the union committee) to accept the company's proposal and sign a 28 month contract. The major proposals and the final settlement are shown in Exhibit 1.

Exhibit 1

Issues	Company's Proposal	Union's Proposal	Final Agreement
Union Security	Status Quo — Modified Union Shop	Union Shop	Status Quo — Modified Union Shop
Wages	Provisions for change based on CPI	Cost of Living	Cost of Living
Shift Differ.	7¢ for 2nd 15¢ for 3rd	10¢ for 2nd 20¢ for 3rd	7¢ for 2nd 15¢ for 3rd
Promote	Seniority & Ability	Seniority	Seniority & Ability
Sat. & Sun. Premium Pay	Status Quo — $1\frac{1}{2}$X for hours over 40; 2X for Sun. as such	$1\frac{1}{2}$X for Sat. as such	Status Quo — $1\frac{1}{2}$X for hours over 40; 2X for Sun. as such
Job Class.	Merit Provision	No Merit	Merit Provision
Arb. of Job Reclass.	Status Quo — No Arbitration of Job Reclass.	Arbitration of Job Reclass.	Status Quo — No Arbitration of Job Reclass.

INCENTIVE NEGOTIATIONS

With contract negotiations not scheduled to begin until late in 1970, management proposed to the union in June that the incentive system be eliminated. Again the Waukegan union quickly accepted the proposal, and new rates went into effect there on July 5; at Lockport, however, settlement was not reached until August 26, new rates going into effect on August 30. Negotiations at Lockport may be followed from company communications:

GORDON PAPER PRODUCTS COMPANY

July 14, 1970

As you know, we met today with your union bargaining committee. We talked over the company's proposal for putting in a new and higher hourly base rate system to replace our present incentive plans.

It was a good meeting. Members of the union committee had studied our proposal very carefully. We talked at some length about many of the details.

Unfortunately no change in a pay system ever pleases everyone. But our proposal offers these advantages:

More than half of you will receive wage increases.

You will continue to earn more than people on the same jobs in other companies in our industry with very few exceptions.

You will be paid more fairly in comparison with each other than under any other system we have ever had.

Your foreman has individual job comparisions of rates Gordon will pay under its proposal and the rates paid by some of our major competitors. He will be glad to discuss them with you and show you how we stand.

July 16, 1970

We had another meeting today with the union bargaining committee. The results of the meeting were disappointing. We have no reason to believe any progress was made in reaching an agreement on the company's proposal for a new wage plan.

We do not know where our proposal stands now. Today was our third meeting with the union. So far they have not told us how they feel about our complete proposal. And they did not ask for another meeting.

I am sure the members of the union bargaining committee and your union steward would like to know how you feel about our proposal.

If there are any new developments, we will let you know.

July 27, 1970

A notice was posted on the union bulletin boards today. It says the union bargaining committee is going to talk with us about "improving" our proposal to get rid of our bonus plans.

Naturally, we were disappointed to see this notice. We hoped the union would accept our proposal. Or if they did not do that, we thought they might ask you to vote on it secretly, just as you do in the election of union officers. As it was, we understand that less than 200 people took part in a standing vote. There are about 850 people in the bargaining unit at Lockport.

We made our proposal to the union on June 16. It is a

fair way to solve a problem which has been bothering all of us for a long time. And it is a complete and a very liberal solution to a difficult problem.

More important, we did not hold anything back when we made our proposal. We don't bargain that way. We believe the union and our employees are entitled to know from the start what our full proposal is on any matter. And that is what we did in this case. We have told all of you what our full proposal is.

I know that a good many of you who did not go to the union meetings have opinions about our proposal. Perhaps you could talk to your union steward and bargaining committeemen about having a full employee vote on our proposal.

If you have any questions about this matter, I know you will find your supervisor and superintendent able to answer them for you.

August 26, 1970

A notice posted by your union announces that the company's proposal to get rid of our bonus plans has been accepted by a majority vote of union members.

Naturally, we are pleased about this development. As you know, we sincerely believe that the new wage system is better for both employees and the company.

We are ready to put the new rates in effect on Monday, August 30, if an agreement can be signed with the union early next week. "Transition pay" checks can be mailed within two weeks after the new rates take effect.

1970 NEGOTIATIONS

Negotiations for a new contract opened in October. The company's strategy was similar to that used in 1968. Negotiations with the Waukegan union were completed on October 29. Again, Lockport proved more difficult.

Those in attendance were the same as in 1968 plus the union's international president. Prior to the first meeting, the company and the union exchanged proposals, and the union distributed its proposals to all employees in a letter. Initial positions and the final settlement are shown in Exhibit 2. As heretofore, management kept supervisors and employees informed as to the progress of negotiations.

Exhibit 2

Issues	Company's Proposal	Union's Proposal	Final Agreement
Union Security	Status Quo — Modified Union Shop	Union Shop	Status Quo — Modified Union Shop
Wages	20¢	50¢	20¢
Holidays	Status Quo (9)	10 Days	Status Quo (9)
Pension	Noncontributory	No Proposal	Noncontributory
Probation Period	Status Quo — (70 Days)	30 Days	Status Quo — (70 Days)
Contract Term	2 Years	1 Year	2 Years

The negotiations opened on October 15 with the company stating, "The facts will substantiate our proposal as a fair and liberal one." When the international president asked for a moratorium on company and union pronouncements, the company answered that "there was no need for a propaganda war but the company might need to write letters to counteract rumors or defend its position."

The company did not draw back from its position except for certain changes in the manner of vesting pensions. The union made some concessions in what union representatives called nonissue areas.

On October 26, the company sent the following letter to the homes of Lockport employees:

> As you know, we are now holding contract negotiation meetings with the bargaining committee from your union.
>
> I thought you'd like to know about the more important proposals the company has made and the reasons we made them.
>
> We drew up our proposals after several months of study. We compared our wage rates and benefits with companies we compete with and which have signed new contracts this year. And we also looked over our benefit plans to see how they needed to be changed.
>
> The proposals we've made to the union are based on this study as well as on four basic ideas I mentioned to you in my last letter. These four ideas are:
>
> 1. What Gordon people need and want.
> 2. Giving Gordon people and the company the best value for money used to pay wages and benefits.
> 3. Distributing the proposals to benefit many Gordon people.

> 4. The effect of the proposals on our ability to compete successfully for the amount of business we need to produce full paychecks for Gordon people.
>
> We think proposals based on such ideas are sound and fair. And such proposals can help both you and the company. A company that is soundly financed and soundly managed offers steady jobs. Gordon always has been able to do this as well as pay wages well above the average for our industry. We want to continue to do this.

The union responded to this letter with its report of bargaining progress. Within two days the company had resubmitted to the employees the union's report with Brian Gordon's penciled comments (see Exhibit 3).

At the seventh and final session, the international president attacked management for lack of flexibility. The company replied by stating that "from experience it knew the desires and the needs of employees, having more access to this information than the union when making these determinations. If the company had offered 10 cents when it could have afforded 20 cents, it would have been dishonest." On November 10, Brian Gordon sent the following letter:

> Contract negotiation talks have ended. The union bargaining committee has said it will take the results to the union membership next Tuesday for voting.
>
> We hope you will vote for the new two-year contract. We think it is an excellent one and that it'll make Gordon an even better place to work.
>
> And we hope you'll vote for it because you too think it's a good contract.
>
> I've written you before that we think the improvements in it are fair and liberal. I'd like to list them again and tell you briefly their advantages.
>
> People who attend the union meetings mext Tuesday will decide if this new and improved contract is to be signed for the next two years. I'm sure you know how important these meetings will be. I hope you will attend them, give your opinions, and vote for the new contract.

On November 17, the membership approved the company's proposals.

DECEMBER 1, 1970

After receiving the news of the vote for contract ratification, Brian Gordon scheduled a meeting with his negotiating team for December 1, 1970. It would be two years before formal negotiations resumed; nevertheless, he wanted to review his team's performance while it was still fresh in their memories. Since 1970 marked the second round of negotiations under his new strategy, he particularly wanted to review it and to discuss any modifications as they planned for 1972.

Exhibit 3

FRATERNAL OF BAG AND CARTON WORKERS

Herbert A. Stewart
Director-Area 3

521 Lakeshore Drive
Chicago, Illinois

REPORT OF THE BARGAINING COMMITTEE
To The Members of Local 1009
Lockport, Illinois, November 2, 1970

A Union Bargaining Committee usually reports to its members at meetings where it can have the benefit of the members' opinions and advice. Due to the fact the Gordon Company has addressed a letter to our members on October 26th, your Committee feels an explanation is in order.

The union got our proposals in writing on Oct. 15. The same proposals were sent to employees on Oct. 26.

The Company's letter was in the mail on the very day your Committee was meeting with the Company. The Union Committee had nothing to report as negotiations neither concluded nor deadlocked. Your Committee had not indicated either acceptance or rejection of the Company's proposals. The fact is the Company has not, even now, answered on some of the Union proposals.

We were doing this at the meeting on Oct. 27. We plan to continue answering their proposals at our next meeting. We haven't told employees anything not told union committee first.

Now let's look at the Company's letter.

Two of their "basic ideas";

1) What Gordon people need and want; and

2) Distributing proposals to benefit many Gordon people,

are what you elected your Committee to tell the Company. For the Company to assume it knows the answers before discussions are completed might well be considered a reflection on the Committee and the members who elect them.

This implies that only the union should know or be allowed to find out what employees need + want. The important thing is that the needs are known and met, regardless whether the union or the Company is the source.

We spent 6 months developing our proposals and we have facts to support them. But we are still open minded on new facts or good reasons for changing our position.

Your Committee wishes to report on progress to date on the Union's proposals. A report by mail cannot be either complete or fair because of limited space but the Company has chosen the method and must suffer its limitations.

First, let us say the Union has asked for nothing, except in total amount, that has not already been granted by major competitors of Gordon.

This is an important exception. The total cost of money items is the most important consideration.

UNION PROPOSALS

1. Union Shop -- The Company objects "in principle". They choose to ignore the more basic principle of democracy on which America is founded and the fact their principle competitors have agreed to this provision. The overwhelming majority of employees voted for the Union Shop in a free and democratic election. Over 90% of eligible empolyees are members.

Is it "democracy" for the company to force employees to join the union?

We can't agree that letters can't be fair. We know they are not complete. That's why we give management people additional details to pass on to employees.

Exhibit 3 (continued)

2. 50¢ General Wage Increase -- The Company offer, 20¢. The Gordon straight time average rate is now \$3.30 per hour. The average for the paper industry is \$3.54 in September 1970 and was \$3.91 in Paperboard Mills in July 1970 according to the Bureau of Labor Statistics, U.S. Department of Labor.

The non-Gordon figures quoted include overtime, shift differential, vacation and holiday pay. The Gordon figure does not. This is obviously an unfair comparison. Comparable figures for Gordon are about 25¢ higher.

.....

Discussions incomplete on distribution of overtime, contract clarification and other matters.

The Union's report is not complete and cannot be under the circumstances, neither is the Company's. The Union does not approve of reporting by mail and does not appreciate the Company's efforts to bargain by mail with the members when these members elected a Committee to represent them.

We are not bargaining by mail. We do think Gordon people have a right to know about the things in bargaining that affect them.

The implication is the Union Committee does not report the facts to the members.

The Union Committee also does not appreciate the Company's invitation to the members to get their reports on progress of negotiations from the supervisors. We understood the supervisors' presence to be to avoid future errors and for a better understanding of the agreement. If they are to use this information to discuss the merits of the proposals during negotiations then the Union is playing against loaded dice and will have to consider ways to balance the situation.

Our letter of Oct. 9 to all Gordon people (including employee members of the union committee) said our foremen were going to attend meetings and would tell employees about them.

Your Committee is endeavoring to secure the best possible agreement as instructed by the members. We are aware no agreement can be reached including all of the Union's demands. We are just as certain no agreement satisfactory to the members can be reached covering only those points mentioned in the Company's letter of October 26th.

Does this mean the union has closed its mind to an agreement based on our proposals?

Your Union Committee has been negotiating in good faith in a reasonable and responsible manner. The Union Committee is not responsible for the present delay in negotiations. When negotiations resume, as they will shortly, your Committee feels it is entitled to the confidence of the members and the respect of the management as demonstrated by deeds not by words alone.

Regional Director Stuart called on Oct. 28 and asked to postpone the meetings until Nov. 8.

Fraternally submitted

THE BARGAINING COMMITTEE
Local 1009

AERO PLUMBING COMPANY (A)

Aero Plumbing Company and M.A. Mayer Construction Company were engaged at El Monte and Downy, California, as contractors in the building and construction industry. At the time of this case Mayer had been engaged as the general contractor in the construction of an apartment building at Glendale, California. In connection with this project, Mayer subcontracted portions of the work to various contractors, including the plumbing work to Aero Plumbing Company.

Aero's employees were represented by the Southern California Pipe Trades District Council No. 16, herein called the Union. It had been the practice of the union to negotiate and enter into a collective bargaining agreement with the Plumbing, Heating and Piping Employers Council of Southern California, Inc., a multi-employer association, herein called the Association. Thereafter, the union had prepared a similar, though not identical, contract, called the standard agreement, which it had submitted for signature to plumbing contractors who were not members of the trade association. Aero and the union had been parties to such a standard agreement which expired on July 1.

Early in July the union sent a copy of the new standard agreement to Aero. On July 12, Harold Mooore, a representative of Plumbers Local 280, a local affiliated with the union, met with Frank A. Calhoun, the president of Interstate Employers Association, Inc, herein called Interstate, and Al Aukerman, secretary-treasurer of Aero. Moore requested that Aero sign the proprosed agreement. After some discussion, Calhoun, as spokesman for Aero, stated that the company was willing to accept those parts of the proposed agreement which related to wages, hours and other terms and conditions of employment. Calhoun went on to state, however, the Aero would not accept certain other provisions of the proposed agreement and these he specified as: (1) the Assocation as agent for the purpose of collective bargaining and adjustment of grievances; (2) a requirement that the employer post a bond; (3) a requirement that the employer pay certain stipulated sums of money to an industry promotion fund; and (4) application of the terms of the contract to cover owners or supervisors of the employer. Calhoun stated Aero had chosen Interstate as its representative and further stated that it would be acceptable to Aero if the union wished to substitute the name of Interstate for that of the Association as Aero's agent for the purpose of collective bargaining and adjustment of grievances. Moore stated that he had no authority to change the proposed contract and declared that this would have to be discussed with the union.

Thereafter, three meetings were held between representatives of the union and of Aero. At each meeting, Aero was represented by Calhoun and Aukerman while the union was represented by Everett Schell, executive secretary of the union; Fred E. Weeks, a representative of Local 761, affiliated with the union; Chester Davies, a representatives of Local 78, similarly affiliated; and Nate Burdett, assistant business manager of the union.

The first meeting occured on July 27. The parties discussed the contract and Calhoun again stated that Aero was prepared to agree to the provisions of the proposed agreement relating to wages, hours and conditions of employment but that it would not accept the four provisions to which it had objected at the time of the meeting with Moore. At the conclusion of the meeting, Calhoun, at the request of Schell, agreed to put Aero's position in writing. On the following day he sent a letter to the union which set forth Aero's position as follows:

Dear Mr. Schell

In response to your request we are submitting in writing our position as stated in conference yesterday.

The Company accepts the proferred Southern California Pipe Trades Agreement only insofar as said Agreement deals with wages, hours of work, and other terms and conditions of employment for the employees of the Company.

The Company does not agree to certain non-mandatory subjects of bargaining which are contained in said Agreement and herewith excludes these items from the Agreement. Specifically these items are as follows:

1. Exclude all mention of the Plumbing-Heating and Piping Employers Council of Southern California in the Agreement relative to their being the agent of the Company for purposes of collective bargaining or adjustment of grievances. You may replace their name with the name of Interstate Employers Association, Inc.

2. Exclude from the Agreement the controls over supervisors and owners of the Company.

3. Exclude the performance bond requirements in the Agreement insofar as the Company is concerned.

4. Exclude the obligation to pay money to an industry promotion fund.

5. Exclude the requirements that owners of the Company pay money to other persons for the "privilege" of working.

Since the company agrees to all wages, hours of work and other terms and conditions of employment for the employees of the Company, (i.e., mandatory subjects of bargaining) as contained in said Agreement it is our position that we now have a written agreement covering the Company's employees.

Yours truly,

Frank A. Calhoun

On August 3, counsel for the union sent the following letter to Calhoun:

Re: <u>AERO PLUMBING CO.</u>

Dear Mr. Calhoun:

I have been asked to respond to your letter dated July 28.

At the outset I wish to point out to you that you have erroneously concluded that there is now in existence a written agreement between you and the Union merely because you have refused to accept certain alleged permissive subjects of bargaining and have accepted what you consider to be mandatory subjects of bargaining. The fact that certain items are designated as permissive subjects of bargaining does not mean that discussion of these items is unlawful, or that collective bargaining is not required if certain alleged permissive subjects of bargaining are rejected.

It is the Union's position that you have a right to refuse to discuss permissive subjects of bargaining. It is also the Union's position that no agreement has yet been reached.

Since the items that you object to afford the employees covered by the agreement a certain degree of financial security and job stability, the Union feels that it is willing to delete any request of the items that you object to in your letter and in lieu thereof, the Union proposes agreement on the following additional items:

1. No transferability of men from the jurisdiction of one union to the jurisdiction of another union.

2. Complete elimination of the grievance and arbitration procedure.

3. Complete elimination of the no-strike clause.

4. The Union shall have the right to strike or engage in economic action for any and all violations of the agreement.

5. Fifty cents ($ .50) per hour in addition to the wages now required by the Master Labor Agreement.

6. An additional 10% of gross wages to be added to the total fringe benefit package.

Your prompt response to this proposal would be greatly appreciated.

Yours very truly,

Eugene Miller

On September 19, the parties again met and discussed the six demands set forth in the union's letter of August 3, which it proposed as substitutions for the provisions to which Aero had objected. The first of these demands was that the transferability of men be eliminated. This referred to the practice of the union to permit an employer who was signatory to the standard agreement the right to disregard geographical boundaries of the various locals within the District Council to the extent of assigning the first and the third man on a job from among his permanent employees. Under this practice, however, the second, fourth and all succeeding men for that particular job were to be secured from the local within whose geographic area the job was located. The union's proposal to Aero, therefore, meant that Aero would not be able to use any of its own employees unless by chance they happened to be members of the particular local which claimed jurisdiction over the area in which the job in question was located.

The second demand of the union was that the grievance and arbitration procedures set forth in the standard agreement be eliminated. Calhoun asked why the union wished to eliminate this matter and the union stated that it was because Aero wanted to choose its own people to sit on the committee.

The third and fourth demands which would eliminate a no-strike clause in the proposed agreement and would grant the union the right to strike for any violation of the contract were discussed together. The union explained that it wished to retain the right to strike if any violation of the agreement occurred and stated that the elimination of a no-strike clause also gave Aero the right to lock out employees.

The parties next discussed item 5, which was the union's demand that the wage rates set forth in the standard agreement be increased by fifty cents per hour. The union explained that its demand meant that Aero was to pay an additional sum of fifty cents per hour per employee the first year; one dollar per hour per employee the second; and $1.50 per hour per employee the third year.

The final and sixth item of the union's demands regarding an additional 10 per cent in gross wages in addition to the fringe benefits included in the standard agreement was then discussed. Calhoun asked if the additional 10 per cent would benefit the employees. Schell replied that it would not and further stated that, since Aero was requesting a separate administration of the contract, this would require a separate trust fund which would require more money to administer. Calhoun then stated that although Aero was requesting that it be represented by Interstate rather than the Association for purposes of bargaining or the adjustment of grievances, it had no objection to the trustees of the various trust funds as set forth in the standard agreement and was willing to accept them. Schell, however, replied, "Well you want to change all the other items. You might as well change this one, too." The parties reached no agreement at this meeting and arrangements were made to meet again on October 4.

When the parties met on October 4, Schell asked what Aero's answers were to the various proposals which had been advanced by the union. Calhoun replied that Aero would agree to item 1 regarding the restriction on the transfer of men but wanted it understood that this did not cover the owners or supervisors of the company. Schell replied that, "if they pick up a tool, they can't work." Calhoun stated that the union had no authority to bargain for owners or supervisors but that Aero had no objection to the union's first proposal.

As to item 2, Calhoun pointed out that grievance and arbitration were among the most important items in a collective bargaining contract and a resort to them would be necessary in order to adjust grievances without having strikes or lockouts. Schell answered, "Well, we have a grievance procedure, but since you don't want that, then we want the complete elimination of it." Calhoun pointed out that Aero was willing to have Interstate act on behalf of the employer and the fact that Aero was suggesting a different employer represenatative did not eliminate the need for a grievance and arbitration procedure. Schell disagreed, however, and stated that the union wanted the right to take economic action.

With regard to the third and fourth proposals of the union that there be an elimination of the no-strike clause from the contract, Calhoun requested that the union modify its position by agreeing to a no-strike clause but excluding from such clause and thus permitting strikes to enforce grievances relating to the employer's failure to pay wages, fringe benefits or travel time. At first Schell agreed to this but after further discussion changed his position and insisted that the union wanted the right to take economic action.

With regard to the union's fifth proposal relating to wage rates, Calhoun stated that Aero would agree to pay the wage rates and all the fringe benefits which were set forth in the standard agreement. Schell rejected this offer and stated it cost the union money to sit there and bargain with Aero and that the employer was going to have to pay for it.

As to the union's last demand regarding an additional 10% for fringe benefits, Calhoun stated that Aero would be willing to pay its share to the trust fund provided for in the standard agreement and would be willing to appoint the existing trustees as its trustees and that there would thus be no need to set up a separate trust fund. Schell replied that the union insisted that a separate trust fund be established and that it would not agree to Aero's participation in the fund provided for in the standard agreement. Calhoun answered by saying that since Aero had agreed to the union's demand prohibiting the transfer of men, it was not likely that any of Aero's employees would receive any benefits from the funds in question because of the short time they would be engaged in construction jobs. He proposed that the union lift this provision and permit Aero to use its employees throughout the area of the District Council and stated that if it did so Aero then could agree to separate fringe benefit package. Weeks responded by saying that if Aero was so interested in the employees, it could pay them the additional wage rates which the union was demanding. And either Weeks or Schell also stated, "Of course, if you don't like this, you can always sign the standard agreement." Weeks also said that if Aero wished to make sure that the employees got the benefits from the separate fund, it could guarantee its men 40 hours per week, 50 weeks per year, and the union might then consider reducing its demands for wages to $5.55 per hour as set forth in the standard agreement but in that event he would to have discuss this separately with the rest of the union committee members.

As the meeting ended, Schell asked one of his colleagues when the union had filed notice with the federal and state mediation services.

When he was told it had been more than 30 days before, Schell declared, "We're free to strike and picket now." Calhoun said he hoped the union would not do so and their differences could be resolved in other ways. Schell replied, "Well, you'll just have to take your best shots because we're apparently not getting anywhere." He further stated, "It's costing us money to sit here. We can't tie up four men like this continuously. You'll just have to take your best shots. If you don't like this, you can always sign the standard agreement." At this juncture, Schell also stated that the union would not sign a different agreement with Aero than it had signed with anyone else.

Late that afternoon, October 4, three of Aero's employees were working on a job site within the jurisdition of Plumbers Local 761. As they were preparing to quit work for the day, they were approached by Don Arnold, business representative of the local, who instructed the three men that they could not come back on the job because Aero had not signed an agreement with the union and that a picket line was going to be established.

On Friday, October 7, Calhoun called Schell and requested that the parties have another meeting. Schell answered that he saw no purpose in it, that the union was not going to change its position. Calhoun replied that they had made some progress at the last meeting and he hoped they could make more. Schell answered that he was afraid that the parties would be wasting each other's time.

On October 11, 1966, Aero signed the standard agreement which had originally been submitted to it by the union.

1979 AUTOMOBILE NEGOTIATIONS (A)

Early in the summer of 1979, the 26-member International Executive Board of the United Automobile, Aerospace and Agricultural Implement Workers of America (UAW), led by UAW President Douglas Frazer, had to determine a bargaining strategy for the imminent contract negotiations with the U.S. auto industry. The current three-year pact was due to expire September 14. Initial meetings with the "Big Three," General Motors, Ford and Chrysler, were scheduled to begin July 16 in Detroit.

INDUSTRY BACKGROUND

Negotiations between the UAW and the major automobile manufacturers are among the most important in the U.S. economy. Not only are the 780,000 UAW workers at the Big Three companies affected, but an estimated 15 million jobs are linked directly or indirectly to motor vehicles and auto sales represent 18% of retail sales in the U.S. In addition, auto settlements influence wage trends in other industries.

ECONOMIC CONDITIONS

The 1979 contract talks followed a year of near-record sales for the U.S. auto industry. Total U.S. sales reached 11.3 million new cars, nearly equalling the 11.4 million unit sales record of 1973. Domestic car sales reached 9.3 million, also the best since 1973. Table 1 shows how 1978 compared to prior year results for the Big Three.

However, performance varied greatly among the top producers. As shown in Table 2, GM had achieved a 5.1% average net profit on sales for the last five years while Chrysler had barely broken even. In 1978, while GM posted record profits and Ford had its second best year ever, Chrysler lost $205 million. Chrysler had incurred losses in three of the last five years.

First quarter 1979 results seemed to confirm this pattern. Compared to the first quarter of 1978, GM's dollar sales were up 20% and profits were up 45%. Ford's sales rose 26%, profits 28%. But Chrysler continued to lose money even with a sales increase of 11%. Although the growth comparisons were distorted by the impact of the severe winter and coal strike in 1978, 1979 began as a good year.

Early optimism quickly gave way to deep concern. Just a few weeks after GM's chairman had predicted a record year for 1979, the market for U.S. cars experienced a severe decline. Unsettling news about the economy and fears of a shortage of oil supplies due to a disruption in Iran weakened the total market for automobiles. By May, unit sale were lagging 1978 sales 9%. At the same time, those who were buying cars were choosing more imported models.

Imports had been gradually increasing their penetration into the U.S. auto market as shown by Table 3. This trend accelerated in early 1979. In March imports captured 22.5% of sales. This held in April and rose to a 24.3% market share in May.

Table 1

Selected Measures of Industry Performance for the Big Three
($ millions)

Year	Net Sales	Net Income	After-Tax Margin	After-Tax Return on Equity (%) Auto Industry	After-Tax Return on Equity (%) S&P 400 Indstrls
1965	$32,771	$3,067.6	9.36%	23.4%	12.6%
1968	44,276	2,661.5	6.01	16.7	12.3
1970	40,732	1,116.8	2.74	5.7	10.3
1973	67,796	3,559.6	5.25	16.9	14.2
1975	68,306	1,315.8	1.93	5.7	12.1
1977	105,862	5,173.3	4.89	19.1	14.0
1978	119,623	4,892.0	4.09	16.3	14.6

Source: Company Annual Reoports and Standard and Poor's, Inc.

Table 2

Performance Variance within Big Three
($ in millions, units in 000s)

Cumulative Results Five Years, 1974-1978	GM	FORD	CHRYSLER
Total Sales	$232,628	$157,095	$55,878
Total Net Income	11,952	4,895	69
Net Income as a Percent of Sales	5.1%	3.1%	0.1%
U.S. Factory Unit Sales:			
Passenger Cars	22,706	13,037*	5,784
Trucks	6,421	6,144*	2,021
Total	29,127	19,181*	7,805

*Includes Ford of Canada.

Source: Company Annual Reports.

Table 3

Import Share of U.S. Auto Market, 1965-1978

1965 - 8.1%	1973 - 15.2%
1966 - 7.3	1974 - 15.7
1967 - 9.3	1975 - 18.3
1968 - 10.5	1976 - 14.8
1969 - 11.2	1977 - 18.6
1970 - 14.7	1978 - 17.7
1971 - 15.1	1979* - 21.8
1972 - 14.6	

*January - June

Source: Ward's Auitomotive Yearbook and "Ward's Automotive Reports."

Japanese automakers made the largest improvements in market share, rivaling Ford's share in total. Table 4 shows that all three major U.S. makers were affected.

At the same time total sales were declining, sales of U.S. made cars shifted more heavily to smaller cars as shown by Table 5. The total share for small cars (subcompacts and compacts) had risen to 48.8% in April and May. Not only were sales moving to the lower margin models, but U.S. manufacturers were producing small cars at capacity and could not meet the additional small car demand.

Another factor affecting the industry's economic picture was the combined effect of productivity changes and increased wages and benefit payments. Productivity data showed a 3% per year gain in output per hour for production workers from 1975 to 1978 (Table 6). (Output per hour actually dropped 1.8% in 1978.) Yet during the same time period, auto workers' wages had increased at an annual rate of 9.7% (Table 7). Their wage position vis-a-vis all manufacturing production workers continued to imporve quite dramatically.

In addition to wage increases, the labor cost for auto workers was raised by the accelerating cost of benefits. Each of the auto companies and the UAW itself compile different commputations of the costs of various benefit programs. This data is closely guarded as the various estimates of cost are a prime area of negotiation in making trade-offs during bargaining. However, there was no doubt that negotiated benefit imporvements were an increasing portion of total compensation. Legally required benefits were also growing at almost the same rate. One industry observer estimated GM's settlement costs as shown in Table 8. By mid-1979, GM spokesmen claimed that average total compensation costs were $15.10 per hour.

Table 4

Percentage of Total U.S. Market
Year-to-Date, May 1979 and 1978

	May 1979		May 1978	
	Month	YTD	Month	YTD
General Motors*	44.6%	45.7%	47.2%	45.8%
Ford*	19.1	20.7	23.2	23.6
Chrysler*	8.9	9.2	11.0	10.8
Toyota	5.5	4.4	4.0	4.1
Datsun	4.9	4.2	4.1	3.3
Honda	3.3	3.4	2.3	2.5
Volkswagen	2.9	3.0	1.7	2.1
(Imported Only)	(1.4)	(1.5)	(1.7)	(2.1)
(U.S. Made)	(1.5)	(1.5)	(-)	(-)
Mazda	1.7	1.3	0.5	0.5
American Motors	1.6	1.3	1.6	1.6
Subaru	1.3	1.2	0.7	0.8
Other Imports	4.6	5.6	4.7	4.9
Total Domestic	75.7	78.4	83.0	81.8
Total Imported	24.3	21.6	17.0	18.2

*Excludes small number of imported models sold by U.S. manufacturers.

Source: "Ward's Automotive Reports," June 11, 1979.

Table 5

U.S. Make Auto Market Segmentation by Size,

YTD May 1979 and 1978

	YTD May 1979	YTD May 1978
Subcompact	22.3%	12.4%
Compact	22.0	24.9
Van	1.4	1.6
Intermediate	27.1	2.1
Full Size	21.3	22.9
Luxury	5.9	6.1
Total(U.S. Makes Only)	100.0%	100.0%

Source: "Ward's Automotive Reports," June 11, 1979.

Table 6

Output Per Hour for Motor Vehicle and Equipment Production Workers	
Period	Annual Percentage Change*
1965-70	1.4%
1970-75	4.4
1965-78	2.9
1975-78	3.0
1975-76	4.9
1976-77	6.0
1977-78	(1.8)

*Calculated on a compound basis.

Source: U.S. Department of Labor, Bureau of Labor Statistics.

(Note: This information is assembled from a variety of sources and compiled by the Bureau of Labor Statistics. The automobile industry does not necessarily agree with this data. The companies profess not to keep their own productivity statistics. Should they refer to such company data during negotiations, they would be required to release that data to the UAW.)

Table 7

Average Hourly Earnings
(Wages and overtime wages only)

					Increase Rate*			Total Increase %	Total Increase $
	1965	1970	1975	1978	1965-1970	1970-1975	1975-1978	1965-1978	1965-1978
Autos	$3.54	$4.76	$7.24	$9.56	6.1%	8.7%	9.7%	270%	$6.02
All Mfg.	2.66	3.46	5.03	6.48	5.4	7.8	8.8	244	3.82
Contract Construction	3.78	5.44	7.49	8.92	7.6	6.6	6.0	236	5.14

*Compounded annual rate of increase.

Source: U.S. Department of Labor, Bureau of Labor Statistics.

Table 8

UAW Contract Settlements at General Motors*

	1970	1973	1976
Straight time	$3.84	$4.78	$5.74
Cost of Living Allowance	.21	.40	1.14
Overtime, Holidays, Vacations	.75	1.17	1.74
SUB,** Pensions, Insurance	.72	1.28	2.20
FICA,*** Unemployment Taxes	.24	.42	.55
Total	$5.76	$8.05	$11.37

*Reported after the fact; not amounts estmated at times of contract signing.
**Supplemented Unemployment Benefits.
***Social Security Taxes.

Source: Ward's Auto World, June, 1979.

THE BARGAINING PROCESS

Collective bargaining involving automobile manufacturers is primarily company-by-company and plant-by-plant. Contracts with General Motors, Ford and Chrysler expire simultaneously while other manufacturers (American Motors, suppliers, and now Volkswagen of America) have separate negotiation periods. No interest has been demonstrated in negotiating an industrywide contract. The UAW is the major union, but the IUE represents some parts plants at GM.

A significant feature of the auto bargaining process is the use of pattern bargaining. The UAW traditionally chooses one auto firm as the target company. Upon winning a settlement at the company, the UAW goes to other members of the Big Three in an attempt to duplicate or even slightly improve the pattern agreement. Since the contracts usually expire just prior to the start of the model year, a strike can mean the difference between a profit or a loss for the year. The union hopes that in this highly competitive industry the target company would give ground rather than be struck and probably lose business to its competitors, who still would be working. The target company would usually be selected by the UAW in late August after preliminary discussions had begun with all three companies. Further negotiations with the companies not selected would be held in abeyance with temporary contract extensions.

In the past, a variety of factors, such as the size of the UAW's strike fund, the economic condition of each of the companies, and the desirability of sharing the burden of strike duty among all workers and companies, have influenced the selection of a target. In 1967, Ford was the target and was struck for 66 days. The result was a major boost in the SUB program but a cap on the cost of living allowance (COLA). In 1970, it was GM and a 10-week strike. The objective was to remove the cap on the cost of living adjustment. Chrysler was picked in 1973, not so much because it was their turn but because the UAW considered them the most suitable. In earlier years the relatively poor financial situation at Chrysler made the UAW reluctant to target them, but in 1973 Chrysler was having one of its best years ever and was making inroads into the small car market, a position it did not want to jeapordize by undergoing a strike. Although a strike resulted, it only lasted nine days and the result was the acheivement of the right for workers to refuse overtime and a 30-and-out retirement program.

In the 1976 negotiations, Ford was again the target. After a four-week strike, the UAW won more time off for workers under a "scheduled paid personal holiday" plan. Company contributions to SUB funds were increased and skilled workers received a larger pay differential. A one-time bonus payment to retirees was also negotiated. In subsequent bargaining, General Motors signed a pledge to remain neutral in UAW organizing drives. (The UAW had accused GM of a "Southern Strategy" of keeping the unions out of new GM facilities in the South by not hiring people with union backgrounds or sympathies.)

Another significant feature of the auto bargaining process is simultaneous but separate national and local bargaining. The local unions hold bargaining talks at individual plants where the emphasis is on seniority, safety, working conditions and other local issues. The local talks have been known to continue past the resolution of national issues and local strikes are not unusual. (For the content of a local agreement, see Exhibit 1.)

1979 UAW OBJECTIVES

Formal development of UAW bargaining objectives is an involved process. Suggestions are made by union locals and are considered at several special conferences and meetings. Advisory committees composed of union members develop resolutions that are offered to the separate skilled trades and production workers conferences for consideration, modification and adoption. These resolutions along with direct suggestions from the locals are reviewed and categorized by a Resolutions Committee for several weeks prior to the National Collective Bargaining Convention. A formal proposal is then submitted to the convention delegates. The International Union officers and staff provide information, leadership, and support during this process.

In 1979, the Resolutions Committee received 1,297 proposals prior to the April convention. Its recommendations were presented in a printed booklet that was read to the convention in sections, with debate open for each section. (However, the convention could only vote for the adoption of the recommended resolutions as a whole.) After two days of discussion, the resolution package was adopted without change.

The adopted bargaining objectives covered all areas of the labor agreement (Exhibit 2). The highest priority items were increases in pensions for both current and future retirees, more paid days off, and a substantial wage increase with improvements in the COLA formula.

PENSIONS

UAW President Fraser had declared that "cost-of-living protection for the retirees shall be the number one priority demand in 1979." In 1976 the UAW decided not to reopen the six-year pension agreement made in 1973 because such an action could have resulted in an injunction against the union forbidding any future bargaining for benefits for retirees. The U.S. Supreme Court had ruled that it was illegal for a union to insist on bargaining for benefits for retirees (on the grounds that retirees are no longer employees). Now, with the expiration of the six-year agreement, pressure from retired members for increases was intense. (There were about 190,000 living retirees from the Big Three companies alone. While not voting on contracts, retired members do vote for local union officers. The UAW has always encouraged its retired members to be active in the union and the union provides several retirement centers.)

Emphasizing the plight of retirees on fixed company pensions (although most have social security benefits which are indexed to inflation) also was a means of welding the often-divergent interests of retirees and employees. Raising the pensions of past retirees might contribute to the likelihood of significantly higher payments for future retirees, who were the current employees. This would maintain a continuing incentive for workers to retire early and thus open up jobs for younger workers.

Moreover, the UAW had been a leader in developing pension concepts ever since pensions became a legally mandated issue of bargaining in 1949. The UAW virtually started the trend toward early retirement by winning monthly pension supplements for early retirees in 1964. But the supplement ends when social security payments begin for the retirees. While social security payments were indexed in 1972 to increase with the cost of living, the corporate pension payments in autos are fixed at the time of retirement.

Pension benefits in the auto industry were already among the best in the U.S. A 30-year worker could collect a pension of $700 monthly if under age 62. The companies also provided medical and life insurance coverage. If an average long-service employee retired at the normal retirement age of 65 (with a spouse at least 62), their total after-tax retirement income would exceed the take-home pay the employee would have received for working full time. Due in a large part to these benefits, the number of individuals receiving pensions at GM had grown from 10% of average employment (excluding retirees) in 1965 to over 31% in 1979. However, inflation had decreased the purchasing power of the benefits since the current benefit levels were negotiated in 1973. Fraser declared that "we did not struggle year after year...to covert that glorious slogan 'Too Old To Work, Too Young to Die' to...'Too Poor to Eat'."

TIMEOFF

In 1976, partly as an answer to demands for more job security, Ford and the UAW had initiated a Scheduled Paid Holidays (SPH) plan which was subsequently adopted by GM and Chrysler. Phasing in seven more days off by the end of the contract (in addition to other holidays and regular vacations), the plan was designed to give workers more paid time off and thereby to create the need for more employees. Days are assigned to workers on a rotating basis to evenly spread the assignments over the days of the week.

This plan was also seen as a major step towards the long-time UAW goal of the four-day work week. In the last contract year, Big Three workers would have 20 paid days off for holidays. With the addition of vacation days, the average Ford worker would have 37½ paid days off during the year, GM workers 39½. The SPH plan provided the administrative mechanism to keep plants operating all week with a variable work force scheduled even within shifts.

A favorable union report on the new paid holiday plan was presented at the 1979 UAW convention. Fraser contended that of the one million hourly people employed in the U.S. motor vehicle industry, 150,000 would be unemployed if the UAW had not negotiated reduced working time over the many negotiations. Now the delegates wanted further days added.

WAGES AND COLA

Wages have always been a major issue in bargaining and 1979 was no exception. Auto workers receive base wages consisting of several components. First, each occupation has a basic straight-time hourly wage rate. Second, an annual "Improvement Factor" is added to this base rate and is awarded in the second and third year of the three-year agreement. The Improvement Factor is an annual increase to improve the workers' standard of living. It has been 3% annually for some time, and was initially designed to reflect the rate of national productivity growth. Finally, base rates are increased by Cost of Living Adjustments (COLA) based on changes in a composite of the U.S. and Canadian governments' Consumer Price Indexes. All of these factors are subject to modification in bargaining as are shift premiums, overtime rates and other items.

Strongest bargaining emphasis is usually placed on the COLA. With accelerating inflation, the potential benefit of COLA to UAW workers was expected to be substantial.

COMPANY CONCERNS

Even before the sales decline of the first part of 1979, automobile industry managers had several concerns that would be presented to the UAW as important issues in the upcoming negotiations.

ABSENTEEISM

Casual absenteeism (unscheduled absences for less than 40 hours duration) had long plagued the auto industry. Because of the assembly-line nature of automobile manufacture, such absences could be extremely disruptive and costly. Over the years, many techniques had been tried to curb these absences ranging from penalties to incentives. In 1976, Ford had proposed the Scheduled Paid Holiday plan primarily to reduce absenteeism.

Apparently, the SPH plan had not been effective in solving the absenteeism problem. At GM, short-term, noncontractual absenteeism increased to 5.8% in the first half of 1979, up approximately 30% over 1976. At Ford, unauthorized voluntary absences and short-term (often recurring) medical absences had increased 25% since 1976. Instead of reducing the problems of short-term absences, the net effect of the SPH plan had been to overlay built-in increased contractual absenteeism on the growing rate of noncontractual absences. (At GM, total contractual and noncontractual short-term absences during the first six months of 1979 were 10.6%.)

To help remedy the absenteeism problem, the auto companies wanted to strengthen provisions allowing termination of employees for absences. They also wanted to tie eligibility for paid time off to good attendance records and tighten rules governing medical absences.

BENEFITS COSTS

An issue of particular importance to the auto companies was the burgeoning cost of employee benefit plans. For example, the costs to GM for pensions, insurance, and supplemental unemployment benefits alone had more than doubled each five years since 1963 (a compounded growth rate of 15% per year). In 1963, those benefits cost $675 per employee. This rose to more than $5,100 in 1978. Employees made no contributions towards paying for those benefits. Costs for social security and other legally mandated benefits were also rising at increasing rates.

The auto companies were looking to find ways to help control the rising benefits costs. One suggested approach was redesigning health plans to encourage more carefully considered use of health care services. Another was elimation of several items of duplication of benfits payments, such as dual payment of Workers Compensation claims to pension recipients and payment of full sickness and accident benefits when social security disability benefits were paid. Some wanted to restrict benefits coverage for new workers until they not only gained experience but also proved dependable attendance. Others felt that the workers should pay a portion of the benefits costs directly and bear part of the burden of cost increases (a demand the UAW had refused before). However, UAW's Fraser had declared that the companies "are in for the longest strike they have ever had if they try to tamper with our (health benefits) system."

OTHER FACTORS AFFECTING NEGOTIATIONS

INFLATION

In early 1979, inflation was accelerating in the U.S. economy. As shown in Table 9, the consumer price index through May was increasing at an annual rate over 13%. This increased workers' demands for COLA formula improvements and changes to the pension plan. One recurring demand was that some type of COLA be added to retirement payments. Such a COLA for pensions would once again break new conceptual ground for contract provisions.

Table 9

Changes in Consumer Prices

Period	Average Annual Percent Change
1968	4.2
1969	5.4
1970	5.9
1971	4.3
1972	3.3
1973	6.2
1974	11.0
1975	9.1
1976	5.8
1977	6.5
1978	7.6

1979:	Change From Preceding Month	Annualized Percent Rate
January	.9	11.4
February	1.2	15.4
March	1.0	12.7
April	1.1	14.0
May	1.1	14.0

Sources: U.S. Department of Labor, Bureau of Labor Statistics.

GOVERNMENT GUIDELINES

In an attempt to control inflation, President Carter had established voluntary wage and price guides restricting wage increases to 7% annually. These had not been well received by any union groups. During the April 1979 National Master Freight Contract negotiations the guidelines had been adjusted to exclude certain types of costs such as increased charges for current benefits, giving rise to "guideline math." The result was that the Teamsters were able to win an agreement of 27.4% over three years (assuming only 6% per year inflation) that was found by the government to be "consistent with the guidelines." The trucking companies, expecting a higher rate of inflation, estimated the cost of the agreement at more than 30% over its three-year term.

In the most recent national negotiation, the Rubberworkers had won substantial gains in excess of 7% per year. The most important change for the Rubberworkers, however, was achievement of a "100% recovery" formula for COLA. The formula was increased from 1 cent for every .30 point increase in the Consumer Price Index to 1 cent for every .26 point increase. The current UAW formula increased wages a percentage that was 80% of the percentage increase in the cost of living.

UAW President Douglas Fraser had been one of the strongest critics of the wage-price guidelines. After the Teamster's settlement he had declared that the guidelines had "self-destructed." He also advised the government to "stay the hell away from our negotiations."

One means the government had used to try to enforce the wage-price guidelines was to deny government contracts to those who violated the standards. A group of unions had won a suit to set aside that enforcement mechanism, but the government appealed and won the right to use that method. All of the large automotive companies had significant government contract work.

LAYOFF AND PLANT CLOSINGS

With inflation soaring, auto sales down, and oil suppplies uncertain, there was growing fear of a U.S. recession. This increased the importance to the UAW of several secondary negotiating objectives: improvements to the Supplementary Unemployment Benefits (SUB) fund and protective measures concerning plant shutdowns.

Just three years after a substantial restructuring of the SUB plan as part of the 1976 bargaining, the SUB fund at Chrysler was in danger of running out of funds by the end of the summer. The SUB fund paid weekly benefits to laid-off workers which, together with state unemployment compensation, equalled 90% of take-home pay. If the fund was at its maximum level, benefits could be paid up to 52 weeks. Due to the drop in auto production caused by auto sales declines, the Chrysler fund had been severly depleted.

Chrysler had also announced that it planned to permanently close the Hamtramck, Michigan facility in 1980. It was the largest auto assembly plant in the country. This announcement, along with increasing industry layoffs and uncertainties over the effects of foreign competition led to more worker demands for protection if jobs were lost. Such protections could take the form of special payments, optional transfer to other facilities, hiring preferences or early retirement.

"SOUTHERN STRATEGY"

In another area related to preserving UAW jobs and memebership, the question of a GM "Southern Strategy" still was not settled. The UAW wanted to insure that the opening of new automobile factories in the Southern states would not dilute its position as spokesman for the majority of auto workers. Workers in the South had historically been less unionized.

During the 1976 negotiations, GM had pledged "to neither discourage nor encourage the Union's efforts in organizing production and maintenance employees traditionally represented by the Union elsewhere in General Motors, but (to) observe a posture of neutrality in these matters." The UAW pledged "to conduct itself in a manner which neither demeans the Corporation as an organization nor its representatives as individuals."

Differences of opinion over GM's actions and intentions persisted. In 1978, GM agreed to allow UAW workers the right to apply for jobs in new plants where they currently worked. Before employees had been required to take time off to travel to the new plants to apply.

In 1979, the issue was still open. A represntation election was scheduled for July 19 (three days after contract talks were scheduled to begin) at the new Oklahoma City assembly plant. The UAW had won only one major organizing victory since the last negotiations in the 1976 election in Monroe, Louisiana. It had recently lost elections in Fitzgerald, Georgia and Clinton, Mississippi. Now the UAW alleged that GM was violating its neutrality pledge and distributing antiunion material. The 1979 negotiation would be another opportunity for the UAW to press for stronger neutrality agreements.

AUTOMOBILE INVENTORIES

The sharp decline in auto sales and the sudden shift to smaller cars during early 1979 was first considered to be a short-term reaction to the oil supply scare. The automobile industry had continued to produce automobiles at a normal rate. When the sales trends continued, inventories reached record levels. Total inventories in May were an all-time record high of 66 days supply. A "normal" level was the 53 days supply of May 1978. Even more serious, the mix of cars in stock weighted towards the larger, slower selling models (see Exhibit 3). These high inventory levels presaged plant shutdowns and layoffs and had to be considered in comtemplating any possible strike strategy.

CHOOSING A TARGET COMPANY

GENERAL MOTORS

In many ways, GM was the most logical target. The company had been consistently profitable and had a record year in 1978. Its return on stockholders' equity had been over 20% for the last three years and first quarter 1979 results were even better. It had consistently increased its share of the domestic car market from a low of 49% in 1974 to 59% during 1979. Clearly, GM could best afford the wage and benefit improvements desired by UAW.

This year, however, there might be a chink in GM's armor despite its size and success. The short supply of the highly successful new "X body" small cars first introduced in the spring of 1979 might make it vulnerable to a possible strike. The very size of GM with over 460,000 UAW workers made a strike against GM more expensive than strikes against smaller companies, but the UAW strike fund would be a historical high of over $293 million by the end of August. Selective "mini-srikes" against critical parts and small car plants might be used to help conserve the UAW rsources.

There was also sentiment that perhaps it was "GM's turn." GM had only been the target twice since World War II, in 1946 and 1970. Both negotiations resulted in expensive, lengthy walkouts. There was little doubt that GM would be a tough adversary. However, some observers felt that the UAW had to select GM as the target simply to prove that it was not afraid to take GM on.

One negative factor was that in past negotiations GM had been more responsive to monetary demands than to social innovations. The prime UAW priority of adding some type of cost of living protection to pensions for already retired employees would certainly break new ground. Some felt, though, that even this change was primarily an economic one.

FORD

Ford was also a potential target company. It had a relatively sound financial base. Ford also would dislike a shutdown if only because it was perennially fearful of giving GM any additional edge in the market-place. However, a 48-day strike had resulted during the last negotiation in 1976 when Ford was the target. With only 197,000 UAW workers, the strike fund would last longer at Ford should a full shutdown take place.

Ford was also the logical place to win a major imporovement in pensions for the already retired. Of the Big Three, it had the lowest ratio of retirees to active workers, so such imporovments would be less expensive for Ford. In addition, Ford had historically been much more open to contract innovations in the past.

An important economic factor to consider would be the potential effect that the U.S. gas-economy requirements might have on Ford. To mandate improved fuel economy, the U.S. government had established corporate average fuel economy standards (CAFE) for the fleet averages of each manufacturer's U.S. sales. Beginning with a requirement of 18 miles per gallon for the 1978 model year, the required CAFE rose to 27.5 mpg for 1985. For every 1/10 mpg below the required CAFE that a company achieved, a penalty of $5 per car sold would be assessed. At a rate of 2,900,000 units sold per year, a miss of only ½ mpg would result in a penalty of $72.5 million. Ford was having a difficult time meeting the 1979 CAFE requirement due to poor sales of Pinto, its subcompact model. In October 1978, Ford had begun limiting sales of larger models and raising prices on larger-engine models. This meant that in the poor sales climate of 1979, Ford had to limit sales of its more profitable larger automobiles. This could easily cause Ford to close down family size car assembly plants and could jeopardize thousands of UAW jobs.

CHRYSLER

Chrysler presented a very difficult problem. At the same time that it was absorbing high losses, Chrysler faced substantial cash needs to retool to keep pace with competition and to meet new governemnt requrements. Also, Chrysler's management was just settling down from the upheaval caused when former Ford President Lee Iacocca was fired by Ford and hired as President of Chrysler in November 1978. Iacocca had made major changes to the executive leadership in the past few months. It was highly questionable whether Chrysler could absorb the kind of settlement GM and Ford could at least tolerate. In fact, Chrysler might be expected to ask for special treatment.

There were precedents for special contract terms and provisions. The UAW had granted concessions to American Motors during periods of financial difficulty. In 1971, the union accepted a four-year contract that limited retroactivity of first-year increases and postponed retirement improvements until the third year. A two-year agreement in 1974 delayed implementation of a new dental plan. In 1977, the UAW signed seven-month and one-year contracts with AMC that matched pay increases at the Big Three but provided no new fringe benefits. However, the most recent AMC settlement, a two-year pact negotiated in 1978, generally followed the Big Three pattern.

The disadvantage of special concessions was that such contracts diluted the strength of pattern bargaining. American Motors, for example, was now effectively excluded as a target used to set new industry standards. With only three large domestic auto manufacturers left, elimination of Chrysler as a "bargaining equal" with GM and Ford would be very undesirable. The goals for Chrysler would have to be very carefully assessed within the context of a general industry strategy of pattern bargaining.

BALANCING A SETTLEMENT

In addition to selection of a target company, the UAW also had to decide on the emphasis of each component of a setlement package. The leaders of UAW knew that they would be highly unlikely to achieve all of their bargaining goals. Yet every objective was the most important to some segment of its diverse membership. So at the same time they would be bargaining for total package gains, they must also consider some type of balance in a settlement. If they set a target of a 30% total increase over three years, this would mean an increase of around $5 per hour. Assuming that this might be won, how should this be apportioned and how should trade-offs be made?

Exhibit 1

1976 LOCAL AGREEMENT between GM ASSEMBLY DIVISION, FRAMINGHAM PLANT and LOCAL #422, U.A.W

TABLE OF CONTENTS

Exhibit 2

WHAT WE WANT IN '79

UAW negotiators will head into bargaining with the major auto and agricultural-implement companies armed with a strong program to deal with the economic distress of union members and their families. Following are highlights of the union's bargaining program for 1979, adopted in Detroit April 17-18:

WAGES AND SALARIES

- A "substantial increase" in wages, protected by provisions for cost-of-living allowance adjustments.
- Updating the COLA formula by using current relationships between the average wage level and the consumer price index, to protect workers more fully against inflation.

REDUCING WORK TIME

- More progress toward reducing hours per worker.
- In addition to pressing for more paid days off, seeking concrete steps to reduce overtime. One approach: demanding compensatory time in addition to premium pay when overtime is worked (for example, a half-hour of compensatory time for every hour of overtime worked).

PENSIONS

- Negotiating increases for retired workers that will preserve their purchasing power.
- Increases for early retirees under age 65, to permit them to exercise their right of early retirement with assurances that their benefits won't be diminished by inflation.

"This is the significance of the slogan 'COLA for Retirees,'" the resolution declares. "We are determined to meet this challenge. It is a top priority."

HEALTH CARE

- Extension of improved prepaid vision-care program to retirees.
- Improved dental coverage and benefits.
- Full payment by employers of Part B Medicare premiums for retirees and spouses as well as for all others eligible for Medicare.

PLANT CLOSINGS

- Prenotification of closings to the union, with an opportunity to negotiate assistance for workers.
- Retraining programs, preferential hiring rights, and other benefits for workers laid off by transfers or plant shutdowns.

HEALTH AND SAFETY

- Stronger provisions to insure workers' right to know about workplace hazards.
- Improvement of company occupational medical programs to strengthen the range and quality of services.
- Spelling out the right of workers to refuse to work on patently unsafe jobs until the hazard is corrected.

OTHER AREAS

- Training, reduction in worktime, and other provisions to help deal with the effects of technological changes on the workforce.
- Strong controls on subcontracting and contracting out.
- Maintenance of the right to strike over work pace disputes.
- Improved group sickness and accident, extended disability, and life-insurance benefits.
- Conversion from the hourly wage system to salaries.
- Inclusion of workers in stock-purchase and profit-sharing programs on an equitable basis.
- Paid educational leave.
- Group legal services.
- Joint union-management study of child-care facilities.
- Strengthening the grievance procedure to deal with discipline problems.
- Provisions to deal with the special problems of skilled-trades workers, technical, office, and professional workers, and other special categories within the union. □

Exhibit 3

Days Supply

GM		FORD		CHRYSLER	
SUBCOMPACT:					
Chevette	19	Pinto	47	Horizon	26
Monza	25	Bobcat	59	Omni	26
Sunbird	18	Mustang	48	Omni	26
Starfire	20	Capri	42		
Skyhawk	38				
COMPACT:					
Citation	22	Fairmont	62	Volare	72
Phoenix	13	Zephyr	85	Aspen	86
Omega	16	Granada	78		
Skylark	15	Monarch	91		
Camaro	37				
Firebird	27				
INTERMEDIATE:					
Malibu	69	LTD II	108	Fury	58
LeMans	60	Cougar	155	LeBaron	90
Cutlass	49	XR-7	147	Monaco	62
Supreme	49	T'bird	157	Diplomat	116
Century	58			Cordoba	207
Regal	54			Charger	186
M.Carlo	117				
G.Prix	84				
FULL-SIZE:					
Chevrolet	121	LTD	109	St. Regis	97
Pontiac	106	Marquis	134	Chrysler	117
Olds 88	53				
Olds 98	69				
LeSabre	93				
Electra	145				
Riviera	38				
Toronado	37				
LUXURY:					
Cadillac	85	Continental	107		
Eldorado	55	Mark V	160		
Corvette	30	Versailles	164		
Seville	100				
PASSENGER VANS:					
Sportvan	130	Club Wagon	88	Voyager	168
				Sportsman	107

Source: "Ward's Automotive Reports", June 11, 1979.

1979 AUTOMOBILE NEGOTIATIONS (B)

UAW SELECTS GM AS TARGET

The International Executive Board of the UAW selected General Motors rather than Ford as the industry's "target" company on August 3, 1979. The UAW had ruled out Chrysler as a strike target when formal negotiations had opened July 16. UAW president Douglas Fraser noted that there were more than twenty GM car models with less than a 60-day inventory. Ford had fewer models in the same position. Fraser also indicated that the UAW would definitely consider a strike that was not national in scope if an agreement should not be reached.

The target announcement followed two months of bargaining that had gotten off to an unusual start. First, the UAW had eliminated Chrysler as a target due to its precarious financial position. Then union negotiators had delayed the first session to protest GM's alleged anti-union tactics at an Oklahoma City assembly plant. Later that week, the UAW won the representation election at that plant.

Those first two months had seen little apparent progress. The UAW had presented each company with a set of demands based on the bargaining goals adopted by its Convention. GM called these demands "unreasonable " and suggested that a "wide gap" existed in the parties' conceptions of a "fair and reasonable settlement." GM reiterated its contention that 1979 was a "year for restraint, for moderation." Ford's position was similar. The auto companies had made counterproposals that the union rejected as insufficient. The most unusual proposal was Chrysler's proposal for a two-year wage freeze which the UAW rejected. July and August also brought news of a continuing decline in car sales and a rise in inflation.

GM SETTLEMENT REACHED WITHOUT STRIKE

GM and the UAW reached a new three-year settlement on the night of September 14, avoiding a national strike. Major new provisions were:

- retirees would receive periodic increases of 24% to 40% over three years (with GM receiving UAW permission to stretch its $8 billion unfunded pension liability over 30 years to reduce current funding requirements);

- scheduled paid holidays would be increased to 26 over three years from 12 in the past three (with other regular holidays, workers would average 23 paid days off per year plus vacations);

- base wages would continue to be raised 3% per year;

- the COLA adjustment would be increased in the third year to 1¢ for every .26 point increase in the COLA- formula;

- 1¢ would be withheld from each quarterly COLA adjustment "to help pay for the costly total benefit package" (2¢ per quarter in the third year);

- health, vision, and dental care plans as well as life and disability benefits were improved;

- GM agreed to permit workers to transfer seniority from existing plants to new ones making similar products (this historically resulted in the quick recognition of the UAW in the new plants);

- GM agreed to contribute benefits of certain tax credits for machinery and equipment investments into a trust fund that would purchase free GM stock for UAW members;

- the UAW agreed to extend by several months the phasing in of wages and benefits for new employees;

- GM and the UAW agreed to set up a joint committee to combat casual absenteeism.

It was estimated that with 8% inflation, this contract would increase average hourly direct labor costs for GM about 33% over the three years.

This contract negotiation had been singularly absent of invective and belligerency. The negotiators first concentrated on noneconomic issues covering general working conditions. The major pension, wage and time-off issues were left until immediately prior to the contract deadline. Relatively early agreements on the issues of procedures for new plants and the conceptual structure of pension increases led to the final peaceful settlement.

FORD FOLLOWS PATTERN

Ford and the UAW reached a new contract following the GM pattern in less than three weeks on October 4. This followed the September 30 announcement that UAW workers had voted 129,374 to 51,391 to accept the GM pact. There were minor changes in the Ford agreement, but the major provisions were identical to GM's.

There had been conjecture that even Ford would be unable to meet the GM terms. When Chrysler's chairman John Ricardo had unexpectedly resigned on September 18, former Ford president Lee Iacocca warned that Chrysler's problems were a sign of fundamental industry ills. "Ford's going to have to start yelling soon they're next." The public focus on financial prospects for the auto industry that had arisen from Chrysler's problems had led some analysts to conclude that Ford indeed faced an uncertain future. Nevertheless, the pattern held.

CHRYSLER WINS CONCESSIONS

With GM and Ford contracts settled, the UAW was confronted with the difficult Chrysler situation. Chrysler had sought U.S. government loan guarantees to aid its financial problems. Early Chrysler proposals were rejected by the Carter administration. As the auto market continued to deteriorate, it appeared that Chrysler's very survival was truly at stake.

Political pressure seemed to demand that Chrysler's workers be willing to make substantial sacrifices before aid would be forthcoming. A quick agreement was needed to even allow the possibility of Congressional action before the Christmas recess. Many felt later action would be too late. Yet Fraser also had to negotiate an agreement that would be ratified by the UAW members. Many workers felt it would not be just for Chrysler workers to earn less than UAW workers performing the same jobs at GM or Ford. Fraser described his strategy for compromise as plans to negotilate a "freeze on purchasing power."

Three weeks following the Ford agreement (ratified on October 22) Chrysler and the UAW agreed on October 25 to a new three-year contract. The new contract provided deferments to wage increases and COLA "travel" (movement of past COLA to base rates), reduced paid holildays, and made other benefit concessions. The UAW contended that these concessions saved Chrysler $203 million over the next three years. The UAW also had agreed to defer about $200 million in payments due from Chrysler to the pension fund.

Fraser said that the UAW had achieved its two major goals: parity with the GM and Ford contracts by the end of the third year, and keeping the COLA clause "pure and untampered." In addition, Fraser was to be named to the Chrysler board of directors and the UAW was given lilmited influence over certain "socially desirable" investments of pension fund money.

GOVERNMENT PRESSURE FORCES NEW CHRYSLER AGREEMENT

Even as the UAW leadership began campaigning for workers to ratify the Chrysler agreement, vocal members of Congress declared that the concessions were not enough. In addition, Alfred Kahn, Chairman of the U.S. Council on Wage and Price Stabililty, declared November 11 that the GM, Ford and Chrysler agreements probably violated Carter's wage guidelines. In Kahn's opinion, the Chrysler contract did "not remotely approach the kind of sacrifice (required) as a condition of being bailed out by the U.S. government."

Chrysler's cash situation worsened daily, auto sales continued to slump and many business and poliltical leaders voiced opposition to government aid for Chrysler. Fraser had to carefully balance several critical objectives. He had to help insure Chrysler received aid but wanted to minimize additional UAW concessions. He wanted to protect the $300 million UAW strike fund which had not been depleted by these negotiations. Some suggested this could be loaned to Chrysler to help protect UAW jobs. He also had to protect his political strength within the UAW and remain credible to the members. One important part of his strategy was to try to maximize the concessions other interested parties must make for Chrysler to receive aid. This included suppliers, bankers, dealers and the states where Chrysler was a large employer.

As debate continued, UAW workers ratified the Chrysler agreement November 16. As the December recess approached, complex aid plans began to take shape.

A compromise plan to give Chrysler $1.5 billion in loan guarantees was passed by Congress December 21. One requirement for the aid was a total of $462.5 million in wage concessions by Chrysler's workers (and $125 million from management employees). Chrysler would also have to obtain $2 billion from nongovernment sources. By January 6, 1980, Chrysler and the UAW had developed a new contract with $243 million in additional concessions. This came almost entirely from the elimination of paid days off, with some from further delays in wage increases. UAW members approved the new concessions January 21.

AFTERMATH

Few would venture to guess the permanent effects of the 1979 contract negotiations. Chrysler's future viabililty was far from certain and Ford clearly was going to have a difficult time staying in the same economic category as GM. Where did pattern bargaining fit in this more diverse company spectrum? Not only were differences developing between companies, but deep rifts had developed between the U.S. and Canadian segments of the UAW (as Canadian members working for Chrysler rejected the January wage concessions reguired for U.S aid). One response of the UAW became clear as Fraser began to attack what he described as the root of the problem: Japanese imports. He urged pressure be brought on Japanese carmakers to set up plants in the U.S. Whether this occurs or not, the structure of the auto industry is likely to be very dilfferent when the 1982 negotiations begin and these differences may substantially change the structure and conduct of industry bargaining.

1980 STEEL NEGOTIATIONS

Steel labor negotiations, which now occur every three years, are among the most important in the United States. The labor contract which results from these negotiations sets the wages, hours, and working conditions not only for the 290,000 steel workers employed by the 9 companies represented in the negotiations, but also for another 190,000 workers employed by other steel companies which later adopt the general terms of the settlement. In addition, the provisions of the new contract become a pattern for settlements in many other industries.

Unlike automobile labor negotiations which are carried on separately by each company, in steel the major companies negotiate jointly as a group with the Steelworker's union. As a result failure to reach an agreement can shut down the entire industry. Because of this industry-wide bargaining and because steel is an essential raw material for so many other industries, steel negotiations impact on the entire economy. A high settlement resulting in sizeable increases in steel prices can have a serious effect on the general price level. On the other hand failure to reach an agreement can result in shutdowns and unemployment not only in steel plants but throughout the economy.

As the parties approached the 1980 negotiations there had been 20 years of relatively stable labor relations in the industry. The last national strike had occurred in 1959. Moreover, in 1977 the companies and the union had agreed that there would be no national strike in 1980 but instead that all unsettled issues would be sent to arbitration for final and binding agreement. Thus, the 1980 steel negotiations would occur in a unique atmosphere. Unlike the situation elsewhere in private industry labor negotiations in the U.S., the threat of the strike or the lockout would not be present as a pressure to force the parties to reach agreement. The reasons for the elimination of the strike and lockout weapons and the effect of such elimination on the bargaining and the settlement will be discussed later.

THE INDUSTRY

In 1976 the American steel industry consisted of 89 companies with basic steel-making capacity. However, the 8 largest companies accounted for 70% of the total production. U.S. Steel, the largest company, accounted for almost one-fourth of the total output.

PRODUCTION

Production of steel is subject to strong cyclical swings. During the 70s the peak of production was reached in 1973 when over 111 million tons were shipped and the low point was reached in 1975 when only 80 million tons were shipped (see Table 1). Compared to 98 million tons in 1978, shipments in 1979 had increased to 100 million tons, but were still considerably below the 1973 peak. As the parties approached the 1980 negotiations, production in the first two months of 1980 showed a drop of 3% compared with the corresponding period in 1979.

Table 1

Steel Mill Product Shipments
and Employment in U.S.

Year	Total Net Shipments (thousands of tons)	Average Number of Employees
1979	100,262	453,000
1978	97,935	449,000
1977	91,147	452,000
1976	89,447	454,000
1975	79,957	457,000
1974	109,472	512,000
1973	111,430	509,000
1972	91,805	478,000
1971	87,038	487,000
1970	90,798	536,000

Source: Annual Statistical Report 1979, American Iron and Steel Institute.

TECHNOLOGY

The technology of steel production has been changing rapidly during the past 20 years. Whereas in 1960 about 90% of all steel was made by the open-hearth process, by 1975 over 60% was produced by the basic oxygen process, approximately 20% by electric furnaces and only about 20% by open hearth. The trend to basic oxygen and electric furnaces is continuing. Another major innovation has been continuous casting which is expected to increase from about 10% in 1978 to 50% by 1985.

The union has not opposed the introduction of technological changes, including the basic oxygen process, the electric furnace and continuous casting. George Moore, Vice President of Bethlehem Steel, has stated:

> "The Steelworkers (Union) rather than attempting to deprive the company of the efficiencies resulting from capital investment in modern facilities, have taken a positive approach in dealing with the impact of new technology on its members."

FOREIGN COMPETITION

The steel industry has been plagued by foreign imports which have made heavy inroads, especially on the east coast and the west coast. As a percentage of total U.S. supply imports increased every year from 1973 (12.3%) to 1978 (18.1%). In 1979, although imports were down, they still accounted for 15.2% of the total U.S. supply (see Table 2).

Industry spokemen maintain that European and Japanese producers have been "dumping" steel on the American market, that is, that they have been selling steel here at prices below their total costs of production. The government initiated a program under which steel imported below certain prices would be subject to an investigation to determine if it was being dumped. However, the trigger prices were based on the cost of steel production in Japan and, according to industry spokesmen, permitted European producers to "dump" steel products "legally" in the U.S. because European costs are considerably higher than Japanese costs.

In March of 1980 the U.S. Steel Company filed suits charging that companies in 7 European countries were "dumping" steel products in the American market. U.S. Steel demanded higher tarriffs to protect American producers. The Carter administration opposed the U.S. Steel Company action and discontinued the trigger price system pending outcome of the suits.

The union has strongly supported management's position that the industry should be protected against unfair competition from abroad. As the 1980 labor negotiations proceeded, imports continued to rise reaching a level of 14.6% in the first quarter of 1980 compared with 12.5% in the corresponding period in 1979.

Table 2

Imports of Steel Mill Products

Year	Imports (thousands of net tons)	Imports % of total Supply
1979	17,518	15.2
1978	21,135	18.1
1977	19,307	17.8
1976	14,285	14.1
1975	12,012	13.5
1974	15,970	13.4
1973	15,150	12.4
1972	17,681	16.6
1971	18,304	17.9
1970	13,364	13.8

Source: Annual Statistical Report 1979, American Iron and Steel Institute.

PROFITABILITY

Over the past two decades return on equity in the steel industry has been considerably below the average return of all U.S. manufacturers (see Table 3). Since 1957 only in one year, 1974, did return on net worth in steel exceed the average of all U.S. manufacturers. Even in that year profits in many industries including oil, paper, drugs and chemicals exceeded those in steel.

However, as the parties began negotiations in February of 1980, the 1979 annual earnings of the steel companies became available and in most cases indicated sizable increases in earnings compared with 1978. Only U.S. Steel indicated a loss for 1979 and this was the result of heavy write-offs on plants which were being closed. Inland, McClouth, and Lukens did report decreases of 17%, 13% and 42% respectively. However, increases reported were as follows: Bethlehem 22%, Armco 11%, National 13%, Republic 9%, Wheeling Pittsburg 160%, Interlake 279%, Kaiser 269%, Colorado Fuel and Iron 28%, and Copperweld 20%.

Table 3

Return On Stockholders' Equity
(percent after taxes)

Year	All Manufacturing	Iron and Steel
1979	16.5	6.8%
1978	15.0	7.3
1977	14.2	0.1
1976	14.0	7.8
1975	11.6	9.8
1974	14.9	17.1

Sources: Quarterly Financial Reports, 1974-1980, U.S. Federal Trade Commission.

EMPLOYMENT

The numbers of workers employed in the steel industry is affected in the short run by the cyclical nature of demand for steel and in the long run by the major techological changes. Productivity per worker has increased over the years and may be expected to continue to increase as the new techniques become fully operative. In 1970 the industry produced 91 million tons with 536,000 hourly paid workers, whereas in 1979 the industry produced 100 million tons with only 453,000 hourly paid workers (see Table 1). Although not opposing the technoligcal changes which have resulted in the increased productivity and decreased employment, the union has tried through collective bargaining to protect its members from loss of income due to both cyclical and technological unemployement.

THE UNION

The United Steelworkers of America (USW) was formed in the 1930s with financial and other support from John L. Lewis and the United Mineworkers. The industry strongly opposed unionization and a bitter and violent struggle occurred. Although U.S. Steel recognized the union in 1937 as representative for its members, the other steel companies continued to resist and it was not until 1941 that the union won NLRB representation elections in the Bethlehem plants. Soon after the Bethelehem elections most of the other steel companies agreed to negotiate with the union. Since 1952 the labor contracts have provided for a modified union shop with the result that union membership now approaches 100% of the hourly-paid work force in the industry.

MEMBERSHIP

USW (with 1.3 million members in 1976) was the largest union in the AFL-CIO and the third largest union in the nation. Only the Teamsters and the Autoworkers were larger. Membership in USW is not confined to the steel industry where, because of declining employment (see Table 1), membership has been decreasing. The union has compensated for this decline by merging with other unions and carrying on active organizing campaigns in other industries. It is estimated that basic steel and iron mining workers now constitute only 35% of the total membership. Although USW has tried to organize the white collar as well as the blue collar workers, its efforts in this respect have not been very successful. Office workers make up only about 3% of the membership.

FINANCES

The USW is in solid financial condition. In 1976 it reported a net worth of $136 million not including $65 million held by local unions. The income is derived mostly from union dues and initiation fees. The initiation fee is $10 and dues are equal to two hours of pay per month. Since the average steel worker's hourly wage in 1979 was $ 11.02 the average monthly dues of members in the steel industry was $ 22.04 per month. The union did not establish a strike fund until 1968. At present approximately 10% of all dues goes to the strike fund. Since the steel industry has not had a major strike since 1959 the fund has grown rapidly . As the union approached the 1980 negotiations the fund was reported to be in excess of $100 million.

CONTROL

Much of the power and authority in the union is centralized in the president and executive board of the international. The international office hires, directs and pays the staff of over 1,000 field representatives and about 500 headquarter personnel. However, the president and other international officers are elected by a national referendum and each district director is chosen by a vote in his own district. (The district directors are members of the executive board.) Reelection of president and other officers in the union has not been automatic. In 1957 a relatively unknown steel worker, Donald Rarick, headed a rank and file dues protest and polled 35% of the vote against the incumbent David McDonald. In 1965 I. W. Abel, who had been Secretary-Treasurer of the union, defeated McDonald by 10,000 votes out of 600,000 cast. In 1969 a relatively unknown staff lawyer, Emil Narick, ran against Abel and polled 41% of the votes. In 1977, when Abel retired, Lloyd McBride, who generally supported Abel's policies, was opposed by Edward Sadlowski, the Director of the union's largest district (the Chicago-Gary area). Sadlowski, who accused the leadership of working too closely with steel management, conducted a very active campaign and, although he lost, received 43% of the 578,000 votes that were cast.

CONTRACT NEGOTIATIONS

In many industries in the United States the major contract negotiations occur at the company or plant level. However, in the steel industry since the middle fifties major issues have been negotiated on an industry-wide basis. In 1980 nine major steel companies were represented by a single four-man bargaining committee composed of two from U.S. Steel, one from Bethlehem and one from Republic. The multi-company committee negotiated with a union committee which represented the hourly employees in all of the 9 companies. Although from time to time the union has threatened to return to company-by-company bargaining, this has not occurred. When the industry bargaining committee has failed to reach an agreement simultaneous strikes have been called at all 9 of the companies. Following the industry settlement, negotiations are still conducted at the company and local plant level but the major issues are settled at the industry level. Nevertheless, on a few occasions strikes have occurred at the local level despite a settlement at the industry level. Before a local union can strike, however, it must have the approval of the national union president.

STRIKES

During the period 1946 to 1959 over half of the negotiations ended in strikes. The last national strike occurred in 1959 and lasted for 116 days. The basic issue in the 1959 strike was the attempt of the companies to eliminate Section 2-B, the local working conditions clause, which restricted managments' right to unilaterally change working conditions, including crew sizes, during the life of the contract. Management insisted that it needed the right to make such changes in order to operate efficiently. However, despite the 116 day strike the companies were not successful in eliminating the local working conditions clause. The settlement which was reached continued Section 2-B in the new agreement and it has not been materially changed since that time. It should be noted that Section 2-B does not interfere with the introduction of new methods or equipment and does permit manning changes which result from such introductions.

Steel industry spokesmen contended that the government forced management to end the 1959 strike by withdrawing their (the industry's) demand for a change in Section 2-B. They saw in the governments action further confirmation of an earlier statement by John A. Stephens, the negotiator for U.S. Steel, who had said that the difficulty for management in steel was that the union would not allow the industry to win a short strike while the government and the industry's customers would not allow it to win a long strike.

Since 1959 there has not been an industry-wide strike in the steel industry. Management's conviction that it would not be permitted to win a strike, as expressed by Stephens, undoubtedly has been an important factor in the 20 years of peaceful settlements. From time to time the settlements have been criticized by government officials and others as having been secured at too high a price. Steel management has strongly resented the government criticism.

Despite a decade of strike-free negotiations in the sixties, the union and the companies came to the conclusion that the very possibility of a strike, the strike threat, was working to their mutual disadvantage. Prior to each contract termination date automobile companies and other users would stockpile large amounts of steel to protect themselves in case a strike should occur. As a result steel production and employment reached very high levels in the months preceding a contract termination date. However, even though agreement was reached without a strike, production and employment dropped heavily once a contract was signed and would not recover for several months. This was attributable to two factors. Once assured of continuation of supply, customers would work off the inventories they had built in anticipation of a possible strike. In addition, a number of users would be committed to forward contracts (made prior to termination) with foreign producers who could have maintained deliveries during a strike of the U.S. steel industry. Pre-termination stockpiling and foreign contracts reduced the demand for domestic steel. In order to avoid this phenomena the parties recognized that steel customers needed to be assured that no strike would occur. The proposal to accomplish this purpose came from I. W. Abel, the president of the union, and, as adopted by the parties in March 1973, became known as the Experimental Negotiating Agreement (ENA).

EXPERIMENTAL NEGOTIATING AGREEMENT

The ENA was designed not only to prevent stockpiling by customers but to avert crisis bargaining and provide a guaranteed base for pay raises. Under the terms of the agreement, bargaining for a new contract would begin February 1. It guaranteed wage increases of at least 3% a year plus cost-of-living improvements for each of the three years beginning with the start of the next contract term, August 1, 1974. In addition, each union member in the basic steel industry received a bonus of $150 in the first pay period after September 30, 1974. The agreement called for nearly all other issues, including any wage increases over the 3% level and impasses on fringes, to be submitted to final and binding arbitration if collective bargaining could not resolve them by April 15, 1974. The arbitration board called for under ENA would have one union-appointed member, one industry-appointed member, and three impartial members appointed with the approval of both sides. Only the three impartial members would vote on key issues. Arbitrators, if utilized, would be required to submit their decision by midnight July 10, 1974. The parties would have until July 20th to agree on the implementation of the arbitrators' award and any issues remaining unresolved were to be referred back to the arbitrators for their binding decision by midnight July 31, 1974.

In return, the union agreed "... not to engage in strikes, work stoppages, or concerted refusals to work in support of its bargaining demands, ..." Individual plant strikes on local issues were not barred although a series of interim deadlines were established to prod local settlements. In addition, approval by the international president would be required before a local strike could take place.

In 1974 the parties reached an agreement without resort to the arbitration procedure and the ENA was extended to cover the 1977 negotiations, thus demonstrating the parties' satisfaction with the new process. In 1977 when agreement in basic steel was reached, again without resort to the arbitration procedure, the ENA was extended to cover the next round of negotiations in 1980. However, ENA did not prohibit strikes over local issues and indeed in 1977 a long strike occurred in the iron ore mines over extending incentives to a greated portion of iron ore jobs.

While the parties continued to differ on the incentive issue a second controversy emerged from the strike. The union and the industry representatives disagreed as to whether the strike was over a "local issue", i.e. whether the strike constituted a permissible strike under the ENA. The merits of the incentive dispute were settled in the late fall of 1977. However, while the parties had already agreed to conduct 1980 negotiations under the terms of the ENA the question of permissible strikes under those terms remained a matter of contention between them. Also, with the approach of 1980 negotiations management began to question publicly whether industrial peace under the ENA had too expensive a price tag.

WAGES-BENEFITS

WAGES

Steel labor negotiations during the seventies have resulted in sizeable increases in wages and benefits for steel workers. Regular straight pay went up from $3.93 in 1970 to $9.82 in 1979, a 175% increase. If shift differentials, Sunday, holiday and overtime premiums are included the hourly pay increased from $4.24 to $11.02 or 160%. If all other payroll costs including holiday and vacation pay are included the total employment cost to the companies increased from $5.68 to $15.92 or 180% (see Table 4). During this same ten-year period the cost of living as measured by the Consumer Price Index rose from 116.3 to 239.9 which was 106%. Thus, whether one considers regular straight time pay, straight time pay plus differentials or pay plus benefits, steel workers have more than kept up with the cost of living during the seventies.

COLA

The 1977 labor agreement contained a cost of living adjustment clause (COLA). The first COLA clause in steel labor contracts was agreed to by the parties in 1956. However, in 1962, in exchange for other benefits, the union agreed to eliminate COLA. During the late sixties and early seventies, as the cost of living began to increase rapidly, the pressure for a COLA clause increased and in 1971 one was again included in the contreact. The COLA clause in the 1977 agreement provided for a 1¢ per hour increase for every .3 point increase in the CPI index. Neglecting other wage increases, the COLA clause alone did not fully compensate the average steel worker for losses in real earnings resulting from inflation.

Table 4

TOTAL EMPLOYMENT COST PER HOUR—WAGE EMPLOYEES IN THE IRON AND STEEL INDUSTRY

Year	Pay for Hours Worked: Straight Time: Regular (1)	Pay for Hours Worked: Straight Time: Shift Differential (2)	Pay for Hours Worked: Straight Time: Sunday Premium (3)	Pay for Hours Worked: Overtime Premium (4)	Pay for Hours Worked: Premium For Work On Holidays (5)	Pay for Hours Worked: Subtotal: Pay For Hours Worked (6)	Comparison: Average Hourly Earnings In Steel (BLS) (7)	Other Payroll Costs: Pay For Holidays Not Worked (8)	Other Payroll Costs: Vacation Pay (9)	Other Payroll Costs: Allowances and Adjustments (10)	Total Payroll Cost Per Hour (11)	Employee Benefits Cost Per Hour (12)	Total Employment Cost Per Hour (13)	Year
1979	$9.822	$.121	$.368	$.427	$.281	$11.019	$10.77	$.247	$1.230	$.055	$12.551	$3.370	$15.921	1979
1978	8.890	.120	.333	.391	.242	9.976	9.70	.194	1.051	.049	11.270	3.033	14.303	1978
1977	8.029	.117	.280	.294	.193	8.913	8.67	.200	1.015	.123	10.251	2.785	13.036	1977
1976	7.247	.115	.249	.239	.148	7.998	7.86	.177	.912	.045	9.132	2.612	11.744	1976
1975	6.634	.080	.218	.171	.124	7.227	7.11	.170	.874	.040	8.311	2.279	10.590	1975
1974	5.921	.062	.212	.235	.120	6.550	6.38	.114	.653	.108	7.425	1.653	9.078	1974
1973	5.159	.062	.135	.218	.114	5.688	5.56	.092	.507	.024	6.311	1.370	7.681	1973
1972	4.813	.060	.087	.161	.100	5.221	5.15	.101	.528	.027	5.877	1.198	7.075	1972
1971	4.242	.060	.075	.126	.071	4.574	4.57	.090	.519	.032	5.215	1.046	6.261	1971
1970	3.926	.054	.071	.118	.067	4.236	4.22	.077	.431	.023	4.767	.910	5.677	1970
1969	3.776	.050	.072	.154	.068	4.120	4.09	.053	.370	.023	4.566	.809	5.375	1969
1968	3.553	.049	.067	.126	.065	3.860	3.82	.049	.376	.018	4.303	.729	5.032	1968
1967	3.398	.048	.063	.091	.056	3.656	3.62	.056	.349	.008	4.069	.689	4.758	1967
1966	3.353	.049	.065	.110	.059	3.636	3.58	.049	.324	.008	4.017	.616	4.633	1966
1965	3.261	.049	.064	.106	.056	3.536	3.46	.048	.343	.008	3.935	.540	4.475	1965
1964	3.177	.049	.061	.090	.054	3.431	3.41	.048	.310	.007	3.796	.559	4.355	1964
1963	3.166	.047	.055	.069	.053	3.390	3.36	.050	.240	.007	3.687	.560	4.247	1963
1962	3.141	.046	.052	.052	.041	3.332	3.29	.058	.224	.008	3.622	.533	4.155	1962
1961	3.054	.045	.050	.048	.044	3.241	3.20	.055	.200	.005	3.501	.488	3.989	1961
1960	2.916	.046	.050	.045	.037	3.094	3.08	.054	.195	.006	3.349	.471	3.820	1960
Incr. 1979 vs. 1960	$6.906	$.075	$.318	$.382	$.244	$7.925	$7.69	$.193	$1.035	$.049	$9.202	$2.899	$12.101	Incr. 1979 vs. 1960
% Incr. 1979 vs. 1960	237%	163%	636%	849%	659%	256%	250%	357%	531%		275%	615%	317%	% Incr. 1979 vs. 1960

Source: Annual Statistical Report 1979, American Iron and Steel Institute.

JOB EVALUATION

In 1980 the steel industry job evaluation plan provided 34 different job classes with an 11.7¢ increment between classes from class 2 to class 34. When originally established in 1947, the increment between the then existing 30 job classifications had been 3.5¢. By raising the increment from time to time the parties were able to offset, to some extent, the narrowing differentials occassioned by negotiation of across-the-board cents-per-hour increases. However, since the 1971 contract the COLA increases have resulted in a serious pancaking of the rate structure despite these sizable increases in the increment.

Basic hourly job classes throughout the steel industry are determined by a job evaluation plan, developed jointly by the industry and the union, which became effective in 1947. The plan, known as the Cooperative Wage Study (CWS) program, assigns more value to the responsibility factors than the job evaluation plans used in most other American industries. As a result, workers share more fully in the benefits of technological change.

INCENTIVES

More than 85% of the blue collar workers in the basic steel industry are on incentive pay. Thus, the base rates provided through the CWS are considerably below what the workers actually earn. The average earnings of $11.02 in 1979 (see Table 4) included incentive pay. Although the use of incentive pay has declined over the years in other American industries the percentage of workers covered by incentives has increased in steel. Neither management nor the union desires to eliminate the incentive system and those workers who are not covered by it would like to get on the "gravey train."

In August 1980 when the 1977 labor agreement terminated a typical steel worker was reported to be earning $25,000 per year. This was considerably above the average in almost any other industry. Only construction and petroleum workers were earning more on an hourly basis. The gap in gross hourly earnings between steel workers and all manufacturing workers increased from 23¢ per hour in 1947 to 86¢ in 1962 and to $3.77 in 1979. Although in 1947 the gross hourly rate of auto workers was slightly higher than that of steel workers ($1,47 compared with $1.45) by 1962 steel workers were earning 26¢ per hour more than auto workers and by October 1979 the gap had increased to 79¢ per hour ($10.59 as compared with $9.80 per hour).

FRINGE BENEFITS

Over the years fringe benefits have become an increasingly significant part of the total employment costs in steel. In 1979 total employment costs had risen to $15.92 per hour compared with $5.68 in 1970 and $3.82 in 1960. Fringes (including shift differentials, over-time, Sunday and holiday pay) had increased from 24% of total employment costs in 1960, to 31% in 1970, to 38% in 1979 (see Table 4).

The increasing cost of retirement pay and medical benefits have contributed strongly to the increase in benefit costs. In August 1979 minimum monthly retirement payments in steel, exclusive of social security, ranged from $135 for the lowest paid employee with 10 yrs of service to $675 for the highest paid employee with 45 years of service. In 1979 employees and their dependents enjoyed a comprehenisive hospital-medical-surgical plan, plus major medical insurance of $30,000 annually and $50,000 lifetime per individual, as well as a liberal dental plan and a vision-care plan.

Two benefit plans in steel deserve special attention. A Supplementary Unemployment Benefits plan (SUB) was negotiated in steel in 1956 following the negotiation of a similar plan in 1955 by the auto industry. In negotiations following 1956 SUB was continually improved and by 1979 a steel worker who became unemployed was eligible for SUB payments for a period of 52 weeks with minimum payments of $125 per week when being paid benefits from the state and $170 per week when state benefits were not available. Moreover, an employee with 20 years of service was eligible for an additional 52 weeks of SUB payments unless the employee was offered appropriate work at another location by the company.

Vacations is an area in which the steel industry has pioneered in two respects: "sabbatical" vacations and extra pay for vacation periods. Regular vacations in the industry range from one week for employees with 1 to 3 years of service to 5 weeks for employees with 25 or more years of service. In 1963 the industry and the union agreed on an innovative vacation arrangement whereby an employee who was on the upper half of the seniority list in a plant would receive a "sabbatical" vacation of 13 weeks once every five years. More recently the parties agreed that employees on vacation should receive a vacation bonus in addition to their regular pay. In 1979 the vacation bonus was $30 per week for summer vacations, $35 per week for spring and fall vacations and $40 per week for winter vacations. Sabbaticals have not been widely adopted elsewhere in American industry and vacation bonuses have met with very limited acceptance.

WAGE AND PRICE GUIDELINES

On March 14, 1980 President Carter announced new wage and price guidelines. The new guidelines would permit annual pay increases within a 7.5 to 9.5 percent range. (The cost of labor contracts with COLA clauses would be determined by assuming that the CPI would increase 7.5% per year.) The new guidelines had been proposed by the Pay Advisory Committee. R. Heath Larry, a former Vice President of U.S. Steel and former chairman of the steel industry negotiating committee, and Lloyd McBride, President of USW were members of the Pay Advisory Committee. President Carter said that the new program would restore "discipline" without imposing mandatory wage and price controls.

It was not clear what effect the guidelines would have on the 1980 steel negotiations. In kicking off the negotiations in February, R. Bruce Johnston, Vice President of Labor Relations for U.S. Steel and chairman of the industry negotiating committee, although recognizing government pressure for wage moderation, had noted that, "the guidelines are loosely defined and loosely administered. I don't expect to have any guideline problems based on what I have observed of other settlements."

UNION DEMANDS

The ENA, as detailed above, guaranteed wage increases of 3% per year and cost of living adjustments during the life of the 1980 agreement plus a $150 one-shot bonus. These ENA increases formed the floor upon which the union hoped to build a much large settlement. Lloyd McBride, President of the USW, stated that the union's demands included:

1. -A substantial wage increase to restore lost purchasing power;

2. -Substantial increases in pension payments for workers who had already retired as well as for future retirees, plus protection of such payments by a COLA formula;

3. -More economic security for workers through liberalization of pensions, disability pay, and SUB;

4. -Extention of the extended vacation plan to include all workers;

5. -Limitations of contracting out of work;

6. -Payment to workers of interest on arbitration awards to compensate for delays in the grievance and arbitration procedure.

The demand of the union for a substantial increase in pension benefits for steel workers who had already retired was interesting because of the law with respect to this matter. The Supreme Court in 1971 had ruled that a company is not required to bargain with a union on this issue. Thus, the steel industry was not obligated to discuss it with the union in the 1980 negotiations. However, over the years the real income of retired steel workers had been severely depressed by inflation. As a result the Wage Policy Committee of the union had placed this demand very high on its list and had indicated that, if necessary, it would forego other increases in order to secure substantial improvements in pension benefits for retired steel workers.

THE SETTLEMENT

On April 14, 1980, one day before the ENA required that all unsettled issues be referred to arbitration, the union and industry representatives announced that a settlement had been reached. As reported later the settlement included the following:

1. Wage Increases:

   -May 1, 1980 - 25¢
   -Aug 1, 1981 - 20¢
   -Aug 1, 1982 - 15¢

   An additional 1¢ increment each year to each job class from Job Class 2 to Job Class 34. (Averages 8¢ per hour per year because of the large number of employees in the lower job classes.)

2. COLA:

   No change in the formula which continues as 1¢ per hour for every .3 point increase in the CPI. COLA accumulations will be rolled into base rates on: May 1, 1980; Aug. 1, 1980; Aug. 1, 1981; and Aug. 1, 1982. The COLA adjustment due May 1, 1980 (about 32¢) eliminated in return for improvements in retirement pay.

3. Retirement Pay:

   a- For workers already retired (150,000):
   Two adjustments which by Aug. 1, 1981 will provide every retiree with benefits equal to $12 per month per year of service (increases ranged from 70% for those who retired before Aug. 1, 1966 to 10% for those who retired between 1977 and 1980).

   b- For future retirees:
   First year of contract - increase of $2 per month per year of service.
   Second year of contract - increase of $1 per month per year of service.
   Third year of contract - increase of $1 per month per year of service.
   By the end of the contract monthly benefits will range, depending on the worker's salary, from $17.50 to $20.50 per month for each year of service.

4. Shift Differentials:

   Afternoon - increased from 20¢ to 30¢ per hour.
   Evening - increased from 30¢ to 45¢ per hour.

5. SUB:

   When state unemployment benefits are received by the worker the maximum benefit will increase in three steps over the life of the contract from $125 to $180 per week.

When state unemployment benefits are not received by the worker the maximum benefit will increase in three steps over the life of the contract from $170 to $235 per week.

Company's contribution increased from 13.5¢ to 17.5¢ per hour until maximum financing is reached.

6. Insurance:

Life insurance increased by $4,500 effective Aug. 1, 1982.

Sickness & Accident benefits increased from a range of $156 - $211 to a range of $211 - $276 per week.

Major improvements in hospital and physician services.

Dental benefit maximum increased from $750 to $1,000.

Visual coverage expanded.

7. Vacations:

-Extended vacations for workers with 25 years of service increased from 13 to 14 weeks.

-Extended vacations for junior employees increased from 3 to 4 weeks.

8. Incentives for Ore Miners:

Incentive opportunities for ore miners increased from 15% to 23% bringing them into full parity with basic steel incentives.

9. Plant Shut Down:

Company must give union and employees at least 90 days notice before closing a plant.

10. Contracting Out:

A pilot study at a particular plant will be undertaken by the parties to determine how to deal with this problem.

11. Safety and Health:

A comprehensive union-management program will be undertaken to decrease safety and health hazards.

12 Labor-Management Participation Teams:

Local union-management teams will be set up in an attempt to improve the quality of worklife.

13. ENA:

No agreement was reached to continue the ENA to cover the 1983 negotiations. Failure to extend the ENA resulted from the inability to agree on the issues on which local unions would be free to strike this year. In 1977, following the signing of the basic steel contract which contained the continuation of the ENA, the international president supported a long strike on incentive coverage by iron ore miners. (See ENA above.) In the 1980 negotiations management refused to agree to an extension of the ENA to cover the 1983 negotiations unless it was assured that strikes on such issues would not occur during the 1980 local negotiations. The national union was unwilling to give such assurances. It is possible that, following settlement of local agreements, the parties may amend the 1980 contract to include an extension of the ENA for negotiations in 1983. However, unless such an agreement is reached, the union will be free to strike at the end of the 1980 agreement on August 1, 1983.

J. Bruce Johnson, chief negotiator for the steel industry, estimated that the wage increases, including the COLA provisions in the 1980 agreement would range from 30 to 37% depending on the rate of inflation. "This is a very competitive settlement", he said, "and is well within the guidelines set by the Carter administration." Johnson had in mind that part of the cost-of-living increase and the increase in pensions for employees already retired were exempt from the guideline formula.

POSTSCRIPT

The United Steelworkers twentieth biennial convention was held in Los Angeles in August 1980. At the time more than 70,000 steelworkers were on layoff and the industry was in the depths of one of its worst slumps ever. Yet the gathering was described in The Wall Street Journal as one of the quietest in steelworkers' history. Dissention and spirited debate which had marked past conventions were avoided in order not to jeopardize the union's ability to win concessions from government to aid the ailing industry and concessions from management regarding the ENA.

Following the convention USW negotiators were to sit down with industry bargainers to attempt to negotiate a renewal of the ENA to cover 1983 negotiations. The Wall Street Journal reported the following on August 8, 1980 as the convention came to a conclusion.

> USW leaders like the ENA. Under it they've won some of the best contracts of any union. But the industry is hinting very broadly that it thinks the ENA is too expensive and will have to be modified extensively if it's going to be used at all in 1983.

MAN-HATTEN ELECTRIC POWER COMPANY

The negotiation of the first contract between Man-hatten Electric Power Company and the National Utilities Union had been a long and at times a very strained process. The parties resolved many issues — some of minimal significance, some of great import. Negotiations had been narrowed to the four issues listed below and with forty-five (45) minutes remaining before strike deadline the pace had picked up. In order to solidify its position, NUU had stated that the strike deadline was firm. In 45 minutes — no contract, no work. Management and the union hoped to come to agreement but neither at too great a sacrifice!

PRESENT POSITION OF THE PARTIES

ISSUE	UNION	MANAGEMENT
Union Security	Union Shop & Dues Checkoff	Open Shop
Layoff	Plant-wide seniority	Job seniority
Wages	15% increase 1st year 10% increase 2nd year 10% increase 3rd year	5% increase 1st year 3% increase 2nd year 3% increase 3rd year
COLA*	No Cap	12 cent cap
	*Parties have agreed to 1 cent for each .4 rise in the CPI (1967 base)	

SECTION III

Contract Administration

IN THE HALLS OF ACADEMIA

The Dean stepped out of his office to discover that at least one dog had left his or her mark in the hall outside his office. In just ten minutes a trustees' committee was due for a meeting regarding the possibility of student unrest. As he decided what to do he heard the custodian, Jim Boydston, whistling in one of the rooms down the hall. He had had words with Jim once before about cleaning up after dogs and wondered what the custodian's response would be if he approached him to clean up the mess.

During the early part of 1971 the canine population on many college campuses had attained substantial size and visability, giving the impression that every undergraduate had at least one dog as a constant companion. At the same time individuals, both on and off campuses, were extremely aware of ecological problems and had become sensitized to the effects of all types of pollution upon the environment. The result of this sensitivity was manifested in a law passed in New York City requiring dog owners, under penalty of fine, to pick up and remove waste materials deposited by their pets. A handful of other cities adopted similar statutes. The pollution which led to these requirements was also at the heart of a management-union disagreement at a large midwestern university.

Custodians employed by The University of Michigan and represented by Local 1583 of the American Federation of State, County and Municipal Employees were unwilling to clean up after untrained dogs who performed their vital functions while visiting various university buildings. One custodian, who also held the position of Grievance Representative, told the dean located in his building that such work was not part of the work required of a custodian. Most custodians were ignoring the remembrances left by man's (and woman's) best friend, as well as the deans' requests to remove same.

Hearing about this controversy, a professor contacted the university's Director of Labor Relations to obtain more information. The Director stated that no grievances had been filed on the matter, or rather, about removing the matter. However, he knew that there had been some "gripes" expressed by various custodians. It was clearly obvious that the custodians were implicitly avoiding any duties involved with the removal of anal wastes left in the halls of their buildings. Management of the Maintenance Department had been told by at least one dean that he (the dean) was tired of having graduate student assistants do the work of custodians, i.e. cleaning up after dogs.

Custodians continued to ignore such situations and said informally the moment they were required to do such cleaning by their supervisor a grievance would be filed.

In addition to their desire to avoid provoking a student confrontation, the university administration knew they could expect little help from the city of Ann Arbor. The state legislature had cut that portion of the university's budget which represented a fee paid to the city in lieu of taxes. Since the city dog warden was employed only two days per week, little could be done to control the canine population.

The dean was wondering what action to take with respect to canine pollution in the halls of academia.

HOPEDALE MINING COMPANY

Charles Dykeman, a handy man at No. 8 mine of the Hopedale Mining Company, was formally discharged on July 8 for having taken home on June 9 and again on June 12, without permission, company materials for his own use. On June 15, Mr. Dykeman was suspended "until further notice"; and, on July 8, twelve days after an informal hearing by management, Mr. Dykeman received written notice of his discharge because "there was no evidence brought out to refute the fact that (he) appropriated company material for (his) own use." Within 24 hours, the Hopedale local of the Ore Miners Union of which Mr. Dykeman was a member, filed a grievance in his behalf under the contract with the company as follows:

> The union is appealing the discharge of Charles Dykeman. It protests his unjustified discharge for a minor infraction of the company's rules and requests his reinstatement with full seniority and all wages lost.

On the same day that Mr. Dykeman was discharged, Edward Truslow arrived at the office of Roger Goodnow, who was manager of the company's industrial relations at Hopedale, as his newly appointed staff assistant. Mr. Truslow had just graduated from a business school, where he specialized in labor-management problems. He was asked to investigate the basic facts leading to Mr. Dykeman's discharge and to recommend suitable procedures to prevent the recurrence of such cases.

Mr. Truslow found living conditions in Hopedale favorable. Although small, the miners' homes were well built, mostly of brick, and pleasantly situated with neat, well-kept yards and numerous vegetable gardens. Community life seemed cooperative and wholesome. About 98% of the working population was employed by the company. Union members and management personnel were well acquainted, called each other by their first names, and often took part jointly in civic affairs.

In proceeding with his investigation, Mr. Truslow noted that the miners, almost to a man, felt that the company had been unjust in discharging Mr. Dykeman. They also resented what seemed to them a changed attitude in management with regard to the personal use of materials. As the case moved up the various steps of the grievance procedure,[1] the union continued to insist that Dykeman's failure to get materials passes was a minor infraction for which discharge was too severe a penalty. Management officials repeated, in turn, their contention that all employees, including supervisors, were required to obtain a pass before taking material away from the mines and that Dykeman's discharge was proper.

[1]There were four steps in the grievance procedure. Any grievance not settled under Step No. 4 of the procedure set forth in the contract might be appealed to arbitration by an impartial umpire appointed by mutual agreement of the parties.

HOPEDALE MINING COMPANY

After all steps in the grievance procedure had been taken without resolving the difference, the union stated that it would resort to arbitration. Mr. Truslow had not participated in any of the grievance proceedings; but, when he learned that on the basis of past experience several months might elapse before the case was heard before an umpire, he was fearful of the possible dangers inherent in such delay. He therefore proposed that another try, perhaps through an informal joint meeting, might be worthwhile. Both management and union officials, though skeptical, agreed to make another effort to settle the dispute "across the table" and consequently requested Mr. Truslow to serve as moderator.

The meeting which was held on August 30, was attended by the following representatives:

For the Company

Edward Truslow, Assistant to Roger Goodnow
Joseph Monahan, Manager of Mine Operations
Carl Wagoner, Superintendent of No. 8 Mine
William Kenney, Captain of No. 8 Mine
Frank Maytag, Shop Foreman
George Readdy, Chief of Guards

For the Union

Vincent Palmer, Local Business Agent
Charles Dykeman, Grievant
Sam Stockmeyer, Miner (open pit)
Andre Mario, Miner (No. 8 mine)

Palmer: Dyke, suppose you start us off by telling us again just what happened on June 9.

Dykeman: Well, it was this way. You see, I had one piece of angle iron that I got out of a scrap pile; it was not a new angle. I had it bent and welded, but before my working hours; I was scheduled on the night turn. And when Bill Kenney saw Eric Kronich and me making it up,—Eric is a welder in the shop, Mr. Truslow--he said, "Who's that for?" Eric told him it was for me. Bill said, "Dyke, you better get a pass for that." I asked Bill to give me the pass but he said "No, you'll have to get it from Carl Wagoner." Well, he wasn't there and when we quit in the morning I didn't see him, so I just took it along. The other piece of angle that the company guard later found in my yard I did not get from the mine.

Truslow: That was your own? You brought it with you to the mine?

Dykeman: Yes, I brought it with me. Well, I didn't find Carl Wagoner so I didn't get a pass for that angle iron. Then Saturday night, June 12, I got the steel sheet. I had asked Bill Kenney about a sheet. He said, "How big?" I told him the dimensions--about 4 by 6 feet and 1/8-inch thick. He said, "That's too much. You'll have to see Carl Wagoner about that." Well, again I looked for Carl Wagoner, and I couldn't find him. But there was the week-end for working in my yard, and I asked Eric Kronich would he help me about the sheet. There were sheets piled up, old ones they used to cover up stuff. I pulled one aside and said, "This will do." It was a 1/16-inch sheet. I wanted a 1/8-inch but they didn't have it. Lunch hour I threw it on the car and took it home.

Palmer: You didn't take the whole sheet, Dyke, did you?

Dykeman: No, it was a piece cut off. Kronich cut it off for me. And the next Monday, Bill Kenney says,, "Wagoner wants to see you, Dyke." I went to see him and Wagoner said, "What business did you have in the shop?" I said, "I was up in the lunch hour. I came up for oil." Then he wanted to know about this angle stuff. After I told him just how it was, he said, "Dyke, I'm going to make you take tomorrow off, and let that be a lesson to you. You know you must not take stuff home without a pass. And you had no right to cut into Eric Kronich's work time. Take tomorrow off."

Well, on Tuesday when I was off I went out in my yard and saw Bill and also George Readdy, the chief company guard, drive up. I had the sheet standing alongside my garage. I didn't hide it. George got out and was looking at it. He said, "Where'd you get it, Dyke?" I said, "Where do you think?" He said, "Where's the angle iron?" I took him over in the field where it was laying and showed it to him and said, "There's one; the other belongs to me." He said, "Dyke, are you going to tell me where you got it?" I told him, "Sure, I got it at the mine." Then they left.

Palmer: Then you were dismissed until further notice?

Dykeman: Yes.

Palmer: Tell Mr. Truslow how many years you have been working here.

Dykeman: Twelve years.

Palmer: Now, Mr. Truslow, I just want Dyke to tell you in his own words why he feels maybe he deserved that one-day suspension Carl Wagoner gave him--but to jump from that to discharge--well, go ahead, Dyke.

Dykeman: Well, Mr. Truslow, you're still new here, but I know all the fellows will tell you--and our bosses will, too--that the company from way back has let us have such scrapmaterials to use in our houses and yards and such things. We've been talking about this thing and so you probably have already heard that as far back as any fellow can remember, we were taking scrap iron and steel and lumber and things like that. I used to be in the paint shop when I was first hired, and plenty of times I even gave the bosses sort of left-over paints in the cans. I remember once I even gave Mr. Wagoner some light buff paint. That is, I gave it to Bill Kenney for him.

Monahan: Now just a moment, Dyke. That isn't the whole story, is it? Isn't it also true that for most of the years you have been working in the mines, no one was allowed to take anything away unless he got a materials pass okaying it?

Dykeman: Well, yes, sir; the company put that in sometime in 1970. But they weren't really strict about passes as regards scrap. Of course, passes were more important on some other things.

Truslow: Now let me be sure I have you straight on that, Mr. Dykeman. Do you mean the fellows make differences between things they feel it's O.K. to take even without a pass, things they have to have a pass for, and things they shouldn't take at all?

Dykeman: Yes, sir, and any of the fellows will tell you the same thing. I remember one time when two guys took off some dynamite caps, and the company discharged them the minute it all came out. Why, the union never raised even any idea of making a grievance out of that. And we all thought the same way about it, even though those two guys were our buddies. We felt bad about it, of course, but we had to admit they did wrong. After all, dynamite is dangerous stuff, with kids around in the yards at home. The FBI could even come into a thing like that.

Truslow: Yes, Mr. Monahan has been going over with me the discharges in the past for taking company materials. (To Monahan) They confirm, Mr. Dykeman, don't they? Two fellows were, as I recall, discharged for taking dynamite caps, weren't they?

Monahan: Yes, Dyke is okay on that--as far as that goes. But you were told by your captain, weren't you, Dyke, that you were not to take away the stuff you wanted, the angle iron and steel sheet, unless and until you got a pass from Mr. Wagoner?

Dykeman: Yes, sir. Bill Kenney told me that and I did try to find Carl Wagoner; I just couldn't.

Monahan: Did you really try very hard, Dyke? And remember it wasn't only one order you simply disregarded. I never have any trouble finding Carl Wagoner when I want to see him. You couldn't find him somehow Wednesday, or Saturday either?

Dykeman: Well, sir, you're the boss and you can keep looking for him. But I had to get back to my work.

Monahan: You weren't so worried about that when you took Eric Kronich off his job to bend your angle iron, were you?

Dykeman: But that was before my shift began.

Monahan: But while he was working. But come back to the question of passes. Granted you tried, really tried, to find Carl, as Bill had told you to—and couldn't. What made you think the alternative was simply to cart off the stuff without the pass?

Palmer: (interrupting): Well, don't think I don't want Dyke to answer that question, Joe. But with Mr. Truslow new here, and trying to help us settle this case fairly, can't we all lay our cards on the table? Dyke--and the union—agree that some stuff should never be taken without a pass. And you will support what Dyke said, won't you? No one in the union ever protested those discharges. But why discharge Dyke for something that you must admit you've never before been so strict about? Sure, the fellows know that since 1970 the company has required passes for scrap materials. But can you say that no one ever took anything off without a pass, when he knew it was scrap and he'd get okayed anyway, and he just couldn't find his captain at the time?

Monahan: There are just a few things wrong with that in Dyke's case; it doesn't quite fit, Vince. You see, Bill Kenney had already refused to give Dyke passes- though, of course, Dyke didn't bother to ask him first. Bill caught him working on the angle iron with Eric Kronich.

Dykeman: Well, it sounds bad when you say Bill "caught" me. I wasn't doing anything lots of the fellows don't always do. You make it sound like a crime, or something.

Monahan: Well, Dyke, lots of people would tell you it is a crime to take property that doesn't belong to you, and a man's work time that you don't pay for, without permission; and when you've been told outright by your captain not to.

Truslow: Were you quite sure in your own mind, Mr. Dykeman, that you were simply doing something the company had tolerated for many years?

Dykeman: I want to be honest in this, Mr. Truslow, and I can see now I wasn't right in everything. But as far as taking the scrap is concerned, well, I'll just leave it to Mr. Monahan and Mr. Wagoner and my own captain here. Was anybody ever discharged for that?

Kenney: Dyke, didn't I tell you the steel sheet you wanted was too big for you to take off on my okay?

Wagoner: Since when is an 8-foot long steel sheet scrap around here?

Monahan: How did you get that sheet from the mines? Tell us, Dyke. Tell Mr. Truslow.

Dykeman: Well, I asked Bill for a 1/8-inch sheet. He said, "That's a big sheet, you better..."

Kenney (interrupting): I said 6-foot was a big sheet, too. Soyou go and have an 8-foot one cut down.

Dykeman: I found it stacked up with other stuff. It's always been all right; but I admit that after Bill told me, I should have waited to get a pass. You see I was building a trailer, and I wanted to work on it. And I did think that there was a good chance Carl Wagoner would say O.K. on the angle iron and the steel scrap, too.

Monahan: How did you get that sheet home, Dyke? Did you try to have anyone else take it home for you?

Dykeman: I did not.

Monahan: You didn't talk to one of the materials handlers about taking that sheet home?

Dykeman: No. (Pause.) Well—yes. Just a minute! I know what you are getting at now. Tony Vespaziani and I were kidding in the lamp house about taking the sheet, and I says, "Well, I can take it home in the truck." And he says, "You better not." So he went down the hole, and that's all there was to it.

Monahan: By "the truck," you mean a company truck? You must remember Mr. Truslow isn't onto all our mine lingo yet.

Dykeman: Yes.

Monahan: How <u>did</u> you take it home?

Dykeman: On the top of my car, on the roof rack.

Monahan: When, Dyke? We want Mr. Truslow to have all the facts in your own words and with your own explanations.

Dykeman: In my lunch period.

Monahan: Is it customary for you to drive home—four miles each way—between three and three-thirty in the morning?

Dykeman: Well, no. But I've already admitted during my hearing that some of the things I did may not have been quite okay. I didn't complain when Carl Wagoner said I'd have to lose a day's pay for them. I could see maybe I had that suspension coming to me. I didn't complain to the union or anything. Of course, I began to suspect something more was up when Bill Kenney and George Readdy came to my house the next day. But I didn't try to hide anything; they'll tell you that. So why was I suddenly discharged when I came back from the "day-off" Carl had given me?

Kenney: Of course you had that steel plunk up against your garage wall, Dyke. You couldn't quite hide it.

Dykeman: But I had told you I took it before. And I showed George the angle iron, didn't I?

Kenney: Yes, but ...

Palmer: I think maybe the best way to show Mr. Truslow the reason the union agrees with Dyke that his discharge, really capital punishment for a mine employee here, is excessive and discriminatory, is to hear now from some of the old-timers about this business of materials and passes. Mr. Stockmeyer has worked in the mines over 25 years. How about taking company property for a fellow's own use, Sam?

Stockmeyer: Well, you take around garden time, until this incident it was a regular thing for an employee to help himself to a shovel and take it home. I know quite a few employees took them home in front of the captains. They'd joke about it. Your captain might ask "Where are you going with that, to dig garden?" And I know one supervisor who ordered two dozen from the storeroom. He said, "We'll need two dozen. I only need six at the mines, but by the time the boys get around to dig garden, we'll only have six left." That's why I say it has been the habit around here. Sometimes they ask the captain if it is convenient. Other times they just think, "Well, everybody else is doing it, we can take it, too." I know there has been pipe taken out, and various materials, and I don't think there was always a pass for it. And I'm including myself in on that statement.

I work in the open pit so I'm not familiar with mine No. 8. I have been working there for 25 years and there never has been anybody discharged for anything like that. A lot of the fellows have shovels, and maybe picks and sledge hammers. If the company wanted to go around to all our homes, like they did to Dyke's and gather the stuff in, they could collect all kinds of materials.

Palmer: How about this business of Dyke and Eric—one fellow making work up that another wants to take home? How about that, Sam?

Stockmeyer: We call that "government work," Mr. Truslow; you'll soon hear that word. I don't think it's serious; it helps keep our town nice, and we all live here. Why, as much stuff is made up for the bosses as for the rest of us, in percentage of men involved, I'd say. Management gets their share of "government work" around here. There's never been any idea of discharge for a thing like that; in fact it's been laughed about a lot. We kid about it.

Palmer: Is Dyke's case the first time the company ever attempted to stop an employee from making up "government work" for another employee?

Stockmeyer: Well, I couldn't say that exactly. They have every once in a while lately, but never before the union was around here. It was the policy of the company that if it wouldn't interfere with the regular repair work, they'd help the employees out such as, oh, maybe a lawn mower that needed welding. All you had to do was ask. And the company never posted notice of any change; that is why I feel that they are discriminating against Dyke, absolutely.

Monahan: I have a few questions to ask Mr. Stockmeyer. I think that the part of his testimony to be underlined is "All you had to do was ask." That seems to apply both to government work and getting passes for materials. Mr. Stockmeyer, are you testifying that it is the practice here to take company property without asking for it?

Stockmeyer: When I said "ask," I mean if it was convenient. Not all the time was the boss asked, and yet they knew the shovels were going away whether they asked for them or not. And never was there any complaint put in by the company. In one particular case, I know of a man carrying a shovel who went by his captain. The captain said, "Oh, I see it's garden time." (Laughter.)

Monahan: How many years ago was that?

Stockmeyer: Oh, let's see, 8 to 10 years ago.

Monahan: Do you know whether or not the employees got materials passes?

Stockmeyer: The only time in the open pit that an employee would make sure to get a materials pass was if he was going to cut himself some lumber off company property. In case he is stopped by the guards he has a pass to show why he is in the company's woods. But Mr. Truslow has heard all about this. We do not say, and never did, that we do not absolutely have to get passes before we take off such stuff like you talked about before. Cutting lumber in the woods like that did get four fellows discharged; they were part of six discharges we never protested. The other two took dynamite, and I'll add something else. We never take copper. It's the same as dynamite and lumber. Copper isn't on the scrap pile; it's stored up in the old engine yard.

Palmer: You said, Sam, the company never indicated any change of policy on taking materials?

Stockmeyer: They never called the union in or let us know they were going to do anything like discharge a fellow for what Dyke did—that kind of thing, I mean.

Palmer: Mr. Mario here is another old-timer in No. 8 mine. How about materials down there, Andy?

Mario: Well it's just like Sam told you about the open pit. Sometimes materials passes are given, and sometimes they aren't. Like Sam says, it's a question of past practice. For example, wood comes up overnight out of the mine and it's laying there, and they put it on the truck and take it down to so-and-so's place. And I don't think a pass was always issued.

Truslow: What about scrap iron?

Mario: If employees want some article made, they get permission, and make it, but I don't think there are passes issued for every article made.

Monahan: Bill, let's hear your complete version of this difficulty that began Wednesday night, June 9.

Kenney: Well, as mine captain it was my practice to stay up above ground until the 11 to 7 shift went down. On June 9 I walked over to the work shop and noticed some angle laid down on cutting horses. I asked Dyke and Eric what they were doing with the angles. Dyke replied that he was making a trailer. I asked him if he had a pass and when he said, "No," I told him to let the angles lay and to see Carl Wagoner about getting a pass. Then I told him to get back on the job. He said he was up in the shop to get some oil.

Monahan: How much angle was there?

Kenney: One piece, roughly 20 feet long, and a couple of shorter pieces. I knew Dyke didn't get that from the scrap pile like Dyke tried to say. We don't scrap 20-foot pieces of angle.

Monahan: O.K. Now tell us about Saturday night, June 12.

Kenney: Dyke asked me for a pass to get a piece of steel sheet for a bed of a trailer. He wanted a 1/8-inch piece, 4- by 6-feet. I told him that was too big for me to make out a pass for and that he should see the superintendent, Carl Wagoner. Dyke turned around and walked out. I thought it over and decided this might need checking. So on Monday I mentioned to Carl (Wagoner) about Dyke being in the shop and Eric Kronich working on the angles and asked him whether Dyke had come for a materials pass. He said he hadn't seen Dyke.

Truslow: As Mr. Dykeman's foreman, you have authority to issue passes?

Kenney: Well, I can issue passes for small items like scrap wood, maybe a bolt or a piece of the scrap pile, worth maybe five or ten dollars in value--but no more.

Truslow: Scrap steel?

Kenney: If it is not too big an item.

Truslow: How big a piece of angle iron could you grant permission for?

Kenney: Probably not over 3 or 4 feet--and that would have to come out of the scrap pile. I wouldn't issue a pass for new stuff.

Truslow: Do you have authority to ask one employee to make up work for another employee?

Kenney: Yes, but I tell that employee there's got to be a pass to cover it.

Truslow: I just want to review all this while we are all together. You have issued passes to other employees?

Kenney: I have issued a lot of passes.

Truslow: Mr. Wagoner, as superintendent of mine No. 8, will you review for us your action after these matters were called to your attention by Mr. Kenney?

Wagoner: Well, Dyke can't say I didn't make things clear to him. I told him right away he had no business working in the shop on his own work during working hours. I told him I was going to give him shrift for working in the shop, but in the course of this conversation, he also admitted to me he had taken the angle--not the steel, mind you, but the angle. Before I decided to do anything about that I thought I'd talk to Mr. Monahan to see if he wanted to go any further. I told him the whole story and also that I had found out on investigation that Dyke had asked this Vespaziani to take the sheet home. Joe (Mr. Monahan) and I decided to send George Readdy and Bill Kenney, not intending for them to search Dykeman's property or his house or his garage, you understand, but just to see what they could see. You know the rest. They came back to me and reported, and we figured we should suspend Dykeman until further notice.

Truslow: Mr. Wagoner, did our long-service employees understand correctly the materials pass system at Hopedale? Was it as they recalled it?

Wagoner: Years ago we sold employees certain things--I mean steel or what not, but we discontinued that. Commodities were scarce and the company just did not want to be in competition with other people. Before that it was just a matter of convenience. Anyway, we discontinued selling entirely in 1972.

Even before that we had materials passes. With these passes we have gone so far that if an employee wants to work on his own car--this is mine No. 8 I am talking about, not the open pit--we give him a pass if he wants to come up off-shift. That permits him to do that. It's the same with these loads of scrap wood. I'd say most employees got passes--and many of them are just for scrap wood.

We tried to help our employees. If somebody had a grate to be welded, he brought it up. As far as management was concerned, we insisted upon passes for that. A man had to have a pass to take it home because he couldn't prove whose it was unless he had the pass. I know several cases where a fellow picked steel plates out of the scrap pile for a battery box. He'd ask for a pass, and we'd even help him weld up the battery box. There are many instances similar to that.

Truslow: What about materials taken without passes?

Wagoner: Well, we began to suspect that; we were sort of up against it though, because certain things you just couldn't keep track of. You couldn't go out to your scrap pile and say somebody took a piece of angle last night, and there's no pass to show it. But we did notice that a roll of canvas, 50 feet long, and some matting for the lamp house had been taken. We were trying to figure how to stop such things.

Now, you take the plant guards. We don't have many.

One is the chief, and the other four are regular guards. We have an awful lot of territory to cover, and on some shifts there's only one guard. Area No. 8 is big; there are no fences around it. You take what Stockmeyer said—in the open pit—sure they might take a shovel home. But at mine No. 8 we'd insist on a pass. Even salvage men get passes. I don't say all the employees are going to see all the passes, but I try to keep check. Readdy sees some of them; some of them he doesn't see. We even issue passes for a loan of a tool, like an air drill or a shovel to dig garden or a saw. The man gets a pass and when those things are returned we mark them off as having come back.

Truslow: Do you have any knowledge about how many materials passes you issue a month?

Wagoner: Probably 30. Most of them are made out by the mine captains. They contact me only on bigger items.

Truslow: Can you recall any discharges for taking company property beyond those six mentioned?

Wagoner: With the difficulty in policing the place it's almost impossible. We caught one crusherman going home with some scrap copper about seven years ago, and he was discharged. Then as you've been told, about four years ago the powder and caps of dynamite were stolen. When those two men were discharged there was no question about it. That's true, as the men have told it to you.

Truslow: Did Mr. Dykeman come to you for materials passes before this incident?

Wagoner: I can't recall his ever asking for a pass. But I have my own ideas about what he's taken and given to other men.

Truslow: What was the value of the material he took on June 9 and 12?

Wagoner: As Bill Kenney said, we "pass" scrap up to $10 usually. Whether we have ever given a pass for $25 worth of material hasn't much to do with a man taking away $25 worth of material without a pass. That's what Dyke did. And we certainly didn't make a practice of issuing passes for new material. When Dyke talks about the steel sheet being scrap, those four by eights were put over the steps to shed water, and that didn't hurt them any more than if they were in the regular pile, where they could get rusty. It wasn't scrap sheet. We intended to use those sheets for general work. But after a 4- by 6-foot piece was cut out of a 4- by 8-foot sheet for Dykeman, you might as well say the 4- by 8-foot was taken.

Truslow: Was that sheet out in the open or in a shed?

Wagoner: Thin sheets are usually stored, but some are in the shop. The one Dyke took was stored. Heavier sheets such as ¼-inch and larger are kept in the open. The reason is rust. If a light sheet is left out, it rusts quicker.

Truslow: Did you ever discipline an employee for making up work around the plant which was not company work?

Wagoner: I don't say that I have directly, but I believe Kenney has. Bill, did you ever discipline that fellow Raehm for doing such work without permission? I know he did it.

Kenney: I told him about it, but I never punished him.

Truslow: Well, Mr. Readdy, let's hear your experience on June 15.

Readdy: When Mr. Wagoner told me to go to Dyke's house, I asked him for a witness to go with me in case I found something and he sent Kenney. Even before I stopped my car, I saw the sheet outside Dykeman's garage. Dyke came walking down and asked me what I was looking for. I said, "A steel sheet taken from No. 8 mine." He asked, "Did I take that sheet out there?" I responded, "That's what I'm trying to find out. Where's the angle iron that you admit taking?" He said, "Over in the field." So Bill and I walked over there with Dyke. I figured there were about 21 feet of angle iron, shaped up into a U, like he said. So I said, "Well, you might as well admit where you got the sheet." And, of course, he admitted he got it at the mine. And so, I went back and reported the incident.

Truslow: Mr. Maytag, as shop foreman I understand you supervised Mr. Dykeman when he worked as a painter?

Maytag: Yes, sir. And Dyke can't say he never was warned about company materials. I had quite a bit of trouble with Dyke's giving paint out in small lots such as pints or quarts. When we were painting the big machine shop he made a practice when a man asked for it to give him a quart or a pint. It took more paint than we had figured for the machine shop. I warned him and told him before he gave any more away to see me or the superintendent.

Dykeman: Just a minute! How many times did you warn me? There was only one time--when the half gallon of buff paint was found out back of the carpenter shop. I was working out of that can. I started putting my stuff away, and when I came back, the paint was gone. Only once did you warn me about giving paint to the fellows. How many times did I ask you whether I should give this fellow or that fellow paint?

Maytag: If I gave you permission it was all right. If I didn't, it was a different story.

Palmer: Mr. Truslow, after hearing all this, once again the union still insists that it was the past practice of the employees to take company property for their own use without passes, and on some occasions to get passes. This is the first time that the company has discharged an employee for taking stuff like Dyke took. Others had done the same kind of thing before him. I hope we can settle this amicably. But if not, I repeat, we shall request arbitration and demand not only reinstatement for Dyke with full seniority and other job rights, but also retroactive compensation for all the time management has made him lose by an unjust, excessive, and discriminatory penalty. Now what do you say, all you men on management's side? How about it?

AMERICAN AIRLINES

On September 12th two employees of American Airlines were discovered by company security guards in the passenger cabin of a Boeing 727 under circunstances which led the officers to conclude the two employees were in the act of pilfering food and drink from the plane. The General Foreman had listened to the employees' explanations and now had to decide on what disciplinary action to take.

Bob Doyle, a plane cleaner assigned to Flight No. 377, was found seated in aisle seat 19-D with a tray containing a Sky Club meal in front of him. Mike Rider, another plane cleaner, had completed his assignment on another plane and came aboard 377. He was found with a partially filled bottle of wine in his hand which he attempted to conceal by placing it on aisle seat 15-D and covering it with a yellow headrest as the officers came down the aisle.

The company had been quite concerned about pilferage of company property because of excessive amounts lost in recent years. Numerous communications had been sent to supervisors and employees stressing Rule #34 (see Exhibit 1) and the rigid enforcement of that rule. One of the memos sent during the last year read as follows:

> ... this policy (Rule #34) will be strictly enforced as to all employees without exception whatever. It will be uniformly enforced as to all employees whether in supervisory, hourly or salaried ranks.
>
> Don't be confused by such rationalizations as "everybody else is doing it" or "it will be thrown out anyway" or any other excuses for theft. Any further incident of theft or pilferage of whatever nature, no matter how small the value of the property involved will result in immediate dismissal of the employee or employees involved. It must be clear that long seniority and a good record will not mitigate the dismissal penalty.

A second communication, a memo from the president, stated in part:

> There is no such thing in American Airlines as petty theft or pilferage. A THEFT IS A THEFT!

Bob and Mike each made a statement when the security officers took them to the General Foreman's office after having been discovered on Flight No. 377. Bob said, "I put the meal in front of me and I was contemplating eating it when the security officers came aboard. I did not eat nor drink anything." Mike stated, "I was looking for a discarded Wall Street Journal and as I came to the back of the plane I saw a bottle of wine more than half empty on a seat. I set it down when the officers came in. I did not eat or drink anything."

Exhibit 1

AmericanAirlines

TO: ALL PERSONNEL

Through the years, American has established the reputation of delivering to its customers a quality product . . . a comfortable flight in well maintained equipment with courteous, cheerful and efficient treatment by all personnel.

That reputation did not come about by accident. It has resulted from the guiding principles of the Company, which include these elements:

1. **INTEGRITY**: to say what we mean, to deliver what we promise and to stand for what is right.
2. **RESPONSIBILITY**: to accept responsibility for our actions and to repose a high level of responsibility in our employees.
3. **VIGOR**: to approach problems with a youthful, enthusiastic, and fresh point of view, and to get things done instead of looking for reasons they cannot be done.
4. **DESIRE FOR BUSINESS**: to demonstrate that we want our customers' trade by going after it aggressively, and by serving our customers cheerfully and thoughtfully.
5. **EXCELLENCE**: to be satisfied with no performance short of the best.
6. **EFFICIENCY**: to attain our goals in the most efficient way.
7. **INNOVATION**: to be receptive to new ideas if they represent better ways of doing things.
8. **CITIZENSHIP**: to do our share in making the communities we serve, and the nation of which we are a part, a better place to live.
9. **STYLE**: to reflect in our manner and appearance the elements which comprise the Character of American Airlines.

These principles provide a general guideline for the conduct of all Company personnel, at every level of the organization. In addition, we have more detailed rules and regulations. Some important ones have been listed below.

Your supervisor is acquainted with the policies of the Company and with its rules and regulations. When in doubt, consult with him. His purpose, as a supervisor, is to aid you in your work for American Airlines.

George A. Spater
President

RULES AND REGULATIONS

ATTENDANCE

1. Report for work on time.
2. Call in when absent and when you expect to be late as far in advance of your scheduled starting time as possible. (Three consecutive days' absence without advising American Airlines will be considered a voluntary resignation).
3. During your tour of duty, remain in the area necessary for the efficient performance of your work.
4. Remain at work until your tour of duty ends unless you are authorized to leave early.
5. Check on or off duty in the prescribed manner and for yourself only.
6. Unauthorized appearance on the premises of the Company while off duty is restricted and your presence must not interfere with the orderly work of others who are on duty.

PERFORMANCE OF WORK

7. Follow instructions received from supervisors. Insubordination will not be tolerated.
8. Use only the machines or equipment to which you are assigned or specifically authorized to operate.
9. Do not enter, climb upon or fly Company airplanes unless authorized to do so.
10. Be sure to observe smoking regulations in all areas in which you work or visit.
11. Wear suitable clothing for your work and take pride in your neatness and appearance.
12. Cooperate with other employees, thus avoiding delays in flights and poor service to the public.
13. Avoid damaging Company property and the property of others.
14. Report any damaged property or defective work immediately upon discovery.
15. Loafing, sleeping on the job or intentional restriction of output is prohibited.
16. Misrepresentation of facts or falsification of records is prohibited.

SAFETY

17. Work carefully. Observe posted or published regulations.
18. Use safety equipment.
19. Report immediately to your supervisor, accidents or injury sustained on the job.

PERSONAL CONDUCT

20. Be courteous and helpful to our patrons, passengers and visitors.
21. Do not make false or slanderous statements about the Company, its employees or patrons.
22. See that your conduct reflects credit upon AA. This includes paying your just debts, thereby avoiding complaint from creditors or garnishment proceedings.
23. Conduct yourself in a moral and decent manner.
24. Consider the welfare of the Company and your fellow employees. Perform no act which is detrimental to either.
25. Reporting for or carrying on work while showing any signs of the use of intoxicants, or knowingly permitting another employee to do so, is prohibited.
26. Possession or drinking of any intoxicants on Company premises at any time, or drinking intoxicants in public while wearing uniform with AA emblem or insignia is prohibited.
27. Distributing, or posting literature on Company property, or posting or removing bulletin board notices requires prior authorization of the Company.
28. Soliciting, collecting or accepting contributions on Company time requires Company authorization.
29. The use of Company time, material or facilities for purposes not directly related to Company business, or the removal or borrowing of Company property without permission is prohibited.
30. Gambling of any kind on Company premises is prohibited.
31. Horseplay, fighting or scuffling on Company premises at any time is prohibited.
32. Threatening, intimidating or otherwise interfering with other employees at any time is prohibited. This includes off-duty periods.
33. Possessing, dispensing or using a narcotic, barbiturate, mood-ameliorating, tranquilizing, or hallucinogenic drug, either on duty or off duty, except in accordance with medical authorization, is prohibited.
34. **Dishonesty of any kind in relations with the Company, such as theft, or pilferage of Company property, the property of other employees or property of others entrusted to the Company, misrepresentation in obtaining employee benefits or privileges, as well as any action constituting a criminal offense, whether committted on duty or off duty, will be grounds for dismissal and, where the facts warrant, prosecution to the fullest extent of the law.**

WILSON DISTRIBUTORS COMPANY (A)

On Ocotber 24, 1979, Mr. Donald Wilson, Vice President of Personnel and Labor Relations of Wilson Distributors Company, was faced with the problem of deciding what action, if any, to take against a company truck driver, Thomas Boling. Boling had been hired by the company approximately six years earlier. He had worked for about one month as a delivery truck driver and then had been transferred to the warehouse where he had worked for approximately one year. At the end of that period he had bid for and recieved another delivery truck driver job which he still held. The job consisted of transporting the company's products from the warehouse to the customers.

Recently, the company had been informed by two of its customers and several of its competitors' salesmen that Boling was offering to sell company merchandise to customers on his delivery route at prices far below the regular prices quoted by the company's salesmen. After reviewing the evidence presented to him by company officials Wilson was convinced that Boling was guilty of this offense. He wondered what he should do about it.

BACKGROUND

The Wilson Distributors Company was a family-owned wholesale distributor to lumber dealers of windows, doors, and related products. It was started in 1904 and in 1979 operated three warehouses, with over-all sales of $15 million. Its main office and largest warehouse (sales of $8 million) were located in Chicago. Initially, Wilson was a retailer, then moved into wholesale distribution, and then into manufacturing, mainly through asssembly. In recent years, company officials had decided to limit their operations to wholesale distribution because of the high labor costs they had incurred as a manufacturer. By 1979 incidental manufacturing operations such as the glazing of purchased glass and the finishing of various pieces of lumber were a very minor part of over-all activity in each warehouse.

The company employed 300 people of whom 175 were in Chicago, including 55 shop personnel (of whom 30 were assemblers), 83 employees in warehousing and shipping (including 18 drivers) and 12 salesmen (classified as office personnel). All non-supervisory warehouse and shop employees belonged to the Carpenter's Union, which had won bargaining rights in 1948. In the past five years, the level of employment had remained constant. There had been no layoffs or terminations because of lack of work and only four disciplinary discharges. The union had appealed only one of the discharges to arbitration and in that case the company's action had been upheld by the arbitrator.

Since the company's primary activity was distribution of assembled products, the Chicago warehouse was usually full of merchandise. As orders were received, they were recorded on order forms which were forwarded to the appropriate departments for processing. When the materials for a particular order were ready for delivery they were collected at the shipping dock. The shippers were responsible for what was then loaded onto each truck. Normally, the driver who was to make the deliveries then backed up his truck to the loading platform and the shippers loaded it. Occasionally, the truck driver assisted the shipper. Sometimes there were no shippers immediately available, and the driver was trusted to load his own truck. Once the truck was loaded, the driver delivered the materials to the company's lumberyard customer. Under a company policy begun about eight years ago, employees who owned homes could purchase a limited amount of company materials at reduced cost for use in their homes. (Boling did not own his own home.) With the exception of these personal purchases, all the materials were delivered from the warehouse in company trucks to the lumberyard companies.

THE PILFERAGE PROBLEM

In the latter part of 1977, management heard through numerous rumors and reports that merchandise was leaving the Chicago warehouse without accompanying order forms. When the annual physical inventory check was concluded in December, company executives discovered that they had suffered inventory losses of approximately $40,000.

Management was of the opinon that such a large loss could not have been due to errors in shipments. Likewise it was convinced that it was not the reuslt of thieves breaking in from the outside because the warehouse was completely surrounded by a high fence and guards were on duty constantly. The company concluded that some of its drivers and warehousemen were colluding to steal and resell company goods.

The reports from customers and competitors regarding Boling were not the first that the company had had concerning attempts of its drivers to sell its merchandise at low prices. In one earlier case a customer had reported that a driver had offered to sell merchandise to his yardman at ridiculously low prices. The customer had claimed that he had threatened his yardman with dismissal if he bought any of the "stolen merchandise." In another earlier case a customer had reported that a driver had approached him directly and had offered to sell him company products "for cash" at very low prices. In still another earlier incident it had been reported that one of the drivers had had business cards printed with his own name and that of a fictitious company through which he proposed to sell merchandise at below normal prices. Although management investigated all of these earlier cases it did not believe that it had sufficient evidence to move against the suspected employees. The company tried rotating employees among the various delivery routes in order to make it difficult for those who were suspected of selling to build up regular customers. This procedure, however, was discontinued because it worked against the company's desire to build long-term good relationships between the drivers and the customers.

THE COMPANY HIRES A SECURITY CONSULTANT

Further checks in the spring of 1978 indicated that the inventory losses were continuing. That summer, an employee confirmed management's impressions that the pilferage was the result of collusion between some of the drivers and some of the warehouse workers. As a result, late that summer, the company hired Security Advisers

Associates (SAA), a firm which specialized in company security matters, to conduct a complete investigation and make recommendations. SAA's study which included a review of company policies and security practices was made known to all personnel. As a part of the study a number of employees were interviewed. As the study began, R. Steven Wilson, Jr., President of Wilson Distributors, sent the following letter to the company's supervisory personnel:

> In recent inventories we have found the actual count of certain items of stock to be quite a bit lower than our stock records showed that we should have.
>
> We did not follow this up at the time, as we felt the shortages were possibly due to clerical differences in our stock records. Recently, however, we have checked several of these items that have been consistently short and we find that shortages also exist in the first eight months of this year.
>
> Of course our stock material is no different than cash. We have periodic audits made of our books and records in the office, which is good business practice, but up to now we have not followed a similar audit approach in the warehouse.
>
> The continued existence of the above condition, added to information received from the outside that our material is being sold by some employees at ridiculously low prices, brings us to the point where we must take action.
>
> We have, therefore, engaged Security Advisers Associates, investigative consultants, to make a security survey.

By November of 1978, the consultants concluded their study. Some of the changes which they recommended to management to stop the illegal disappearance of material were as follows:

1. Start checking the truck loading process on a random basis;

2. Install a guard house at the gates and a procedure for checking materials entering and leaving;

3. Institute pre-hiring checks on all prospective employees;

4. Arrange for a larger loading area on the shipping platform so that when goods are left on the platform to await loading, there is no confusion about which truck they are for, and so that supervisors can be sure no extra materials are being placed on trucks;

5. Check the shiping operations during the lunch hour break;

6. Make it an ironclad rule that a trucker may not load his truck.

Company officials put the first three of these suggestions into effect, but decided not to implement the rest. They agreed that the loading area was too small and confused and thus comparatively easy for pilferage, but felt it would be too costly to enlarge it significantly. Similarly, they chose not to prohibit any driver from loading his own truck, even though there were no available shippers, although they recognized certain security problems. Management also decided against checking the shipping area during the noon hour. The did not consider this a serious security problem since there was usually a lot of activity at the warehouse during the lunch hour and someone trying to steal materials was likely to be seen by another employee or a commercial visitor.

THE WALSH DISCHARGE

In September, 1979, compnay officials uncovered a serious shortage of one of their products. This product was one which had also been disappearing in large quantities in the two previous years, so managment believed that the pilferage problem was continuing. Early in October the manager of one of the company's lumberyard customers notified the Wilson managment that one of its drivers, Anthony Walsh, had delivered some company materials to one of the lumberyard employees. The lumberyard was on Walsh's regular route, but he had not been scheduled to make any stops there that day. The materials were transferred to a private gargage in another part of the city the next day, Saturday. Shortly thereafter, local police entered the garage with a search warrant and dicovered stolen company material worth approximately $1,000. Company officials examined the stolen material and found that the boxes had been marked for a comapny cutstomer on another route, but the order numbers which had been written beside the customer's name were fictitious. A local handwriting specialist, who had frequently given expert testimony in court, was retained by the company, and she was able to match the handwriting on the box with that of one of the company's warehousemen, Jack Blake.

While company officials immediately discharged Walsh, they decided not to take any immediate action against Blake. They wanted to be positive before they confronted him and they also hoped to discover first whether others in the warehouse had colluded to steal company property.

No court action was initiated against Walsh. The lumberyard manager did not want to be identified as the informer. He indicated that although one of his employees had agreed to take material stolen from Wilson, the employee was a trusted one of the lumberyard, and one they did not wish to antagonize. Management believed civil action against Walsh would be fruitless without the lumberyard manager's testimony.

About two weeks later, Blake purchased some company materials for his own use, and then told his supervisor he was leaving work early to take his wife and baby to the hospital. Management asked their security consultants to follow him and they traced him to a bar where he was observed transferring the materials to another man's car. After remaining at the bar for several hours, Blake left and went to another bar where he worked evenings. He remained there for his night job. Management suspended Blake for three days for lying as to the reason he had to leave work and for breaking company rules by giving to another person the material that he had purchased at low rates for his own use.

When they told him of his suspension, company officials also questioned him about the stolen material they had uncovered, and said that they had good reason to believe that he was involved. They told him about the results of the handwriting analysis they had performed, and urged him to admit he had colluded to steal the materials. He denied stealing the material and refused to implicate others. When Blake did not report back to work after his three-day suspension, he was fired. Neither Walsh, Blake, nor the union entered a grievance.

THE CASE AGAINST BOLING

Throughout the early part of October 1979, John Wilson, Vice President of Sales, had been receiving information from the salesmen of other companies that Wilson drivers were again selling company goods at unusually low prices. On the morning of Ocotber 14, a customer told him that the company's truck driver, Thomas Boling, had offered to sell company merchandise below cost to one of the employees of the customer. Accompanied by a representative of SAA, Wilson visited the customer's place of business. Both the customer and his employee told them that Boling had offered to sell the employee merchandise at about half price.

Also on Ocober 14, Alan Conway, Treasurer and Credit Manager of the company, received a call from another customer claiming that the company's regular driver, Boling, had offered to sell him company merchandise at a substantial discount. Three days later, another SAA investigator interviewed this customer. The customer positively identified Boling from a photograph taken by SAA consultants and repeated that Boling had approached him with an offer of merchandise at half price. In his report of this interview to the Wilson management, the SAA consultant stated that he was sure the customer was telling the truth.

On the morning of October 24, Donald Wilson was becoming increasingly concerned about Boling's actions. Although Wilson believed that some of the other drivers had been stealing company property for some time, he thought that Boling's approaches to customers had been very amateurish, and probably were his first attempts. Wilson realized also that the company had no direct evidence that Boling had actually stolen company property but only that he had attempted to find buyers for such material. On the other hand, Wilson felt that strong action against Boling, if successful, would serve as a forceful deterent against the other drivers who were engaging in dishonest activities but against whom the company had been unable to secure any substantial evidence. Wilson read the section of the labor agreement on discipline and discharge (see Exhibit 1) and wondered what action he should take.

Exhibit 1

Article VI Miscellaneous

It is agreed that the Employer has retained the usual management rights and that the right to manage the Employer's business and direct the working force is vested exclusively in the management of the Employer, which right shall include, but shall not be limited to, the right (except insofar as limited herein) to suspend, discharge, or otherwise discipline for just cause; to transfer or layoff because of lack of work or for other legitimate reasons; to plan, direct and control its operations; and to change methods, processes, equipment or facilities; provided, however, that this will not be used for the purposes of discrimination against any employee or to avoid any of the provisions of this agreement or the obligation to bargain collectively concerning changed wages, hours, or working conditions.

SUBURBAN TRANSIT COMPANY (A)

On the afternoon of August 2 James Geimer, General Manager of Suburban Transit, sat back in his chair to reflect on his meeting earlier that day with the representatives of the Amalgamated Transportation Workers (ATW). Two grievances submitted by the ATW had been discussed at length; one concerned the discharge of a driver for alleged intoxication. The second dealt with the discharge of a janitor for use of methadone (see Suburban Transit (C)). Union President Ralph Schroeder had threatened to take one or both cases to arbitration, if the company did not offer a "fair settlement".

Suburban Transit, a privately owned company, operated buses in a large metropolitan area. As a pulic utility, it was licensed by the State Public Service Commission to provide safe, adequate, and impartial service to the public. The company operated under the regulations of the Commission. On an ordinary day it transported almost 40,000 passengers within a large suburban area and between the suburbs and the downtown area.

John Walker, Vice President of Local 469 of ATW, reported for work at Suburban Transit's main garage from 11:00 A.M. to 2:00 P.M. as a "cover" man; if a scheduled driver did not report for a trip or if a driver had to be withdrawn for illness or some other reason, the "cover" man would take over the work. During the three hours Walker was not needed as a "cover".

At 2:00 P.M. Walker was scheduled to go on a regular "run". When he did not appear at his bus on time, the dispatcher notified Gary Zook, the Superintendent of Transportation. Zook called Walker on the public address system, but he received no reply. Zook asked one of the men to look around for Walker; the man returned saying that Walker was in the Drivers' Room. He added that he thought he was drunk. Zook himself went down to the Drivers' Room and saw Walker slouched over a table with his head resting on his arm. Zook walked over and put his hand on Walker's shoulder; Walker looked up at him and then put his head back down. Zook left Walker, found a "cover" man, and drove to City Hall, where they met the bus driven by Ralph Schroeder, President of Local 469, ATW. Zook replaced Schroeder and asked him to drive back to the garage with him. On the way back Schroeder asked, "What's up, Gary?" Zook replied, "Walker is drunk in the Drivers' Room." "You're kidding," Schroeder fired back, "I saw him at one o'clock and he was cold sober." "See for yourself," Zook responded.

When the two men walked into the Drivers' Room, they found Walker drinking a cup of bullion soup. Zook walked over and asked him, "What's the story?" Walker replied, "I'm crocked. So what?" Walker made some abusive remarks to Zook, before Schroeder interrupted, "Pull yourself together, Johnny, and get out of here." Walker took his advice and the other two men went their respective ways.

When Walker reported for work the next day, he found that he had been suspended. Walker went to Zook's office and apologized for his abusive remarks; he asked for reinstatement. Zook told him that he could resign voluntarily and that if he did not do so he would be fired. Walker refused to quit, and Zook handed him a letter of dismissal.

Two days later the union filed a grievance stating that the company did not have "sufficient cause" for discharging Walker (see Exhibit 1). A week later Zook met with Schroeder and Walker to discuss the grievance, but their differences were not resolved. As the second step in the grievance procedure, a meeting was held at the company's main office. The union was represented by Schroeder, Walker, and James Beamer, another employee. The company was represented by Geimer, the General Manager, and Zook.

Geimer: Let's get down to the first item of business today, the grievance over the discharge of John Walker. What do you have to say for yourselves?

Schroeder: We say that Brother Walker should not have been discharged. The Company acted without "sufficient cause" and so it violated the Agreement.

Zook: Being drunk at work is a serious matter. We cannot have men under the influence of alcohol while they are at work. And so we have to get tough with anyone who violates Rule 22. (See Exhibit 2).

Schroeder: We realize that alcohol and work don't mix. But you are overlooking some important details in this case. In the first place Walker did not drive a bus under the influence. Nor did he make any attempt to do so.

Zook: But he was drinking before he was scheduled to drive, and he did drink on Company property.

Schroeder: Wait a second! Did you see him drinking on Company property?

Zook: No, I didn't.

Schroeder: Did anyone?

Zook: No one admits it. But one of the men came back and said he saw Walker drunk in the Drivers' Room about two o'clock.

Schroeder: Look, I saw Johnny about one o'clock, and he was sober. And you saw him an hour later and thought he was drunk.

Zook: Well, he was. I went down to the Drivers' Room about 2:20 P.M. and his head was on the table. When he looked up at me, his eyes were glassy and he smelled of alcohol.

Schroeder: Did he say anything?

Zook: No.

Schroeder: Was anyone else around?

Zook: No, the room was empty. That's when I decided to get you into the picture. When we got back, Walker looked a little better than when I left. His eyes were still somewhat glassy, and he still smelled of alcohol.

Schroeder: He looked more sick than drunk to me. I didn't smell any alcohol.

Zook: He did say "I'm crocked."

Schroeder: If he had said, "I'm sick," you would not be making such a big deal out of this whole thing.

Zook: But he did say it, Right?

Schroeder: You're emphasizing that point too much. Besides, he did not slur any of his words. And when he left the property, he didn't stagger or weave. He was probably taking his medicine. What is that stuff you take, Johnny?

Walker: I have two kinds. This is one, and here is the other.

Zook: (examining the two bottles) The date on this one prescription is two years ago.

Walker: The guy at the pharmacy fills it for me regularly. I don't have to get the prescription renewed.

Zook: This is a red herring. You were drinking on the job before you were scheduled to go out. And for that reason I fired you.

Schroeder: What did you put down on the daily record sheet?

Zook: J. Walker, sick at 2:00 P.M. We don't list anybody as drunk. They're listed as either sick or missing. Anyone who informs us is marked "sick". The "no show" guys are listed as "missing". Walker was given credit for three hours on the job, and then dismissed as sick.

Walker: Well, I am sick. I have the gout. It comes on me at night. There are some mornings my joints are so sore that I can hardly get out of bed. Sometimes my wife or one of the kids has to help me get up. I've been hospitalized four times with gout. The first time was ten years ago. The last time was earlier this year when I was in the hospital for 10 days and home for 20 more.

Schroeder: You're right about the sickness. I've seen you some days and you look like your walking on eggs. I feel sorry for you.

Zook: You have been absent a lot: 52 days since January 1. And you didn't work 61 days last year. Most of those days you were listed as sick. I also notice that you were out a number of Mondays.

Walker: Gout accounts for 90% of my absences.

Zook: But we are really talking about alcohol because too much sauce causes the gout.

Schroeder: There are other causes of gout. Look it up on the medical books, if you don't believe me.

Zook: Johnny, are you saying that you don't drink?

Walker: No, I take some whisky once in a while.

Zook: How much do you drink?

Walker: Not a whole lot.

Schroeder: You're trying to scapegoat him. (Turning to the other employee) Jim, you have been working here more than 15 years. Have you ever seen alcohol on Company property?

Beamer: Yes, a number of times.

Schroeder: Have you seen people on Company property with alcohol in them?

Beamer: Yes, I have.

Schroeder: Have any of these cases been recently?

Beamer: A few have.

Schroeder: To your knowledge, has anyone ever been disciplined for these things?

Beamer: No. At least, I don't know of anyone who has.

Zook: We discharged old Fritz.

Schroeder: And then you took him back.

Zook: We took him back because he agreed to go through the AA program. Besides, his case was different from Walker's. He had been drinking before he came on the premises. And, furthermore, he wasn't being paid while hewas here. Nor was he scheduled to work that day. Actually, he was discharged for excessive absences. But as a matter of fact, he had been hitting the bottle pretty hard.

Schroeder: How many employees have been discharged for offenses other than taking fares in the last five years?

Zook: Two, I think.

Schroeder: And now you are tring to get rid of Walker.

Zook: I warned him on July 7.

Walker: I don't remember a warning. You spoke to me about absences and lack of cooperation. I have not been a discipline problem in the 34 years I have spent with the company. I have never received a written reprimand or anything worse.

Schroeder: What is his record as a driver?

Zook: Very good. He has never had an accident charged to his record.

Schroeder: Any complaints from the public?

Zook: We get very few complaints about his driving and his work with the public. But he is still a poor employee. Look at all those absences. We can't run a company like this.

Schroeder: This man has 34 years service with the company, and to want to drop him two years before he becomes eligible for a pension.

Zook: We have to look to the future. A guy with a booze problem is a real risk for the company. What if he smashes one of our buses into a light pole or somebody's store? We have a reponsibility to the public. The State Commission could make life miserable for us. We have to be careful.

Schroeder: You don't do it by being harsh with a fifty-six year old man with eight kids.

Zook: Don't give us the hearts and flowers routine.

Schroeder: I'm not. I'm just telling you that you're too hard on Walker, and any arbitrator in this country will see it our way. He did not take a bus out. He did not endanger anyone's life or health or property.

Zook: But he was on duty under the influence of alcohol. You have to admit that, Ralph. Besides, he was drinking on company property. And we have to do something about it. We are cracking down on discipline. That's why we asked the union board members to help us by policing their own departments.

Schroeder: You're not going to improve discipline around here by discharging a fifty-six year old man with eight kids. The penalty is too severe. If he had said "I'm sick" instead of "I'm crocked", we wouldn't even be here right now.

Zook: Don't forget all the absences: 113 days in 18 months. That is a lot. Johnny is a good driver, but a terrible employee.

Schroeder: And so you are going to put him on the street after 34 years of service. Its guys like you that make unions necessary.

Zook: Save the rhetoric for next Labor Day. Do you have anything more to add?

Schroeder: Not a thing. You know that we are going to arbitration if you don't put Brother Walker back to work.

Exhibit 1

Pertinent Contract Clauses

Article VII. Management's Rights

Paragraph 7.1 The right to hire; promote; discharge or discipline for sufficient cause and to maintain discipline and foster efficiency in its operations is the sole responsibility of the Company. It is understood that the Company will not use these rights to discriminate against Union members because of their association with or activity for the Union.

Article XIV. Grievances

Paragraph 14.3 In the case of discharge of an employee, reasons for such discharge shall be given the employee on request, and upon his written request the officers of the association shall be furnished with the same information in writing within 24 hours after such request has been made.

Paragraph 14.4 Until a member of the association has served his probationary period of 31 days and has been accepted by the Company as a regular employee of the Company, the officers of the Company shall be sole judges of all questions concerning such member.

Exhibit 1
(continued)

Article XV Offenses and Hearings

Paragraph 15.1 When a member of the association is summoned to the general office to answer to any charge or charges, it shall be as soon as possible after the offense was comitted and in no case later than 7 days after the matter has come to the attention of the officials of the Company and it has been reasonably possible to reach the man. No action will be taken based solely on a written complaint unless the persons complaining have sent name and address and the employee has had a chance to read the complaint.

This Does Not Apply
To Fare Inspections

Paragraph 15.2 Entries shall not be placed against the discipline record of any member of the association until such member has been given the right of a hearing and the defense, if any, is to be briefly recorded with the charge.

Exhibit 2

Pertinent Company Rules

11. Suspension and Dismissals

Violations of rules, disobedience of orders, or neglect of duty may be considered sufficient cause for discipline or dismissal.

22. Intoxicants or Drugs

The use of intoxicants either before reporting for duty or while on duty, or the excessive use of intoxicants at any time, or the carrying of intoxicants about the person while on duty or on the Company property is prohibited, as is the use of harmful or habit-forming drugs.

SUBURBAN TRANSIT COMPANY (C)

On the afternoon of August 2, James Geimer, General Manager of Suburban Transit, sat back in his chair to reflect on his meeting earlier that day with the representatives of the Amalgamated Transportation Workers (ATW). Two grievances submitted by the ATW had been discussed at length; one dealt with the discharge of a janitor for the use of methadone. The second concernecd the discharge of a driver for alleged intoxication (see Suburban Transit (A)). Union president Ralph Schroeder had threatened to take one or both cases to arbitration, if the company did not offer a "fair settlement".

Suburban Transit, a privately owned company, operated buses in a large metropolitan area. As a public utility, it was licensed by the State Public Service Commission to provide safe, adequate, and impartial service to the public. The company operated under the regulations of the Commission. On an ordinary day it transported almost 40,000 passengers within a large suburban area and between the suburbs and the downtown area.

BACKGROUND

George Potter, a thirty-one year old worker, had been on and off drugs over a number of years. He started smoking marijuana when he was fifteen; the frequency of his use of marijuana varied over the next five years. At age twenty he took up heroin and rapidly reached the point where he was taking at least one dose a day. During these years he was arrested and convicted of possesion of marijuana, for larceny, and for breaking and entering. By his own admission he stole to pay for his usage of soft and hard drugs. When he was twenty-three, George voluntarily went to the Federal Public Health Service Hospital at Lexington, Kentucky, to "kick the habit." For six months he went through the course of treatment which included methadone dosages and group thereapy. Two and a half years after his return to society he resumed the use of heroin and the criminal activity related to it. Within a year he was arrested for breaking and entering; for this he was convicted and incarcerated for 18 months. After his release he was placed on probation for two years. His Probation Officer, Charles Harvey, urged him to get a job; Potter did so, finding work as a janitor at Acme Manufacturing Company. He was discharged six months later for frequent absences from work. Harvey suggested that he apply at Suburban Transit, and he gave him the following letter to present to the company's personnel department:

> This letter will introduce Mr. George Potter, who is on parole under my supervision for the next 17 months for the crime of breaking and entering. He has had previous work experience as a janitor at Acme Manufacturing Co. He lost the job there due to absenteeism, but he realizes now that he must work or be returned to the institution. He is aware that missing work will not be tolerated.
>
> Potter's employment record is fair from the standpoint

of the quality of his work, and he seems to be a fair employee prospect.

Any assistance you can give him will be appreciated.

Potter went to Suburban's offices and applied for a job. During an employment interview he gave the letter to the company representative. At the Medical Department he told the First Aid Attendant that he had been treated for heroin addiction at the Lexington, Kentucky hospital five years previously. Potter explained, "I was hooked on 'h' for three years and then I turned myself in. But I haven't been on it since I got out of jail." All of these remarks were written on his medical record card along with this observation: "No evidence of needle marks on his arms."

Potter was hired as a janitor in the garage. Within his first year he was disciplined three times for absenteeism: an oral warning after six months, a discharge which was reduced to a 26-day suspension after seven months, and another written warning after thirteen months. After this Potter reported for work regularly.

Eight months after he was hired Potter was given a Confidential Security Information Card. One question on the card was: "Have you ever been arrested and convicted of a violation of a Federal or State law?" On Potter's card an "x" had been typed in the box marked "No". Potter signed the card and turned it in at the personnel office.

Eleven months after he was hired Potter resumed his use of heroin. Twelve months later he decided that he wanted to "go straight" and he went to the Metropolitan Drug Abuse Center (MDAC). He was placed in a methodone maintenance program, in which he received a daily dose of methadone sufficient to control his desire for heroin. In the treatment at the Lexington hospital methadone was administered over several months to detoxify the patient; in a maintenance program the patient's use of methadone would continue indefinitely.

A month later Gary Zook, Supervisor of Transportation, posted the following notice on several bulletin boards at the garage and other locations:

> Unathorized possession, distribution, or use of any drug anywhere on Company premises is a grave potential safety hazard. Let me remind you of Rules 11 and 22.
>
> 11. <u>Suspensions and Dismissals</u>
>
> Violations of rules, disobedience of orders, or neglect of duty may be considered sufficient cause for discipline or dismissal.
>
> 22. <u>Intoxicants or Drugs</u>
>
> The use of intoxicants either before reporting for duty or while on duty, or the excessive use of intoxicants at any time, or the carrying of intoxicants about the person while on duty or on the Company property is prohibited, as is the use of harmful or habit-forming drugs.

Just to be perfectly clear I add this:

> Any employee found possessing, dispensing, using, or under the influence of any drug on Company property without proper authorization from the Company's Medical Department is subject to immediate discharge.

Two weeks later a Suburban employee was suspended after traces of methadone were found in his urine specimen. The man's claim that the specimen was Potter's, not his own, led to an investigation. Potter admitted that he was participating in a methadone treatment program conducted by MDAC; at this time the company discovered the full record of Potter's arrests and convictions. On July 15 Potter was discharged for the following reasons:

> -On the Company premises under the influence of a dangerous narcotic drug.
>
> -Falsification of your arrest and conviction record.
>
> -Your prior record of misconduct.

Within two days and with the support of the local union, Potter filed this grievance:

> My discharge violates the Agreement because the Comapny does not have sufficient cause for such action. The Company was aware of my problem when they hired me and therefore I ask to be reinstated to my job and reimbused for the loss of earnings that I may suffer and that the violation notice be rescinded and stricken from my record.

When a meeting between Gary Zook and Ralph Schroeder, local union president, failed to resolve the issue, the grievance was taken to the second step. At this meeting the company and the union presented the following arguments.

THE COMPANY'S ARGUMENTS

Dr. Theodore Stone, the Company's Plant Physician, outlined the effects of heroin and indicated some consequences in the work situation.

> A person who uses heroin goes through a regular reaction cycle. At first the person becomes euphoric, then drosy, then relatively "normal", and finally pained by withdrawal symtoms. This cycle takes six to eight hours. Most experts agree that addicts are functionally disabled. The addict may be able to get to the plant, but he can hardly concentrate on his responsibilities to his fellow employees and to the Company, if he is euphoric, drowsy, or craving another dose. His reflexes are not as quick and accurate

> and his span of concentration is reduced considerably. And so the addict is clearly a menace to himself and to those around him.

To this Zook added a further threat to the company: that the addict frequently steals company property or sells narcotics to others to support his own habit. Zook went on to mention that discharging a heroin addict was a wide-spread accepted practice in industry. He cited several examples in local firms during recent months.

Then Dr. Stone went on to explain the effects of methadone as presented in several well-known pharmacological textbooks and journals.

> Ingestion of methadone produces the same symptoms as heroin except that they are less pronounced and less severe. Methadone caused euphoria, a decrease in coordination, an analgesic reaction, and an impairment of consciousness and judgment. Further, it alters the intelligence or the intellectual processes of the person. In general the drug is effective over a three of four hour period. Unless another dosage is provided, the person experiences an insatiable need for heroin. Hence, it is a fair assumption that a person addicted to methadone will use heroin sometime in the future.

Dr. Stone added that he had examined some methadone addicts.

The company representatives went on to point out that Potter had falsified his record by turning in the Confidential Security Information card without reporting his previous record. Potter, they argued, deceived the company by not changing the response from "No" to "Yes". Finally, they pointed out that he had been disciplined three times for absenteeism. The combination of methadone addiction, conviction record, and absences made him so undesirable that the company had sufficient cause to discharge him.

THE UNION'S ARGUMENTS

Union representatives agreed with the company men that methadone was an addictive narcotic, but they disagreed on its effects on the user. In support of their position they called upon Dr. Ronald Eckstein, a staff member at MDAC, who stated:

> The use of methadone in a supervised methadone maintenance program does not produce any of the symptoms associated with heroin. The patients with whom I have been working have not experienced euphoria, or loss of coordination, or impairment of judgment, or alteration of intelligence. To my knowledge these observations can be supported by known clinical experience. My conclusion is that people on a methadone regimen can function normally without any special risk to themselves or others.

In response to Dr. Stone's comments, Dr. Eckstein asserted that methadone is effective for a period of 24 to 36 hours and further, that methadone taken orally under close supervision does not produce a euphoric reaction in the patient. He went on to cite a report from the Columbia University School of Public Health issued a year earlier; the report summarized the results of a four-year methadone treatment program at Beth Israel Medical Center:

> ... the success of the methadone-maintenance treatment program far outweigh the failures. ... A majority of the patients completed their schooling or increased their skills and have become self-supporting. The pattern of arrest has decreased substantially. Less than one percent of the patients who have remained in the program have reverted to regular heroin use. ...

Another piece of evidence introduced by the union representatives was the "Methadone Primer" published by the City Department of Health. In part it said:

> ... a person on methadone maintenance can operate a motor vehicle or handle industrial equipment without endangering himself or others. ...his intellectual functioning is not impaired. ... tests have demonstrated that, in most cases, the coordination and the reaction speed of patients are normal. ... Ephoria may occur in the earliest stages of treatment, during the period when the dosage is being gradually increased to the stabilization level. However, controlled use of methadone does not cause a euphoric reaction, once stabilization is reached. It appears, too, that once the body develops a methadone tolerance, the drug does not mask pain or cause drowsiness. In some cases the coordination and reaction speed of the person on methadone maintenance may not be normal, but in general the disabilities of heroin are not replicated in methadone maintenance.

In a rejoiner Dr. Stone was careful to point out that these findings were tentative. He went on to note that the Food and Drug Administration had restricted methadone to "investigatonal use" because, in its words, "despite recent research gains, there remains inadequate evidence of long-term safety and effectiveness." Dr. Stone concluded his remarks with this observation, "At the present moment it is impossible to say with certainty that in the long run methadone is actually beneficial."

In regard to the falsification of Potter's record, Schroeder argued that it was a company mistake. He reminded management of the letter which Potter provided at the time of his employment. In any case, he argued, Potter's action in not correcting the answer on the card does not warrant a penalty as severe as a discharge.

Exhibit 1

Pertinent Contract Clauses

Article VII. Management's Rights.

Paragraph 7.1 The right to hire; promote; discharge or discipline for sufficient cause and to maintain discipline and foster efficiency in its operations is the sole responsibility of the Company. It is understood that the Company will not use these rights to discriminate against Union members because of their association with or activity for the Union.

METAWORK INCORPORATED

Mr. William Miles, Personnel Manager, was considering what disciplinary action he should take with respect to employees who had engaged in a recent strike against Metawork Incorporated. He was wondering if his actions had caused the men to walk out, and if so how this should affect his decision. He also was concerned about the degree of disciplinary actions-what should he do about Hausman- about Mazzo- about the other union officers and about the employees who engaged in the work stoppage. He reviewed the events leading up to the incident hoping to gain insight as to what course of action to take.

On March 26, 1980 Metawork Incorporated informed Local 227 of the International Ferrous Workers of America (IFWA) that the company would reduce the crew size on the annealing furnaces from 3 to 2 men. Paul Hausman, the union's business manager, met with Bill Miles and objected to the reduction in manning; claiming that an oral agreement had been reached seven years earlier not to reduce crew size below 3 men. Since Mr. Miles had not been on the labor relations staff at the time of the claimed agreement he agreed to postpone the reduction pending an investigation of Hausman's claim. On April 23rd Hausman was informed by the company the investigation did not support the union's contention that such an agreement had been made and the company, therefore, intended to reduce the size of the crew effective Monday, April 26, 1980.

Paul Hausman contacted some of the furnace workers during the weekend and related to them the company's intention in spite of the agreement they had reached a number of years ago. On Monday morning April 26, 1980, the two employees assigned to the annealing furnace, Frank Lane and Bob Hand, refused to operate it. They walked over to the next aisle where Hausman was working, spoke with him briefly and told their foreman that they still refused to operate the furnace with only two men. Lane and Hand were suspended from the plant and told that management would inform them later regarding the disciplinary action which would be taken against them. The company also suspended Paul Hausman at 1:00 P.M. claiming that he told the two employees to refuse to work.

At approximately 1:30 P.M. five of the six executive board members of the union met with the personnel manager. (The absent member, Charlie Ball, worked the the second shift from 3:00 P.M. to 11:00 P.M.) They requested Mr. Miles to revoke the suspensions. Bill refused to do so and reminded the board members of their responsibilities under the no-strike clause of the labor agreement (see Exhibit 1). Following the meeting with Bill Miles almost all of the employees, including the five members of the executive board, stopped work and left the plant.

Jeff Mazzo, one of the union officers not on the executive board reported for work at 3 P.M., his normal shift. Management claims that Jeff was at that time acting business manager of Local 277. The company based this on an agreement reached with the union in September 1979 to the effect that Mazzo would substitute for Hausman when the latter was absent from the plant. A notice embodying this agreement had been sent to all foremen, to Hausman and to Mazzo on

September 23rd stating, in part, that "whenever he (Hausman) is absent from the plant, J. Mazzo will be Acting Business Manager." Mazzo came into the plant at his usual time but then turned around and walked out. According to the general foreman, Jeff waved to the other employees to leave the plant. Most of them, including Charlie Ball, walked out.

Later that afternoon the union leaders informed the employees that they were holding a meeting at St. James Hall. The meeting was attended by Hausman, Mazzo and the other local union leaders but a majority of the employees were not there. Hausman and the other leaders did not urge the men to return to work, but did arrange for another meeting to be held the following day and to be attended by the union's International Representative, Gus Leber. The company had already sent telegrams to Mr. Leber and the international headquarters informing them of the strike and urging them to get the men back to work.

On Tuesday afternoon a second union meeting was held and was attended by Mr. Leber who urged the employees to return to work. Hausman, Mazzo and the other local union officers supported Leber's position. The employees voted to return to work on Wednesday morning and Leber so informed the company.

Bill Miles was happy that the company could resume production tomorrow. As he expected, contacting the IFWA headquarters brought an end to the walkout. However, he still had to decide what action to take, if any, because of the walkout.

He decided to send telegrams to Hausman, Lane and Hand informing them to return to work on Wednesday and adding the phrase "pending further disposition of your case" in Hausman's notice. He reviewed the language of the agreement in an attempt to determine the responsibilities of the various individuals who participated in the stoppage. He also reviewed the personnel files and discovered Paul Hausman had received a written warning on an earlier occasion because he had violated Article VII. Jeff Mazzo had received prior warnings for violating Article VII and had also been given a two-week disciplinary suspension—a penalty which was later upheld in arbitration.

Bill took up a pencil and started sorting the facts. He knew his decisions had to be well analyzed and properly substantiated.

Exhibit 1

Pertinent Contract Clauses

Article VII- NO STRIKE, NO LOCK-OUT

1. In view of the mutual interest of the Company, the Union and employees in the maintenance of uninterrupted production, the Company agrees that there shall be no lockouts, and the Union agrees they will not cause or sanction or take part in any strike, walk-out, work stoppage, slowdown or picketing for the duration of this Contract or any extenstion or renewal thereof. All disputer shall be handled in accoradance with the terms of the Grievance Procedure contained in this Contract.

2. The Union and its members, individually and collectively, agree that if there is a violation of this clause any and all employees violating this clause will be subject to disciplinary action by the Company, including discharge, suspension for a period of up to but not exceeding six (6) months, or complete loss of seniority. Employees shall have the right of appeal through the Grievance Procedure of the contract. Neither the Union nor its officers shall be held responsible for the action of any individual employee unless such action shall have been ordered or directed by the Union and/or any of its officers, in violation of this clause, and the Union shall take all reasonable action to bring employees back ti work.

3. If the Union sanctions or takes part in any strike, walk-out, picketing, work stoppage or slowdown, all provisions of Section VI (Union Sercurity) shall be immediately terminated.

Article IX- GRIEVANCE PROCEDURES

1. A grievance is defined to be any controversy between an employee or employees and the Company as to any matter relating to working conditions or any controversy between the Union and the Company involving the interpretation, application or violation of any provision of this Agreement or of any supplemental agreement.

2. Any griveance, as defined above, which arises shall be settled in accordance with the grievance procedure steps set forth in paragraph three (3) below. However, a grievance must be taken up at the earliest practical date, but in no event later than ten (10) working days from the date on which the employee(s) affected or the Union's Business Manager knew of, or should reasonably have had knowledge of, the existance of the condition giving rise to the grievance; otherwise the grievance shall be deemed not to exist.

Exhibit 1
(continued)

Article XX- MANAGEMENT'S RESPONSIBILITY

The right to hire, reassign, promote, and for just and lawful cause to demote, layoff, discharge and suspend, and the management of the plant, and the direction, disposition and number of the working forces shall remain vested solely and exclusively in the Company, but each employee covered by this Agreement shall possess the right to appeal as provided by the terms of this Agreement.

WILSON CEMENT BLOCK COMPANY

The Wilson Cement Block Company owned fifteen side-o-matic trucks which were used to haul its product (various types of cement blocks) to its customers. Side-o-matic trucks are heavy, open-end vehicles equipped with a fifteen foot boom for loading and unloading the blocks.

Mr. Pierre Brock was employed by Wilson as an operator of one of these trucks. At the time of his discharge on December 6, he had been employed by the company for approximately eight years. He had been driving a side-o-matic truck for the past six years.

The accident which resulted in Mr. Brock's discharge occurred Thursday morning, December 5. On that morning Brock took a load of blocks on his truck to a building site about 30 miles away. He unloaded some of the blocks at the building site and was told by one of the construction supervisors to deliver the rest to the other side of the building. Brock started to drive the truck around the building. As he turned the corner, the side-o-matic boom crashed into the wall, causing serious damage to the building and to the vehicle. Brock was able to disengage the boom from the building and to drive the truck to the other side of the building.

Mr. Brent Rankford, the company's superintendent of manitenance and transportation, was sent to the site where he examined the truck and observed the damage to the building. He estimated the costs to repair the truck at over $1,800 and was told the building damage amounted to about $5,000.

Rankford claimed that Brook told him that when the accident occurred he had boom pointed toward the back of the truck. Rankford said that the accident couldn't have happened that way, because the front of the boom was smashed in.

Rankford instructed Brock to unload the rest of the blocks by hand and to drive his truck back to the plant, where Mr. Rankford directed forman Robin Bowman to assign Brock to another side-o-matic for the remainder of the day. The next day when Brock returned to work, Mr. Rankford discussed the accident briefly with him and told him he was discharged. Brock's foreman later sent a notice of discharge to Brock by registered mail, and a copy to Timothy Buckmore, chairman of the Union's grievance committee. It said:

> You are hereby discharged for your negligence in operation of side-o-matic truck on Thursday, December 5, 1979.
>
> /s/ Brent Rankford,
> Superintendent,
> Maintenance and Transportation

Brock promptly appealed his discharged in accordance with the grievance procedure under the collective bargaining agreement between the company and Local 981, International Brotherhood of Teamsters, Chauffeurs, Warehousemen and Helpers of America. Having been unsuccessful in the first two steps of the procedure the union dropped the case. However, Brock, supported by five other drivers, appealed on his own behalf, contending that the union leaders had conspired with management to deprive him of employment. Brock was a charter member of the Fraternal Order of Construction Material Haulers, a militant splinter group in the Teamsters Union that grew up following the area-wide negoiations of 1978. The Fraternal Order had a number of special demands that they felt had not been recognized by the parent union. Among these was the right to process individual grievances to arbitration with or without union representation.

ADDITIONAL FACTORS

1. Brock's Explanation

Brock denied that he ever had a conversation with Rankford as to how the accident occurred. Later, after he was discharged, Brock told grievance chairman Buckmore that the boom had been pointing straight forward when he started to move the truck from the first to the second unloading site. He admitted that he had not locked the boom into poisition. He had forgotten to disengage the hydraulic take-off which allowed the boom to swing, and guesses that one of the buttons on the control box, which was in the back of the truck, was activated as a result of the control box hitting a cable or the side of the truck.

2. Mechanic's Explanation

According to Wayne Hooper, the company's chief mechanic and a member of the union, Brock's story of how the accident occurred was a fabrication. Hooper contended that if a side-o-matic truck is operated while the hydraulic take-off is activated a loud whine could be heard, and it is likely that severe damage to the transmission and to the hydraulic equipment would result. He said the whine would be evident to the driver and indicated that although the truck had been badly damaged the transmission and hydraulic equipment were not affected. Furthermore, Hooper contended that it was unlikely that a button on the control box would activate itself by hitting a cable or the side of the truck.

"But" said Hooper, "we have to watch this guy, because if we don't hear his case the Fraternal Order may stage a wildcat. The internal union feuding could result in violence and, possibly, more accidents and equipment damage."

3. Safety Instructions

All drivers of side-o-matic trucks were given standard written safety instructions by the personnel department. Drivers were required to obvserve three rules whenever the truck was to be moved forward. One, the boom was to be locked into position pointing directly forward. Two, the hydraulic takeoff was to be disengaged so that there was no chance of the boom being activated even if the control button were accidentally bumped. Three, the control box was to be hung onto a bar provided in the back of the truck. Brock admitted that he knew about these rules and admitted that he had neglected to effect any of the three precautions, but claimed he had never received written instructions from the personnel department. There was general agreement that any one of these three actions would have prevented the accident if it occurred in the manner described by Brock to Buckmore.

Company personnel agreed that drivers of the side-o-matics did not always secure the boom in place when travelling short distances, especially around the company's loading area. Rankford admitted that he knew it happened at times and that he had never disciplined a driver for it.

4. Previous Accidents

This was not the first accident that Brock had since he began driving the side-o-matic. The company claimed they kept a record of all accidents, no matter how minor.

On May 5, 1975, a cement block fell from Brock's truck and damaged the bumper of another car. The company supplied ropes to each driver and charged the driver with the responsibility to make sure each load was secure. Mr. Brock contended that there were times when ropes were in short supply and that he had complained on several occasions about the problem.

On April 20, 1976, when Brock was delivering blocks at a building site, his truck slid back into another car damaging the windshield and body of the car.

On September 8, 1976, Brock claimed he injured his leg when his foot slipped off one of the foot pedals in the truck. The company doctor found that Brock had broken his ankle and he was out of work collecting compensation for nearly two months.

On February 11, 1977, Brock's truck dropped back at a traffic light and damaged the hood of the car behind him. This accident, as well as those of May 5, 1975 and April 20, 1976, resulted in insurance claims against the company, and all were verified through the company's insurance carrier.

5. Previous Disciplinary Action Against Brock

Mr. Leary, president of the company, said that on each of the occasions listed he talked with Brock and Ray Hudley, former business agent of the union, and told them that Brock's accident record would have to improve. Leary contended that Brock also had been warned several times about taking time off on the road when he was supposed to be driving the truck. Prior to the February 11, 1977 accident Brock was not given any written warnings or any other form of discipline.

As a result of the February 11, 1977 accident Mr. Leary said that he had given Brock a written warning, a copy of which was sent to Hudley. A copy of the warning, taken from Brock's personnel file, read as follows:

> Investigation shows that February 11 accident which caused serious damage was due to your negligence or poor driving. You are hereby warned that further negligence may result in your discharge.

Mr. Brock himself denied that anyone ever talked to him about his previous accidents or that he had received any written warnings. He did not deny that the accidents occured and admitted that Mr. Leary had talked to him once or twice about not getting back on time after he was out on the road. Hudley, not a member of the Fraternal Order, said that Brock had received the warning and that he, Hudley, had talked with Brock about it.

6. Disciplinary Action Against Other Employees

Company representatives all agreed that, in general, the company had been lenient with its employees in the past. Only two instances could be recalled where truck drivers were discharged for disciplinary reasons. Neither involved side-o-matics.

On March 25, 1975, David Madson, a truck driver, was discharged following an accident due to his negligence and because he was under the influence of liquor at the time. Madson had thirteen months of seniority at the time, but had no previous record of infractions.

In 1970 another driver, Jonas Herbert, had been discharged because of negligence, but he was later reinstated as a result of arbitration - the arbitrator pointing to Herbert's long service 15 years as the primary reason for reinstatment.

There was one other case on the company's records where a side-o-matic driver had serious accident. That incident was also caused by the failure of the driver to lock the boom in position. Jeremy Le Brow, an employee with twelve years of seniority, was delivering blocks to a construction site. After unloading the blocks LeBrow neglected to realign the boom and secure it - rather he left it protruding from the side of the truck and drove away. After driving several blocks the boom struck a building, shattering several windows and severing a pipe which, in turn, activated the entire fire preventive sprinkler system. More than $3,000 worth of water damage resulted. LeBrow was suspended.

Although LeBrow had twelve years of seniority at the time of the accident, he had only been driving a side-o-matic for three days. He had applied for the job and was initially turned down by the company because he had no previous experience. When LeBrow insisted on driving - claiming that his long seniority entitled him to the chance - the company finally agreed. On reviewing the accident Mr. Leary, the company president, said the company should assume partial responsibility - that they should never have permitted LeBrow to operate a side-o-matic. Leary agreed to reinstate LeBrow after five days on the condition that he would not be permitted to drive a side-o-matic in the future.

Mr. Leary drew a distinction between the LeBrow and Brock cases - saying that Brock was an experienced driver, well acquainted with safety rules and skilled in operation of the vehicle. Brock's accident, in Mr. Leary's opinion, was an example of gross negligence.

7. Relevant Contract Provision

Article XII - POWERS AND DUTIES OF THE EMPLOYER

The employer retains the exclusive right to manage the business, assign work, and to direct the working forces. The employer, in the exercise of its rights, shall be expressly limited by the provisions of this agreement. The right to manage the business and plant, and to direct the work force includes the right to hire, suspend or discharge for proper cause, and the right to relieve employees from duty because of lack of work or for other legitimate reasons.

Article XV - GRIEVANCE PROCEDURE

Any matters arising from the interpretation or application of this agreement shall be taken through the following grievance procedure:

Step 1. Between the employee presenting the grievance and his foreman.

Step 2. If an adjustment is not reached in Step 1, the complaining employees together with the Chairman of the union grievance committee shall take the matter up with the superintendent of the department in which the grievance arises.

Step 3. If adjustment is not reached in Step 2, the Chairman of the union grievance committee shall take the matter up with the company president who may call in other representatives of management to consider and attempt to adjust the grievance.

Step 4. If no adjustment is reached in Step 3, the Chairman of the union grievance committee may appeal the matter to arbitration, except that no grievance shall be subject to arbitration unless the grievance has been actually referred to arbitration in writing with notice to the other party within ten (10) days after the decision at Step 3 is delivered.

8. Precedent

This was the first instance where an employee sought to bring a grievance on his own behalf.

Exhibit 1

BROCK'S PERSONNEL RECORD

Name: Pierre G. Brock
Date of Birth: August 27, 1936
Date of employment: January 12, 1971
Married: three children

Work History

Classification	Department	Date	Rate
Laborer	012	1/12/71	$4.88
(Merit increase)		4/ 1/71	5.03
Fork truck	211	7/20/71	5.34
(General increase)		5/ 1/72	5.49
Outside driver	211	2/12/73	5.70
(General increase)		5/ 1/73	5.96
Side-o-matic	044	11/22/73	5.96
(General increase)		11/30/74	6.36
(General increase)		11/30/75	6.51
(General increase)		4/30/77	6.65
(General increase)		11/30/78	6.85
(General increase)		11/30/79	7.13

Education:
High School (did not complete)

Previous Work Experience:

Gas Station Attendant	1956 - 1957
Garage Mechanic	1960 - 1970

Service:

U.S. Marine Corps	1957 - 1960
Honorable Discharge	

Exhibit 2

NATIONAL LABOR RELATIONS ACT Section 9(a)
Representatives and Elections Sec 9. (a) Representatives designated or selected for the purposes of collective barganing by the majority of the employees in a unit appropriate for such purposes, shall be the exclusive representatives of all the employees in such unit for the purposes of collective bargaining in respect to rates of pay, wages, hours of employment, or other conditions of employment: Provided, That any individual employee or a group of employees shall have the right at any time to present grievances to their employer and to have such grievances adjusted, without the intervention of the bargaining representative, as long as the adjustment is not inconsistent with the terms of a collective bargaining contract or agreement then in effect: Provided further, That the bargaining representative has been given opportunity to be present at such adjustment.

BORDER STATE BUS COMPANY (A)

On Thursday afternoon, October 11, John Benson, President of the Border State Bus Company, called a meeting of the top officials of his company to decide what action, if any, to take against one of their employees. The employee, William S. King, 36, had been a bus driver for the company for thirteen years. On October 5 King had been identified by local public news media as the Acting Grand Dragon of the state branch of the recently activated Ku Klux Klan and also as a bus operator for the company. During the next few days many complaints were received by telephone at the company's headquarters. However, the company took no immediate action hoping that the storm would blow over. Instead, the public reaction continued to mount. In addition to general protests, management was informed, not only by citizens and customers, but also by some of its own bus drivers that they feared violence would occur unless King was removed from his job. Management learned also that there was talk of a wildcat strike and that black citizens, who made up 50% or more of its customers, were threatening an economic boycott.

On the morning of October 11, the company received a telegram from the local chapter of the National Association for the Advancement of Colored People (NAACP) protesting the employment of King on public buses which were used by blacks. At 12:45 p.m. that day the local secretary of the NAACP telephoned the office of the company's president and reported that the NAACP had received a number of calls from bus drivers informing her that the men were talking about a wildcat strike.

Shortly after 2:00 p.m., Benson, who had been away from the office most of the day, returned to his desk. Upon learning what had happened that day, he called a staff meeting for 2:30 that afternoon to review the situation in detail. As he listened to the reports and advice from the other management officials, Benson wondered what action he should take.

The Border State Bus Company was a public utility operating passenger buses in one major city in the state. As a public utility it had to provide safe, adequate, impartial service to the public, and was subject to certain statutory requirements. In recent years, a Metropolitan Transit Authority had been set up as the governing administrative body for the company. It took over the authority which had previously been exercised by the Public Service Commission under the State Public Service Commission Law. The law provided in part that no public utility could "discriminate against or cause any undue or unreasonable prejudice to any person" (see Exhibit 1). Blacks comprised 44% of the population of the city and about 50% of the patrons of the bus line.

Amalgamated Bus Driver's Union, Division 38, was the collective bargaining agent for the 1,200 bus operators, of whom 540 were black. The collective bargaining agreement of September 30th also took note of the particular duty of a public transportation company to service the public adequately. Article IV, Section 3 said, in part, that the union and its members were to render faithful service in their respective positions, cooperate with management in the effective operation of the business, and "foster friendly relations between the company and the general public." It further stated that the employees were to "be courteous to passengers and to others with whom they (came) in official contact; (and they were) at all times (to) seek to protect the property of the company from injury at their own hands or at the hands of others..." (see Exhibit 2).

At the start of October, the newspapers and radio and television news programs in the city reported that there were indications that an effort had begun to activate a chapter of the Ku Klux Klan in the state. On the morning of October 5th, radio announcements identified the Acting Grand Dragon of the state branch of the Ku Klux Klan as William S. King, a Border State Bus Company bus driver. Afternoon newspapers also carried the story, with a statement by King that the Klan intended to institute a program to "let people know what the Klan stands for and give them an opportunity to join."

That day, company officials at the downtown headquarters received a number of calls from persons who identified themselves only as patrons of the company. The callers expressed concern and apprehension over the fact that the company employed a man who held the position King was reported to hold.

The next morning, Saturday, October 6th, King went to the office of his supervisor, Don Fuller, Manager, Southern Division of the company. During their discussion the subject of his connection with the Klan was brought up and King asked what was the company's attitude toward his activities. Fuller said that the company had no objection to anybody belonging to any organization as long as it did not affect their job and as long as the activities of the organization were not conducted on company time or property.

That evening, a rally was held on an open field outside the city which attracted 2,000 persons for what the newspapers described as "an evening of race baiting and cross burning by Ku Klux Klansmen." The press reported excerpts from the speech delivered by King as follows: "We will not entice violence, but we won't walk away from it either... Forward the white race. Segregation forever."

When John Benson, President of the Border State Bus Company, got to his office on Monday morning, October 8th, he learned that the company had received a great number of calls over the previous weekend complaining about the fact that the leader of the Klan was an employee of the company and involved in the transportation of the public. That day, additional calls came in from the public inquiring about the situation, expressing alarm that King was an employee and asking what action the company planned to take. Management officials made no comments to any caller. During the non-working hours that he was away from his job, King was interviewed by television, radio, and newspaper reporters about his planned revival of the Klan. The public news media continued to focus attention on the story.

On Tuesday, October 9th, Benson received a telephone call from a white employee asking that King be discharged and disclosing that a number of black bus operators had approached the National Association for the Advancement of Colored People asking that a mass demonstration be held to protest King's employment. The employee also said he was concerned that violence might erupt between members of the union or between the public and the company, if King remained employed. Following this conversation, Benson called a meeting of the company officers to discuss what they should do. It was concluded that although the situation appeared to be worsening, it would probably subside. They agreed not to take any action.

Following the October 9th staff meeting, and throughout the next day, Wednesday, October 10th, company executives received a steadily increasing number of telephone calls. These calls came from private citizens, as well as from white and black bus operators, and members of the press. Patrons of the bus line called to complain about the continued employment of King, and threatened to boycott the service for fear they might be exposed to violence caused by King or by people whose beliefs were diametrically opposed to King's.

In addition to complaints from the bus-riding public, other bus operators phoned company officials to express their fears. Typical of the white operators who called was the statement of one man who spoke to Harry Smith, Superintendent of Transportation, and said:

> "Mr. Smith, I don't know this fellow King. They may think I am King and I just don't appreciate having to drive a bus and have somebody throw a brick through the window. I don't know whether you are aware that that is going to happen but it is exactly what is going to happen. We are afraid."

During this period the company had a number of calls also from the local newspaper, radio, and television reporters. The newsmen informed management that they had received reports that the employees were planning a wildcat strike and that the black community was planning to boycott the buses. They asked the company for a statement regarding what action, if any, it planned to take. The company representatives replied that the company wished to make no statement at this time.

Company officials were aware that union leaders were also receiving complaints during this period from both white and black members. At a special union executive board meeting held on October 8th, King was asked to reaffirm the oath of loyalty he had taken when he joined the union which stated he held no ill feelings toward any member because of race, creed, or color. King renewed this loyalty oath and signed a pledge card again. He stated that he was a Klan member, but felt no ill will toward either the union president, Francis X. O'Brien, who was Catholic, or the union lawyer, Hyman Goldberg who was Jewish. In fact, he added, he had nothing against any Catholic, Jew or Black union member. At the next regular union meeting, October 9th, the executive board recommended that no charges be filed against King. This motion was approved by the members. However, the membership also passed a resolution condemning the Klan.

At 8:05 a.m. on Thursday morning, October 11th, the company received a telegram from the NAACP requesting an immediate investigation of the King situation. Shortly after 12:45 p.m., the secretary and legal representative of that group telephoned company headquarters and left a message for the president, John Benson, who was away from his desk. The NAACP leader said that her organization had been receiving numerous calls from black and white bus operators about a possible wildcat strike if the company did not discharge King immediately. She also said the NAACP felt management had an obligation to act quickly, and that she had expressed this sentiment in telegrams to the state Public Service Commission and the Metropolitan Transit Authority.

At approximately 2:00 p.m., Benson returned to his office and learned of the morning telegram and recent phone call. He immediately called a staff meeting of the top company officials to reappraise their earlier decision in light of subsequent events.

While waiting for the other members of management to arrive, Benson had his secretary get King's work record from the personnel office. The employee had been a bus driver for the company for 13 years. During that period, his performance had been about average. Ten years earlier, he had been suspended for a short period of time for having assaulted an elderly black passenger.

Benson also noted that King had arranged to begin his vacation this year at the conclusion of his work on Friday, October 12th. This seemed to Benson to introduce an additional problem if management chose to discharge King. Under the contract, and employee became ineligible for his paid vacation if he was discharged for just cause prior to the start of his vacation. Thus, if management chose to discharge King at once, he would lose the paid vacation to which he otherwise would have been entitled.

Immediate discharge of King presented still another problem. The labor agreement provided that when discharge was contemplated an employee should be suspended until such time as the union had been notified in writing and given an opportunity to request a hearing. If a hearing was requested discharge would not be effective until after the hearing. (See Exhibit 2.) In past cases when discharge was contemplated the company always had followed this procedure and merely suspended the employee pending a hearing.

As the meeting got under way Benson was informed by Don Fuller that King was that very afternoon driving a bus and that his shift would not end until 5:00 p.m. As Benson heard the reports, the danger of violence, a strike, and a boycott all appeared to him to be imminent. He doubted that those who were threatening to participate in these actions could be placated as long as King remained an employee of the company, even a suspended employee. He wondered what management should do.

Exhibit 1

Public Service Commission Law

Article 53
Section 14 - Preferences and Discrimination

(A) Preferences and discrimination prohibited. No public service company shall (with the exceptions listed in the following subsection) directly or indirectly, by any means whatever (including but not limited to special rates, rebates, drawbacks or refunds) in respect of any service rendered or commodity furnished by it:

Exhibit 1
(continued)

(1) Charge, demand or receive from any person a greater or less compensation than from any person under substantially similar circumstances;

(2) Extend any privileges or facilities to any person except such as are uniformly extended to all persons under substantially similar circumstances;

(3) Give any undue or unreasonable preference to or discriminate against or cause any undue or unreasonable prejudice to, any person, locality, or particular class of service.

Exhibit 2

Article IV of the Labor Agreement

Section (2). The union further recognizes that the power of discipline is vested exclusively in the company. The company agrees that discharge will be for just cause. Where disciplinary action is contemplated, the following procedure shall be adhered to:

(a) In the event disciplinary action is to be taken against an employee, which may result in suspension or discharge, final action will be withheld until such time as the union office has been notified in writing and given an opportunity to determine whether or not it desires that a hearing be held for such employee.

(b) It shall be incumbent upon the company to serve this written notice to the union office within one (1) day (except Saturdays, Sundays and Holidays) after the employee has been interviewed on the infraction which causes the need for contemplated discipline.

(c) If the incident is one of a more serious nature which may result in the discharge of the employee, the employee may be withheld from active service pending a hearing and final action, payment or nonpayment for the lost time to be a part of the final determination.

Section (3). The union convenants that its members shall render faithful service in their respective positions and shall cooperate with the management in the effective operation of the business; foster friendly relations between the company and the general public; that they shall be courteous to passengers and to others with whom they come in official contact; that they shall at all times seek to protect the property of the company from injury at their own hands or at the hands of others...

JOHNSON CHEMICAL COMPANY

Mr. Thomas Stamp had been chosen to arbitrate two grievances by the Johnson Chemical Company and the Independent Chemical Workers Union (ICWU), Local 483, in accordance with Article XI of the parties' collective bargarining agreement. The grievances, although not factually identical, were similar in nature and each was presented at the arbitration hearing conducted on April 22, 1979. Tom Stamp believed that the issues involved in these cases were among the most interesting and difficult issues he had been faced with in some time. He was aware of the fact that the grievants had filed charges with the Equal Employment Opportunity Commission shortly after the arbitration hearing. He wondered what significance, if any, he should give to considerations other than the facts and arguments raised by the representatives of the company and the union. In particular should Title VII[1] have any bearing on discharge of Mr. Epstein or Mr. Perkins, the grievants? He pondered these questions as he finished sorting the facts and began to formulate his decision.

The Johnson Chemical Company owned and operated an agricultural chemical manufacturing plant at Storrs, Michigan. In December, 1978, approximately 320 people were employed by the company; 120 employees were in supervisory clerical and technical positions and the remaining 200 were employed in production, warehousing and maintenance functions.

The production, warehouse and maintenance employees were covered by a three-year collective bargaining agreement, dated March 1, 1978, between Local 483 and Johnson Chemical Company. The union had been certified by the National Labor Relations Board in 1958 and acted as the exclusive bargaining agent for all of the company's production, warehouse and maintenance employees since then. The two grievants, Howard Epstein and William Perkins, were members in good standing of Local 483 of the ICWU when they were discharged by the company.

---

[1]Title VII of the Civil Rights Act of 1964 provides in part as follows:

Sec. 703.

(a) It shall be unlawful employment practice for an employer:

(1) to fail or refuse to hire or discharge any individual, or otherwise to discriminate against any individual with respect to his compensation, terms, conditions, or privileges of employment, because of such individual's race, color, religion, sex, or national origin; or

(2) to limit, segregate, or classify his employees in any way which would deprive or tend to deprive any individual of employment opportunities or otherwise adversely affect his status as an employee, because of such individual's race, color, religion, sex, or national origin.

JOHNSON CHEMICAL COMPANY

Sometime in December of 1978 the company was commissioned by Farmers Cooperative, Inc., a large agricultural supplies wholesale firm, to develop and produce a new nitrogenous fertilizer. Under the terms of the arrangement, Johnson Chemical Company was promised a long-term (and apparently lucrative) contract to supply the fertilizer to Farmers Cooperative, if it could first develop, produce and ship 200,000 pounds of the new fertilizer on or before November 1, 1979. To ensure production which would be adequate to meet the November 1979 shipping deadline, Johnson advised all of its production department employees that, commencing January 16, 1979, they would be required to work a six-day week, Monday through Saturday, inclusive. The affected employees were told that the required Saturday overtime policy would continue for a period adequate to assure the necessary production, which was estimated at the time as anywhere from six months to one year.

At all times prior to January 1979, all departments in the plant had been scheduled on a five-day week, Monday through Friday, working one shift from 7:30 a.m. to 4:00 p.m. Before January 1979, the company had occassionally scheduled daily and weekend overtime, as business required; however, it had never previously required all of the employees in a department to work Saturday or Sunday overtime during any given weekend.

Howard Epstein, an Orthodox Jew, had been hired by the company in June 1968, and was the second most senior employee (of twelve) working as a chemical operator in the company's production department. Before January 1979, Epstein had worked daily overtime whenever he was scheduled, but when offered Saturday work in the past he had always refused due to his religious beliefs. The company had never questioned his prior refusals to work Saturday overtime because on every occasion they were able to schedule a less senior man within the department to perform the required work.

Upon learning of the company's new policy, Epstein went to see George Fiske, Plant Personnel Manager. Epstein explained to Fiske that his religious beliefs prevented him from working on Saturdays, the Jewish Sabbath. Epstein offered to work more daily overtime to make up for any time missed on Saturdays. Fiske explained to Epstein that he sympathized with him, but that the company desperately needed a full crew working on Saturdays, and therefore it could not possibly excuse him from the Saturday work.

Mr. Epstein was absent from work on January 16, 23, and 30, 1979, all Saturdays. On his return after each absence, he was issued a disciplinary warning notice and was advised that his continued refusals to work would result in his discharge. After missing work on Saturday, February 6, 1979, Epstein was discharged for "refusal to work a reasonable amount of overtime" per Article IX, Section 6, paragraph (e) of the contract. Epstein filed a grievance on February 8, 1979, alleging that his discharge was unlawful under the contract.

William Perkins was hired by the company on June 17, 1978 as a laborer in the warehouse department. He was the least senior man in his classification (which included forty other employees). On or about January 7, 1979, Perkins joined a group called the "Evolutionary Naturalists." The members of this group, numbering nearly 900 in the state of Michigan, apparently reject what they term as "the corruption of modern society." The Fundamentalist for Evolutionary Naturalists, which Perkins claimed as the group's "bible," states that:

> An Evolutionary Naturalist is a revolutionary against the greed, corruption, racism, hate, poverty, and war in modern society. He actively opposes all forms of traditional social and political tenets. . . An Evolutionary Naturalist believes only in the divinity of man and nature. He aspires only for truth, beauty and goodness. The universe is conceived of as an indefinitely extended creative process, always tending to higher levels of development. The basic role of man is to be the chief agent of the evolutionary advance on earth through the application of his intelligence to the problems of life on earth and through the building of a better world. . . when life on earth veers from a course of truth, beauty and goodness, then the existing traditions must be rejected. . . An Evolutionary Naturalist must oppose illegal wars, depose ignoble politicians, and upset established life styles. To this end, an Evolutionary Naturalist may not engage in labors of the day or gainful employment on any Wednesday between the hours of noon and midnight and he must fast and meditate during this period ...

After joining this sect, Perkins informed Fiske that henceforth he would have to leave work every Wednesday at 11:30 a.m. for religious reasons. Perkins offered to make up this time by working either Saturday or Sunday in his own department, or by replacing Epstein in the production department on Saturdays, or by reporting in four hours early on Wednesdays. Fiske replied that he was not going to foul up his schedule to accommodate every fanatic working for the company.

Perkins left work at or about 11:30 a.m. on January 13, January 20, and January 27, 1979, all Wednesdays. Upon his return after each absence, he was issued a disciplinary warning notice, and after the January 27 absence he was given a two-day disciplinary suspension. After leaving work on February 3, 1979, Perkins was discharged for excessive absenteeism in violation of Article IX, Section 5 of the contract. He personally filed a grievance on February 5, 1979.

Neither the Epstein nor the Perkins grievance was settled in the grievance procedure and the union demanded arbitration. The company and union agreed to consolidate these cases for the purpose of arbitration and selected Thomas Stamp to decide the issues.

Shortly before the hearing, Perkins told the union that he wished to present his own case to the arbitrator and retain his own counsel. The union president, John Bain, informed Perkins that this was neither possible nor necessary, since the established procedures had been utilized for many years to adequately represent the employees in the unit. Neither Perkins nor his counsel appeared at the arbitration hearing, but the union did present his case to the arbitrator.

The company argued at the hearing that under Article VII of the contract it has both the right to discharge for proper cause and to schedule the working hours of the plant. Under Article IX, Section 5, the company contended that Perkins' failure to work Wednesdays falls under the category of excessive absenteeism and thus is proper cause for discharge. It further contended that under Article IX, Section 6, clause (e), Epstein's refusal to work Saturdays constitutes a refusal to work a reasonable amount of overtime and, therefore proper cause for his discharge.

The union countered that Epstein's refusal to work Saturday overtime is not "unreasonable" per Article IX, Section 6, clause (e) of the contract, because he offered to work more daily overtime to make up for the time missed on Saturdays. The union also contended that Perkins' refusal to work Wednesday afternoons is not "excessive absenteeism" under Article IX, Section 5 because he too agreed to work at other times to make up for the time missed on Wednesdays. Further, even if such absences are characterized as "unreasonable" or "excessive," the union believed that these absences were motivated by sincere religious beliefs and that under Article IX, Section 6, clause (d), and Article IX, Section 5, such absences must be excused. Thus, the Union stated that there is no proper cause for either discharge under the contract.

Exhibit 1

Miscellaneous Contract Clauses

Article VII

MANAGEMENT RIGHTS

The Union hereby recognizes that there continue exclusively in the Company the traditional rights of management to manage the business and to direct the working forces, including, but not limited to, the rights to plan, direct, and control plant operations, to decide the operations or services to be performed in or at the plant by employees of the Company; to schedule the working hours; to hire, promote, demote and transfer employees; to suspend, demote, discipline or discharge employees for proper cause, or to relieve employees because of lack of work or for other legitimate reasons; to make and enforce reasonable shop rules and regulations not inconsistent with the provisions of this Agreement; to introduce new and improved production methods, materials, or facilities; or to change existing production methods, jobs, materials, or facilities; limited only by the express language of this Agreement and provided, however, that such rights shall not be applied to conflict with any express provisions of this Agreement.

Exhibit 1
(continued)

Article IX

HOURS OF WORK and OVERTIME

Section 1. The work week shall run from Monday through Sunday, inclusive, and it shall begin with the commencement of the first shift on Monday; the work day shall be the consecutive 24 hours beginning with the employee's schedule starting time.

Section 2. Insofar as production is needed, the normal working hours shall be eight per day, exclusive of a one-half hour unpaid lunch period, and shall be forty per week consisting of five consecutive work days. Nothing in this Agreement shall be construed as a guarantee of hours of work or pay, nor a right to pay for time not worked. Overtime or premium pay shall not be pyramided.

Section 3. The starting time for the day shift shall normally be 7:30 a.m. In the event that the Company deems it necessary to schedule a second shift, the starting time for said second shift shall normally be 4:00 p.m. Employees who are assigned to work a second shift and who are scheduled to commence work on or after 4:00 p.m. shall be paid a shift differential of fifteen cents (15¢) per hour for all hours worked on that shift.

Section 4. Overtime premium shall be paid as follows:

(a) For all hours worked in excess of eight (8) hours in any one work day - time and one-half (1½) times the employee's regular straight-time hourly rate.

(b) For all hours worked in excess of forty (40) hours in any one work week - time and one-half (1½) times the employee's regular straight-time hourly rate.

(c) For all hours worked on Saturday- two (2) times the employee's regular straight-time hourly rate.

(d) For all hours worked on Sunday- two and one-half (2½) times the employee's regular straight-time hourly rate.

Section 5. All employees are expected to work regularly (according to their work schedules) and on time. Excessive absenteeism or tardiness will be grounds for discipline; however, absences which have been excused in advanced for good reason shown or absences which are expressly recognized and condoned under this Collective Bargaining Agreement (such as Sick Leave, Leaves of Absence, Authorized Union Business Time, Funeral Leave, Holidays, Vacations, etc.) will not be charged against the employee.

Exhibit 1
(continued)

Section 6. The Company shall determine when overtime shall be worked and shall schedule such work. In the assignments of overtime, the following rules shall apply:

(a) The Company will divide overtime as equally as is feasible among qualified employees in each department.

(b) A refusal by an employee to accept an overtime assignment shall result in the employee being "charged" with such assignment for the purpose of equalization of overtime.

(c) It is recognized that because of the requirements of customers, it is not always possible for the Company to give advance notice to employees that overtime work will be necessary. The Company, however, agrees to use its best efforts to notify eachemployee required to work overtime at least two (2) hours prior to the end of the employee's work shift, and not later than 1:00 p.m. of the working day immediately preceding a Saturday, Sunday or holiday.

(d) Reasonable requests to be excused from overtime work will be honored; however, if because of this, there are not enough qualified employees among the remaining employees left to do the overtime work, then the lesser senior qualified employees in the department and on the shift involved shall be required to work the overtime, starting with the least senior of such employees.

(e) An employee offered overtime, and who refuses to work a reasonable amount of overtime, consonant with the business needs of the Company and after he has been given advance notice, may accordingly be disciplined by the Company.

Article X

GRIEVANCE PROCEDURE

Section 1. For the purposes of this Agreement, a grievance is defined as any dispute or difference of opinion between the Company and the Union or between the Company and any of its employees covered by this Agreement involving the meaning, interpretation or application of the provisions of this Agreement.

Section 2. The grievance procedure shall be the sole method by which said disputes or differences of opinion shall be resolved.

.....

Exhibit 1
(continued)

Section 5.

(a) Any employee who is discharged shall, upon his request, be granted an interview not to exceed forty-five (45) minutes, with his department Shop Steward before he is required to leave the plant. Upon request of the Shop Steward, the Company will furnish to said Steward a written statement of the reason for the discharge.

(b) If an employee believes he has been unjustly discharged, he shall reduce his grievance to writing and have it submitted to the Director of Personnel or his designated representative within five (5) days after he leaves the plant. Thereafter, if such grievance is not satisfactorily resolved, it may be appealed by the Union directly to arbitration.

Article XI

ARBITRATION

Section 1. Grievances which have been processed through the grievance procedure set forth in Article X of this Agreement, but which have not been settled in accordance with the terms of that Article, may be appealed by the Union to arbitration. In order to appeal a grievance to arbitration, the Union shall, within ten (10) working days after receipt of the Company's final answer, give written notice to the Director of Personnel of its desire to arbitrate.

.....

Section 4. The arbitrator shall have no right to amend, modify, nullify, ignore or add to the provisions of this Agreement. The arbitrator shall act in a judicial, not legislative, capacity, basing his decision on this Agreement and without amending, subtracting from, or changing this Agreement. His decision and award shall be based solely upon his interpretation of the meaning or application of the terms of this Agreement to the facts of the grievance presented. No liability shall accrue against the Company from a date prior to the date the grievance was presented, or in disciplinary cases, to the date of the discipline (and taking into consideration interim compensation and efforts by the aggrieved to mitigate damages). If the matter sought to be arbitrated does not involve an interpretation of the terms or provisions of this Agreement, the arbitrator shall so rule in his award and the matter shall not be further entertained by the arbitrator. The duly rendered award of the arbitrator shall be final and binding on the Company, the Union and the employee or employees involved.

ADELPHI COMPANY (A)

Frank Latta, President of Adelphi Company, was concerned with the company's loss of market share and a trend of steadily declining profits. After interviewing a number of management consultants Frank decided to hire Professor Darcey Coyle of the Hartford Graduate Center to assist management in determining why the company had become less competitive. Frank also asked Professor Coyle to evaluate any recommendations which would improve Adelphi's performance.

Adelphi Company, located in western Connecticut, employed 1,200 employees to manufacture a line of semi-durable products which was sold to other industrial firms. During the last three years the company had experienced a gradual increase in sales but a decrease in profits while employment had remained fairly constant. Last year the company reported annual sales of $60 million (a record) with a net profit-before-taxes of $1.6 million.

In his initial meeting with Professor Coyle, President Latta described Adelphi's situation and expressed his concerns.

> Darcey, four years ago the total market for our products was about $200 million and Adelphi had 25% of it. Today the market is $300 million and we've got 20% of it. So, in spite of increasing sales, we're getting a decreasing share of the market. That makes our sales peak sound a bit less impressive, doesn't it? Yet to retain this declining portion of a growing market, it has been necessary for us to hold our selling prices almost constant while our costs for raw materials, wages and other expenses have been rising constantly. At the same time, our major competitors are meeting and often beating our prices and delivery terms.
>
> Our competitors are all publicly held firms, and from what I've seen of their financial statements, they all seem to be doing better than Adelphi.
>
> It looks to me as if our overall wage costs are out of line. On the other hand, our average hourly wage rate of $7.00 is close to the average for the industry and I feel our people are good workers. However, we seem to get less output per dollar of wages than our competitors. For some time we have been averaging five hours of overtime per worker per week.
>
> Maybe Adelphi just needs better first-line supervision and tighter scheduling. I think the salaries we pay our foremen and general foremen are competitive, $16,000 and $20,000 per year, respectively, but I'm not sure of the competition. I do know we pay our division managers competitively. Last year we hired a new manager, Bruce Moore, for $36,000 per year. By the way, you might wish to start your investigation by talking with some of our

> division managers. I'd suggest you spend some time with Bruce and get to know his operations.

Professor Coyle followed the president's advice and arranged a meeting with Bruce Moore. The initial meeting went well and Bruce agreed to spend time with Darcey over the next few months explaining his operations and allowing the consultant to observe his various activities.

Bruce Moore was 35 years old and the Manager of Division E, one of nine Adelphi manufacturing divisions. Moore took charge of Division E and its 110 employees about ten months ago when he came to Adelphi. Before joining Adelphi, he was production control manager of an electronics firm in Springfield, Massachusetts. During one of their conversations Bruce told Professor Coyle about his ideas regarding Work Sampling techniques and his desire to get his supervisors interested.

> A little over two months ago I brought up the idea at one of our division meetings, and I had the feeling that the supervisors were afraid that I was trying a gimmick that could be used as a club over them.
>
> For that reason I told them I would be a guinea pig and have a Work Sampling study made of myself. I wanted to show them that it really didn't hurt. Of course, I didn't expect to learn much by studing my own activities, but I thought the test would demonstrate the simplicity and usefullness of the Work Sampling technique.
>
> So, the next day I asked my secretary, Louise Pierce, to make up 480 small, separate slips of paper. On each slip of paper was typed a time. The time on the first slip was 8:01 a.m.; the second slip, 8:02 a.m.; the third 8:03; and so on to the 240th slip which was marked 12:00 noon. Then she slipped to 1:01 p.m. for the 241st slip and continued for each minute of the afternoon to 5:00 p.m. for the 480th slip. These times correspond to my theoretical working hours during the day. I eliminated the period between noon and 1:00 p.m., because I'm often at lunch then. Of course, this doesn't cover my work after 5:00 p.m. which is a fairly normal occurrence. However, I thought the regular working hours would be good enough for the demonstration. Then Louise folded each of the 480 slips and put them into a carboard box.
>
> Frank Mather and Joe Hanson are the two supervisors who report directly to me. Since I wanted to sell them on the plan, I decided to try to get them involved and interested. On Friday, Frank, Joe, Louise and I got together in my office. I showed them the cardboard box. I shook it to mix up the slips, and then asked them to help me in drawing out time slips for ten samples per day for the first week of the study.
>
> Joe is an ex-screw machine operator in his mid-forties and he reacts fast. "Do you mean that you called us in here to help you pull fifty pieces of paper out of a cardboard box? That's funny, real funny. What are you trying

to prove?"

Joe has seen right through my little game--and it irritated me. I told him, "I thought four heads might be better than one, but maybe you don't have anything to contribute."

Frank stepped in at that point, probably to save my red face.

"Aw, come on," he said. "It won't take long if we don't yak about it. I'll draw the ten slips for the first day."

Frank reached into the box and counted out ten slips.

I said, "Okay, now unfold them and arrange them in sequence, the earliest time first."

When he finished, I copied the times. They were 8:02, 8:53, 9:23, 9:41, 11:34, 1:10, 1:15, 3:56, 4:00, and 4:35.

I refolded the slips and tossed them back into the box.

Then it was Joe's turn and he grudgingly picked out ten slips. When they were arranged in order, the times for the second day were: 10:31, 10:54, 11:08, 1:48, 2:15, 2:27, 3:03, 3:16, 3:26, and 4:26.

We went on with the drawing for Wednesday, Thursday, and Friday. As I copied down the last figures, Joe asked, "Why go through all this? Why not just do a ckeck every hour on the half-hour or something? And why put back the slips after the draw for every day?"

Well, that was a break, because Joe was getting interested--at least a little bit--and I got a chance to say something about random sampling versus stratified sampling.

I turned to Louise and gave her the listing of ten times a day for the entire week. She looked a little startled when I told her that the study would start on the following Monday and that she would handle it. I pointed out that the first time for Monday was 8:02 a.m., the second time was 8:53 a.m., and so on. I said, "At exactly 8:02 a.m., I want you to find out what I am doing and write it down. You do the same thing at 8:53 a.m., and at each of the ten times during the day. On Tuesday, you do the same thing with the new list of times. At each of the times, if I'm not in sight, telephone me; if you can't get me on the telephone, page me over the P.A. system. Keep trying until you get me."

Joe started laughing. He said, "I'll bet there will be a few times that you'll say that your activities are miscellaneous."

Louise was worried. She asked, "What if I miss a time? I _do_ have _other_ work, you know, so it would be easy to miss one."

Right then and there, I took off my wrist alarm watch, handed it to her, and told her to get use to it over the weekend. I told her that after each check on me, she could set the alarm to the time listed for the next sampling.

> For the first few days of the study, Louise had a lot of questions. I took quite a ribbing, especially from my own supervisors. I thought, "Fine, at least they are interested enough to make cracks about it."
>
> Even the president, Mr. Latta, said he'd heard some rumors and asked what I was up to. When I said that I hoped Work Sampling could show me what some of our problems were, he said, "By now you ought to know what your problems are and start getting rid of them. This Work Sampling sounds like a waste of valuable time. And you say this study of yourself is a demonstration? A demonstration of what?"
>
> I must have looked shocked because after that outburst, Mr. Latta smiled, put his hand on my arm and said, "All right, study yourself. Study your navel for all I care. But get the work done."
>
> Remember, Darcey, I started this study on myself to get things rolling, it wasn't supposed to prove anything. But something interesting has developed.
>
> We took a total of 50 samples a week, 10 samples per day, right? Well, in Week Number One, I was caught twelve times in third-step grievance meetings. Think that's bad? Let's get the list out for the seven weeks of the study. Here we are. Out of 50 samples for each week, I was tied up in third-step grievance meeting as follows:
>
> Week 1 - 12 times
> 2 - 24 times
> 3 - 10 times
> 4 - 17 times
> 5 - 8 times
> 6 - 21 times
> 7 - 13 times
>
> That's a total of 105 times out of 350 samples in seven weeks that I was checked off as being in grievance meetings. That's 30%. According to the arithmetic of Work Sampling, that's not just an accident.

Bruce showed Professor Coyle a copy of the grievance procedure and arbitration language from Adelphi's collective bargaining agreement (see Exhibit 1). He went on to explain that grievance meetings were held on company time. Although Bruce had no record of first step activity, he was aware that of the grievances reduced to writing, few were settled in Step Two of the procedure. Also, the amount of time required to hear a grievance in the second step was about the same as the time required in the third step of the procedure.

After briefly discussing the results of the work sampling, Professor Coyle suggested that he and Bruce independently attempt to determine the costs attributable to the processing of grievances at Division E. Bruce agreed and furnished Darcey with the following annual salaries—Assistant Division Manager—$26,000; Personnel Representative--$20,000. Bruce told Darcey that his

(Bruce's) secretary also took notes at third step meetings and her salary was $14,000 per year.

Bruce Moore and Darcey Coyle agreed that, prior to their next meeting, each would prepare an estimate of the costs of grievances and a list of recommendations concerning these costs. They would devote their next meeting to comparing their cost estimates and evaluating their respective recommendations.

Exhibit 1

Article XIII
GRIEVANCE PROCEDURE

Sec. 1. Complaints and grievances arising between an employee or group of employees and the Company shall be disposed of as follows:

Sec. 2. STEP ONE: The aggrieved employee shall take the grievance to his foreman within five (5) work days after the circumstances giving rise to the grievance first occurred. The foreman shall give his answer to the employee within three (3) work days.

STEP TWO: If the grievance is not settled in STEP ONE, it shall be reduced to writing, signed by the employee and his Union steward and presented to the foreman within three (3) work days. The foreman shall add his answer to the grievance and forward it to the general foreman with a copy to the Union. Within five (5) work days, a meeting between the aggrieved employee, his Union steward, the department foreman, and the general foreman will be held to resolve the grievance. The general foreman will give his answer within five (5) work days from the conclusion of the meeting.

STEP THREE: If the grievance is not settled in STEP TWO, it may be presented to the Division Manager or his designated representative within five (5) work days from receipt of STEP TWO answer. A meeting between Company officials--Division Manager, Assistant Division Manager, Personnel Representative, General Foreman, and Department Foreman--and Union representatives--two Union Executive Committee Members, the Steward and the grievant--will be held within ten (10) work days after receipt of appeal. Within five (5) work days following this meeting, the Division Manager will give his answer to the Union.

Sec. 3. A grievance must be referred to the next step as provided above or it will be considered settled on the basis of the last answer given. If a grievance is not answered by the Company within the time limits above stated, it shall be considered granted.

Exhibit 1
(continued)

Article XIV
ARBITRATION

Sec. 1. If a grievance involving the interpretation and application of a specific provision of this Agreement has not been settled after being fully processed through the grievance procedure set forth above, then the Union may submit such grievance to arbitration by giving written notice thereof to the Company not later than two (2) weeks after the completion of STEP THREE. The grievance shall be considered as having settled in STEP THREE unless it is so submitted to arbitration within such time limit. No questions relating to arbitrability shall be subject to arbitration hereunder.

Sec. 2. The choice of the arbitrator shall be by agreement of the parties. However, if such agreement has not been reached within one (1) week after the receipt of such written notice submitting the grievance to arbitration, the grievance may be referred by the Union to the American Arbitration Association for the selection of an arbitrator in accordance with the rules, then obtaining, of said Association applicable to labor arbitrations. Any arbitration hereunder shall be conducted in accordance with such rules, subject to the provisions of this Agreement. The parties shall share equally in the compensation and expenses of the arbitrator. The award of the arbitrator on any grievance properly submitted to him hereunder shall be final and binding upon the parties.

Sec. 3. Each grievance shall be separately processed in any arbitration proceeding under this Article.

Sec. 4. There shall be no right to arbitration to obtain, and no arbitrator shall have any power to award or determine, any change in, modification or alteration of, addition to, or subtraction from, any of the terms of this Agreement.

TARBO LUMBER COMPANY

On the afternoon of April 11, Robert Murray, Vice-President of Personnel for Tarbo Lumber Company, sat back in his chair to reflect on his meeting earlier that day with the representatives of the International Brotherhood of Woodworkers (IBW). Two grievances submitted by the IBW had been discussed at length; the first concerned work done by less senior employees when more senior men were on layoff; the second dealt with the efforts of an older carpenter to transfer to a lower grade, less demanding job. Union representative Thomas Gleason had threatened to take one or both cases to arbitration, if the company did not offer "a fair settlement." (See Paragraphs 131 and 132 in Exhibit 1).

1. INSIDE WORK BY THREE DRIVERS

Background

Tarbo was a distributor of building materials for local contractors and building supply retailers in a large metropolitan area. Some of the doors, windows, and other accessories were shaped, assembled and glazed by the company, but much of the material was sold in the same form in which it was received. The company maintained a large warehouse where its merchandise was stored and from which it was shipped to its customers in its own trucks. It had 18 trucks, 13 of which required a Class II license to operate and 5 of which were "straight jobs" which required only a Class I license, the ordinary kind. By custom, these five vehicles were given to the drivers with the most seniority. The company regularly scheduled 17 trips on Thursdays and Fridays, 16 on Tuesdays and Wednesdays, and 14 on Mondays. When business was good, two trucks were often needed for one scheduled trip.

The chauffeurs who drove the trucks were in the same department as the other warehouse employees. The warehouse jobs and their corresponding hourly rates were as follows:

Dispatcher	$8.06	Checker	$7.52
Office Shipper	8.06	Forklift	7.32
Shipper	7.52	General Help	7.02
Stockman	7.52	Porter	6.68
Chauffeur	7.52	Watchman	6.54

When the chauffeurs were not driving, they did the same work as general helpers in the warehouse, e.g. unloading trucks, filling orders, and so on. When the chauffeurs performed these "inside" jobs they continued to receive their usual rate.

For many years the company had carried only one spare driver. However, three years ago it decided that it should operate with 18 regular drivers and 2 spares. But last summer when the superintendent was sick for several months, the company had a total of only 18 drivers, including the spares. With this number it had difficulty making all of its deliveries; because of vacations and absences some trips were actually missed.

A number of the men who now worked jobs in the warehouse had been drivers for the company in the past, and had bid into the "inside" jobs when their seniority enabled them to do so. Several of these retained their Class II licenses which permitted them to operate the large trailer trucks. When Bill Mooney, department foreman, who had worked his way up from general helper and had been a driver for a number of years, got into a particularly tight spot, he prevailed upon some of his old friends to drive for a day or two at their regular rate. However, the "inside" men objected to being transferred to "the street" even temporarily and generally they did not perform well when asked to do so. An increasing number of them avoided the possibility of temporary transfers to driving by failing to keep their Class II licenses. For renewal of a Class II license one had to take an annual physical examination.

The superintendent returned to work on August 11 of last summer; two weeks later the company posted openings for two spare chauffeurs. In the past, drivers' jobs had been filled by bids from warehouse employees in lower paying jobs, but this time none of them bid for the open positions. As a result, the company went to the open market and hired an experienced driver, Buzz Meyer. In December the company lost two of its drivers and it posted another notice in the warehouse, but no bids were received. Concerned by this the management announced that the company would put anyone who wanted to drive in a one-month training program, but none of the employees volunteered. The company again went to the outside and hired two experienced drivers, Joe Brennan and Moe Reese. With the acquisition of these two men, the company had 19 drives, including one spare.

In February, Pete Moss, the union steward for the drivers, asked the superintendent, Matthew Cook, when another spare driver would be hired. Cook replied that he would do it as soon as he had completed preparations for the summer vacations (see Paragraph 40 of Exhibit 1).

In March the volume of business declined and the company decided to reduce its work force. With less material entering and leaving the warehouse, fewer workers were needed to unload and sort the incoming shipments and to load all outgoing trucks. However, the number of delivery trips per week did not decrease, although the average trip was lighter. In fact, with business slack, the customers expected the service to be better than in prosperous times. In accord with the management decision, the following notice was posted:

> <u>To Warehouse Employees:</u>
>
> We regret to announce that the Company finds it necessary to reduce its work force at once.
>
> Accordingly, on March 13, the Company will layoff nine men from the Warehouse. Inasmuch as three of the men hold a classification of Chauffeur, we shall post a notice of job vacancies for chauffeurs as per Paragraph III of the Union Contract and will temporarily rehire these three on March 16 pending final selection of qualified employees from within the working force of the warehouse department. If there are no qualified applicants for these

> vacancies, we shall retain these men as chauffeurs during the duration of the layoff.
>
> The Company anticipates that further cutbacks will not be necessary. While the duration of the layoff depends on general conditions, the Comapny is hopeful that it may be able to recall all personnel no later than the beginning of the summer vacation season.

Accordingly, the nine men with the least departmental seniority were laid off (see Exhibit 2).

On Monday, March 16, the company posted the following job openings notice:

> There are openings for two (2) chauffeurs and one (1) spare chauffeur. Any qualified man in the warehouse having a Class II license may apply in writing. Please get the application from Matthew Cook.

Six of the men still employed in the warehouse had been drivers for Tarbo, but none of them bid for the three jobs. Instead, four others bid: Dennis Ahern, who had not been laid off and who had a Class II license and three year's driving experience with a previous employer, Meyer, Brennan, and Reese. The jobs were given to the first three.

On March 24, Dowling, Hunter, and Leonard, who had been laid off filed a grievance, alleging that the company had denied them their seniority rights. In particular they said:

> Junior men have filled the vacancy of senior men on layoff from March 21 in the warehouse. This action by the company violates Article XI, Seniority, of the Labor Agreement. We request that we be returned from layoff and compensated for all lost pay.

The grievants pointed out that Meyer and Brennan were spending part of their time doing the same kind of work that they had done in the warehouse before they were furloughed.

On April 3 the company posted a bid for an additional spare driver. Reese, the lowest man on the seniority list, was the only bidder; he had a Class II license and had had several years' driving experience before coming to the company. This brought the number of drivers and spares to 20.

Discussion of the Grievance

Attempts by the company and the union to settle the grievance informally were not successful, and so the union asked that it be place on the agenda for a formal grievance meeting which was scheduled for April 11. Representing the union for this grievance at the meeting were: Thomas Gleason, International Representative; Al Arens, Local President; Peter Moss, Steward for the drivers; Bill Wolsey, Steward for the "inside" warehouse employees; and the three grievants. Representing the company were Robert Murray, Vice President for Personnel; Matthew Cook, Plant Superintendent; and Bill Mooney, the Warehouse Foreman.

Murray: We have your grievance about the layoffs in the warehouse, but we don't agree with it. In fact, we don't understand why these men are grieving.

Gleason: Well, you are violating the seniority clause of the contract by having Meyer, Brennan, and Reese do the general helpers' work when these three senior men, Dowling, Hunter, and Leonard, are on layoff. Look at the contract language, (Gleason read Paragraph 110 of Exhibit 1.) Now, in this case, I'm sure you'll agree that Dowling, Hunter, and Leonard have more seniority than Meyer, Brennan, and Reese. I'm sure that you'll also agree that Dowling, Hunter, and Leonard can do the warehouse work. They were doing it just before they were laid off. Yet these three senior men are now out of work and the very same type of work which they did is being done now by men with less seniority. In effect, you have denied them their seniority rights.

Cook: We haven't really denied anyone their seniority rights, Tom. Meyer, Brennan, and Reese are working because they're chauffeurs. We dropped nine guys from the warehouse, and we followed seniority exactly.

Gleason: We admit that you followed seniority in the original layoff, and we're not arguing about that. What we are arguing about is that after laying off nine you turned around and violated the contract by putting guys with less seniority back doing work in the warehouse jobs that had been done by men with more seniority.

Cook: Look, Tom. We need drivers. We posted the job openings for drivers as the contract provides. Dowling and the others had a chance to bid on those jobs. But they didn't. And we took the guys who were willing and able to drive.

Gleason: OK, but there is a hooker here. They did not have Class II licenses.

Cook: We offered to put people into a training program and the offer still stands. They can learn to handle one of the big rigs.

Gleason: You're asking for miracles. Driving one of those things is tough work, even when you are used to it. What you could have done was switch drivers around. Take three of the guys with II licenses off the small trucks. Then put Dowling and the boys on the small ones; all they need for them are Class I license, which they have already.

Cook: That is not the way we have been working it. The small trucks go to the five most senior drivers. That has been a practice for a long time. You know if we changed that we have plenty of complaints from the other drivers.

Gleason: Look, there are half a dozen "inside" men who have Class II licenses. You don't have to have all these low seniority men driving trucks. You can move some of the insiders onto the trucks as they're needed. You're always telling us about your right to move people around. What is it? The management's rights clause that you forced us into (Paragraph 64 of Exhibit 1) lets you do it. Why are you ignoring it now?

Mooney: We'd have even more problems if we started forcing people to drive when they don't want to. I have enough trouble when I try to get someone to fill in for just one or two days. And, when we have transferred people back to driving regularly, it hasn't worked out. They don't want to do it. They call in sick or they screw up orders. They just don't get the job done. It causes us more headaches than it's worth. We'd rather have people who are willing to drive.

Gleason: What you are really saying is that you don't want to bite the bullet and do what you have to do. And, so these three senior men have to sit on their hands with no pay while three junior men perform their work. That's not fair and you know it. It violates the basic principle of the seniority clause.

Cook: Now let's get something straight. In the first place we have the right to temporarily use people in various jobs. When drivers are not on the street, they are helping out in the warehouse. This is the quid pro quo of the work guarantee. (See Paragraph 22 of Exhibit 1.) We can guarantee 40 hours a week only if we can shift people around as the need arises.

Gleason: That's exactly our point, Matt. You do have the right to move people around to fill in. So you didn't have to hire all these new drivers. You got along with two spares for a long time by using the "inside" men who could drive when emergencies arose. If you did that now, these three senior men would be doing the warehouse work instead of these extra new drivers.

Cook: We have always had the practice of putting drivers to work in the warehouse, when they weren't pushing a rig. Things are no different now than they were a year ago. Take Meyer, for example, he still spends 60% of his time on the truck.

Gleason: How about Brennan?

Cook: He's on the street 60% of the time.

Gleason: And Reese?

Cook: A little less than 50% of his time is spent on the truck.

Gleason: So the lowest man on the seniority list spends more than half of his time in the warehouse doing the same work as these three senior men used to do.

Cook: You seem to forget two things. First, prior to last summer we had 18 regulars and 2 spares. So having two spares is not unusual. Second, your own steward requested a second driver, and now we have responded to that request. We said that we would get a second spare before the vacation period and we did. You guys cannot have your cake and eat it too!

Moss: Sure, I bugged you about adding another spare driver, but that was way back in February, when there was more than enough work for everybody. We don't want new spare drivers in our group if it causes senior "inside" men to lose their jobs. Some of those "inside" men with Class II licenses can fill in. In the warehouse we've never objected to that.

Dowling: Look here! Reese is doing exactly the same work that I did, yet he is the lowest man on the seniority list. Brennan and Meyer are spending a lot of their time doing what I did before the layoff.

Cook: But we gave all three of you the chance to learn to drive a truck and none of you wanted to do it. We agree that the seniority rights of the workers are important, but we must have the flexibility to run the company efficiently. Otherwise, we'll all be looking for new jobs.

Gleason: We've gone a long way to help you with efficiency around here, but there has to be a limit somewhere. We cannot allow you to lay off men who have been here for two years while newcomers are doing their work. The seniority clause has to mean something. That's what the contract is all about, and we're going to see to it that it's lived up to.

Murray: Is there anything else you want to add?

Gleason: One final word. If Dowling, Hunter and Leonard are not put back to work and paid for the time they lost, we are going to arbitration. Seniority is one of the basic rights of the employees, and we are not going to stand by idly while you take it away from them.

Murray: OK, I guess we've covered that one. We'll give our answer as soon as we've had a chance to review it again.

2. BIDDING DOWN BY A CARPENTER A

Background

The Tarbo Company served as wholesaler for several nationally advertised door and window frames. In addition, the company assembled regular size door and window frames which it sold under its own trade name. As a service for its customers the company also cut and assembled special size doors and window frames.

Because of the higher profit margins on its own brand name regular-size frames, the company decided to expand its marketing effort on these items. A special sales promotion program was developed, which by February had paid off in a considerably increased demand for these products. As a result it was necessary for the company to increase production which required an increase in the number of assembler jobs. On February 4, three Assembler A jobs were posted for bid.

Only three bids were received for the new assembler jobs, two from Assembler B employees and one from James Lewis, who held the classification of Carpenter A and worked on the custom frames. The rates of the different classifications were:

Carpenter A	$8.80
Assembler A	8.20
Assembler B	7.80

The seniority of the three bidders was:

James Lewis	-	37 years and 8 months
William Brundon	-	4 years and 1 month
Timothy Leary	-	3 years and 3 months

Management accepted the bids of the two general helpers but refused to consider Lewis' bid. Instead it hired a new man for the third job and continued Lewis as a Carpenter A in the custom frames area.

On February 10, Lewis filed the following grievance:

> The Company violated Paragraph 110 of Article XI of the Contract by refusing my bid for the Assembler job and hiring a man from the outside for it. (See Exhibit 1 for Paragraph 110 of the Contract.)

Discussion of the Grievance

Attempts to settle the grievance in the informal stage of the procedure were not successful so the union asked that it be placed on the agenda for the April 11 meeting. Representing the union at the meeting for this grievance were: Thomas Gleason, International Representative; Al Arens, President of the Local; Dennis Dillon, Steward of the Carpenter Shop; and James Lewis, the grievant. Representing the company were Robert Murray, Vice President of Personnel; Matthew Cook, Plant Superintendent; and John Weber, Foreman of the Carpenter Shop. The discussion of the grievance follows.

Gleason: The second and last item on our agenda for today is James Lewis' grievance. I've looked into this one and I don't think the company has a leg to stand on. Paragraph 110 clearly says, "Department seniority shall apply to the filling of all job vacancies provided that the employee has the qualifications to perform the job." Now certainly Brother Lewis has the seniority. How long have you been working here, Jim?

Lewis: Over 37 years and all that time in the Carpenter Shop.

Gleason: So you give these jobs to two helpers who have over 30 years less seniority than Jim and then you go out and hire a man who has no seniority at all. This just doesn't make sense. I'm sure you people don't claim that Jim can't do the job as well or better than the other three men. After all, you're paying him as a Carpenter A now. Jim, how long have you been a carpenter?

Lewis: All together, about 20 years. I've been on it steady for the past 15 years. There was a year or two before that when work was slack that I had to go back to assembler work.

Gleason: So you've actually done the assembler job in the past?

Lewis: Oh, yes. I worked on it for a number of years before I bid on the carpenter job, and then, as I said, when work got scarce some years ago I was transferred back to it.

Gleason: Did the company ever complain about your work as an assembler?

Lewis: Oh, no. Pat Gallagher, the foreman then, said my work was very good and suggested I bid for the carpenter job.

Gleason: Jim, the assembler job pays less money than the carpenter job. Do you want to tell us why you want it?

Lewis: Well, it's a lot easier job. On the custom work most of the frames are bigger and heavier. We have to move them around. Some of them are really heavy. Then we have to carry the power tools all around and they're heavy too. There's a lot more moving around and carrying things than over in assembly. Over there you can sit down and work a lot more of the time. It's a lot nicer place to work, too. The Custom Shop is on the north side near the big doors and in the winter it's drafty and cold. There's a lot of dust in the air too, because of the sawing. Well, I'm over 60 now and I don't need the extra money so I'd rather have the easier job.

Gleason: That's our case, Bob, and I don't see how you can sit there and say you're not violating the Contract by refusing Lewis' bid.

Murray: Well, you obviously overlooked Paragraph 112 of the Contract (see Exhibit 1). That last sentence was added in the negotiations before the last one to protect management's investment in the training and development of its employees. We get a man like Jim Lewis who comes in here as a helper with no training at all. So, the company spends a lot of time and money training and developing him and we move him up the line from helper to Assembler B to Assembler A to Carpenter B to Carpenter A. At each stage he becomes more valuable to us because he can do more. We have to protect that investment in him. And that's why we put that last sentence into the Contract. We can't afford to have these guys moving into lower rated jobs.

Gleason: Your idea of Paragraph 112 is sure different than what we had in mind in the union when we agreed to it. I took part in those negotiations and it was our idea that we didn't want men using their seniority to bump across departments and job progressions. In this case, Lewis is in the same department and the same job progression.

Murray: I agree it was partly for the purpose you say, Tom, but it was also to protect our investment in training men for the higher job. At least that's the way we understood and that's what the language says. It definitely states that a man assigned to a <u>lower paying job</u> shall have preference. And that's the way we've interpreted it for five years now. We went over the files and I have six cases here where we refused to permit a higher-paid man to take a lower-paying job, even though he was the senior bidder. In not one of these was a grievance filed.

Gleason: We'd like some time to look these over. (A short recess was held while the union representatives examined the six files after which Gleason resumed.) Well, we think Lewis' case is different than any of these six. In each one of them a lower-paid man in the job progression was bidding for the job. In this case there was no lower-paid man bidding for it. You went outside and brought a man in from the street rather than give the job to Lewis. I don't see how you can read that into the last sentence of Paragraph 112. Certainly, Lewis ought to have preference over outsiders. Paragraph 110 says seniority will prevail in case of promotions and Lewis had 30 years of it compared with none for the man you gave the job to.

Murray: I was in the negotiations too. In fact, I wrote and the company proposed Paragraph 112, and our purpose in getting it in the Contract was to protect us from the loss of our investment in the training and experience of higher rated employees. That was the purpose of it and these six cases show that the practice has been not to permit employees to bid down. To permit Lewis to do it now, would create a precedent we just couldn't live with.

Gleason: Well, I guess we've said all we have to say on this one except I can tell you that unless the company changes its position, Bob, it goes to arbitration.

Murray: OK, we'll give you our answer in a few days.

Exhibit 1

Pertinent Contract Clauses

Article II, Hours

Paragraph 22. Any employee who reports for work shall be guaranteed a minimum of eight (8) hours work each day; and all employees are hereby guaranteed a minimum of forty (40) hours work or pay in any weekly payroll period, however, this clause will not apply to a stoppage of work beyond the Employer's control; such as a hurricane, wind or fire or any Act of God.

Article IV, Vacations

Paragraph 40. The vacation period for summer vacations during the term of this agreement shall be from June 1 to September 30. The vacation period for winter vacations during the term of this Agreement shall be from January 1 to March 31.

Article VI, Miscellaneous

Paragraph 63. It is the intention of the parties hereto that the operation of the plant shall continue as heretofore, except as abridged by the Agreement, and all employees covered by this agreement may be temporarily transferred from one department to another at the discretion of the Employer.

Paragraph 64. It is agreed that the Employer has retained the usual management rights and that the right to manage the Employer's business and direct the working force is vested exclusively in the management of the Employer, which right shall include, but shall not be limited to, the right (except insofar as limited herein) to suspend, discharge, or otherwise discipline for just cause; to transfer or lay off because of lack of work or for other legitimate reasons; to plan, direct and control its operations; and to change methods, processes, equipment or facilities; provided, however, that this will not be used for the purpose of discrimination against any employee or to avoid any of the provisions of this Agreement or the obligation to bargain collectively concerning changed wages, hours or working conditions.

Exhibit 1
(continued)

Article XI, Seniority

Paragraph 110. The rule of departmental seniority shall prevail. In the event work becomes temporary or seasonally slack and it is necessary to reduce the work force, in laying off men and putting them back to work, departmental seniority or length of last continuous service shall be followed. Departmental seniority shall apply to the filling of all vacancies provided the employee has the ability and qualifications to perform the job. If no employee in the department requests or qualifies for the job, the Company retains the right to hire new personnel to fill the job. If the Employer and the Union are unable to agree on the ability and qualifications of the employee to perform the job, the dispute shall be submitted to arbitration in accordance with the Arbitration Clause of this Agreement.

Paragraph 111. Notice of a job vacancy, whether by reason of management's decision to replace an employee whose employment has been terminated or to create a new job, shall be posted by the Employer on the bulletin board within seven (7) days after such decision and shall remain posted for a period of two (2) weeks, but the Employer may fill such vacancies or new positions immediately pending final selection of an applicant. The job shall be awarded, if a qualified employee in the department has applied for it, within three (3) weeks from the date the job is posted. Any employee in the department desiring to fill any such posted vacancy or new position shall make application in writing.

Paragraph 112. Permanent vacancies are normally filled by promotion in the line of progression on job sequence within a department. The most senior qualified applicant who is permanently assigned to a lower-pay job classification within the department shall have first preference for the opening.

Article XIII, Disputes

Paragraph 130. The Union and the Employer agree that the terms and conditions of this Agreement shall be binding upon all the employees in the bargaining unit and upon the Employer and that except as provided in this Article neither the Union, its agents nor the employees shall directly or indirectly initiate or participate in any strike, stoppage of work, slow-down or curtailment of plant work or of any other Company work and that the Employer agrees that there shall be no lockout during the adjustment of any controversy concerning a violation of any terms of this Agreement.

Exhibit 1
(continued)

Paragraph 131. Should any difference arise between the Employer and the Union or any employee of the Employer which is not adjusted between the employee and his foreman, the employee shall submit his grievance in writing to the Plant Superintendent on a form furnished by the Employer. A representative of the Union shall meet promptly with a representative of the Employer to discuss the grievance and endeavor to work out a satisfactory settlement.

Paragraph 132. If the representative of the Union and the representative of the Employer are unable to settle the grievance in the manner provided in Paragraph 131 within thirty (30) days, the grievance may be submitted to arbitration in accordance with the procedure prescribed in this Article. The request for arbitration may be made by the Union or by the Employer by notification in writing to the other Party within five (5) working days after the final meeting between the representative of the Union and the representative of the Employer as provided in Paragraph 131. Within ten (10) working days after said notification the Party requesting arbitration shall execute and mail a written request to the Federal Mediation and Conciliation Service, Washington, D.C. 20260 for the appointment of an arbitrator, a copy of which shall be simultaneously mailed to the other Party unless during the said ten (10) day period the Union and the Employer mutually agree upon an arbitrator. The request for arbitration shall state the known facts concerning the alleged grievance and the remedy or the relief sought by the Party requesting arbitration.

Paragraph 133. The authority of the arbitrator shall be limited to the question or questions which are submitted. The arbitrator shall be bound by the provisions of this Agreement and he shall not have any authority to establish wage rates nor to add to, subtract from, modify or otherwise change any of the terms or provisions of this Agreement including but not limited to the schedule of wages as provided in Article X. The arbitrator shall mail his decision in writing to the Union and to the Employer within fifteen (15) days after the final submission. The decision by the arbitrator shall be final and conclusively binding upon the Employer, the Union and the aggrieved employee. The expense of the arbitrator and of the arbitration hearing shall be shared equally by the Employer and by the Union.

Exhibit 2

Warehouse Department Seniority List as of March 1

Name	Job	Name	Job	Job Designations	
Hoyt	D	Lehman	Ch	C	Checker
Flynn	OS	Wright	Ch	Ch	Chauffeur
Carpenter	OS	Kessel	Ch	D	Dispatcher
Hendley #	S	Sanderson	Ch	F	Fork lift
Souza	S	Ronan	F	GH	Gen. Help
Woods	S	Wells	F	OS	Off. Shipper
Babcock	S	Morris	F	P	Porter
Lounsbury	St	Madigan	F	S	Shipper
Ryan	St	Bellhamer	F	St	Stockman
Northrop	St	Tremblay	GH	W	Watchman
McKenna	St	Dennahey	GH		
Vasseur	St	Kemper	GH		
Kelly #	St	DelDotto	GH		
Glardo	St	Donohoe	GH		
Harold #	St	Russell	GH		
Oliver	St	Ahern	GH		
Hammond #	St	White	GH		
Artley	St	Thompson	GH		
Dineen	St	Imhoff	GH		
Donovan	St	Rizzo	W		
Lynch	C	LaNassa	GH		
Levitt #	C	Madill	GH		
Arvey	C	Ryan	GH		
Dolan	C	LaRosa	W		
Morgan	C	Beals	GH		
Campbell #	F	Hanley	GH		
Dowd	Ch	Manhoney	P		
Bradley	Ch	Stevenson	GH		
Aiken	Ch	Brown	GH		
Moss	Ch	Twisser	W		
Murphy	Ch	Rubino	GH		
Chisolm	Ch	Villiani	GH		
Edwards	Ch	Dowling	GH		
Richards	F	Hunter	GH		
Schultz	Ch	Leonard	GH		
Benvenuto	W	LeBrun	GH		
Alves	F	Meyer	Ch		
Cody	Ch	Dewey	P		
Libens	Ch	Brennan	Ch		
Harvey	Ch	Alberts	GH		
Arenella	Ch	Reese	Ch		

# Indicates employees with Class II licenses who are not chauffeurs.

GROTON CHEMICAL COMPANY (A)

On August 22, 1977 the following grievance was presented to the supervisor in the maintenance department:

> I contend that the company is wrong in not awarding me the No. 2 mechanic-carpenter job. I further contend that I'm the senior bidder and have the qualifications for the job. I have worked as No. 2 mechanic-carpenter in construction for a number of years.
>
> /s/ William W. Fite

The mechanic classification at the Groton Chemical Company covered a variety of skills such as mechanic-electrician, mechanic-painter and mechanic-carpenter. Each mechanic skill classification was divided into three levels depending upon the amount of skill required. Thus, a carpenter might be rated as a mechanic-carpenter No. 1, mechanic-carpenter No. 2 or mechanic-carpenter No. 3.

The mechanic-carpenter No. 1, which was the highest carpenter classification, required that a worker be able to read blueprints, lay out his or her own work, do his or her work with a minimum of supervision or, when necessary, direct the work of No. 2 and No. 3 carpenters.

The No. 2 carpenter worked under supervision, was given specific instruction, and only rarely was he or she required to work alone. The No. 2 carpenter was expected to exhibit some skill and ability in the use of carpenter tools.

The No. 3 position represented, for the most part, beginners in the craft. Workers in this classification had to exhibit only rough skill and ability in the use of carpenter tools, and they always worked under supervision with specific instructions. Most employees who did carpenter work started in this classification and were advanced as they exhibited greater skill. The relative skill difference between the No. 2 and No. 3 positions, however, was not as great as the difference between the No. 1 and the No. 2 positions.

The hourly rates paid the three positions were as follows:

Mechanic-carpenter No. 1	$6.67
Mechanic-carpenter No. 2	$6.38
Mechanic-carpenter No. 3	$6.12

The company, after determining the amount of work likely to be required in each grade of carpenter work, established the number of jobs needed in each classification. Thus the company increased or decreased the number of jobs in a classification according to the needs of the company. For example, if the need for work in the No. 1 classification jobs was decreased the company eliminated some of the No. 1 positions. The displaced workers bid for other jobs, usually by bumping out No. 2 carpenters who in turn might bump No. 3 carpenters. When the need for No. 1 carpenters increased the No. 2 carpenters bid for the new jobs.

GROTON CHEMICAL COMPANY (A)

Early in August the company determined that there was sufficient demand for No. 2 class carpenter work to warrant the addition of three additional jobs in that classification. On August 8 the company posted Notice #307. (See Exhibit 2.) Award Notice #307 was posted on August 19. (See Exhibit 3.) Exhibit 4 contains the employment record of four employees who had bid for the jobs.

At the time of posting, Fite was working as a mechanic-painter No. 3 at $6.12 per hour. When Fite was first hired, he was hired as a mechanic-carpenter No. 2, and remained in that position until 1949 when he was forced to take a lower rated, lower paying job as a result of a decrease in the work force. He returned to the No. 2 job in 1958, only to be removed from it two years later when management claimed that he did not exhibit the required qualifications. In 1964 he was again given a No. 2 carpenter-mechanic position which he held until there was a reduction of the work force in 1975. At that time, Fite was given the No. 3 painter job which he was holding at the time the grievance arose (Exhibit 5 presents contract clauses which might reflect on this issue).

THE THIRD STEP GRIEVANCE MEETING

At the September 22nd third step hearing, the parties were represented as follows:

Company

(1) Robert Fayer, Assistant Personnel Manager
(2) James Hale, Maintenance Superintendent

Union

(1) George Davis, Union President
(2) Harry Tomason, Chief Steward
(3) Ray Fox, Grievance Committee Member
(4) William Fite, Mechanic-painter and Grievant

Davis: This doesn't make sense to me at all. The company agrees that Fite has the seniority. But that's not all. Fite has been a No. 2 carpenter before. In fact, the record shows that he's had about 18 years of it. In 1963 the company gave him the No. 2 classification, and he kept it until 1975 when the job was abolished. He must have done the job O.K. or the company would have taken him off.

Hale: Well, our experience with Fite shows clearly that his abilities aren't equal to those of Scannel, Kingley or White. These three men have qualifications close to those required of a No. 1 carpenter, whereas Fite is barely above the No. 3 carpenter requirements.

Fayer: Awards made on the three No. 2 mechanic-carpenter jobs were in accordance with Article 5, paragraph G of the present contract which reads, "Promotions and transfers shall be made on the basis of relative ability, training, safety, knowledge, efficiency, and physical fitness provided that when the above qualifications are equal, plant-wide seniority shall be the determining factor. Qualifications acquired outside the plant must be authenticated." Fite does not possess as much ability as the three junior employees who were asssigned to the job openings.

Tomason: Fite's past performance as a No. 2 mechanic-carpenter must have been satisfactory.

Fayer: I take exception to that statement. On more than one occasion Fite had been told that his work was unsatisfactory.

Davis: If that's true, why wasn't Fite removed from the job under Article 5, paragraph O of the contract?

Fite: The only time anybody talked to me about my work was when I bid on a No. 1 mechanic-carpenter job in 1970.

Hale: That's not right! Bailey talked to you, Fite, and so did Stern, your foreman. They both approached you about your poor performance.

Fite: Stern never talked to me!

Hale: Fite is just marginally qualified as a No. 2 carpenter. The company would have removed him under Article 5, paragraph O of the contract if his job hadn't been abolished before such action could be taken. Several people talked with Fite trying to get him to improve but he never did. In 1960 Fite was removed as a No. 2 mechanic-carpenter, because he didn't possess the qualifications for the job. Ten years later Fite bid on a No. 1 job and at that time he was advised that the company was considering removing him from his No. 2 carpenter classification, because his work was not satisfactory. Fite went ahead and entered a grievance because we didn't award him the No. 1 job. Here is a copy of the 1970 grievance (See Exhibit 1). Again in March 1975 in the presence of Edwards (union president) and Conner (steward), Fite was told that he was failing to show evidence of his ability to do No. 2 work and that if his work did not improve the company would have to consider removing him from the classification.

Fayer: Fite has been on the job a considerable length of time, and he has certainly had ample time to prove his ability to do the job; however, he has not done it and therefore it is evident that he does not possess the qualifications necessary to do the job.

Davis: It is hard to believe that some of the abilities and traits of the men working with Fite have not been adopted in Fite's performance. (There was general agreement from members of management that it was hard to understand but that Fite had failed to show improvement during the years.)

Hale: In Fite, all factors including quantity, quality, knowledge and cooperation are poor and in addition, Fite goldbricks. Other men in the carpenters' gang don't like to work with him, because he doesn't carry his share of the work.

Davis: Who are the men who don't want to work with him?

Hale: The company doesn't want to put an employee on the spot, so I won't mention any names.

Fox: I can't understand why Fite was permitted to hold a No. 2 carpenter's job after he was removed from that classification in 1960.

Fayer: Obviously an error was made in allowing Fite to return to the classification after being removed from it, but it would be equally wrong to permit him to return to this classification at this time, because he is not qualified to successfully perform the duties required by the job. Many times the union has requested that the company give consideration to advancing employees who were not part of the mechanics training program.

Most of the older workers are not graduates of the program and have acquired their skills on the job. We recognize that the training accorded to the graduates of the training program (such as the three selected to fill the three carpenter jobs) often makes them better qualified to fill openings and hence receive promotions. We have always reviewed the records of those individuals who have not been through the training program, and certain advancements have been made. The union could not expect the company to automatically put employees back on the job when they don't have potential for advancement and especially when they are not even qualified for the job which they bid.

Hale: I'd like to point out some specific instances to the union that I think reflected some of Fite's shortcomings. On September 11, 1975 Fite was supposed to be working on the roof of the Tower Concentrate Building, but he just stood on the scaffolding. He went for a smoke while the others worked and in general stood around most of the time instead of helping with the repairs on the roof. The next day, September 12, he was put to work repairing a roof on one of the River Experimental Labs. During that assignment Fite spent much of his time in the smoke shanty. On September 13, a Saturday - on overtime - he was found loafing in the carpenter and pipe shop. On September 19, he was assigned to help dismantle the Blasting Supplies Lab. He finished that job about 2:30 p.m. and admitted loafing in the lab for the balance of the day. Even as painter, there have been numerous cases when he hasn't remained on his assigned job.

Fayer: These traits are certainly not desirable and definitely raise a question about the man's ability, interest and cooperative spirit.

The union requested a short recess after which Davis stated:

> The union feels Fite is qualified as a No. 2 carpenter, because he has worked in that classification for approximately 18 years; and, having been hired as a No. 2 carpenter originally, Fite certainly should have been awarded the job. The union wants a step four hearing.

On October 5, a fourth step grievance meeting was held. Present for the company were: Jim Jason, Labor Relations Manager, Joseph Lowenberg, Plant Manager, Robert Fayer, Assistant Personnel Manager, and James Hale, Maintenance Superintendent. Present for the union were: Martin Shaper, Regional Director, District #50 USWA, Davis, Tomason, and Fox.

Exhibit 1

1970 WILLIAM FITE GRIEVANCE

The grievance submitted by Fite, dated June 18, 1970, read as follows:

> The company having posted three No. 1 carpenter jobs for bid only awarded two of these jobs and both of the awards were made to employees of lesser seniority than I have. I contend that I should have been awarded one of these jobs, both on my seniority and my qualifications. I am at present a No. 2 carpenter and have worked as a No. 2 carpenter for some time here at the plant. Therefore, with the experience I have on the job I feel that I should have been awarded one of these jobs.

Extracts from the June 1970 Grievance Meeting

Mr. Bailey, Fite's foreman, stated that the quality of Fite's work had not been satisfactory, that he had failed to carry out instructions, and that he had been observed to be argumentative when receiving instructions. Specific mention was made of a recent job in which he had failed to brace a water line properly while an excavation was being made underneath the line.

Fite asserted that in the latter instance he had complied with the general foreman's exact orders. Bailey, however, pointed out that had Fite displayed No. 1 carpenter's qualifications he would have recognized an obvious need to use a different method of bracing and would have brought the matter to the attention of the foreman. Bailey further stated that he had difficulty in keeping Fite at work. The union argued that Fite should be awarded a No. 1 job and that the incentive of the higher rate would encourage him to do a better job in the future.

The grievance went to the second step, and the union wanted a more explicit definition and description of Fite's failure to measure up to the requirements of a first-class carpenter.

Turner cited a recent job in the Blasting Supplies Works handled by Fite and a helper as evidence of Fite's ability. Bailey stated that the particular job demonstrated Fite's lack of ability. The work had been laid out by a leadman after which Fite and a helper spent over a week doing a simple job which should have been completed in about four days. Turner then characterized that statement as evidence that Fite was being watched and checked with more thoroughness than other carpenters.

It was felt by management that the case involved no question of relative qualifications but was only a challenge to their right and their ability to judge whether an employee did or did not possess qualifications. The company refused to change their position. The grievance was finally withdrawn by the union.

Exhibit 2

NOTICE #307

The following jobs are open for bid, under the terms of the contract, effective August 8, 1977. All bids or withdrawals of bids must be deposited by 12:30 p.m., August 15, 1977.

PLEASE INDICATE JOB LETTER ON BID

Job Letter

Blasting Supplies Division

A. MATCH HEAD MACHINE ADJUSTER — Temporary Vacancy
$6.12 — Needed - 1 — To replace: 26 G. Lutz

B. WIRE OPERATOR -
Folding Machine Runner — Temporary Vacancy
$6.00 — Needed - 1 — To replace: 329 J. Toy

Dynamite Division - Powder

C. POWDER OPERATOR #1 - Gel. Cart. — Temporary Job
$6.35 — Needed - 1

D. POWDER OPERATOR #2 - Gel. Cart. — Temporary Job
$6.25 — Needed - 1

E. POWDER HELPER - Gel. Box Pack — Temporary Jobs
$6.14 — Needed - 2

F. POWDER HELPER - Powder Pool — Temporary Jobs
$6.14 — Needed - 2

G. POWDER HELPER - Hand Pack — Temporary Job
$6.14 — Needed - 1 — To replace: 42 H. Long

H. SHELL HOUSE HELPER — Temporary Job
$6.10 — Needed - 1

I. BOX PRINT HELPER — Temporary Vacancy
$6.10 — Needed - 1 — To replace: 32 J. Stein

Engineering Division

J. MECHANIC #2 - Carpenter — Temporary Jobs
$6.38 — Needed - 3

K. LABORER — Temporary Jobs
$5.84 — Needed - 2

______________________________ PERSONNEL MANAGER

Exhibit 3

AWARD NOTICE #307

Job Letter

Dynamite Division - Powder (continued)

I. 1 - BOX PRINT HELPER - T.V.

154	L. Job	10-14-66
42	H. Long	9-12-69
82	A. Frable	10- 3-69
213	R. Stellfox	5-27-70
224	F. Hinkle	7-31-71
250	C. Christian	10-12-71

Awarded to: L. Job

Engineering Division

J. 3 - MECHANIC #2 - Carpenters - T.J.

176	W. Fite	8-18-44
99	C. Scannel	7-13-51
771	F. Kingley	10- 4-51
343	F. Bain	9-21-54
98	A. White	8-21-57
275	N. Barton	6-11-63
300	J. Vadner	5-22-70

Awarded to: C. Scannel
F. Kingley
A. White

K. 2 - LABORERS - T.J.

140	J. Spudis	5-28-70
135	F. Mlynek	5-28-70
309	J. Domashevitz	6-13-73
271	H. Berger	8-31-73
231	D. Correll	8-31-73
211	R. Clemson	8-31-73
198	G. Tonkin	8-31-73

Awarded to J. Spudis
J. Domashevitz

____

PERSONNEL MANAGER

Exhibit 4

PERSONNEL DATA

Employee #343 Frank Bain Date Hired 9-21-54

Date	Classification	Specialty
	Cap Helper	
4-30-53	E.B.C. Foreman	Soldering & Sulfuring
7-14-59	E.B.C. Leadman	E.B.C.
6- 5-62	E.B.C. Operator	Trucker - Caps
10-18-65	E.B.C. Leadman	#2 Pack House
10-12-70	Ordinace Operator #1	Primer Line
2-25-72	Leadman #1	Labor Gang
5- 5-72	Truck Helper	Powder - Trans. Dept.
7-16-72	Mechanic #3	Carpenter
4-13-73	Truck Helper	Safety
4- 4-74	Mechanic Helper	Electrician
5-21-74	Truck Helper	Safety
11-28-74	Mechanic #3	R.X.L.
9-25-75	Truck Driver	Safety
4- 1-76	Mechanic #3	D & D Section
6-17-76	E.B.C. Operator	Pack House Operator
7-29-76	Mechanic #3	D & D Section

NOTE: Bain claimed Mechanic #2 - Carpenter job on March 15, 1973. Claim was denied on qualifications.

Employee #771 Frank Kingley Date Hired 10-4-51

Date	Classification	Specialty
	Powder Helper	
	Acid Helper	
	Acid Operator	
9-19-67	Truck Driver	Construction
10-12-69	Mechanic #3	Carpenter
9-12-74	Mechanic #2	Carpenter
10- 3-75	Truck Driver	Safety
8-18-77	Mechanic #2	Carpenter

Exhibit 4
(continued)

Employee #99 Charles Scannel   Date Hired 7-13-51

Date	Classification	Specialty
	Shell Helper	
	Shell Operator #2	
	Shell Helper	
12-15-66	Truck Helper	Safety
10-12-69	Mechanic #3	Carpenter
9-11-74	Mechanic #2	Carpenter
10- 1-75	Truck Helper	Safety
8-18-77	Mechanic #2	Carpenter

Employee #98 Arthur White   Date Hired 8-21-57

Date	Classification	Specialty
	Shell Draw Helper	
1- 9-66	Cap Operator	
4-19-66	Acid Helper	Finish House
8-29-67	Truck Helper	Safety - Trans. Dept.
6-19-69	Truck Driver	Safety - Trans. Dept.
11- 1-69	Mechanic #3	Carpenter
6-16-70	Mechanic #2	Carpenter
10- 3-75	Truck Driver	Safety - Labor Dept.
10-16-75	Laborer	Janitor - Dyn. Div.
8-18-77	Mechanic #2	Carpenter

Exhibit 5

PERTINENT CONTRACT CLAUSES

Article V

. . . . .

E. When job vacancies occur or a new job is created, the job will be posted.

Employees shall prepare bids or withdrawals in triplicate, depositing original in the Company box, duplicate copy in the Union box, and retaining the triplicate copy. All bids or withdrawals shall be available for inspection by the departmental steward at the latter's request.

Copies of all job notices and job award notices shall be furnished to the Local President and Chief Steward.

In considering bids for vacant jobs, the Company will consider seniority and qualifications.

There shall be no interference by Company or Union with any employee in the exercise of his or her right to bid for or to claim a job.

The company shall either post job awards within five (5) full working days after the bidding period expires or post notices stating why awards are being delayed.

. . . . .

G. Promotions and transfers shall be made on the basis of relative ability, training, safety, knowledge, efficiency, and physical fitness, provided that when the above qualifications are equal, plant-wide seniority shall be the determining factor. Qualifications acquired outside the plant must be authenticated.

In the application of the above factors governing the promotion and transfer of employees by bid and award, the Company agrees that such factors will be determined and applied in a fair, unbiased, and nondiscriminatory manner. The above is a statement of policy and shall not change the intent of the preceding paragraph.

H. In all cases of layoff or rehire, the seniority of employees involved shall be considered on a plant-wide basis and shall be the determining factor. However, if there is any job opening or job vacancy that cannot be filled by employees within the bargaining unit, or by qualified employees who have been laid off, the Company may retain present employees with lesser seniority who are qualified to perform the work or then hire new employees. However, an open or vacant job will not be awarded to an employee if there is another employee with greater seniority on furlough, or laid off, who has qualifications to perform the work in the vacant or open job. Grievances with respect to the judgment of employees' qualifications for these purposes shall be subject to the full grievance procedure, including arbitration, except for those job classifications which are designated with an asterisk in Appendix "A," in which case the plant manager shall be the sole judge and his decision shall not be subject to the grievance procedure beyond the first three steps. Senior employees who have been laid off or who are on furlough, will be notified by the Company of job vacancies or job openings for which they have qualifications. Such employees will be given twenty-four (24) hours from the time of notification to advise the Company of their intentions with respect to the open or vacant job.

. . . . .

O. If an employee who has been awarded a job is unable to satisfactorily perform the work, the management may:

1. If he is on a temporary job, transfer him to his permanent job, or,

2. If he is on a permanent job, transfer him to the Labor Gang, Powder Helper Pool, Transportation Department or Utility Pool. Such transferee must make reasonable efforts to acquire a regular job by bid.

Article XX

TRAINING

Mechanics Training Program - A Mechanics Training Program is hereby established with the following objectives:

1. To exercise due care in the selection of applicants for training in skilled trades.

2. To provide for suitable instruction and training which, upon completion, will result in first-class mechanics fully capable of meeting the demands of their occupations.

3. The parties agree to adopt a Training Procedure, copies of which will be given to the Union officials and stewards. They also agree to establish a Training Committee with advisory functions as set forth in the Training Procedure. Membership of the Committee shall be as follows:

   Two members representing the Union Two members representing the Management One Chairman (Personnel Manager)

4. The Training Procedure may be amended at any time by mutual agreement of the Company and the Union. The Union in this case shall mean the Grievance Committee.

GROTON CHEMICAL COMPANY (B)

On August 9, the following grievance was presented in the Acid Department of Groton Chemical Company's Pennville Plant:

> We, the Undersigned, take exception to the practice of the company insisting upon Acid Leadmen doing our work. This consists of transferring acid over Saturday and Sunday, weekends, when we are obliged to remain home.
>
> This constitutes our daily work, two shifts per day when Leadmen do not transfer acid. We, therefore, contend that any work of this nature which occurred over a weekend period rightly belongs to us as contracted overtime and cannot be performed by the Leadmen who again by contract are not allowed to replace any employee for a shift or part of a shift.
>
> On Saturday, August 6, the Acid Leadmen performed the following work:
>
> (1) Pumped mix from mix and weigh Scale Tank #3 to Tower and Cascade Storage Tank.
>
> (2) Pumped from Tank #5 to Scale Tank #1.
>
> (3) Pumped twice neutralizing Tank #3 to storage tank or truck.
>
> Each of these jobs takes approximately $1\frac{1}{2}$ hours.
>
> Signed Fred Scherer
> Signed Anthony Vancura
> Signed Joseph Cooper
> (Steward)

The manufacture of dynamite requires the use of certain acids among which are nitric, sulphuric, and mixtures of these two. At the Pennville Plant there was an operation where some of these acids were produced for use within the plant as well as for outside sales. The grievants and the leadmen referred to in the grievance were employed in this operation.

As part of the operation it was necessary to transfer the liquids from the storage tanks to the scale tanks where they were weighed and mixed, from the scale tanks to storage tanks, and also to and from tank trucks and tank cars. Some years ago these transfers were accomplished with compressed air and the operation became known as "acid blowing" and the operators as "acid blowers."

At the time of the grievance, acid transfers were accomplished by electric pumps. The employee performing the pumping set the lines and the valves so as to direct the flow of the liquid to the proper tank, started the flow of material, and then traced the line to see that the liquid was flowing as intended, without leakage. During the pumping the employee had no active duties but was responsible for the operation and had to be on hand in case of emergency. When pumping to the scale tank the operator had to stop the process when the required quantities had been delivered.

Acid blowers were employed on the second and third shifts (8 a.m. to 4 p.m. and 4 p.m. to midnight) Monday through Friday. During that time most of the pumping was performed by them although some was done by the acid operators and the leadmen. It was sometimes necessary to pump acid, however, when the acid blowers were not at work, and the leadmen had performed the task at those times (see Article II, Exhibit 1). There were four acid leadmen who worked a schedule so as to cover the three shifts, seven days a week. One of them was always present at the plant during normal operations. Leadmen, acid blowers and acid operators were hourly paid employees and in the bargaining unit. Acid blowers and operators were paid $6.19 per hour, while leadmen received $.45 above that rate.

THE SECOND STEP GRIEVANCE MEETING

On August 20 a second step grievance meeting was held to discuss the acid blowers' grievance. The parties were represented as follows:

Company

(1) Frank Kirsten, Plant Personnel Director
(2) Tom Walton, Senior Supervisor
(3) Leo Lowery, Acid Supervisor

Union

(1) George Davis, Union President (worked in the acid area)
(2) John Cooper, Acid Area Steward
(3) Fred Scherer, Acid Blower
(4) Anthony Vancura, Acid Blower

After Kirsten read the grievance Cooper asked Scherer to explain the men's complaint.

Scherer: Well, as the grievance says, last Saturday the leadman spent over four hours doing our work. This is the work us acid blowers do during the week. When there's work like this to be done on Saturday, we should be called out. We didn't mind the leadman doing a little job once in a while, but this thing has grown and grown until it's beyond all reason. It isn't fair. Other groups get called out. Why shouldn't we? I can tell you one thing, the leadmen are plenty sore about all this extra work too. How are they supposed to get their regular work done?

Lowery: Fred, you fellows are wrong when you say we are loading up the leadmen with more and more pumping over the weekends. I have the figures for the past two years here and you're welcome to look them over. Sure, last Saturday was heavy, but there have been other Saturdays just as heavy in the past, and the figures don't show any general increase over the past two years.

Cooper: How much time do your figures show the leadmen spent on pumping last Saturday?

Lowery: The day leadman reported a total of three hours. This included pumping the tube twice which is not included in the grievance.

Cooper: Well, whether it's been going on for two years or not it's asking too damn much of these men to have the leadmen do them out of that much Saturday work. After all, it's their work. I understand the leadmen also operated the neutralizer on Saturday. How can you expect the leadmen to do their regular work?

Lowery: We've had no complaints from the leadmen. They're not overworked. After all, the leadman is a higher paid classification, and under the contract we have the right to ask him to do this kind of work. It's no different than it's always been.

Davis: The men tell me that when Sam Sessions was acid supervisor he made an agreement with them that the leadmen would not pump over two hours on Saturday. If there was more than two hours pumping the blowers would be called out.

Kirsten: Was that a written agreement, George? Do you have a copy of it?

Davis: Of course it wasn't written. It didn't have to be written. Sam was as good as his word and that's heck of a lot more than you can say about some people around here today. I can see we'll have to get everything down on paper from now on. I resent this whole business. Every time our men mention an understanding that was made in the past you as much as say we're a bunch of liars.

Kirsten: Now, George, I didn't say that, at all - but this is the first time I heard of such an understanding and I wonder if it had been formalized. After all, in the last grievance Ray asked me if I had a written record of the agreement made by the clean-up crew.

Scherer: You can't deny this is our work. We do it all week, but almost never are we called out on Saturday any more. We're just interested in coming out here and doing our work. We're being done out of four hours at time and one-half almost every Saturday.

A recess was then called during which each side reconsidered its position. Following the recess a further discussion was held but no agreement was reached.

GROTON CHEMICAL COMPANY (B)

THE THIRD STEP GRIEVANCE MEETING

At the third step grievance meeting, which was held on September 22, the parties were represented as follows:

Company

(1) Frank Kirsten, Plant Personnel Director
(2) Leo Lowery, Acid Supervisor
(3) Ted Walters, Senior Supervisor
(4) C.L. Hoover, Superintendent, Dynamite Division

Union

(1) George Davis, President of the Union and Grievance Committee Chairman
(2) Harry Tomason, Chief Steward
(3) Ray Fox, Grievance Committee Member
(4) Joseph Cooper, Acid Area Steward
(5) Fred Scherer, Acid Blower

Kirsten read the grievance and stated that the company could not agree to it.

Cooper: The acid leadmen are doing more and more work which belongs to the men, not just pumping acid, as the grievance says, but on Saturday afternoons they act as storeroom helpers, and on the evening and night shifts they run the neutralizer.

Davis: The contract says you can't replace another employee for a part of a shift, but that's exactly what you're doing. You're replacing not just the blowers, but neutralizers and storeroom attenders. In the case of the neutralizers you're replacing a man for a whole shift. As I said in the other grievance, we give you fellows a little finger and you take the whole damn hand.

Lowery: George, the amount of work done by the leadmen has <u>not</u> increased. You can look at the records. It's true the blowers don't get as much overtime as they used to get. But that's not because the leadmen are working more. We used to have the tank trucks come in here on Saturday and Sunday, and the blowers were called in to load them. Recently we worked it out so we don't have to have the Saturday and Sunday shipments. Also as you know our production of acid is down so there just isn't as much pumping required.

The acid leadmen are not doing any more work. It's true that they get things out of the storeroom when there's an emergency but that's nothing new. They've been doing that for years. Matter of fact, they used to do it all day Saturday but now we have a storeroom attendant out here Saturday morning.

Fox: The storeroom work is completely outside the acid department. He has no business over there at all. The men tell me that one Saturday the acid leadman made 35 trips to the storeroom. That doesn't make sense. And what about the neutralizer? What's the leadman doing on that?

Walters: Well, we reached an agreement on that a couple of years ago - the leadman can operate the neutralizer when he has time. You remember when we settled that, Joe.

Cooper: Sure, we agreed he could do it in his free time, but it's like George says, you fellows are taking advantage of it. Some days now the leadman turns out a full shift's operation. Heck, we never had that in mind.

Kirsten: George, you said we are violating the contract. We don't agree. As we read paragraph 2 of Article II (see Exhibit 1) we have every right to use the leadmen this way. The last sentence which you refer to was not meant to cover this kind of situation.

It was adopted to cover a situation where a member of the work force was required to discontinue work during a shift, or who failed to report for scheduled work on a day. We agreed that leadmen would not do the work of an absent employee. That's not the case here at all.

Walters: Leo and I have looked over the production schedules and we can arrange things so that the tower and cascade concentrator won't have to be operated over the weekend. That will decrease the pumping by leadmen over the weekend, but, of course, it won't result in any more overtime for the blowers. We can fit it into their regular work schedule during the week.

Davis: Is there an overtime distribution plan in effect in the acid area?

Lowery: Yes, we have one. Joe and the boys drew it up, and I agreed to it after a couple of changes. We don't have any trouble with it as Joe will tell you, but we just haven't had any overtime for the blowers recently. That's no fault of the plan. It works O.K.

Davis: How can you say there's been no overtime for the blowers with all this Saturday pumping?

Cooper: As I recall it, our overtime plan said leadmen should not share. I'm trying to find it - yes - here it is, Item 7 says "Production leadmen will not share time in operational overtime duties."

Davis: Well, there it is in black and white, Frank. You don't have to take our word for it this time. I think you'll have to agree that these overtime plans are part of the contract. It's spelled out here in Article IX (see Exhibit 1).

Kirsten: We agree, George, that the overtime plans are binding but we don't agree that the overtime plan has any bearing on this case.

Hoover: What you want in this grievance would increase our cost of making acid and we just can't afford it, especially with costs rising so fast these days. The margins are low here. The competition is tough. We've already lost some of our outside customers, and the company is even buying some of its own acid outside. That's why the blowers' overtime is down. If we have to bring the blowers out here on Saturday and Sunday every time there's a few hours of pumping there'll be less work, not more, for everybody.

A recess was called during which each side discussed the grievance. When the meeting reconvened no agreement could be reached, and the union asked Mr. Kirsten to schedule a fourth step meeting.

The fourth step meeting was held on October 5. Present for the union were Martin Shaper, Regional Director, District #50 USWA, Davis, Tomason, and Fox. Present for the company were Jim Jason, Labor Relations Manager, Joseph Lowenberg, Plant Manager, Kirsten, and Hoover.

Exhibit 1

Sections from the current agreement between the United Mine Workers of America and Groton Chemical Company (Pennville Plant).

Article II Recognition

Leadman shall perform the duties of working gang boss or leader. He shall exercise the authority to assign work and direct the performance thereof; to supervise the quality of workmanship and to maintain order, reporting any violation of rules. It shall be his responsibility to maintain standards of production, both quantity and quality, as established by the Company, and to report to his foreman or supervisor any conditions which prevent the attainment of such standards of production. If such conditions result from the action of an employee, or employees, the leadman may consult with the departmental steward. A steward must be present whenever an employee is reported by the leadman for either violation of rules or for causing conditions detrimental to standards of production.

Supervisory duties as defined above shall be the primary function of a leadman. However, time not spent in the performance of supervisory duties may be spent in manual work, and there shall be no limit placed on the amount of time spent in such work. Leadmen will not be used to replace employees who are absent from work for a complete shift or who are required to discontinue their regular work for the balance of a shift, unless such leadmen are the only qualified employees available for that shift.

Article VII Reporting Pay

(a) Any employee not being notified at least two (2) hours before starting time of his regular shift not to report for work and reporting, shall be given four (4) hours work or shall be compensated for four (4) hours at his straight time rate unless the Company's failure to notify him shall be for a cause beyond the Company's control, in which case the employee shall be compensated for two (2) hours at his straight time rate. Employees so reporting will be provided with transportation if there are no other means of transportation available.

(b) Employees reporting for work as provided in paragraph (a) above or employees who are called out to work on a day that has not been scheduled for work will be compensated for either four (4) or two (2) hours in accordance with paragraph (a) above, on the following basis:

(1) For reporting on Saturday or Sunday, compensation at the rate of time and one-half, subject to qualifying for such pay as provided in Article XI of this Agreement.

Exhibit 1
(continued)

(2) For reporting on the seventh consecutive day worked in his regularly scheduled workweek, compensation at the rate of double time, subject to qualifying for such pay as provided in Article IX of this Agreement.

(3) For reporting on any other day, compensation at straight time unless the employee has worked forty (40) hours or more on the preceding days in that week in which case his reporting pay shall be at the rate of time and one-half.

Article IX Hours of Work

Overtime work will be distributed equally as far as possible on a departmental basis. If requested by the Union, a cumulative record of overtime worked by every employee in a department will be posted and a copy will be sent to the Local Union President. The employees of a department may submit a plan for the distribution of overtime for all employees within such department within two (2) weeks of the effective date of the contract. However, the plan, if once approved by the Company, may not be changed for the remainder of the contract term. In any department where no overtime plan is in effect, and no plan is submitted by any such department and approved by the Company, the overtime will be distributed by the Company in accordance with provisions of this Agreement.

Article XIII Union

(a) The Union recognizes the responsibilities imposed upon it as the exclusive bargaining agent for the employees, and realizes that in order to provide maximum opportunities for continuing employment, good working conditions, and better than average wages, the Company must be in a strong market position, which means it must produce at the lowest possible costs consistent with fair labor standards. The Union, through its bargaining position, assumes a joint responsibility in attainment of these goals.

(b) The Union therefore agrees that it will cooperate with the Company and support its efforts to assure a full day's work on the part of its members; that it actively will combat absenteeism and any other practices which restrict production. It further agrees that it will support the Company in its efforts to eliminate waste in production; conserve materials and supplies; improve the quality of workmanship; prevent accidents and strengthen good-will between the company, the employees, the customer, and the public.

SOUTHWESTERN BELL TELEPHONE COMPANY (A)

In July, 1975, M. B. Kleypas, Division Plant Manager for Southwestern Bell's Kansas City Plant Division, was trying to decide which individual to choose to fill a recently vacated switchman position in his downtown district. Openings were normally filled on the basis of the seniority of qualified applicants. However, a recent Consent Decree entered in the U.S. District Court for the Eastern District of Pennsylvania had committed the company to a model Affirmative Action Program (AAP) which established a target number of minority personnel for all the company's job classifications. At present, the division was three people below the agreed-upon number for switchman. A qualified minority applicant was available, but he had considerably less seniority than several white applicants.

Kleypas was convinced from past experience that selection of a minority worker would prompt an immediate grievance from the union, Local 2369 of the Communication Workers of America. The division had lost two similar grievances in the past but was nevertheless committed to meet its utilization targets. Kleypas wondered what to do: should he award the job according to seniority or should he award it to the minority applicant?

THE CONSENT DECREE

In 1970 American Telephone and Telegraph Company (AT&T) sought rate increases for long distance service from the Federal Communications Commission (FCC). The Equal Employment Opportunity Commission (EEOC) intervened in the proceedings, registering opposition to the increases on the grounds that AT&T was guilty of race and sex discrimination in its employment practices in violation of Title VII of the 1964 Civil Rights Act.[1] Public hearings were then held, these ending in early 1973 when an agreement was forged between the FCC, EEOC, AT&T and the Departments of Labor and Justice.[2] This then was formalized by a Consent Decree entered in the U.S. District Court for the Eastern District of Pennsylvania. The Decree established a model program on which AT&T's affirmative action programs would be based. Company efforts to achieve the goals of the programs would be monitored by several government agencies, and jurisdiction of the matter would rest with the District Court.

AT&T revised all of its affirmative action programs to conform to the model program, and these revisions applied to all the company's subsidiaries. Among the revised objectives were these:

---

[1]Prior to 1972 the EEOC did not have the authority to bring suit itself against an individual company. The AT&T rate hearings gave the EEOC its first forum to bring charges of discrimination against AT&T.

[2]The union was not a party to the Consent Decree.

> The Equal Employment objective for the Bell System is to achieve, within a reasonable period of time, an employee profile, with respect to race and sex in each major job classification, which is an appropriate reflection of proper utilization....
> This objective calls for achieving full utilization of minorities and women at all levels of management and non-management and by job classification at a pace beyond that which would occur normally; to prohibit discrimination in employment because of race, color, religion, national origin or sex, and unlawful discrimination because of age; and to have a work environment free of discrimination.

A demographic study was made in each community where AT&T operated so that percentages of minority workers and women could be identified. Similar statistics were also compiled for each of the company's 15 job classifications, and the percentages were compared. When the comparison disclosed under-utilization of minorities or women in a classification, goals, intermediate targets and time frames were then established to increase the employment of such persons in the affected job classification and bring the work force in that classification up to the community profile. The goals were projected on one-, two-, and three-year bases. They were "neither rigid nor inflexible quotas but objectives to be pursued by mobilization of available company resources for a good faith effort."

The switchman's job was in Classification 7. This classification was referred to in the Consent Decree in the following manner:

> (Part A-III) B. In filling vacancies in ... job classifications 6 and 7, candidates for promotion shall be evaluated on the basis of net credited service and best qualified, unless a lower standard of qualification is provided in a collective bargaining agreement or pursuant to Bell Company practices. However, if any Bell Company is unable to meet its intermediate targets within the stated time frames using these criteria, it will use only the criteria of net credited service and a basic qualified criterion and, if necessary, will seek new hires who meet at least the basic qualified criterion. Efforts to achieve intermediate targets should be substantially uniform throughout the appropriate time frame. Each Bell Company agrees to notify the appropriate collective bargaining representative of its employees prior to promoting or transferring persons in AAP job classifications 6 and 7 on the basis of net credited service and basic qualifications.

> (Part B-II) D. This Decree shall not be interpreted as requiring the abandonment of any provisions in any Bell Company's Collective Bargaining Agreement(s) except as required to maintain compliance with Federal Law, Executive Orders and regulations promulgated pursuant thereto pertaining to discrimination in employment. All of the Bell Companies' obligations in this Decree are required for compliance with Federal Law provided however, that nothing

> in this Decree is intended to restrict the right of the Bell Companies and the collective bargaining representatives of their employees to negotiate alternatives to the provisions of this Decree which would be in compliance with Federal Law.
>
> To the extent that any Bell Company has in effect a posting or bidding system, said system shall continue to be used. Provided, however, that such system will be modified to the extent necessary to conform with Part A, Section III of the Decree. ...

THE SELECTION PROCESS

According to long-standing practice in the Bell system, when division management was notified of a job opening, they, in turn, notified the union and a management group called the Placement Bureau. The Placement Bureau screened employee transfer requests and determined whether the persons applying were qualified for the openings requested. This was done without regard to departmental lines. At the same time the union posted a job bid sheet and subsequently submitted to management a list of interested bidders. The Placement Bureau then screened these requests and submitted its own list of qualified applicants. Regarding the switchman opening, Mr. Kleypas received lists from the union and the Placement Bureau, both of which contained the name of F.F. Schick, an employee with a continuous service date of July 1, 1948. He had served as a switchman from 1952 to 1959. The only minority member whose name appeared on both lists was L.B. Hogan, a black who had a continuous service date of February 11, 1969.

UTILIZATION GOALS

There were 19 black workers in classification 7 at the beginning of the year. One of these 19 had quit in early June. The utilization goal was 21 employees by the end of the year. No black person had successfully bid into a classification 7 job during the first six months.

THE COLLECTIVE BARGAINING CONTRACT

There were three pertinent sections of the union contract all in Appendix C:

> 7.01 Length of service shall be taken into account in the treatment of employees covered by this Appendix insofar as the conditions of the business and the abilities of the employees permit.
>
> 8.03 Following the receipt of such list (of applicants for a vacancy)...the Company shall be free to fill the vacancy by selection of an employee named on the list, or by selection of another employee taking into account length of service insofar as the conditions of the business and the abilities of the employees permit. The Company shall notify the Union of the selection, and the reason therefor if the selection is not made from the Union list.

> 8.07 The decision of the Company on any of the matters under the foregoing paragraphs of this Part 8 shall be controlling unless the Company is shown to have acted in bad faith. A charge of bad faith shall be subject to the grievance procedure...and to the arbitration procedure. ...

PAST GRIEVANCES

Past arbitration decisions revealed the existence of two related cases. In 1972, before the Federal Order, a promotion grievance was upheld by an arbitrator who stated that the seniority clause of the contract was not affected by the then-existing affirmative action program.

A second case, also involving a promotion, was settled in early 1973 in favor of the union. At that hearing, the arbitrator refused to consider the Consent Decree as admissible and decided the case solely on the contract language.

Mr. Kleypas was not sure if these decisions would have any bearing on the present situation if he chose Hogan for the job. He had to decide soon because the position was an important one, and the workload was exceptionally high for the division at that time.

HULL MANUFACTURING COMPANY (A)

The U.S. Government owns a number of ammunition plants which are operated under contract by private companies. One of these plants, Yankee Ordinance, is located at Harbor City in the northeastern part of the country. Since 1951 Yankee Ordinance has been operated under contract by Hull Manufacturing Company, a conglomerate with headquarters in Chicago.

Over the years since 1951 Yankee has turned out a variety of shells and other military supplies for the Government. Specifications for these products are developed by the armed forces and bid on by Yankee and other producers. The Yankee plant covers many acres. The various production lines are in separate buildings sufficiently far apart so that an explosion in one line will not affect another. Actually Yankee has had an extremely good safety record, in part because both the management and the employees are conscious of the danger of the materials with which they work.

In 1974 Yankee had approximately 500 professional and management employees and 1,800 other employees for a total of 2,300. The 1,800 non-professional and non-management employees were organized into nine unions which included five craft unions, a guards union, a firefighters union, the Teamsters, and the Munition Workers Union of America (MWUA). The production, stores, inspection and maintenance labor employees, a total of about 1,000, were represented by the MWUA. Approximately 30% of the employees in the MWUA bargaining unit were black.

The number of employees at Yankee had varied greatly over the years depending on the need of the armed services and also the ability of the Company to compete successfully for bids. In the early fifties during the Korean conflict employment reached 7,000 and then dropped to less than 1,000 in the late fifties and early sixties. By 1963, however, it had risen to almost 4,000 but by 1965 it had dropped down to about 3,000. Starting in 1966, employment increased rapidly again reaching a peak of 11,000 in early 1969. In late 1969 and 1970, there was a rapid decline to about 4,000 and since then until 1974 a slow decline to the 2,300 level in late 1974. Although the above figures indicate the general trends they do not tell the whole story. Within any one year production and employment could vary considerably depending upon the success or failure of the Company in securing orders through competitive bidding. (See Exhibit 1)

The 1,000 employees represented by the MWUA were employed in four separate divisions: Labor, Stores, Production and Inspection. The majority of the employees were in Production. In each of the departments each job had a single hourly rate. In 1974 the rates for jobs in the four departments had the following ranges:

Labor - \$3.15 to \$3.57
Stores - \$3.15 to \$4.04
Production - \$3.64 to \$3.95
Inspection - \$3.57 to \$5.27

The labor contract between Hull and the MWUA provided that the seniority date of each employee "shall be the date of his most recent hire or transfer into the bargaining unit." However, each of the four departments constituted a separate seniority unit. When a job became available in one of the four departments it was posted for bidding and was awarded to the qualified employee with the greatest bargaining unit seniority in that department. However, if there were no qualified bidders within the department the job was then opened for bidding by employees in the other three departments and awarded to the qualified employee with the greatest bargaining unit seniority.

When a job was discontinued, the employee had the right to displace the employee with the least bargaining unit seniority in the classification, but if he or she could not qualify by seniority and experience within that classification, then to displace the least senior employee in another classification in the department. Finally, if the employee did not have the seniority and qualifications to displace anyone in the department, he or she had the right to displace the least senior employee in classifications in other departments.

In all of the departments except Inspection an employee could bid into the department without passing a test. However, prior to 1970 in order to enter the Inspection Department an employee first had to pass a qualifying test and then spend six months as a Quality Control (QC) Inspector Trainee before moving to the Quality Control (QC) Inspector job (see Exhibits 2 and 3 for job descriptions). Employees who bid for the QC Inspector Trainee jobs were given the right to take the test on the basis of their bargaining unit seniority. The labor contract provided that:

<u>Article VII, Seniority Rights</u>
<u>Section M3</u>

In the Inspection Division, the Quality Control Trainees shall be selected by a qualifying test on the basis of their seniority. The Quality Control Trainees shall have less seniority than Quality Control Inspectors, but all time accrued as Quality Control Trainees shall be credited to them. The Quality Control Trainees seniority shall be from the date of their entry into the Division (as Trainee) and any recalls to the Division shall be on the basis of seniority. The Quality Control Trainees shall have bidding rights on the basis of their seniority. The placing of Quality Control Trainees immediately prior to completion of their training period shall be done in this manner:

After all available jobs have been bid and filled and vacancies are still left open, the Quality Control Trainees shall be placed on these jobs on the basis of seniority. This shall be done prior to completion of the training period. The training period shall be for a period of six (6) months.

Upon completion of the training period, the former Quality Control Trainee's seniority shall be that of his most recent date of hire as employee of the Company.

The test for entrance into the QC Inspector Trainee job was developed by the company's Personnel Department (see Exhibit 4).

From time to time the questions in the test were changed so that they could not be passed on from one examination group to the next. Employees were given 40 minutes to complete it. The passing grade was 70.

The QC Inspector Trainee job carried the hourly rate of $3.57 for the second three months. The job of QC Inspector carried a rate of $4.07. Compared to the jobs in the three departments other than Inspection, QC Inspector carried a high rate. Only one job in the other three departments carried a rate as high. However, the QC Inspector was the lowest paying job in the Inspection Department other than trainees and clerks. There were actually seven higher classifications in Inspection, the top rate being $5.27.

The company had had no trouble getting bids for the QC Inspector Trainee job even though employees who were successful often had to take a cut in pay for the first three months of the training period. However, although 30% of the employees in the bargaining unit were black only a small number of them bid for the QC Inspector Trainee jobs and a still smaller number succeeded in passing the test. In 1974, of the 250 employees in the QC Inspector classification only 12, or less than 5%, were black. It was well known among the workers that the questions in the qualifying exam contained the types of problems which were covered in the last year of the local high schools and that very few black employees had graduated from high school.

In 1970 the company presented an Affirmative Action Program to the Office of Federal Contract Compliance (OFCC). The OFCC requested additional information regarding any tests which were required of employees before hiring or promotion and pointed out that such tests would not be approved unless they were validated. The company had not validated the QC Inspector Trainee test and was of the opinion that it could not be validated. The company informed the OFCC that the test would be discontinued. The company's Affirmative Action Program was then approved.

For several years following 1970, because of the production level at the plant, the company had no need to increase the supply of QC Inspectors. As a result no bids were posted for QC Inspector Trainees during that period. In the spring of 1974 the company and the union negotiated a new three-year labor agreement. The question of the test for QC Inspector Trainees did not arise during the negotiations. The new contract continued without change Section M3 of Article VII.

In the fall of 1974 production began to increase and management decided more QC Inspectors would be needed in the future. As a result the company posted a bid for QC Inspector Trainees. The bid indicated that no qualifying test would be required. Instead of the usual test the company used a questionnaire (see Exhibit 5). The bidders were called into the Personnel Office two or three at a time in order of their bargaining unit seniority and asked to fill out the questionnaire. If an employee answered all the questions in the affirmative and was able to write legibly he or she was accepted into the training program. As a result 29 employees including 15 blacks were awarded jobs as QC Inspector Trainees. The seniority roster of the new 29 QC Inspector Trainees is shown in Exhibit 6.

On November 10, 1974, Mary Fox, a QC Inspector on the second shift, filed the following grievance:

> I feel it is necessary that the same test should be given to trainees as was used in past practice. The change in procedure is contrary to the contract, not acceptable to the union, and is discriminating in nature.

The grievance received strong support from Louella Brown, the Chief Steward of Inspection, and also from John Curtis, the President of the local union, both of whom were also QC Inspectors. Fox, Brown, and Curtis were white employees. Data from their personnel folders are shown in Exhibit 7. Management was surprised by Brown's and Curtis' action because it had been of the opinion that the union was opposed to any kind of qualifying tests.

At the third and last step of the grievance procedure which was held on December 18, 1974, the following discussion occurred among Mary Fox, John Curtis and James Lewis, Plant Personnel Director:

Mary Fox: I filed this grievance because I believe what the company is doing is a clear violation of the contract which stipulates that a qualifying test must be given to an Inspector Trainee. Since there is just a questionnaire used now, it really isn't a qualifying test that someone can pass or fail. Anyone can pass the questionnaire. Now that's discriminatory. It's not fair to the rest of us who had to pass a real qualifying test.

I took the qualifying test back in 1968. The last time it was given was the last time trainees were hired in 1969. I understand that in 1970 the company unilaterally eliminated the test because of the Civil Rights Act. That was over four years ago. Why hasn't the company developed a new test and had it approved by Civil Rights? It's had plenty of time to do it.

Jim Lewis: Mary, we had no choice. We had to eliminate that test. Otherwise the OFCC wouldn't OK our Affirmative Action Plan and all of us would have been out of work. They insisted that if we used a test it had to be validated, that is we had to prove that it really tested the ability to do the inspector job. We don't think you can have a test in this case that can be validated. We're surprised at the Union's position, John. We always thought you were opposed to qualifying tests of any kind and, Mary, we don't understand why you're grieving. You don't indicate in your grievance that you've been harmed in any way.

John Curtis: Well, Jim, it's clearly a violation of the contract. That's why the union's supporting it and it's discriminatory, too, because these new people don't have to pass a test now and we did. But basically it's a violation of the contract and you just can't do that. The contract says in plain English (reading from contract), "Quality Control Trainees shall be selected by a qualifying test." All we're asking is that you live up to the contract.

Lewis: Well, John, I understand from Jerry Thomas who was Personnel Director in 1970 that he talked to you about discontinuing the test at that time and that you raised no objection.

Curtis: He never talked with me about it. The first time I heard about it was when the new group of trainees were awarded the jobs without tests. Look, Jim, you just can't break the contract like this. You're always reminding us that we have to live up to it. Now it's your turn. If you want to change it we'll be glad to bargain with you about it when the contract runs out in 1977, but you can't change it unilaterally now. We're prepared to go to arbitration on this one and I'm sure we can win it. The contract is crystal clear.

Lewis: Well, John, I don't think an arbitrator is going to tell us to violate the law which is what you're asking us to do. Anyhow, we'll take a further look at it and give you our answer in a few days.

Exhibit 1

Hull Manufacturing Company Yankee Ordinance Division Personnel Strength

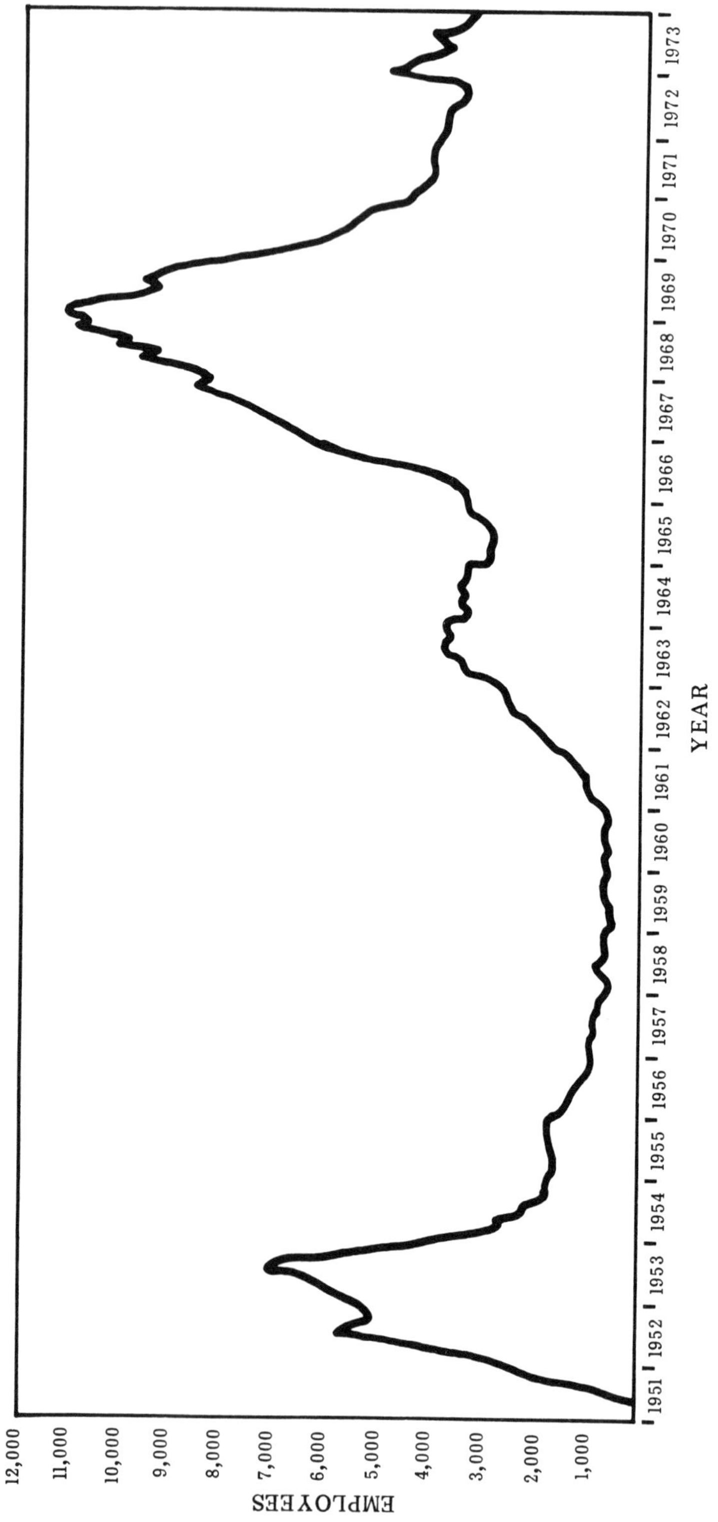

Exhibit 2

JOB TITLE: QUALITY CONTROL INSPECTOR

STATEMENT OF DUTIES

Serves under the general supervision of Chief Inspector or Assistant Chief Inspector, performing duties of a Quality Control Inspector engaged in all or some combination of the following:

Inspects components received, work in process on load lines; and/or receipt of material in Preliminary Inspection;

Understands and operates Quality Control Stations on any load line as set up by the Quality Control Section;

Determines that no defective material is used or produced and that production workmanship is of high quality;

Responsible for compliance with Ordnance Specifications, Standard Inspection Procedures and Drawings;

Performs other related duties of the same level of difficulty when assigned by supervisor.

Must have at least (6) six months on-the-job experience as Quality Control Trainee or equivalent experience in a similar Ordnance Installation.

Exhibit 3

JOB TITLE: QUALITY CONTROL INSPECTOR TRAINEE

STATEMENT OF DUTIES

Under direct supervision of higher grade Inspectors, performs inspection on components received, work-in-progress, materials received in Preliminary Inspection and finished ammunition. May assist Component Inspectors and Quality Control Inspectors in more involved inspection methods; may operate training in Inspection and Quality Control techniques from higher grade inspectors and/or in training classes. Upon satisfactory completion of training courses and six (6) months satisfactory service as Quality Control Inspector Trainee, shall be promoted to Quality Control Inspector classification.

Exhibit 4

QUALIFICATION & APTITUDE TEST

QUALITY CONTROL TRAINEE

NAME____ DATE________________

Answer the following questions in the blanks provided.

1. Express the following as a two digit decmal number.
   A. 74%_________
   B. 1/20_________
   C. 13/16_________

2. A man has 4 yards of twine. How many packages can he wrap if he uses 4/5 of a yard per package?

____

3. You buy 2 packages of cigarettes for 27 cents and give the storekeeper $1.00. How much change do you get back?

____

4. How many cubic inches in one cubic foot?

____

5. To Contradict is to: (a) deny, (b) admit, (c) reveal, (d) suspect?

____

6. An Aperture is an: (a) ending, (b) opening, (c) oracle, (d) exercise?

____

7. Concurrent means most nearly: (a) rebellious, (b) capable, (c) simultaneously, (d) conscientious?

____

8. A Hypothesis means most nearly a: (a) fact, (b) supposition, (c) statement, (d) discussion?

____

9. A production line will produce 5,000 units per shift. Your sample rate is 4%. How many samples will you be required to inspect per shift?

____

10. The correct spelling of the following word is: (a) Indianapolis, (b) Indinapolis, (c) Indianpolis, (d) Indianapolus?

____

11. Compute the percent of rejects of the following:

No. Inspected	No. Rejects	Percent
600	3	______
100	15	______
5	3	______
250	5	______

12. How many square feet in a square yard? ______

13. At the rate of 15 miles in 10 minutes, how far will a tank go in one hour?

____

14. Divide 50 by $\frac{1}{2}$ and add 4. ______

15. Perform the following:
A. 17.62 + 0.2 ______
B. 1.017 - .0006 ______
C. 1/6 X 5/8 ______
D. 3 divided by 1/16 ______

16. The correct spelling of this word is: (a) concurence, (b) concurrance, (c) concurrence, (d) concurance?

____

17. At the time that a bush 4 foot high cast a shadow 3 ft. long, a tree casts a shadow 36 ft. long. How high is the tree?

____

Exhibit 5

QUALITY CONTROL TRAINEE QUESTIONNAIRE

YES NO 1. Do you want to become a Quality Control Trainee?

YES NO 2. Can you read?

YES NO 3. Can you write?

YES NO 4. Can you add?

YES NO 5. Can you subtract?

YES NO 6. Can you multiply?

YES NO 7. Can you divide?

YES NO 8. Can you figure percentages?

9. Read aloud the statement of duties for a Quality Control Trainee.

10. Copy the statement of duties in your handwriting.

Exhibit 6

QUALITY CONTROL INSPECTOR TRAINEES
SENIORITY LIST 11/1/74

(M indicates Minority Employee)

Name	Plant Seniority Date
1. Mark Jones (M)	4/10/51
2. John Dixon (M)	8/10/51
3. William Mason (M)	8/11/52
4. Thomas Bryant	8/15/52
5. Mary Barton (M)	9/11/52
6. William Washington (M)	10/10/52
7. John Craft	3/10/53
8. Oneida Barton (M)	5/20/53
9. Bertha Jackson (M)	5/20/53
10. Emma Parsons	4/20/53
11. Carl Jackson (M)	4/20/62
12. John Smith	4/20/62
13. Donald Bryant	2/20/63
14. Susan Howe (M)	2/29/63
15. Mary Hanson (M)	2/29/63
16. Sarah Parker (M)	2/29/63
17. Jim Foster	3/10/63
18. Jim Fisher (M)	4/ 9/63
19. John Carter	5/ 4/63
20. Florence May	5/20/63
21. Brian King	5/20/63
22. Susie Bye (M)	5/20/63
23. Cynthia Rowan	5/20/63
24. Katy Pierce (M)	5/20/63
25. Marie Smith	5/20/63
26. Nancy Barton	5/10/66
27. Betty Truman (M)	5/10/66
28. John Falter	6/11/66
29. Irene Marks	6/11/66

Exhibit 7

DATA FROM PERSONNEL FOLDERS OF MARY FOX, LOUELLA BROWN, AND JOHN CURTIS

Mary Fox:	Date of hire - 9/10/66 Hired as Production Clerk Bid for QC Inspector Trainee - 11/5/68 Passed QC Inspector Test and was awarded QC Training Job - 11/10/68 Advanced to QC Inspector - 5/11/68

Louella Brown:	Date of hire - 8/22/53 Hired as Production Clerk Bid for QC Inspector Trainee - 2/8/59 Passed QC Inspector Test and was given QC Training Job - 2/18/59 Advanced to QC Inspector - 8/19/59

John Curtis:	Date of hire - 4/19/64 Hired as General Laborer Bid for and Promoted to Semi-Skilled Laborer - 3/15/65 Bid for QC Inspector Trainee - 6/11/67 Passed QC Inspector Test and was awarded QC Training Job - 6/23/67 Advanced to QC Inspector 12/24/67

WHAT IS THE PROPER CHAUFFEUR'S RATE?

The employer, Mavrakos Candy Company, is a manufacturer of candy, employing about 150 persons and disposing of its product primarily through its own retail stores owned and operated in the city and suburbs of St. Louis. The local union became a unit of the International Brotherhood of Teamsters by a process of affiliation. In May of 1976, six months after signing the last two year agreement, the local membership gave up its independent status by voting to formally affiliate with and become part of the Teamsters' union.

The parties began negotiations for a new agreement in the fall of 1977. Negotiations were somewhat more heated than in the past and continued for two weeks beyond the October 31 expiration date. The very last issue in contention was the rate of pay applicable to the chauffeur classification. Agreement was finally reached on a new two year contract to be retroactive to November 1, 1977. The contract provided a flat 38 cents per hour increase of wages of the preexisting rates for all employees except the chauffeur. An increase of 35 cents per hour was provided for the second year. The company had insisted that the chauffeur's increases should be limited to those figures; the union had contended that his increases should be much greater. Unable to agree upon a rate for the chauffeur the parties decided to resolve the impasse by submitting that issue to arbitration. The preexisting rate for the chauffeur was $5.15 per hour.

The classification of chauffeur includes only employees who are delivery truck drivers. Ordinarily the company employs not more than one full-time and one part-time employee in this category. However, at the time of the hearing, seasonal needs just prior to the holidays required the services of two full-time and one part-time employee.

The chauffeur operates a 2½ ton truck and his principal duty is the cartage of candy from the employer's manufacturing plant to its various retail outlets. At the factory he loads his truck alone and arranges the load on the truck, according to destinations; at the retail store he unloads with the aid of the porter. The individual freight bundles which he must handle weigh from ten to sixty pounds. At times he hauls items such as peanuts and oil from cold storage to the factory. The job involves not only the obvious necessity of knowing the district and its various traffic conditions and regulations, but also great care in arranging the order of deliveries and the arrival of goods at proper destinations to meet the business needs of the various outlets. In the past, the one permanent chauffeur has been called upon to give his judgment as to the qualifications of other prospective drivers. The ordinary care of the delivery truck is a garage operation in which the driver has no part. For reasons previously stated, the rate established by this arbitration will apply in all probability to only one regular full-time driver and to one part-time driver. The regular full-time driver entered the employ of the company in December, 1969, at which time his wage rate was $3.82 per hour.

COMPANY'S POSITION

In support of its position Mavrakos Candy Company referred to the rates established in the first union contract in November 1969. The rates for the chauffeur and production employees in the factory established a differential of $1.00 per hour in favor of the chauffeur. The company then showed that as wages increased over the succeeding seven years, the same differential was maintained. In other words, in each contract since 1969, the chauffeur received the same dollar increase in hourly wage rates as did the production workers. The company argued that this showed an industrial pattern settled and established by the parties in five successive contracts.

The company further contended that to accord the chauffeur an increase of more than 40 cents per hour would create inequities within its organization or within the bargaining unit. The chauffeur's rate under the company's proposal would be $5.53 per hour. The parties have agreed upon, and included in their contract, a rate of $6.15 for the stockman and $6.41 for the shipping clerk. The company pointed out that stockmen and shipping clerks generally have advanced to such positions from that of truck driver and have enjoyed a higher wage rate because in each such position they carried much more responsibility than in driving. Hence, an increase of much more than 40 cents for a chauffeur would eliminate almost entirely an already well-established differential favorable to a person of more skill and responsibility and so place a junior on practically the same wage level as his senior. The company regards the whole matter as a type of job evaluation already well established by the prior conduct of the parties and well justified on the basis of its own business knowledge as to the relative responsibilities of the several jobs.

UNION'S POSITION

On the other hand, the union takes the position that a rate of $5.53 is not enough for a truck driver. It points out that other candy manufacturing companies pay much more, e.g., the Switzer Candy Company rate is $7.20 and the Chase Candy Company pays $6.90. The union also noted that in the case of the Switzer Candy Company negotiations for an increase are now pending. In addition, the union argued that the prevailing wage rates of local truck drivers in the area generally are much above $5.53. Unionized drivers in the St. Louis area are paid as follows in the industries noted:

Berwery	$7.30
Frozen Food	$7.41
Grocery	$8.46
Packinghouse	$7.76
Plumbing Supply	$7.20

The company differentiates its position from that of the other candy manufacturers mentioned by pointing out that the products of these other manufacturers are machine-made, and each is engaged in mass production and distribution. On the other hand Mavakos produces only hand-made candy of the finest quality, and its average retail sale is less than one pound.

JONES COMPANY

The Jones Company, located in a major eastern city, supplied processed meat products to the hotel and restaurant trade. Due to increased sales in 1980, Peter Jones, the President of the firm, decided it was necessary to modify his processing operations in order to handle the additional volume. He was convinced that existing operations could not be expanded to accommodate the necessary increase in volume because of limited floor space in the plant.

After some investigation and study management adopted a new assembly line system of operation in the spring of 1980. The assembly line system resulted in greater production in the same amount of floor space. However, the new method of processing beef and other meat also caused a realignment of job duties. Employees were given specific duties of a more narrow scope than had been the case under the old craft system. Formerly one man performed a variety of operations while in the new system he was required to perform repeatedly a limited, specific task.

The Loin Department was affected by the changes in the production system. Under the old craft system employees had not been confined to a specific task. Usually a loin was broken down completely by three meatcutters and, on occasion, one cutter performed the entire job. Under the new assembly line system the work was divided into five separate and distinct operations. The impact of these changes on the existing job structure and the wage structure resulted in a dispute between the company and the union which represented Jones' employees.

Employees of the Jones Company were represented by the United Food and Commercial Workers. At the time of the reorganization an agreement dated May 16, 1979, was in effect between the parties. That agreement included the following clauses:

ARTICLE 17
<u>ARBITRATION</u>

<u>Section (a).</u> All disputes arising in the Employer's establishment or place of business which cannot be adjusted between the Employer and a Union representative within 72 hours shall be referred to arbitration...

ARTICLE 30
<u>WAGES</u>

<u>Section (a).</u> Effective May 9, 1979, all regular Employees shall receive an increase of fifty five (55) cents per hour.

<u>Section (b).</u> Effective May 9, 1980, all regular Employees shall receive an increase of forty five (45) cents per hour. The increases granted on May 9, 1980 are to be added to the classifications hereinafter listed in Article 30.

Section (c). The following are the classifications and rates in effect at the Employer's plant as of May 9, 1979:

Class A Cutters	$6.87
Class B Cutters	6.25
Hamburg Men	5.80
Poultry Men	5.65
Truck Drivers	5.65
Freezer Men	5.65
Summer Help	4.50
Common Labor Help	4.50
after 30 days	4.80

The aforesaid rates reflect the increase granted pursuant to the provisions of Article 30, Section (a) as herein above set forth.

ARTICLE 33
DURATION

This Agreement shall take effect as of the day and year first above written and shall continue in full force and effect until May 9, 1981.

The parties' dispute over the introduction of the new production system concerned the impact it had had on James Farrow. Jim Farrow was hired in September 1979 as an experienced trimmer and paid $5.80 an hour. Within the two week trial period the company informed the union that Farrow was not qualifying for the job. There was, however, another employee, then on vacation, who wanted to try out for the job. The parties agreed that Farrow could stay on the job until the other employee returned to work. At that time Farrow would have the option of leaving the company or taking a Common Labor Help job at $4.80 per hour. When the time came, Farrow elected the latter and he worked on that job until June 1980.

In the meantime the company had proceeded to realign its production process during the spring of 1980. It also engaged the National Metal Trades Association (NMTA) to study the new job structure and to develop a new rate structure on the basis of job evaluation principles. The NMTA recommended a new job rate structure with labor grades running from Grade 9 (bottom) to Grade 3 (top) and using the contract's Common Labor Help rate for Grade 9 and the contract's Class A Cutters rate for Grade 3. The rates for the intermediate grades (8 to 4) ran as follows: $5.65; $5.95; $6.30; $6.65; $7.00 (These rates included the May 1980 increase). It should be noted that at no time did the company propose that the personal rates of the employees be reduced because of any change in the wage structure made to reflect the new system.

One of the functions separated out to be performed as a distinct job was that of kidney removing. Under the old system this was a function performed on the loin by either a Class A

Cutter or a Class B Cutter, as one of the several things they did on the loin. A Class A Cutter was understood by the parties to be a general all-around man who could perform all operations on the loin in the most efficient manner. A Class B Cutter was understood to be a man who was not a Class A Cutter. Removing kidneys was one of the less skilled operations performed by these cutters.

In June 1980, Farrow was assigned to the new line to do kidney removing. He was paid the rate of Common Labor Help with the understanding that the rate for Kidney Remover, once agreed to by the parties, would be made retroactive in his case to June 2, 1980. It appears that for a limited time Farrow may have boned some loins as used to be the custom under the old system when demand was high. He stopped doing this when it came to management's attention. The boning operation was one of the more skilled cutter functions.

The company and union representatives discussed the job classifications and rates which the company proposed to adopt because of the change in production methods. The parties proceeded on the basis that unless they reached complete agreement on all aspects, there would be no agreement. At the outset they discussed Farrow and could not agree on his case. Although in the NMTA structure Kidney Remover was classified in Grade 8 at $5.65 per hour, the company proposed to the union that Farrow recieve $6.10 per hour. This was the fair and proper rate for Farrow, the company said, because it was the rate being paid others in the Grade 8 jobs. The company did not intend to concede by this proposal that this was the proper rate in relation to the NMTA studies, but rather that this was the most practical rate to pay Farrow.

The union took the position that Farrow was doing work which, under the contract, called for him to be a Class B Cutter, and insisted that he should receive that rate, $6.70 per hour. Just as the parties were unable to agree upon the proper rate for Farrow, they were unable to agree on modifications in their contractual wage structure to take into account the newly established alignment of functional assignments in the plant. The union's wage administration expert visted the plant but still no agreement could be reached. Finally, in July, the parties gave up trying to reach agreement and it was left that individual problems would be handled as they arose on a case by case basis. The union took the position that, in the absence of agreement in these sessions, the job classification structure in the agreement had to be determining. Unable to agree upon the proper rate for Jim Farrow, the parties submitted the following issue to arbitration:

> How shall James Farrow be classified, and at what rate shall he be paid?

The classifications in the agreement, with the exception of Hamburg Men, were long standing ones. The Hamburg Men classification was added during negotiation of the present agreement and was the only change in the company's classifications despite a union demand during the 1979 negotiations that changes be made in several classifications.

At the arbitration hearing the parties' argued as follows for their respective positions.

THE UNION'S POSITION

The union argued that the issue was not whether Farrow was a good cutter. A greater principle was involved - whether or not the union had a contract upon which it could rely. The parties had discussed classifications in the negotiation of their 1979 agreement. They reached agreement on a job and wage structure and the subject was closed for the duration of the contract. Stability of an agreement was important to both sides; both "bought" the 1979 agreement and must live with it. When the company asked the union to negotiate in June of 1980, the union had no obligation to negotiate. It did so strictly on the understanding that there had to be total agreement or no agreement at all. Total agreement was not reached by the parties. Therefore, the current contract must govern in the present case.

According to the union, the contract made Farrow a Class B cutter because he did work which, under the contract, was mutually understood to be a task performed by the cutter classifications. The parties had no misunderstanding. The only classifications which applied until May 9, 1981, were those listed in Article 30 of the contract unless, by mutual agreement, the parties added to or changed that list. No mutual agreement was reached.

The union contended that it had no quarrel with the company's attempt to improve efficiency or to rearrange the production process. However, if the company were allowed to install a unilaterally-developed job classification system based on job evaluation, then the union had no contractual rights. The union had a contract and the company knew it, as indicated when the company attempted to get the union to negotiate a new structure. That effort failed. Regardless of whether or not the union might be stupid not to have agreed with the company's proposals, no theory, legal or otherwise, would allow the company to install the Kidney Remover classification and rate without the union's agreement. Such a finding would mean that collective bargaining was a nullity.

The union argued further that, regardless of the desirability of the company's proposal, the arbitrator lacked power under the agreement to put it into effect. If he ruled in favor of the company, he would have said, in effect, that the company had no obligation even to talk with the union about the matter. The company, by its action in approaching the union, acknowledged such an obligation. Agreement with the company's position by the arbitrator would constitute a rewriting of the parties' contract and the introduction, through the back door of arbitration, of a job evaluation plan. The arbitrator could not do this, the union contended, even if he thought the results would be good. In the union's view, the Farrow matter was a test case. The fact that Article 30 of the agreement had an effective date of May 9, 1979, precluded either the company or the arbitrator from changing the classification system after May 9, 1979. To do so would make a mockery of the classifications and rates contained in the contract. The union sympathized with the company's position, but stated that no new system could be forced down the union's throat. The union urged the arbitrator to classify Farrow as a Class B Cutter under the parties' contract.

THE COMPANY'S POSITION

The company argued that the basic problem involved recognizing the industrial facts of life. It stressed that the parties have had a good relationship and have proceeded in good faith. It acknowledged that the union had a contract. However, the company contended that the fundamental conditions which prevailed in May 1979 when the contract was negotiated, had changed. What was true on May 9, 1979, was no longer true in June 1980. In May 1979 there was no such thing as a Kidney Remover about which the parties could have bargained. After the plant had been revamped the Kidney Remover classification was established and Jim Farrow actually performed that job. The situation had changed from one in which a worker did multiple tasks to one in which a worker specialized.

The company denied that it had attempted to impose standards on the union. Standards refer to performance. Rather, the company had sought to classify jobs under certain degrees of labor skill. The company denied that it had attempt to rewrite the contract. Instead, the company insisted it had tried to have the contract applied in accordance with the actual situation. It stressed that with the change in production processes the actual job structure had changed. This change insured jobs for more people and required that a job progression be recognized which which would permit orderly upgrading of people to better positons. The company emphasized that it had not arbitrarily realigned jobs and rates, but that technological changes produced new jobs which must be recognized under the agreement. It agrued that it neither ignored the contract nor attempted to act unilaterally. It had tried to develop proposed classifications and rates which were within the framework of the agreement and, at the same time, recognized the changed industrial facts of life in the plant.

The company did not wish to go to arbitration. It tried to negotiate these necessary changes with the union and failed. Therefore, it had the right to bring the matter to an arbitrator. Arbitration, the company pointed out, was the safety valve in the contract. There existed a bona fide dispute under the contract, and Article 17 provided that all such disputes were subject to arbitration.

With specific reference to Farrow, the company stressed that originally Farrow was hired at the Hamburg Men rate to do trimming. He proved he was not qualified to do that work. The union never challenged that decision. The company denied that the contract made Farrow a cutter because kidney removing was low in skill requirements. Also, prior to the present contract, even helpers had cut meat scraps for catfood. Farrow performed a job which did not exist when the current agreement was negotiated. He was not a Class B Cutter.

In the company's view, the contract constituted a "living

document" and, as such, must take into account a job which did not exist when the contract was negotiated. Although the correct, "scientific" rate for Farrow as a Kidney Remover was $5.65 per hour, the company said it had been more that fair in proposing $6.10 for Farrow as a practical rate consistent with the contract. The company asked that its proposal be upheld by the arbitrator.

MAR-AERO CORPORATION (A)

In September 1980, Mr. Robert Wells was in charge of the introduction of a new printing press at Mar-Aero Corporation's Springfield, Massachusetts plant. One of Mr. Wells' duties, as Staff Assistant to the Controller at Springfield, was the supervision of the Stationery Department which was responsible for printing material used by the various departments. Under his direction the department's Model 1250 Multilith Press was replaced by a newer, superior model, the 1275 Multilith Press.

Prior to the introduction of the new multilith press Jim Lux, Multilith Operator, Class 1, operated the Stationery Department's Model 1250. As well as running the 1250 for about six hours per day, Jim performed related duties such as operating multigraph machines, collators, staplers and cutters. Most of the plates used in the printing process were made by an outside lithographic firm which picked up the copy to be reproduced and instructions concerning same from Jim daily. Lux did a small amount of plate making. Occasionally he would show the two Multilith Operator, Class 2 employees how to operate the various pieces of equipment.

The old Model 1250, which cost approximately $3,000, was capable of making a one-color impression on an 8½"x11" sheet of paper at a speed of 6,000 sheets per hour. If a two-color job was to be done, one color would be printed one day, there would be an overnight drying period and the second color done the next day. On this model if the plate was out of line, Jim could adjust the paper as much as 3" to accommodate the error.

Jim Lux had been with the Mar-Aero Corporation for four years following his nine years with the United States Air Force. Jim had performed the same type of work in the service; in fact, he had operated a Model 1250. The instruction provided by the government through a two-week formal training program, as well as on-the-job training, provided Jim with much printing knowledge and skill. This experience was more than adequate for his duties in Mar-Aero's Stationery Department.

Mar-Aero Corporation manufactured defense and commercial products. In addition to manufacturing inertial guidance systems, airborne fire control systems and hydraulic controls for the government, Mar-Aero also produced fuel injection systems, automotive electrical equipment and carburetor parts for commercial customers. Total sales from the products produced at its three locations, of which Springfield was one, amounted to over $200 million dollars in 1978.

In Springfield, the Amalgamated Electrical Workers (AEW), Local 622, represented a bargaining unit consisting of clerical and office employees as well as the production and maintenance employees. Appendix B of the collective bargaining agreement between Mar-Aero and Local 622 contained a listing of Job Groups and their respective job evaluation point ranges and salary ranges (see Exhibit 1). The parties' agreement also stipulated that salaries were "...set in accordance with the classification of the job laid out and described in Appendix B of the contract." The job description of Multilith Operator, Class 1, appeared in Appendix B as follows:

Job -	Multilith Operator, Class 1
Description -	Sets up and operates Multilith and Multigraph Machines with some supervision. May occasionally supervise the Class 2 operator on set up and machine operation. Handles clerical duties connected with machines.

The job of Multilith Operator, Class 1, had been evaluated a number of years ago when a job evaluation system was installed by a Boston consulting firm, Research Associates Incorporated (RAI). The job was classified in Job Group 10 (see Exhibit 2 for SCHEDULE OFOFFICE CLASSIFICATIONS) but, unfortunately, the original evaluation of the job, completed by RAI, had been lost. Following the initial installation by the consultants, the Personnel Office took over responsibility for administering the job evaluation system (see Exhibit 3 for the Mar-Aero job evaluation manual and Exhibit 4 for the salaried job evaluation form used by the Personnel Office).

The acquisition of the new Model 1275 Multilith Press was viewed as an impressive addition to the department. Jim and his supervisor, Bob Wells, both knew this was a very superior machine and that it would be possible to do work formerly done by outside firms.

The 1275, which cost Mar-Aero $9,000, could be described as two of the old 1250 models put together. Since it had two printing heads it was possible to do two-color work in one run or to print on both sides of a sheet in a single run, thus eliminating delays for drying time. The 1275 took larger sheets, 11"x17", and could operate at speeds up to 7,000 sheets per hour.

During the first few months of use many problems were encountered with the new machine. The majority of these start-up problems were corrected by the company from which the machine was purchased; the other problems were reduced as Jim learned the more complicated adjustments associated with printing with this machine.

In the use of chemicals, far better results were obtained by varying the chemicals supplied by an outside firm. Jim pointed out that much greater attention had to be given to the handling of ink - the increased speed made ink control more critical in determining the final result. The adjustment of the spring controls, by trial and error, were more complicated - the new machine contained eight devices compared to the old machine's single control. Plate alignments demanded greater accuracy because of the dual head printing. On the 1275 Jim was allowed a tolerance of only 1/64" for the paper from one end of the machine to the other. Through trial and error and increased experience on the 1275, Jim was finally eliminating the production problems he originally faced.

In early December Jim discussed with Mr. Wells the changes caused by the 1275. It was possible to do in four hours what formerly took two days due to the increased speed, double printing and the increased sheet size. Mr. Wells realized that because of the capability of the new machine the department could turn out more production in the course of a week with Jim spending less time on the 1275 than he had spent on the old 1250. He did agree with Jim that the work had become much more intensive.

Prompted by his belief that the new machine had added to the responsibilities and requirements of Jim's job, by the numerous start-up problems, by an earnest attempt to do right by his subordinates, and by his unfamiliarity with job evaluation, Mr. Wells sent the following memorandum to the Personnel Office:

December 20, 1980

To: Personnel Office

From: Robert Wells, Staff Assistant to the Controller

The current requirements covering Mr. Lux's job are not covered adequately in his present classification. With the introduction of the 1275 Dual Head Multilith Machine, we now encompass work formerly performed by Off-set Printers at a much greater cost. The operation of the equipment requires a thorough knowledge of the inks and papers attendant to the sophisticated reproduction of printing. It would be impossible for anyone with a like classification to perform to the requirements of the Sales Department in its demand for service literature.

In view of the foregoing, I would appreciate your efforts in rewriting and upgrading the particular job.

signed: Robert Wells
Assistant Controller

Exhibit 1

JOB GROUPS AND SALARY RANGES

Job Group	RAI Point Range	SALARY RANGES (Effective May 12, 1980 through April 27, 1981)						
6	52-59	$258.00	$263.60	$269.20	$274.80	$280.40	$286.00	$291.60
7	44-51	239.20	244.00	249.00	254.00	259.00	264.00	269.00
8	37-43	207.60	211.60	215.70	219.80	223.90	228.00	232.10
9	31-36	197.60	201.00	205.00	209.00	215.00	217.00	221.00
10	26-30	191.60	194.90	198.60	202.40	206.60	210.00	213.80
11	21-25	186.20	189.90	193.20	196.90	200.60	204.30	
12	17-20	180.20	183.20	186.60	190.10	193.60	197.10	

Exhibit 2

SCHEDULE OF OFFICE CLASSIFICATIONS

Job Group No.	6	Planner, Class 1A
Job Group No.	7	Dispatcher, Class 2 Group Leader Planner, Class 1 Sales Assistant, Class 1
Job Group No.	8	Sales Assistant, Class 2 Traffic Clerk, Class 1 Microfilm Operator
Job Group No.	9	Accountant Blueprint Leader Cost or Price Leader Planner, Class 2 Plant Engineering Clerk Traffic Clerk, Class 2 Tape Librarian
Job Group No.	10	Accounting Clerk Cost or Price Clerk Factory Payroll Clerk, Class 1 Group Leader Mail Clerk & Messenger Leader Multilith Operator, Class 1 Purchase Clerk Production Planning Clerk Electronic Acct'g Machine Operator D P Control Clerk Public Typist Clerk, Class 1
Job Group No.	11	Chief Telephone Operator General Office Clerk, Class 1 Multilith Operator, Class 2 Stenographer, Class 1 D P Control Clerk, Class 2
Job Group No.	12	Blueprint Machine Operator General Office Clerk, Class 2 Keypunch Operator Telephone Operator Flexowriter

EVALUATION SCALE FOR SALARIED JOBS

<table>
<tr><th colspan="3">FACTORS</th><th>DESCRIPTION</th><th colspan="6">POINTS</th></tr>
<tr><td rowspan="22">A. RESPONSIBILITY</td><td rowspan="12">A-1 SUPERVISION</td><td rowspan="4">Supervision Over Others</td><td>Add Together Where Both Types of Supervision Are Involved</td><td>Up To 10*</td><td>11-25</td><td>26-50</td><td>51-100</td><td>101-200</td><td>Over 200</td></tr>
<tr><td>None</td><td>0</td><td>0</td><td>0</td><td>0</td><td>0</td><td>0</td></tr>
<tr><td>Partial Supervision</td><td>1</td><td>2</td><td>3</td><td>4</td><td>5</td><td>6</td></tr>
<tr><td>Full Supervision</td><td>2</td><td>4</td><td>6</td><td>8</td><td>10</td><td>12</td></tr>
<tr><td rowspan="4">Hiring And/Or Firing</td><td>Ranges Indicated Are Points Obtained From Prior Factor</td><td colspan="2">1-6</td><td colspan="2">7-12</td><td colspan="2">13-18</td></tr>
<tr><td>None</td><td colspan="2">0</td><td colspan="2">0</td><td colspan="2">0</td></tr>
<tr><td>Partial Responsibility</td><td colspan="2">0</td><td colspan="2">1</td><td colspan="2">2</td></tr>
<tr><td>Full Responsibility</td><td colspan="2">1</td><td colspan="2">2</td><td colspan="2">4</td></tr>
<tr><td rowspan="4">Training New Employees</td><td>None</td><td colspan="6">0</td></tr>
<tr><td>Up To 10% of Time</td><td colspan="6">1</td></tr>
<tr><td>25% - 50% of Time</td><td colspan="6">2</td></tr>
<tr><td>75% - 100% of Time</td><td colspan="6">3</td></tr>
<tr><td rowspan="6">A-2</td><td rowspan="6">Company Property</td><td></td><td colspan="2">Slight Risk</td><td colspan="2">Moderate Risk</td><td colspan="2">Serious Risk</td></tr>
<tr><td>Not Over $ 300</td><td colspan="2">0</td><td colspan="2">0</td><td colspan="2">1</td></tr>
<tr><td>$ 300 to $ 5,000</td><td colspan="2">1</td><td colspan="2">2</td><td colspan="2">3</td></tr>
<tr><td>$ 5,000 to $ 10,000</td><td colspan="2">2</td><td colspan="2">3</td><td colspan="2">4</td></tr>
<tr><td>$ 10,000 to $ 100,000</td><td colspan="2">3</td><td colspan="2">4</td><td colspan="2">6</td></tr>
<tr><td>Over $ 100,000</td><td colspan="2">4</td><td colspan="2">6</td><td colspan="2">8</td></tr>
<tr><td rowspan="5">A-3</td><td rowspan="5">Company Operations</td><td>Use Only Highest Rating If More Than One Check Mark</td><td colspan="2">In Department</td><td colspan="2">In Other Department</td><td colspan="2">To Future Progress</td></tr>
<tr><td>Minor Influence</td><td colspan="2">1</td><td colspan="2">2</td><td colspan="2">3</td></tr>
<tr><td>Moderate Influence</td><td colspan="2">3</td><td colspan="2">5</td><td colspan="2">6</td></tr>
<tr><td>Important Influence</td><td colspan="2">5</td><td colspan="2">8</td><td colspan="2">12</td></tr>
<tr><td></td><td></td><td></td><td>Great Influence</td><td colspan="2">6</td><td colspan="2">10</td><td colspan="2">15</td></tr>
<tr><td></td><td rowspan="4">A-4</td><td rowspan="4">Safety And Welfare</td><td>None</td><td colspan="2"></td><td colspan="2">0</td><td colspan="2"></td></tr>
<tr><td></td><td>If Responsibility Attaches Incidentally To Supervision such as Order Dept. Mgr.</td><td colspan="6">Rate 1/4 of The Base Supervisory Rating (A-1)</td></tr>
<tr><td></td><td>Jobs Engaged In Safety & Welfare, e.g., Nurse, Guard, Safety Director, Etc., Rate As Follows -</td><td>To 10%
1</td><td>11-25%
2</td><td>26-50%
3</td><td>51-75%
4</td><td colspan="2">Over 75%
5</td></tr>
<tr><td></td><td>Use This Factor For Safety & Welfare Committee Work</td><td colspan="6"></td></tr>
</table>

*Indicates number of employees supervised.

	FACTORS	DESCRIPTION	POINTS
B. REQUIREMENTS	B-1 Educational Requirements	Use Only Highest Rating If More Than One Check Mark	
		Grammar School	0
		High School	4
		Part College	6
		College Graduate	10
	B-2 Skill, License, Or Specialized Knowledge	As Required By Such Jobs As -	
		Adding Machine, Ditto Machine, Checking Or Proofreading	1
		Filing, Comptometer, Typing, Calculator, Key Punch, Sw. Bd.	2
		Bookkeeping, Stenography, Transcribing, Detail Drafting	3
		Printing, Picture Projection, Librarian, Physical Education	4
		Accounting, Sales, Mach. Shop Practice, Registered Nurse	5
		Credits, Com. Law, Time & Mot. Study, Finance, Sales Eng.	6
		Patent Law, M.E., E.E., Ch.E., Personnel Management	7
		Special Industry Skills Where Supply Is Limited, e.g. Ceramics, Control Inst., Rubber Compounding, Plant Physician	8
	B-3 Experience	No Experience	0
		Up To One Year	3
		One To Three Years	6
		Three To Five Years	9
		Five Years	12
		Five To Seven Years	15
		Seven To Nine Years	20
		Ten Years Or Over	25
	B-4 Learning Time	Less Than One Month	0
		Two To Three Months	1
		Six Months	2
		Twelve Months	3
		Over One Year	4

FACTORS			DESCRIPTION	POINTS	
B. REQUIREMENTS (con't.)	B-5 PERSONAL CAPACITY	Careful, Watchful, And Accurate	Use Only Highest Rating If More Than One Check Mark	Work Checked	Work Not Checked
			Carelessness Causes Additional Work In Department	1	2
			Carelessness Causes Delay In Prod., Costs Or Loss of Business	2	3
			Carelessness Causes Inconvenience To Customers	3	4
		Initiative	Work Largely Of A Routine Character	1	
			Work Of Same General Character, Involves A Minor Problem	2	
			Work Of Same General Character, Involves Important Problems	4	
			No Regular Routine, Many Problems Requiring Initiative	6	
		Breadth Of Vision	Familiar With Own Work Only	0	
			Familiar With All Work In Department	1	
			Familiar With Work In Several Departments	3	
			Familiar Wit Company's Major Operating Policies	5	
		Ingenuity	Some	2	
			Fair	6	
			High	10	
C. CONDITIONS	C-1	Working Conditions	Private Or Semi-Private Office	0	
			General Office, Laboratory, Factory Area With Pleasant Cond.	1	
			Factory Area With Moderately Pleasant Conditions	2	
			Factory Area With Unpleasant Conditions, Traveling	3	
			Add For Sitting - 0 Walking Or Standing - 2		
			Add For Risk/Personal Injury - Little-0, Moderate-1, Great-3		
	C-2	Public Contact	Work Requires Little Contact With People Outside Company	0	
			Job Brings Me Into Direct Personal Contact Each Day	Less Than 3 Times	More Than 3 Times
			Customers And Prospects	4	8
			Suppliers	2	4
			Applicants	1	2
			Others	2	4
	C-3	Confidential Data	Minor Items e.g., Wages, Salaries, Current Prod. Schedules	0	
			Some Information Re. Major Organization Changes Or Other Data Which If Disclosed Would Have Serious Internal Effects	2	
			Information Re. Future Products & Future Prod. Schedules	4	
			Confidential Data If Disclosed Would Seriously Affect The Company's Future Progress	6	

MAR-AERO CORPORATION (A)

Exhibit 4

SALARIED JOB RATING - SUBSTANTIATING DATA

DATE ____________________ JOB ____________________

		FACTORS	PTS	BASIS OF RATING
A. RESPONSIBILITY	A-1 SUPERVISION	SUPER-VISION OVER OTHERS		
		HIRING AND/OR FIRING		
		TRAIN NEW EMP.		
	A-2	COMPANY PROPERTY		
	A-3	COMPANY OPERATIONS		
	A-4	SAFETY AND WELFARE		
B. REQUIREMENTS	B-1	EDUCATION REQUIREMENTS		
	B-2	SKILL, LICENSE OR SPECIALIZED KNOWLEDGE		
	B-3	EXPERIENCE		
	B-4	LEARNING TIME		
	B-5	CAREFUL WATCHFUL ACCURATE		
	PERSONAL CAPACITY	INITITIVE		
		BREADTH OF VISION		
		INGENUITY		
C. CONDITIONS	C-1	WORKING CONDITIONS		
	C-2	PUBLIC CONTACT		
	C-3	CONFIDENTIAL DATA		
		TOTAL POINTS		SALARY RANGE NO.

SUPERIOR PACKING COMPANY

Richard Habert, an employee of Superior Packing Company, was terminated when the company discontinued operations at its plant in Fresno, California. The union which represented Mr. Habert, Butchers Local 776 of the Amalgamated Meat Cutters and Butcher Workmen, requested the Pension Board which administered the Superior Packing Company Employees' Pension Fund to grant Dick Habert a pension upon his termination. The pension requested was refused by the Pension Board. In order to obtain a pension for Habert the union attempted to implement the provisions of the grievance and arbitration procedure of its collective bargaining agreement with Superior Packing Company.

The company advised Local 776 that it could not grant Habert a pension and that it would not voluntarily agree to arbitrate Habert's pension claim. The union then filed a petition to compel the company to arbitrate the dispute. The union's petition, after being denied by the lower courts, was finally granted by the Supreme Court of the State of California and Mr. John Brice was appointed to hear and decide the case.

At the arbitration hearing Superior Packing Company raised a threshold question claiming that the dispute was not arbitrable under the terms of the parties' agreement. After reviewing the evidence and arguments on the question Mr. Brice ruled that Dick Habert's pension claim was arbitrable. Mr. Brice then turned to the merits of the dispute. Specifically Brice had to determine the following issue:

> Is Mr. Habert entitled to the pension claimed?
> If so, what remedy, if any, is appropriate?

Dick Habert was born May 3, 1916, and began working for the Superior Packing Company in June 1944 as an hourly-paid employee at Columbus, Ohio. Ten years later Dick was transferred to Fresno, California under an agreement with the employer that all accrued rights and seniority would be maintained from his original date of hire. Superior terminated operations at its Fresno plant on April 1, 1971, and Habert was terminated and paid three weeks vacation to which he was entitled under the provisions of the collective bargaining agreement. Thus, Habert was terminated as an employee of the Superior Packing Company on April 1, 1971, not because of an act on his part but because the company closed that plant and terminated its Fresno operations.

The collective bargaining agreement, effective March 23, 1970 to August 31, 1971, in addition to the three weeks vacation, also made provision for severance pay. Section 21(a)(1) of the agreement provided that:

> Severance pay shall be paid to employees having one or more years of continuous service who are permanently dropped from the service of the Company because of a reduction in forces arising out of the closing of a department or unit of the business or as a result of

technological changes and when it is not expected that they will be reemployed.

Habert's employment with Superior was terminated under circumstances which entitled him to this separation pay. Dick, however, rather than taking the severance pay, promptly requested the alternative provided in Appendix I of the agreement.

Appendix I of the collective bargaining agreement described changes which had been made to the rules and regulations of the Superior Packing Company Employees' Pension Fund in January 1967. Among those changes was language which provided a deferred pension payable at age 65 in lieu of separation pay. The language stated, in part:

> Vested Pensions
>
> An employee who is covered by the Agreement and whose employment is terminated with the Company under circumstances which entitle him to separation pay at the time when he has: (A) attained age 55, and, (B) completed 25 or more years of credited service, will be entitled to a pension upon his attaining age 65 equal to that determined in accordance with Paragraph 2 hereof, based on his continuous service on the date his employment terminated.
>
> The benefit payable under this paragrph is to be an alternative to the presently available separation pay and the election of the alternative of the pension benefit or of separation pay must be made within 18 months from the date the employee's employment is terminated.

The Pension Board refused Habert's request for a pension on the grounds that he had not reached the age of 55 on the date of his termination, the age specified in the pension plan as one of the requirements for eligibility. The union then demanded that the company recognize Habert's request, but the company also refused.

The company argued that the Pension Board ruled correctly, and in the only manner which it could, consistent with the agreement and the pension plan. The company pointed out that the provision of the plan under which Mr. Habert claimed a vested pension required that his employment be terminated at the time when he had "attained age 55." Dick had been terminated on April 1st and he did not turn 55 years old until May 3rd.

Management added that court and arbitration cases were abundant on the point that a claimant must meet the age requirements specified in a pension plan in order to be eligible for a pension. It disturbed management to think that if Habert were awarded a pension when he was more than a month short of the age requirement, other employees who failed to meet the requirements by a larger margin might also be entitled to a vested pension.

The company noted that many arbitration awards and decisions insisted upon literal compliance with the conditions precedent to vesting of a pension, even though such insistence had left the employee with no benefits after termination. Habert was not in that position. Appendix I stated "the benefit payable under this paragraph (Vested

Pensions) is to be an alternative to the presently available separation pay." Even the California Supreme Court had assumed that the alternative of separation pay was substantially equivalent to the vested pension claimed. Therefore, the denial of Habert's claim did not impose a harsh result upon him.

Superior Packing Company contended that vesting occurred when payments could be claimed absolutely and the contingencies were conditions precedent to that event. Unlike vacation benefits which could be considered as accrued on a day to day basis, pension benefits were defined by certain eligibility requirements. Unless and until all pension requirements were fulfilled, there was no individual to whom a pension was owing; vacations accrued, whereas pensions were contingent.

The company concluded that the collective bargaining agreement with Butchers Local 776 demonstrated the intention of the parties not to require the company to make a discretionary decision to grant an ineligible employee a pension. The obligations of the Superior Packing Company with respect to the pension fund were set out very precisely in Section 16(e). That section of the agreement stated:

> The Company's liability with respect to pension benefits shall be limited to its obligation to make contributions to the fund as provided herein.

Butchers Local 776 strongly disagreed with the company. The union believed that Habert had been but six working days from his 55th birthday when terminated and not more than one month as management stated. The union also viewed the collective bargaining agreement as bilateral in nature, with each party performing certain duties in exchange for performance by the other party. In this case Habert had performed his promise to the fullest extent allowed. His performance over a period of many years was merely six days short of "full" performance due to the slight deficiency. Superior had bargained essentially for twenty-five years of service before it would grant a pension and had obtained an excess of twenty-six years of service from Habert. Certainly the company had received its bargained-for exchanges. The age requirement was more in the nature of a condition than a promised performance, since Habert's being over 55 years old provided no benefit to Superior.

In any contract, the union contended, there was a burden on each party to allow the other to perform within the limits of the contract. If one party prevented the other from performing, the party who prevented the performance cannot later use the failure of such performance as a defense. The company cannot assert as a defense that Habert failed to comply with some non-essential condition for receiving a pension. There was a long-standing policy in the law to avoid forfeitures whenever possible. Local 776 also noted that Superior Packing Company was only one week short of having made all of its contributions to the plan on Habert's behalf. Surely, no great burden of paying a large lump sum suddenly was placed upon the company.

If Habert were deprived of his pension, the company would benefit directly from the forfeiture for it was clear that under the plan forfeitures reduced the company's contributions. Superior would be unjustly enriched if it were allowed to fire an employee just before that employee became entitled to a pension. A ruling against Habert would allow the company to retain a substantial portion of the compensation which it had agreed to furnish to Habert over the years.

The union also argued that national policy favored the vesting of employee benefits to prevent unjust enrichment by employers. Regulations issued by the U.S. Treasury to assist in interpreting the Internal Revenue Code of 1954 defined the national policy as favoring the vesting of pension benefits under the Code. This policy was further defined in a bill introduced in the U.S. Senate on May 2, 1968. The Pension Benefit Security Bill, drafted by the U.S. Department of Labor, provided criminal sanctions for funds which did not provide for vesting of benefits after a certain period. The purpose of such a national policy was to prevent what Superior sought to impose upon Habert. Dick could not now earn another pension in any other industry because of his limited industrial useful life. The company had taken the best he had to offer and now sought to line its own pockets with part of the compensation implicitly promised to him.

Lastly, the union characterized as specious one of the issues raised by the company. The company had questioned the effect that granting Habert's pension would have on other employees who failed to meet the requirements for a vested pension. The union argued that only one employee was involved, that there was no problem with a huge sum payable immediately to numerous claimants. The question was not the broad one urged by the company: "How close to full performance is close enough?" Rather the question was: "Was Habert's virtually complete performance enough?"

Mr. Brice now had to decide if Dick Habert was entitled to the pension which he had requested.

SECTION IV

Intra-Union Relationships

INTERNATIONAL ASSOCIATION OF MACHINISTS (A)

STRUCTURE AND ADMINISTRATION

The International Association of Machinists (IAM), with a membership of over 800,000 was the fourth largest union in the United States during the 1960s. The structure of IAM was based upon some 1,900 local unions, known as local lodges, which varied in size from as few as 15 to as many as 10,000 members. The intermediate structural unit of IAM was the district lodge. The district lodge was a delegate body made up of representatives elected from affiliated local lodges within the transport system, industry, or locality in which the district lodges were established.

The national central unit within the union's structure is known as the Grand Lodge of the International Association of Machinists and Aerospace Workers. The Grand Lodge consists of the international officers, the staff appointed to assist them, and the convention of representative delegates from local lodges. The powers of the Grand Lodge are stipulated in the IAM's constitution.

Normally the legislative function which establishes the policies found in the constitution has been initiated by the quadrennial convention of delegates. Amendments to the constitution may also be proposed directly by the membership. Prior to 1967, all amendments to the IAM constitution had to be approved by a membership vote through a referendum. This post-convention referendum was eliminated, however, when the membership approved a constitutional amendment proposed by the Executive Council.

The constitution states that between conventions all executive powers of the Grand Lodge are vested in the Executive Council. The Council is composed of the eleven (11) elected international officers: the International President, the General Secretary-Treasurer and nine (9) General Vice Presidents. The Executive Council fulfills its duties through periodic meetings and through the administrative organization of the Grand Lodge.

The administrative organization of the Grand Lodge is predominantly based upon a geographical delineation. The Grand Lodge is divided into seven territories, including Canada. The exception to this rule is the Transportation Department. This department was established in 1952 with the purpose to protect the interests of the membership in the railroad and air transport industries. This industrial department exercises authority in those industries throughout the country, thereby overlapping many geographical territories.

The International President assigns a General Vice President to supervise the activities of all the lodges in one of the seven territories or the transportation department. Each of the eight General Vice Presidents so assigned has been relatively dominant in his designated territory.

The pinnacle of administrative authority within the hierarchy is vested in the three remaining Executive Council members: the International President, a General Vice President assigned to assist the president directly, and the General Secretary-Treasurer. These three officers maintain offices at the national headquarters of IAM in Washington, D.C., from which they administer the national organization. Although each individual Vice President is subordinate to the international officers at headquarters, the entire Executive Council remains the union's supreme governing body between conventions.

APPOINTED REPRESENTATIVES

In order to properly service the needs of the membership and fulfill their own administrative responsibilities, the elective officers of IAM have employed a staff of appointed employees. The clerical and technical staff employed at headquarters numbered approximately two hundred individuals. An audit program of the financial condition of the local and district lodges is conducted by the General Secretary-Treasurer with the aid of some twenty Grand Lodge Auditors.

The activities of the Grand Lodge with respect to the expansion of the union, organization of members, grievance representation, National Labor Relations Board representation, and negotiation with employers falls upon the shoulders of the field staff. This staff, as of June 1966, consisted of approximately three Press Representatives, two hundred Grand Lodge Representatives, and forty Special Representatives (Special Representatives are essentially apprentice Grand Lodge Representatives). The Press Representatives were news media specialists assigned to assist the Special and Grand Lodge Representatives with their field activities, especially with the drafting of handbills and press releases.

Each Grand Lodge Representatives (GLR) usually has been assigned to work under one of the General Vice Presidents or to some special task under the direct supervision of the International President. The representatives working in the field have been supervised by the Vice Presidents but occasionally assignments have been made by the President. The representatives are required to submit weekly activity and expense reports to their supervising Vice Presidents and to the International President.

These appointed officials direct organizational campaigns, negotiate and sign contracts on behalf of IAM, attend conferences and meetings, police adherence by local and district lodges to the IAM constitution and policies, act as trustees for delinquent locals and district lodges, and supervise these lodges in organizing, electing officials, handling grievances and arbitration and directing approved strikes.

The position of Grand Lodge Representative has been established under the IAM constitution. Article VI, Sec. 2, reads as follows:

Chief Organizer

> Sec. 2 The I.(nternational) P.(resident) shall be the chief organizer of the G.(rand) L.(odge) and shall have full control of all G.(rand) L.(odge) R.(epresentatives) and of all organizing. He shall provide suitable

> literature for organizing purposes and have the authority when conditions warrant to appoint G.L.R.s and assign them to such localities and for such particular terms and duties as shall be for the best interests of the IAM. All of which shall be subject to the approval of the E.(xecutive) C.(ouncil).

IAM membership is a required qualification for the position of Grand Lodge Representative as stated in Article VI, Section 8 of the constitution. It states:

> Grand Lodge Representatives
>
> Sec. 8. G.L.R.s appointed by the I.P. under authority of Sec. 2 of this Article shall be members in continuous good standing for at least 5 years immediately prior to their appointment, free from delinquencies of any nature to any L.(ocal) L.(odge), D.(istrict) L.(odge) or the G.(rand) L.(odge).

JOB SECURITY AND POLITICAL ACTIVITY

The Grand Lodge Representatives' need for job security was demonstrated during the aftermath of the 1961 international elections. Roy M. Brown, a General Vice President of IAM since 1942 and supervisor of the Southwest Territory, was notified, prior to the 1961 elections, that the Executive Council would not support his candidacy for re-election to the office. Among other things, the split between Brown and the administration stemmed from the expulsion of a member who had brought charges of misusing funds against a district officer in California. Brown responded to the council's notice by announcing his candidacy for the office of General Secretary-Treasurer in opposition to the incumbent, Elmer E. Walker. A number of Grand Lodge Representatives working in the Southwest Territory actively supported Brown in his bid for international office.

The 1961 election results were certified on June 15, 1961, in Washington, D.C., and they indicated that Walker had defeated Brown by almost a 3 to 1 margin. International President Albert J. Hayes wrote that same day to a number of the Grand Lodge Representatives who had supported Brown, notifying each that his services as Grand Lodge Representative were terminated "as of midnight July 31, 1961." No reasons had been given for the termination nor had a hearing been held. On August 11, 1961, six Grand Lodge Representatives demanded of IAM specific charges in writing, time to prepare their defense and a full and fair hearing. They received no reply to their demands.

In accordance with the qualifications for their position, the six Grand Lodge Representatives were members of the IAM. The length of membership, as of 1963, and the original date of employment as Grand Lodge Representative for each are as follows:

	Length of Membership	Date of Employment
Mr. King	20 years	May 1, 1951
Mr. Anderson	27 years	July 1, 1957
Mr. Lindsey	25 years	May 5, 1942
Mr. McGraw	22 years	June 1, 1945
Mr. Skagen	21 years	March 1, 1945
Mr. Truax	26 years	August 1, 1944

As members of IAM these six Grand Lodge Representatives sought relief in District Court under the Labor-Management Reporting and Disclosure Act of 1959 (LMRDA or Landrum-Griffin Act). They charged IAM, Albert J. Hayes, the International President, and Elmer E. Walker, the General Secretary-Treasurer, with violation and conspiracy to violate their rights protected under the LMRDA. The core question before the U.S. District Court was:

> "Was the discharge of plaintiffs without written specific charges nor a reasonable time to prepare a defense nor a full and fair hearing and for the sole reason that plaintiffs supported Brown in an election for Union office violative of plaintiffs' rights and redressable by federal court action?"

Title I of the LMRDA, the "Bill of Rights of Members of Labor Organizations," declares the congressional intention that every member will have complete freedom in voting and expressing himself concerning union elections, election issues and candidates for election. Section 101(a)(5) of the Act states:

> (5) Safeguards Against Improper Disciplinary Action. No member of any labor organization may be fined, suspended, expelled, or otherwise disciplined except for non-payment of dues by such organization or by any officer thereof unless such member has been (A) served with written specific charges; (B) given reasonable time to prepare his defense; (C) offered a full and fair hearing.

Based upon the undisputed facts, the District Court found that the six union members had been disciplined without service of written specific charges, without a reasonable period of time to prepare their defenses and had not been offered a full and fair hearing. IAM demurred, contending that Section 101(a)(5) applied solely to membership rights. However, the court found no such restrictive construction, pointing out that the statute declared that "No member of any labor organization may be ... disciplined;" it did not declare "may be disciplined solely as to rights of membership."

The Court stated:

> There is an inextricable link between each plaintiff's status as a member and as an employee or officer of the Union, i.e., Grand Lodge Representative. To say that it

> does not impose discipline upon a member to deprive him of the advantage of employment by the organization to which he belongs and of which he must be a member as a qualification for employment, is to deny that inextricable link. Even if there were no such link, deprivation of employment can be a most effective means of disciplining a member. And if an underlying purpose of the statute be, as it so plainly is, to protect free elections within labor organizations covered, as defendant Union is, what better means of forestalling such freedom than to discharge members from positions of value to them and of influence in a union for no reason other than support of a losing candidate for union office?

IAM pointed out that under its constitution employment as a Grand Lodge Representative was wholly at the discretion of the International President. The Court, however, stated that:

> Implicit in the power of any officer of an organization to employ personnel at discretion and at will is the limitation that they are to be employed to carry out the purposes of the organization. When an officer asserts that the broad discretion to hire and fire, granted to him by the organic law of a union, may be exercised without restraint or limitation against open and honest union election activities of employee-members of the union, he urges a doctrine which finds support neither in law nor in sound union tradition.

The District Court, finding that these GLRs rights under Section 101(a)(5) of the LMRDA had been violated, did not rule on claimed violations of other provisions of the Act. It denied cross-motions for summary judgment and a motion by IAM for dismissal. However, no remedy was granted, for the court believed an immediate appeal from its order would materially advance the ultimate termination of the litigation and resolve the question of law concerning these employee-members' right to relief under the Act. An interlocutory appeal by IAM to the Circuit Court of Appeals followed the order of the District Court.

The 9th Circuit Court of Appeals stated in its decision dated June 23, 1964, that Section 101(a)(5) of the LMRDA did not apply to summary removal of union officers. However, the Court held applicable Sections 101(a)(1) and (2) which guaranteed equal political rights to union memebers and Section 609 which imposed a prohibition on certain discipline exercised by a union.

Congress did not intend Section 101(a)(5) to preclude a summary removal of a member from union office. When considering the Act, Congress was concerned that such preclusion would permit wrongdoing union officials to remain in office while the time-consuming "due process" requirements of the section were met. In order to meet this objection, the Conference Report on the Act stated that Section 101(a)(5) "applies only to suspension of membership in the union; it does not refer to suspension of a member's status as an officer in the union." The Circuit Court stated that, "Congress' primary concern was that Section 101(a)(5) should not bar summary removal of union officials suspected of malfeasance, but the means Congresss chose to accomplish its purposes was to wholly exclude suspension or removal from union office from the category of union action to which Section 101(a)(5) applied." Thus the Circuit Court overruled the findings of the District Court with respect to this section of the LMRDA.

The Circuit Court ruled that the employee-members had succeeded in establishing claims under Section 101(a)(1) and 101(a)(2) and 609 of the Act. Sections 101(a)(1) and (2) read as follows:

> Section 101(a)
>
> (1) EQUAL RIGHTS - Every member of a labor organization shall have equal rights and privileges within such organization to nominate candidates, to vote in elections or referendums of the labor organization, to attend membership meetings and to participate in the deliberations and voting upon the business of such meetings, subject to reasonable rules and regulations in such organization's constitution and by-laws.
>
> (2) FREEDOM OF SPEECH AND ASSEMBLY - Every member of any labor organization shall have the right to meet and assemble freely with other members; and to express any views, arguments, or opinions; and to express at meetings of the labor organization his views, upon candidates in an election of the labor organization or upon any business properly before the meeting, subject to the organization's established and reasonable rules pertaining to the conduct of meetings. Provided, that nothing herein shall be construed to impair the right of a labor organization to adopt and enforce reasonable rules as to the responsibility of every member toward the organization as an institution and to his refraining from conduct that would interfere with its performance of its legal or contractual obligations.

IAM agreed that the right to engage in intra-union political activity, such as that engaged in by the six representatives, was guaranteed to members by the above sections of the Act. At the same time, IAM argued that these rights do not extend to members who are also officers of the union. The Circuit Court, however, pointed out that Sections 101(a)(1) and 101(a)(2) apply to every member and had been adopted to strengthen internal union democracy. An exclusion of officer-members, as suggested by IAM, would deny protection to those best equipped to keep union government vigorously and effectively democratic. The Circuit Court ruled IAM's position invalid, holding that Sections 101(a)(1) and 101(a)(2) do apply to officer-members.

IAM further contended that Section 609 of the Act should have the same restrictive interpretation as the Circuit Court had found in Section 101(a)(5).

Section 609 reads:

> It shall be unlawful for any labor organization, or any officer, agent, shop steward, or other representative of a labor organization, or any employee thereof to fine, suspend, expel, or otherwise discipline any of its members for exercising any right to which he is entitled under the provisions of this Act. The provisions of Section 102 shall be applicable in the enforcement of this Section.

IAM believed the words "otherwise discipline" in the above section must be read as they were in 101(a)(5) so as to exclude summary removal from union office. It is plausible that the words were used with the same meaning; it is also plausible that these identical words were used with quite different meanings. The Circuit Court reviewed the legislative history of the statute in order to resolve the question.

The Congress imposed a limitation upon "otherwise discipline" in Section 101(a)(5) in order to preserve the union's power to <u>summarily</u> remove officer-members. That section referred to procedural due process. Section 609, on the other hand, made no reference to the procedures to be followed in the disciplining of union members. This latter section is an enforcement provision, effectuating rights conferred in other sections by making it unlawful to punish members who seek to exercise such rights. The Circuit Court found nothing in the legislative history to indicate that Congress wished to preserve an unrestricted power in the union to discipline officer-members. "Thus to construe Section 609 to exclude from its coverage dismissal from union office would immunize a most effective weapon of reprisal," stated the court.

IAM put forth an additional argument, that to extend Section 609 to cases of dismissal from union employment would create a potential conflict of jurisdiction between the courts and the National Labor Relations Board. IAM based this argument on the fact that the actions which the representatives had accused IAM of committing might constitute an unfair labor practice by the union-employer (IAM) under Section 8(a) of the National Labor Relations Act. The Circuit Court held that "Congress was aware that the rights conferred by the Labor Management Reporting and Disclosure Act of 1959 overlapped those available under state law and other federal legislation, and expressly provided that these rights were to be cumulative." Section 609, therefore, included removal from union office within the meaning of the words "otherwise discipline."

The U.S. Circuit Court of Appeals affirmed the District Court's conclusions, although for different reasons, and the Supreme Court of the United States refused a writ of certiorari on November 2, 1964. The representative's right to relief under the Labor Management Reporting and Disclosure Act of 1959 was established under Section 102 of the Act, which reads in part:

> Sec. 102. Any persons whose rights secured by the provisions of this title have been infringed by any violation of this title may bring a civil action in a district court of the United States for such relief (including injunctions) as may be appropriate.

The case was remanded to the District Court for the granting of appropriate relief and remedies.

JOB SECURITY AND FISCAL PROBLEMS

A second event which adversely affected the job security of representatives involved fiscal difficulties of the Grand Lodge of the International. In November of 1964 a membership referendum vote had been conducted in order to secure approval to increase the per capita tax from two dollars to two dollars and fifty cents per month. IAM had hoped to secure additional income because its expenses over the preceding two years had exceeded its income by about two million dollars. The members, through a referendum tabulated in December 1964, rejected the proposed increase and the Executive Council endorsed a retrenchment program. Since income could not be increased, expenses had to be reduced.

One of the steps taken to reduce expenditures was the elimination of Grand Lodge financial support of the employees of local and district lodges. Under a long-standing policy the Grand Lodge had been assuming one-half the salary, up to fixed maximum contribution, of business agencies established by the subordinate units. This financial assistance was granted provided the particular Business Representative, General Chairman or Organizer was persona grata with the Grand Lodge. This practice was discontinued in the effort to reduce expenses.

Another attempt to achieve fiscal balance involved the clerical and field staff of the Grand Lodge. Their numbers were reduced by 10 to 20 per cent. Attrition played a major role in the reduction of both the clerical staff and the staff of Grand Lodge Representatives with employees over age 60 encouraged to retire before the mandatory age of 65. However, the desired staff reduction could not be accomplished solely through attrition and layoffs became necessary.

The clerical staff reduction did not cause much of a problem. Clerical employees were laid off in accordance with the seniority provisions negotiated between IAM and the bargaining representative of the clerical staff, Local 2, Office Employees International Union. On the other hand, the Grand Lodge Representatives were not represented for collective bargaining purposes and similar provisions rationalizing the basis for layoffs had not been established for the field staff.

The General Vice Presidents, as supervisors of the territories, were instructed to adhere as closely as possible to the principle of seniority. The nature of the work performed by the field staff, however, precluded strict observance of last-hired-first-furloughed rule. Some representatives were involved with impending negotiations; others could not be removed because of peculiarities associated with their assigned positions. Thus in accommodating the desired reduction of field representatives the principle of seniority was violated.

One year after the defeat of the referendum the international made a second attempt to increase revenue. The membership, through a second referendum vote conducted in January 1966, approved the per capita tax increase to two dollars and fifty cents per month, effective April 1, 1966. As a result of this increased income general increases in fringe benefits and pay were granted the field-staff employees effective April 1, 1966. The staff was increased in graduated steps, new people were added, and most of the staff members on layoff were recalled by the summer of 1966. The few representatives not recalled to duty were notified that their services had been unsatisfactory prior to the approval of the per capita tax increase.

INTERNATIONAL ASSOCIATION OF MACHINISTS (B)

The structure and administration of the International Association of Machinists as well as some political and fiscal problems which affected the job security of IAM representatives are described in INTERNATIONAL ASSOCIATION OF MACHINISTS (A).

NEW LEADERSHIP AND STAFF ORGANIZATION

The International Association of Machinists (IAM) announced in February 1965, the unopposed nomination of P.L. (Roy) Siemiller and Matthew DeMore as successors to President Hayes and General Secretary-Treasurer Walker, respectively. Messrs. Hayes and Walker retired on June 30, 1965, in accordance with the union's rule of mandatory retirement at age 65. Mr. Siemiller and Mr. DeMore assumed the duties and responsibilities of their offices on July 1, 1965.

During their first month in office the new administration realized fully their roles as top management of IAM. The officers were informed of an effort to organize the members of the field staff for the purpose of establishing a collective bargaining relationship with IAM. The campaign to organize the staff representatives into a "second-generation union", the IAM Representatives Association, was led by Franklin W. Nix, a Press Representative assigned to Atlanta, Georgia, headquarters of the Southern Territory. In addition to his activity on behalf of the field staff, Mr. Nix initiated an unremitting attack upon his superior, General Vice President George Watkins. This attack will be described separately below.

On July 9, 1965, a meeting was conducted in Washington between Nix, General Secretary Matthew DeMore and General Vice President Ross Matthews. At the meeting Nix informed DeMore and Matthews that he was heading up a movement to organize a Grand Lodge Representatives Association. Nix also gave them a copy of a 12-page organizing letter addressed to the field staff and informed them the letter would go into the mail either that day or the following day.

On July 10, 1965, Nix sent to President Siemiller a registered letter in which he informed Siemiller of the organizing activities in behalf of the Association and warned him that if IAM resorted to reprisals counter-measures would be taken. These measures might include charges under Section 8(a)(1),(3) and (5) of the National Labor Relations Act as well as picketing in front of International's offices, and other publicity in the major areas of membership.

Nix wrote to President Siemiller on July 18, 1965, and requested recognition of the Association as the bargaining representative of the field staff in the Southern Territory. Siemiller denied the request on July 26 and expressed his doubt that the Association represented a majority of the employees in an appropriate bargaining unit.

The IAM Executive Council met on September 1 and 2, 1965.

Because of the charges made by Nix against Vice President Watkins (discussed below) the council decided to relieve Watkins of his assignment over the Southern Territory and also to divide that territory, adding various portions to other contiguous territories. The portion east of the Mississippi River was added to the Great Lakes Territory under the supervision of Vice President Floyd Smith. Nix was later assigned to Smith's staff.

On January 6, 1966, Nix met with Siemiller, Matthews, and DeMore in Washington to discuss the Watkins situation at which time Nix also brought up the organizing effort. Nix stated at the meeting that he had had ample time to think about the organizing movement and had come to the view that the Association would be political in nature, and detrimental to IAM. He felt that its formation was a mistake and that he would disband it. Nix suggested alternatively that Siemiller recognize an informal committee through which the representatives could present grievances. Siemiller refused the request, stating that any representative could discuss problems with him or the vice president supervising the representative's territory.

On January 26, 1966, Nix filed a representation petition with the National Labor Relations Board (NLRD) seeking a nation-wide unit of Grand Lodge Representatives, Special Representatives, and Press Representatives of IAM. On the same day Nix wired Siemiller on behalf of the Association and claimed majority representation. He sent a second telegram which read, in part, as follows:

> Lack of any concessions whatever, even to a committee which would not have bound you to anything, unacceptable to organizing committee. I am bound to my commitment to them to petition. I have therefore this date filed petition with the Atlanta Board. Your denial of the existence of a commitment, signed by you, A.J. Hayes and Elmer Walker, and which I had personally seen, also convinces me beyond any doubt that oral promises of the "my-door-is-open" type of staff consideration, would be meaningless....

Based upon the Association's demand for recognition the IAM filed an employer's petition on February 9, 1966.

One official of IAM was shocked by the organizing activity. He believed the organizing activity to be the work of a small group of professional employees such as Nix, who were, by nature, malcontents. He stressed a difference between the professional employees and the representatives. Unlike the Grand Lodge Representatives, the professional employees were not required to be members of IAM as a condition of employment. They were usually granted membership after having been hired. However, because of their lack of identification with the union prior to their employee status, their loyalty and dedication were far different from that of the Grand Lodge Representatives. This official did not believe that the Association would win a representation election.

IAM announced in the February 24, 1966, issue of The Machinist that the referendum election held among its members in January was successful. The membership had increased the per-capita tax to two dollars fifty cents per month and passed a proposition which raised the salaries of the International Officers, Grand Lodge Representatives and Grand Lodge Auditors. These salaries were fixed by the IAM constitution, amendment of which was necessary to make increases. The increases, in accordance with the constitution, went into effect April 1, 1966.

The above action had no effect on the salaries of Special Representatives or on the per diem and expense allowances because these matters were not covered by the constitution. However, the Executive Council decided to upgrade all Special Representatives to Grand Lodge Representatives and to increase the per diem and expense allowances, effective April 1, 1966.

On February 24, some 54 Special Representatives were informed of their reclassification and of their raises which ranged from $1,000 to $4,000 per year. On March 8, IAM notified all Grand Lodge Representatives, Grand Lodge Auditors, and Special Representatives that, in accordance with the Executive Council's decision of February 8, the per diem allowance was increased from $20 to $24 per day and the incidental expense allowance from $7 to $8 a day, also effective April 1, 1966.

The National Labor Relations Board conducted hearings on the representation petitions in February and March, 1966. NLRB members McCullock, Fanning and Zagaria heard the case and their Decision and Order was issued June 10, 1966.

During the hearings IAM contended (even though it had filed a petition requesting an election) that no question of representation existed under the law. IAM argued that the IAM Representatives Association was not a labor organization within the terms of the National Labor Relations Act; that the employees in the requested unit were managerial and/or supervisory personnel and, therefore, not employees under the Act; and that the IAM Constitution barred the representation petitions since this document specified the terms and conditions of employment.

The Board disagreed with IAM and found that a question existed concerning the representation of employees within the meaning of the Act.

The members of the Board ruled that the IAM Representatives Association constituted an organization in which employees participated and that it had been recently organized for the purpose of dealing with employers concerning wages, hours, and conditions of employment. It was true the IAM Representatives Association had no constitution or elected officers; however, meetings for those eligible for membership had been conducted, and the Representatives Association had been the petitioner in the case. Therefore, the Board held the Association was a labor organization within the meaning of the Act.

The Board also found no merit in the contention that the constitution of IAM should act as a bar to the proceedings. The constitution was not a collective bargaining agreement between an employees' bargaining representative and an employer.

The parties disagreed on the description of an appropriate bargaining unit. The IAM Representatives Association wished to include Grand Lodge Representatives, Special Representatives and Press Representatives of the IAM field staff in the United States. Their petition excluded Grand Lodge Representatives and Special Representatives assigned to Vice Presidents as assistants, to the Washington headquarters staff, and those assigned to the transportation department in Chicago; Grand Lodge Auditors; office and clerical employees; professional and technical employees of headquarters staff; guards; and supervisors. IAM on the other hand defined the unit to include all Grand Lodge Representatives, Special Representatives, and Grand Lodge Auditors in the United States and Canada. IAM also believed that the Press Representatives, as professional employees, should be excluded from the unit.

The Board found that all field Grand Lodge Representatives and Special Representatives employed in the United States constituted an appropriate unit. Canadians were excluded because they worked exclusively in Canada and under the direction of the Canadian Vice President. Since the parties were unable to agree upon inclusion or exclusion of certain other classes of employees as listed above, such determination was made by the Board.

The NLRB included in the unit the following:

(a) Assistants to the Vice Presidents--Each vice president in charge of a territory designated one or more Grand Lodge Representatives as assistants. No special qualifications were required and since the duties, pay, benefits and supervision of these assistants were similar to those of other Grand Lodge Representatives, they were included in the unit.

(b) Headquarters Staff--Five of the ten Grand Lodge Representatives and one of the three Special Representatives assigned to the Washington headquarters were included. All of these employees performed special assignments. However, the six employees included spent substantial time coordinating and participating in organizing and negotiating in the field.

(c) Transportation Department Representatives--The Grand Lodge Representatives assigned to the transportation department often crossed the boundaries of the various territories. The duties of the representatives in the air and railroad industries, while requiring such movement, were similar to those of the other Grand Lodge Representatives. Therefore, GLRs assigned to the transportation department were included.

(d) Press Representatives--The three Press representatives specialists in public relations and press media, assisted field representatives with organizational work, strikes, and negotiations under the immediate supervision of their territorial Vice Presidents. The salary of the Press Representatives was not set by IAM's constitution. However, other terms of employment were similar to those of the Grand Lodge Representatives. At times the Press Representatives substituted for the headquarters' newspaper staff. While the newspaper staff spent only about five per cent of the time away from Washington, the Press Representatives spent most of their time in the field and, therefore, were included in the unit.

The NLRB excluded from the unit the following:

(a) Grand Lodge Auditors--The Grand Lodge Auditors received the same pay as the GLRs. However, the auditors were appointed and supervised by the General Secretary-Treasurer; their assigned areas were not coextensive with regions supervised by the Vice Presidents; and their primary function was the auditing of local and district lodges. They were excluded from the unit.

(b) Headquarters Staff--Six of the thirteen representatives on the Washington staff were included above. The remaining seven employees rarely engaged in field work. The Board ruled they possessed little "community of interest" with field representatives and excluded them.

The unit appropriate for the purposes of collective bargaining within the meaning of the Act was described by the Board as follows:

> All Grand Lodge, Special, and Press Representatives employed by the Employer in the United States and Puerto Rico; but excluding all similarly classified employees employed exclusively in Canada, those employed in unrelated specialized assignments at Headquarters, Grand Lodge Auditors, office clerical employees, professional and technical employees, guards and supervisors as defined in the Act.

The eligibility of certain International Association of Machinists employees on lay off since 1965 and those discharged in 1961 was questioned. The Board ruled that both groups could vote in the representatives election, subject to challenge. It was not clear whether those separated in 1965 had been terminated or temporarily furloughed. The employee status of those discharged in 1961 was contingent upon the verdict in their District Court action under the Labor-Management Reporting and Disclosure Act of 1959, described in the (A) case.

The election was conducted by mail ballot July 28, 1966, and the following vote resulted:

Votes for IAM Representatives Association	108
Votes for No Union	91
Challenged Ballots	16
Void Ballots	3

The IAM Representatives Association was certified by the NLRB as the bargaining agent for the unit on August 5, 1966. Plato Papps, IAM Chief Counsel, said that the results of the vote would be honored; and the staff union was recognized by IAM.

One high-ranking official of the IAM explained the results of the election as force of habit, i.e., given the chance, any union representative would vote for a union. He did not believe the Association was a necessity, however, since the employees already belonged to the best labor union in the United States, the IAM. He believed that 95 per cent of the employees were good, loyal individuals but "off the beaten path" on this issue. He thought "They had lost a little bit of the philosophy which had brought them into the union movement."

He also envisioned many problems resulting from the election. The democratic atmosphere within IAM had been generated from the established policy that the members "call the shots." The members direct the policies of the IAM through the constitution which was revised only through membership referendum. Since the qualifications, wages, pensions, expenses and other terms of employment for the employees in the unit were set by the constitution, this IAM official believed that the area for bargaining was limited. He argued that the collective bargaining relationship and the constitution were incompatible on a number of issues.

Local Lodge 1853 located in Chico, California, disagreed with the views expressed by the Grand Lodge. This was not the first time this local expressed opposition to the administration, as witnessed by the members' 99 to 1 vote in support of Roy Brown who ran against the administration's slate in the 1961 elections. Robert Neiter, President of the local, voiced support of the IAM Representatives Association in the local's publication as follows:

> An election was held and our Grand Lodge Representatives now have their own union. Now after spending time and effort in representing the rank and file membership, they can turn their own problems over to a representative of their own. In plain language, they have a union that will protect them from their own union employers.
>
> Events in the past decade have definitely pointed out the need of such an association. It just doesn't make sense to protect the job security of others, when your own job security is tied to the whims of our International President and/or his Executive Council.
>
> Credit where credit is due: Franklin Nix, who so ably handled the work of cementing together and forming the new organization, is to be congratulated on winning the election, and thanked for his many hours, weeks and months of hard work leading up to the election. But let's not neglect to give a great deal of credit where due, the brutal tactics of past President Hayes and past Secretary-Treasurer Walker, at least in my estimation,

these two were the contributing factors that made the election possible as well as the winning of it.

FRANKLIN W. NIX

Franklin W. Nix had been employed by IAM as Press Representative since May 1955. He had been assigned to IAM's Southern Territory and worked out of its headquarters in Atlanta, Georgia, until the territory was abolished in September 1965. The Southern Territory was discontinued by an Executive Board decision in response to certain charges made by Nix against his superior, Vice President George Watkins. These charges were part of Nix's unremitting attack upon Watkins conducted concurrently with the staff organizing effort initiated by Nix.

The events which led to Nix's attack began with the appointment of Watkins as supervisor of the Southern Territory on June 14, 1964. The territory had been supervised from December 1963 until the following June by William Sewell as acting Vice President. Sewell, a Grand Lodge Representative, remained as Watkins' assistant.

On July 3, 1965, Nix called President Siemiller in Washington and in his absence talked with General Vice President Ross Matthews. Nix informed Matthews that he had documentary proof which showed that Watkins was engaged in a concerted campaign to debunk Siemiller, Matthews and DeMore. Matthews authorized Nix to come to Washington and both Matthews and DeMore met with him on June 9, 1965.

At the July 9 meeting Nix turned over to the two international officers copies of a number of pages of Watkins' personal diary. Watkins maintained a loose-leaf diary concerning things he wanted to remember and things he wished to note. The entries which Nix had copied were of two general types. One type concerned political matters at the highest level of the IAM organization and reflected Watkins' personal ambitions and his dislike for other international officers. The other type concerned his personal life and experiences. Nix's selection was of material which would suggest that Watkins was both incompetent and psychotic. Nix developed his thesis that Watkins was unfit to administer the Southern Territory.

DeMore questioned Nix as to how he obtained Watkins' confidential notes. Nix stated that he had made photo copies on a machine in the office. Nix also mentioned for the first time his organizing activities on behalf of the staff (see above).

On July 12, DeMore and Matthews reported their conversation with Nix to President Siemiller. They expressed their reactions to Nix having had taken private and confidential notes. Matthews expressed amazement to Nix's action; DeMore was quite upset because he had once been the victim of a similar act by a subordinate. The three officers agreed that Nix should be fired for extracting and copying Watkins' diary entries. However, they believed that because of Nix's simultaneous organizational activity his discharge at that time would result in an unfair labor practice charge against the IAM.

On August 13, 1965, the IAM Executive Council (excepting

Watkins) met in Chicago. The council was given a full report concerning Nix's charges against Watkins and concerning the manner in which Nix had obtained his material. The council was unanimous in its decision to discharge Nix. However, the members accepted Siemiller's counsel against discharge at this time because of Nix's organizing campaign.

Nix intensified his attack upon Watkins in an 8-page letter addressed to Siemiller. Siemiller and the other Executive Council members received the letter during a meeting of the Executive Counsil in Los Angeles in early September 1965. In the letter Nix accused Watkins of fraud, double charging, and incompetence. Nix also included in his letter comments on the organizing campaign.

Nix's letter was discussed at the council meeting on September 1st in Watkins' presence. Watkins informed the council that the information which Nix copied could have been obtained only by removing them from inside his desk. The council was unanimously of the opinion that Nix should be fired, but was again persuaded by Siemiller's view that it would be imprudent to effectuate the decision at that time. Because of the nature of the serious charges of fraud made against Watkins the council decided to relieve him from active duty and his assignment over the Southern Territory. The council also divided that territory and amalgamated the various portions with contiguous territories.

The nature of the accusations against Watkins prompted Siemiller to authorize a hearing at which Watkins could face his accuser and clear his name. On September 14, 1965, Siemiller appointed Vice Presidents Ross Matthews, Gilbert Brunner, and Floyd Smith as a committee of three to conduct an investigation of the Nix charges, and to make a complete and detailed report of their findings. The committee convened on September 22 at the Washington headquarters.

Nix and Watkins testified before the committee and, upon Nix's suggestion, Sewell also appeared. Witnesses were not sworn during the four days of hearings, but Nix and Sewell made lengthy statements in support of Nix's charges and Watkins defended himself in a like manner. The transcript covered over 500 pages.

On November 26, 1965, Nix wrote Siemiller requesting a meeting off the record to discuss matters before any action was taken regarding Watkins. The request finally resulted in a meeting on January 6, 1966. During the meeting Nix stated that he had practically been fired since he had not been given an assignment since August, even though he was drawing pay. Siemiller commented that Nix could have and should have been fired for taking documents from Watkins desk. Nix also mentioned that since he had achieved his objective of having Watkins removed from the Atlanta office he had lost some of his interest in the organizing campaign.

On January 12, 1966 the committee investigating the charges against Watkins issued a 24-page report. The committee cleared Watkins of the accusations of fraud but found that he had violated IAM policy by discontinuing a prior practice of remitting to the General Secretary-Treasurer all reimbursements from the Federal Government and by establishing an unauthorized emergency fund. The committee also commented at length on the role which Nix had played and censured him severely.

The Executive Council considered the report on February 9, 1966. The council adopted the report as its own, continued the division of the Southern Territory, returned Watkins to active duty, and once more deferred discharging Nix (because of his surreptitious removal of documents) due to the coincidence of Nix's organizing activity.

On August 31, 1966, following the representative election (see above) Siemiller wrote Nix the following leter:

> For approximately 1 year now the Vice President who has the responsibility for supervising and assigning the work force in the territory in which you are located, has advised that he has no assignments where he needs a Press Representative. He further advised that he had never worked with a Press Representative and had no desire for one now. Therefore, in view of the fact that there is no need for your services for our union, this is to notify you that your services are terminated, effective the 15th of September....

Nix had been discharged by IAM. However, he maintained his membership in the union. Nix had mentioned a District Lodge President in a few of the letters he had issued during the campaign. On the basis of these letters the District Lodge President filed charges of misconduct against IAM member Franklin Nix. A trial committee was convened and a hearing held.

On November 10, 1966, the trial committee reported a guilty verdict and recommended Nix's expulsion from the IAM. The membership of Nix's local union concurred by secret ballot as provided by the constitution and Nix was expelled from membership. Nix filed charges under the Labor Management Reporting and Disclosure Act of 1959, in which he sought injunctive relief against expulsion from the union and punitive damages.

The U.S. District Court issued its decision on January 9, 1967. The Court found that Nix's expulsion was in violation of his right of free speech and free expression of opinion under the LMRDA; that Nix was within his right to sue; and, having been unlawfully expelled from the union and denied the right of free speech, he was entitled to injunctive relief.

Fulton Lodge No. 2 (Nix's local) and IAM were ordered by the District Court to reinstate Franklin Nix to membership and to remove all related proceedings from its records. The union, its officers, agents, servants and members were further enjoined from interfering with Nix in his right to speak, publish or or disseminate his views on union matters.

THE COLLECTIVE BARGAINING RELATIONSHIP

The IAM Representatives Assocation conducted an election following its certification by the NLRB. Nix was elected Secretary-Treasurer and William Sewell, and IAM employee for 15 years, was elected Chairman of the Negotiation Committee.

On November 21, 1966, Sewell requested IAM to furnish the association with bargaining unit information concerning the classification of employees, and the policies and procedures relating to hire, tenure of employment, promotions, transfers, demotions, recalls, and furloughs. IAM refused to furnish this information.

On December 5, 1966, the representatives association requested IAM to notify the association prior to making any changes in the status of any employees in the unit. IAM refused. The association also requested the policies and procedures relating to the determination of rates of pay, the costs of the Group Insurance Plan, the costs of the Grand Lodge Travel Insurance Plan, the costs of the Auto Liability Insurance and information regarding the Grand Lodge Pension Plan. IAM also refused this request.

President Siemiller wrote to Sewell on December 13, 1966, criticizing Sewell's weekly report of December 3. His criticism was directed at the general statement which Sewell used to describe his organizing activity during the week. Siemiller suggested that such generalizations were resorted to only to cover up lack of performance. Sewell had been using the same type of language in submitting his weekly reports since 1951 without any prior criticism.

Sewell received a letter from Siemiller dated December 22, 1966, which made reference to reports that Sewell was opposing an administration proposal to eliminate the post-convention referendum. Sewell was requested to inform the President's office if he had been advising Local Lodges against the proposal and, if so, to give his reasons. Sewell replied on December 27, stating that he had discussed the referendum with many individuals in an opposing approach, but had not discussed it with Local Lodges. He also pointed out that his view was consistent with the view expressed by the Executive Council during the 1964 convention.

On January 4, 1967, Siemiller discharged Grand Lodge Representative William Sewell with the following letter:

> I have before me your letter dated December 27, 1967 (sic 1966) within you advise that you refuse to carry out the decision of the Executive Council in supporting the forthcoming Referendum.
>
> Grand Lodge Representatives are on the staff for the sole purpose of assisting the Executive Council, including the International President, in carrying out their duties and responsibilities. Many times it is necessary to make new decisions regarding various subject matters, depending upon the period of time we are living in. In the instant case it was the best judgment of the Executive Council that the time had arrived when we should modernize our Union and do away with the post-convention referendum.
>
> Your position, as stated in your December 27, 1966 letter, together with admitted actions, is insubordination. Therefore, for this reason, your appointment with the International Union is terminated immediately upon receipt of this letter.

Thus Sewell, an employee for 15 years, and an employee who had served three times as acting Vice President of the Southern

Territory, was charged with insubordination and covering up his lack of performance, and was terminated.

Unfair labor practice charges were filled with the National Labor Relations Board. The Board consolidated these charges with charges filed previously by Nix and issued a complaint against the IAM. The complaint alleged the IAM had discharged Nix and Sewell because of their union activity; had repeatedly refused to furnish bargaining information as required by the National Labor Relations Act, and had unlawfully announced and granted general increases in fringe benefits and pay to unit employees during the organizational campaign (April 1966). The NLRB had to conduct hearings on these charges. If the Board ruled that the International Association of Machinist, as an employer, had violated the NLRA then the Board also had to decide what remedies, if any, were appropriate.

UAW PUBLIC REVIEW BOARD (A)

At its Sixteenth Convention in 1957 the United Automobile Workers (UAW) established a Public Review Board (PRB) "to provide close public scrutiny of the UAW and to insure the best possible conduct of its affairs."[1] Section 1 of the new Article 31 of the UAW Constitution stated in more detail that the reasons for establishing the PRB were:

> For the purpose of insuring a continuation of high moral and ethical standards in the administrative and operative practices of the International Union and its subordinate bodies, and to further strengthen the democratic processes and appeal procedures within the union as they affect the rights and privileges of individual members or subordinate bodies.

Article 31 provided that the PRB should consist of seven members, including a chairman. The members were to be proposed by the President of the International Union, subject to approval by the International Executive Board (IEB) for ratification by each biannual convention. Membership on the PRB was limited to:

> Impartial persons of good public repute, not working under the jurisdiction of the UAW or employed by the International Union or any of its subordinate bodies.

Although it was not a requirement of the Constitution, in practice the PRB always included one Rabbi, one Priest, one Minister, and four educators or jurists.

Under the Constitution the PRB was empowered to hear and render decisions on the following matters:

> 1. Appeals from decisions of the International Executive Board (IEB) in cases involving an alleged violation of an individual's rights as a member of the union or the alleged violation of the rights of a local or other subordinate bodies of the International;
>
> 2. Appeals from decisions of the IEB in cases involving alleged violation of any UAW ethical practices code;

---

[1]At least four other unions, all AFL-CIO affiliates, have established public review boards: the Upholsterers' International Union, the Marine Engineers' Beneficial Association, the Packinghouse, Food and Allied Workers, and the American Federation of Teachers.

3. Submission of an ethical practices matter by the IEB;

4. In the absence of an appeal from or submission by the IEB, any complaint of alleged violation of ethical practices which, in the judgment of the PRB, the IEB had disposed of without adequate action.

However, in the area of collective bargaining, the PRB's power was quite limited. The only jurisdiction expressly accorded to it related to appeals from the "action or inaction relative to the processing of a grievance" and required a charge "that the grievance was improperly handled because of fraud, discrimination, or collusion with management." The Constitution further provided that "in no event shall the Public Review Board have the jurisdiction to review in any way an official collective bargaining policy of the International Union."

With respect to matters within its jurisdiction, the PRB was given the authority to hold hearings and to render "final and binding decisions." It was also given the authority to "formulate such rules of procedure and establish such practices as are necessary to facilitate its proper functioning." Finally, the International Secretary-Treasurer was instructed to deposit to the account of the PRB "the necessary funds required by the budget submitted by them." During its first ten years the PRB heard approximately 180 cases. The decisions rendered by the PRB and its annual report were mailed to each member of the UAW and were made available to the news media.

UAW PUBLIC REVIEW BOARD (B1)

RIGHT TO MEMBERSHIP

Arnold Smith became a member of the UAW in March when he was hired at one of Ford's plants. The following December he was elected recording secretary of the 3,000-member local. In February of the following year, however, he was discharged by Ford on the charge of having falsified his employment application.[1] The union processed a grievance on Smith's behalf, arguing that the charge was merely a ruse and that the real reason for discharging him was his militancy on behalf of his union. The grievance was finally taken to arbitration and the arbitrator ruled in favor of the company.

Despite the termination of his employment, Smith continued to serve as recording secretary of the local. Then in November he was elected president of the local, a full-time job. He retained this office for two years when he was defeated in his bid for re-election. Three weeks later, although his dues were paid and he had announced his intention to the membership to continue as a member in good standing, the local's financial secretary issued him an honorable withdrawal card, thereby terminating his active status in the union. Smith appealed the secretary's action to the local membership which voted 35 to 26 to sustain the issuance of the withdrawal card. He then appealed the membership's action the International Executive Board (IEB). The IEB denied his appeal on the ground that the issuance of a withdrawal card to a discharged member was a matter wholly within the discretion of that member's local. From this decision Smith appealed to the PRB.

The union's position was as follows:

1. The right of a discharged member to maintain his membership in the UAW was wholly dependent upon the will of the membership of his local. This was clear from Article 17, Section 2 of the Constitution (see Exhibit 1) and the following Interpretation of the International President which had been issued in 1951 and had been ratified by the IEB (see Article 13, Section 8 for the International President's duties of interpretation):

> Members who may be elected to a national, state or local legislative body or who are engaged in work which promotes the programs and policies of the organization or who are discharged from their employment should be exempt from the issuance of an automatic withdrawal card.

[1]Under educational experience, Smith had said he had only a public school education, when, in fact, he was a college graduate.

> The decision in these cases is left to the discretion of each local union. Any member may, however, appeal any decision made in this respect as provided for in Article 32 of the Constitution.

Smith's position could be summarized as follows:

1. He obtained membership in the union in accordance with constitutional requirements, for at the time of his application he was a worker in and around a plant under the jurisdiction of a local union of the UAW (see Article 6, Section 23 in Exhibit 1). Having thus obtained membership, the union could not lawfully have deprived him of his membership without proper cause.

2. Article 17 (see Exhibit 1) did not on its face create any basis for the issuance of a withdrawal card to a discharged member. On the contrary, the section specifically provided for the right of a member who was laid off from his plant to maintain his good standing by paying dues. Only members who had voluntarily separated themselves from the UAW's jurisdiction were to be issued a withdrawal card automatically.

3. The International President's 1951 interpretation of Article 17, Section 2 was not applicable because its terms were inconsistent with the "plain meaning" of the language which it was supposed to interpret. If the interpretation was to have any application at all, it should have been considered solely as a device to permit locals to protect themselves from members who purposefully sought to abuse the right to retain membership following a contrived discharge to further their own political ends.

4. The IEB really denied his appeal because he had opposed some of the International Union's policies including the placing of an administratorship over his local and the rules and procedures developed for reporting out resolutions at conventions which he had vocally attacked at the convention.

Exhibit 1

SELECTED CLAUSES FROM UAW CONSTITUTION

ARTICLE 6 - MEMBERSHIP

Section 2 Any person eligible to become a member of the International Union who is not affiliated with any organization whose principles and philosophy are contrary to those of this International Union as outlined in the Preamble of this Constitution may apply for membership to the Local Union having jurisdiction over the plant in which he is employed. The applicant must, at the time of application, be an actual worker in and around the plant. All applicants for membership in any Local Union of the International Union shall fill out an official application provided by the International Union, answering all questions contained in auch application, and shall sign a promise to abide by all laws, rules and regulations and the Constitution of the International Union. All applications thus received shall be referred to the Local Union for consideration, and shall be acted upon as soon as possible, but not later than sixty (60) days from the date the application is received by the Financial Secretary of the Local Union.

ARTICLE 13 - DUTIES OF INTERNATIONAL OFFICE, INTERNATIONAL PRESIDENT

Section 8 He shall decide disputes or questions in controversy, including all questions involving interpretation of this Constitution, except such cases as follow the procedure and conditions as outlined in this Constitution, all his decisions being subject to appeal, first to the International Executive Board and then to the Convention. Notice in writing of appeal of any decision of the International President must be filed with the International Secretary-Treasurer and the International President within thirty (30) days from date of decision.

ARTICLE 17 - HONORABLE WITHDRAWAL TRANSFER CARDS

Section 2 Any member laid off from his plant but regularly employed on jobs outside the jurisdiction of the International Union shall take an honorable withdrawal transfer card, or in order to maintain himself in good standing in his Local Union, shall pay dues in accordance with Article 16 and Article 46.

Any member who has voluntarily separated himself from the jurisdiction of the UAW shall be issued a withdrawal card immediately by his Local Union. The above shall not apply to those members who are employed by or officially represent the UAW.

Exhibit 1
(continued)

ARTICLE 32 - APPEALS

Section 2 Any member of any Local Union or unit of an Amalgamated Local Union who wishes to challenge any action, decision or penalty of that body must, in all cases and procedures where no other time limit is specifically set forth by this Constitution, initiate the challenge before the appropriate body of such Local Union or unit within sixty (60) days of the time the challenger first becomes aware or reasonably should have become aware of the alleged action, decision, or penalty of that body.

Section 3 Any member of an Amalgamated Local Union wishing to appeal from any action, decision or penalty of his unit shall first appeal such action, decision or penalty to the Amalgamated Local Union's delegate body, where such exists, or the general membership meeting, where no delegate body exists. This appeal shall be taken by submitting a written notice of appeal to the Amalgamated Local Union's Recording Secretary within thirty (30) days of the unit's action, decision or penalty being appealed from .... An appeal from the decision of the Amalgamated Local Union shall be carried to the International Executive Board.

Section 6 Any member wishing to appeal from the action, decision or penalty of his subordinate body shall do so in writing within thirty (30) days after the aforesaid action, decision or penalty. He shall send such appeal to the Recording Secretary of the subordinate body. The appeal shall set forth the basis upon which appeal from the action, decision or penalty of the subordinate body is taken. The International President shall secure from the subordinate body a complete statement of the matters in issue, including copies of all charges, and any records, minutes, transcripts of testimony, and other material relating to the appeal.

Section 9 Any subordinate body or member thereof wishing to appeal from any decision of the International Executive Board or an International Trial Committee may, in all cases, take such appeal to the Constitutional Convention of the International Union. The appellant shall, however, have the alternative of appealing such decision of the International Executive Board or an International Trial Committee to the Public Review Board established in Article 31 of this Constitution in the following cases:

Exhibit 1
(continued)

* * * * *

(b) Those cases decided by ... the International Executive Board, which concern action or inaction relative to the processing of a grievance, in which the appellant has alleged before ... the International Executive Board that the grievance was improperly handled because of fraud, discrimination, or collusion with management.

(c) In any case in which the International Executive Board has passed upon an appeal from the action of a subordinate body.

Section 12 . . . . In cases that . . . involve the processing of grievances, the Board . . . shall first determine whether the specific allegation upon which the appellant claims the Board's . . . jurisdiction to be based is, or is not, true. If such allegation is found to be true, the Board . . . shall proceed to dispose of all facets of the appeal; provided that in no event shall the Public Review Board have the jurisdiction to review in any way an official collective bargaining policy of the International Union. If the Board . . . shall decide that such jurisdictional allegation is not true, it shall dismiss the appeal in which event the appellant shall, within thirty (30) days of notification of such dismissal, be entitled to appeal the matter to the Constitutional Convention of the International Union; provided that in such appeal, the appellant may not again raise any issue which the Board . . . negated in its decision dismissing for lack of jurisdiction.

Section 13 It shall be the duty of any member or subordinate body who feels aggrieved by any action, decision, or penalty imposed upon him or it, to exhaust his or its remedy and all appeals therefrom under the laws of this International Union prior to appealing to a civil court or governmental agency for redress. Failure to comply with this duty shall be cause for suspension or expulsion, or for revocation of charter, by a two-thirds (2/3) vote of the International Executive Board insofar as imposition of any such penalty is not inconsistent with any applicable laws.

UAW PUBLIC REVIEW BOARD (C1)

RIGHT TO GOOD FAITH REPRESENTATION

Bruce Wagner was a former president of one of the UAW's locals. While serving his term as president, Wagner was elected business agent (a full-time, paid position) of a local of another international union. He then requested a leave of absence from his employer, which was granted.[1] His letter of request indicated no specific duration of the leave. However, the company had on file an unsigned Request for Leave of Absence Form which read in part:

> I request a leave of absence for the period and reason indicated below:
>
> Time-off requirement: two years.
>
> Reason for request: to accept union office for a two-year period as specifically covered in the current labor-management agreement.
>
> I understand this leave, if granted, will be subject to the following conditions: My employment will terminate if I do not return to my job on xxxxxxxxxxxxxx the first work day after the week it expires. If an emergency prevents my return, I will immediately request a renewal of this leave. The company may or may not grant such request, depending upon the facts. (The x'd out portion read: "or before".)

The request form was unsigned, and Wagner denied that he had submitted it.

Ten months later Wagner terminated his employment with the other union and told the company that he desired to cancel his leave and return to work. The company denied his request, taking the position that he had been granted a leave of absence for two years and, therefore, he could not return until the end of that period. Wagner then filed a grievance but the company denied it for the same reason, whereupon Wagner requested that the matter be submitted to arbitration. The union leaders consulted the union's attorney who advised them that, in his opinion, there was only a fifty-fifty chance of winning Wagner's case.

---

[1]The Collective Bargaining Agreement provided:
At the request of the union, a leave of absence for a period of two (2) years shall be granted by the company to any one (1) employee in any year elected to union office.

On August 21, the local's executive board voted not to arbitrate the case. Four days later, the UAW regional director wrote the local union president that, in his opinion, the grievance warranted submission to arbitration. The letter concluded with the statement that, if Wagner appealed the disposition of the grievance, the local union would need to be able to show it had given "as much consideration and support (to) this grievance as it (had) to other grievances of a similar or less serious nature...."

On August 31, the time for submission of the grievance to arbitration expired without the local union having taken any action. On September 4, the local requested an extension of time for appealing to arbitration. The company denied the request two days later. On September 12, the local executive board again voted not to take the grievance to arbitration. At the regular membership meeting held that day the membership also voted not to submit the grievance to arbitration. The regional director told Wagner that he could still achieve arbitration by filing a new grievance, but he declined to do so, claiming the membership's vote effectively "precluded (him) from renewing (his) request and filing a grievance, since the decision (already had been) made that (his) grievance would be dropped prior to arbitration."

In October, Wagner told the regional director he wished to charge the local with failure of proper representation and asked for a complete investigation. At a meeting between the Regional Director and the local's executive board held on October 30, the local president argued that under Article 32, Sections 2 and 6 (see Exhibit 1), Wagner's appeal was untimely. Nevertheless, the case was processed to the IEB, which on May 20 issued its decision holding that the failure of the local to process Wagner's grievance to arbitration was "a deliberate abrogation" of his rights. The local was directed to process a new grievance on his behalf and also to "make him whole for all wages he had lost from July until his date of return to work, less any period of time (he) might have been sick and less any compensation he might have received from other jobs during the period." The local union then appealed this decision to the PRB.

The local's position could be summarized as follows:

1. The appeal to the IEB was untimely (see Article 32, Exhibit 1).

2. Wagner had failed to pay his union dues from February through August 7, at which point he paid a reinstatement fee and dues in excess of $50. This gave them the impression that they "were not wanted or needed until he wanted to come back to work."

3. It was by no means certain that his grievance against the company could have been won in arbitration, the local's attorney having indicated that in his opinion there was only a fifty-fifty chance of winning.

4. Wagner, when president, did not advise the local executive board of his intention to request a leave of absence nor did he actually submit his resignation as president until six months after the leave became effective.

5. Wagner never appealed to the local union as required under Article 32, Section 2 (see Exhibit 1).

The IEB argued as follows:

1. The PRB had no jurisdiction over this appeal because there was no claim, or evidence to support a claim of fraud, discrimination, or collusion with management (see Article 32, Section 9 (b), Exhibit 1);

2. Under the facts of the case, the local's refusal to process the grievance to arbitration despite the admonitions of the regional office was indefensible.

The PRB agreed to hear the case first and then decide the issue of its jurisdiction. If it found that it had no jurisdiction in the matter, it would, of course, make no ruling and the IEB ruling would stand.

Exhibit 1

SELECTED CLAUSES FROM UAW CONSTITUTION

ARTICLE 32 - APPEALS

Section 2 Any person eligible to become a member of the International Union who is not affiliated with any organization whose principles and philosophy are contrary to those of this International Union as outlined in the Preamble of this Constitution may apply for membership to the Local Union having jurisdiction over the plant in which he is employed. The applicant must, at the time of application, be an actual worker in and around the plant. All applicants for membership in any Local Union of the International Union shall fill out an official application provided by the International Union, answering all questions contained in such application, and sign a promise to abide by all laws, rules and regulations and the Constitution of the International Union. All applications thus received shall be referred to the Local Union for consideration, and shall be acted upon as soon as possible, but not later than sixty (60) days from the date the application is received by the Financial Secretary of the Local Union.

Exhibit 1
(continued)

Section 6 Any member wishing to appeal from the action, decision or penalty of his subordinate body shall do so in writing within thirty (30) days after the aforesaid action, decision or penalty. He shall send such appeal to the International Union President and should send a copy of the appeal to the Recording Secretary of the subordinate body. The appeal shall set forth the basis upon which appeal from the action, decision or penalty of the subordinate body is taken. The International President shall secure from the subordinate body a complete statement of the matters in issue, including copies of all charges, and any records, minutes, transcripts of testimony, and other material relating to the appeal.

Section 9 Any subordinate body or member thereof wishing to Appeal from any decision of the International Executive Board or an International Trial Committee may, in all cases, take such appeal to the Constitutional Convention of the International Union. The appellant shall, however, have the alternative of appealing such decision of the International Executive Board or an International Trial Commitee to the Public Review Board established in Article 31 of this Constitution in the following cases:

. . . . .

(b) Those cases decided by ... the International Executive Board, which concern action or inaction relative to the processing of a grievance, in which the appellant has alleged before ... the International Executive Board that the grievance was improperly handled because of fraud, discrimination, or collusion with managment.

(c) In any other case in which the International Executive Board has passed upon an appeal from the action of a subordinate body.

UAW PUBLIC REVIEW BOARD (D1)

DISCIPLINE FOR WORKING DURING STRIKE

Chris Braithwaite, David Bryant, John Jensen, Tony Nash, and Harold Norman were all hourly-rated supervisors at one of the plants of a company whose bargaining unit employees were represented by a local of the UAW. Hourly-rated supervisors constituted the first line of supervision, and the positions were filled by promotion from the bargaining unit. Under the terms of the collective bargaining agreement, hourly-rated supervisors retained seniority in the bargaining unit and held honorable withdrawal transfer cards from the local during their tenure as supervisors (see Article 17, Exhibit 1).

In April, May, and June the local struck the plant as part of a nationwide strike arising out of a dispute over the terms to be included in a new master contract. Prior to the commencement of the strike, union and management officials discussed the nature of activities which would be permitted at the various plants during the course of the strike. Certain oral understandings were reached. Later there was some dispute as to precisely what had been agreed to at the time. However, the parties were in accord that one of the understandings was that hourly-rated supervisors would be permitted to cross the picket lines and enter the various company plants throughout the course of the strike. Whether any agreement was also reached concerning what would be the nature of their activities was later disputed.

After the strike had been in progress for some weeks, hourly-rated supervisors at the plant were instructed by their superiors to perform certain production work which normally would have been done by members of the bargaining unit. The work was performed as instructed.

Following the conclusion of the strike, the company found it necessary to reduce its first line supervisory staff at the plant. As a result, some of the hourly-rated supervisors who had crossed the picket lines and performed bargaining unit work during the strike were returned to the bargaining unit. As the above named employees returned to the bargaining unit, they were charged by the union with having committed acts detrimental to the interests of the union by performing production work during the strike at the same time that they held honorable withdrawal transfer cards. In accordance with the UAW Constitution, a trial was held. At the trial, the local union president, acting as spokesman for the charging parties, stated that Braithwaite, Bryant, Jensen, Nash, and Norman had crossed the picket line and had performed production work. While he said he had seen them cross picket lines, he admitted that he had not seen them do bargaining unit work. He did not present any witnesses who had seen the accused employees performing such work. In addition, the local did not offer as evidence the testimony of any members who might have heard through conversations with others that these men had done that with which they were accused. Instead, the local president indicated it was "common knowledge," shared by all members of the local, that the accused members had done bargaining unit work during the strike. At the conclusion of the local union president's presentation, the defense lawyer requested that the trial committee direct that the charges be dropped for failure to introduce any conclusive evidence in support of the charges. This the trial committee refused to do. The defendants' counsel then proceeded to present the accused's defense. Through the testimony offered by defense witnesses, it was established that all of the defendants had in fact "operated" the plant as charged. In addition to admitting readily that they had performed bargaining unit work, each of the accused employees defended the work they had done. Subsequently, each man was convicted, and fined $100, payable under penalty of suspension. On appeal, the IEB upheld the action of the local union. The five employees then sought review by the Public Review Board, which agreed to hear the case.

At the hearing the employees argued that their convictions should be set aside for the following reasons:

1. The local trial committee was prejudiced, for one of its members had stated for the record that he knew before the trial commenced that the accused employees had committed the acts with which they were charged.

2. The verdict was contrary to the evidence in that the local had failed to offer any evidence to prove the charges. Early in its existence the Public Review Board had held that every union member accused of wrongdoing was entitled to a full and fair trial in accordance with the union's trial procedure, "to protect to the fullest the rights of an individual member against error that might more easily occur in a less formal type of hearing." While the UAW Constitution set forth no explicit requirements concerning the trial proceedings, the International Union did prepare and distribute to its locals a booklet entitled "Guide to Local Union Trials" which set forth suggested procedures for all stages of a trial. The Guide provided that, following the opening statements:

> The accusing member shall then present evidence supporting his charge. Insofar as possible, such evidence should be limited to testimony of witnesses or presentation of authenticated documents. Witnesses should take an oath swearing to tell the truth. After each of the accusing member's witnesses has testified, the accused member may cross-examine. If a member of the trial committee feels that additional questions should be asked, he may ask them directly of a witness.
>
> The trial committee is not bound by the rules of evidence prevailing in courts of law but may receive any evidence—oral or documentary—that the members of the committee would consider if they were making a decision involving an extremely important personal

> affair. Hearsay evidence is not excluded (hearsay evidence is given when a witness testifies about what another person has told him rather than what he did, or saw himself). Trial committee members, of course, may consider such evidence as less weighty than direct evidence, inasmuch as the person being quoted is not present to be cross-examined.

It was plain from this that while the Guide contemplated a somewhat less rigid procedure for the presentation of evidence than would be followed in a court of law, the word "trial" rather than "inquiry" was used in the Constitution. Therefore, such proceedings should have been conducted in substantial conformity with the usual procedure connoted by "trial," including a consideration of the "evidence" presented. The local was deficient in this area because the "accuser" produced no evidence whatsoever. Having heard no evidence, the trial committee was obligated to dismiss the charges.

3. The action of the local was discriminatory because hourly-rated supervisors at other plants covered by this local were not similarly charged although they did the same work.

4. The local's action was contrary to the pre-strike understanding between management and the union wherein it was agreed that hourly-rated supervisors would be permitted to cross the picket line and perform limited production work.

5. Regardless of any obligation they owed the union by virtue of holding honorable withdrawal transfer cards, they were not answerable to the union for acts committed in the course of the discharge of their supervisory responsibilities. The responsibility of the supervisor was wholly to management; the union could not intervene in this relationship. To give the union the right to impose a penalty upon a member by reason of an act pursuant to supervisory responsibility, in effect, conferred upon it the right to exert a measure of control over the affairs of management quite beyond the rights conferred upon it by the collective bargaining agreement. A supervisor could not serve two masters, particularly when the interests of each would often be in direct conflict. Inevitably, the situation would arise as in this case where a choice would have to be made--and there was no real choice: Should he refuse to act as directed by his superior, the supervisor naturally was subject to discipline, including discharge; if discharged, the union could provide him no protection. It was entirely unreasonable for the union to expect to have exacted control over those to whom it could offer no protection. They also challenged Article 17, Section 10 of the Constitution (see Exhibit 1) and urged the PRB to strike it down.

The IEB, for its part, argued as follows:

1. The evidence conclusively established that the defendants operated the plant as charged;

2. This conduct was clearly detrimental to the collective interest of the members since it interfered with the economic pressure which the union was trying to apply to the company at that time;

3. The Constitution expressly held a member responsible for the acts which he committed while holding a withdrawal transfer card;

4. The dilemma the defendants alleged was simply one facet of a choice they had to make for themselves.

Exhibit 1

SELECTED CLAUSES FROM UAW CONSTITUTION

ARTICLE 17 - HONORABLE WITHDRAWAL TRANSFER CARDS

Section 10 A person who has deposited his honorable withdrawal transfer card and thus resumed membership in the Union shall thereupon be subject to charges and trial for acts or conduct detrimental to the interests of the Union or its members, committed while he was out of the Union on honorable withdrawal transfer card. The provisions of Article 30 shall be applicable in such cases.

UAW PUBLIC REVIEW BOARD (E1)

DISCIPLINE FOR CROSSING PICKET LINE

Eugene Desmond and Carl Morse were members of Local 2783 of the UAW and were employed as electricians at a Chrysler plant. Each was also a member of a local of the International Brotherhood of Electrical Workers (IBEW) and worked for building contractors from time to time at hours which did not interfere with their jobs at Chrysler.

On May 31 the contract between UAW Local 528 and the Welch Company expired. At about this time the Welch Company decided to abandon its plant and build a new one in another city, approximately 50 miles away. Construction on the new plant was begun on August 4, with the company temporarily occupying rented quarters in its new home city until completion of the new plant in November. About 80 per cent of the managerial and supervisory employees were transferred, but Welch refused to take its bargaining unit employees, or recognize or bargain with Local 528 with respect to its new work force. A Local 528 picket line which had been set up at the old plant location was then moved to the new site, but it proved ineffective in preventing building trades employees belonging to various construction unions from entering upon the job site.

Charges were filed with the National Labor Relations Board against Local 528 claiming it was coercing and restraining employees in the exercise of their rights by engaging in certain forms of violence, threats, and intimidation in connection with its picketing activities at the old plant location. These charges were not contested by the union, and the local was found to have violated Section 8(b)(1) A of the National Labor Relations Act. No similar charges were filed concerning the picketing by Local 528 at the new site.[1]

During the period of time that Local 528 had a picket line set up at the Welch Company's new plant site, Desmond and Morse were in the employ of Bond Electric Company (whose employees were represented by the IBEW), a construction contractor engaged in the wiring of the new Welch plant. Desmond was also steadily employed at the Chrysler plant, but Morse was on layoff. Both employees crossed the Local 528 picket line several times to perform their duties for the Bond company. Morse at first refused to cross the

[1]Charges were also filed by Local 528 against Welch allenging a violation of the National Labor Relations Act through the refusal of the employer to bargain with the representative of its employees. An NLRB Trial Examiner found violations of the Act and ordered the company, among other things, to bargain with Local 528 as the representative of its employees at the new site and, upon application to return to work, re-employ its former employees at its new facility. This decision was reversed by the NLRB which, contrary to the Trial Examiner, found no unfair labor practice to have been committed by the company in connection with its move.

line but later did so when escorted by his IBEW business agent.

On April 26 charges of conduct unbecoming a UAW member were filed against Morse and Desmond for consistently having crossed a picket line of a sister local. The local union trial committee found them guilty as charged on June 21 ruling that (1) the evidence clearly established that they had crossed the picket line; (2) the picket line was legitimate and authorized; and (3) their act "beyond any doubt whatsoever...did constitute conduct unbecoming a member of this UAW union." The verdict was approved at a membership meeting soon after, and the two men were suspended indefinitely from membership in the union. Desmond and Morse appealed their convictions to the IEB which on April 5 of the following year issued its decision upholding the local's verdict. The IEB ruled that by crossing an authorized picket line of the UAW the two men had subjected themselves to discipline by the UAW. The Executive Board also observed that strenuous efforts had been made to obtain the cooperation of the local building trades council in respecting the local 528 picket line. No agreement had been reached, however, since the construction locals had insisted as a condition for their observing the picket line that concessions be made by the UAW with respect to the installation of machinery at various plants in the area.

Desmond and Morse then appealed to the PRB, and a hearing was held on November 1. At the PRB hearing, they argued as follows:

1. The picket line was found to be illegal under the laws of the United States and hence they could not be held accountable for crossing an unlawful line.
2. The union's action against them was discriminatory since other employees who had crossed the picket line were not similarly charged. (Another employee who was also an electrician employed at the Chrysler plant testified that he too had worked for Bond during this period and had crossed the picket line. He was not charged with conduct unbecoming a union member, however.)
3. The union's action was unlawful. When working for an employer whose employees were represented by another labor union, Morse and Desmond were outside the jurisdiction of the UAW and not subject to its control nor answerable to it for their actions. Furthermore, the work involved was not work which belonged to the bargaining unit represented by local 528 and would not have been performed by those bargaining unit employees. It was entirely new construction work and this did not harm the interests of the UAW since it did not diminish the work of the local 528 membership.

The IEB, however, argued that Desmond and Morse were accountable to the UAW for their actions, and that the discipline metered out was justified. They urged the PRB to uphold the convictions.

UAW PUBLIC REVIEW BOARD (G1)

ELECTION CHALLENGE

On September 11 an election for the office of president of Local 1500 of the UAW was held as part of the local's general elections. Following the closing of the polls, the ballots cast were sealed in the ballot box uncounted and the box was deposited for safekeeping with the local county sheriff. The tabulations made the following day for the office of president showed:

Robert Shay	801
Gus Jones	762

The accuracy of the tabulations was attested to at that time by observers present on behalf of both candidates. Thereupon, the ballot box was returned to the custody of the county sheriff and on the following day the results for the other offices were tabulated. After completion of this count, all ballots were returned to the box, the ballot slot in the box was sealed and the box was left locked, but otherwise unsecured, in the local union hall.

On September 14, Jones, who was then the incumbent president, called the chairman of the election committee and advised him that, in view of the closeness of the election results, he was considering requesting a recount. Jones also asked that the ballot box be returned to the sheriff's office until the question of a recount was decided. The election committee chairman told him, however, that adequate precautions had been taken to insure the safety of the ballot box.

On September 16, Jones filed a formal written application for a recount. At a special meeting held that day the election committee voted to deny Jones' request. The reasons given for its action were that extreme care had been exercised in the counting of the ballots and that, at the time, all observers present had indicated their satisfaction with the accuracy of the results. When his request for a recount was denied by the election committee Jones attempted to secure the intervention of the International President, Walter P. Reuther.

On September 19, Reuther sent a telegram to the election committee instructing them to conform with the provisions of the local by-laws.[1] The chairman of the election committee sent a

[1]Article 5, Section 8 of the local by-laws provided:

> Any candidate shall have a right to petition for a recount. Petitions must be filed with the election committee in writing within three (3) days after the official results of the election are posted. The petition must set forth briefly the reasons for seeking a recount. The petitioner shall pay the expense for a recount within a period of three (3) months. If the recount changes the outcome of the election, the local union shall then bear the expense.

telegram to Reuther the next day and informed him that the membership had overwhelmingly adopted the report of the election committee which included a refusal of a request for a recount. He further indicated that he feared a recount would have a damaging effect on the local, and pointed out that two representatives of Jones' slate had been present during the tabulations and had agreed with the method and results of the election. Reuther sent the following telegram to the chairman of the election committee on September 21:

> You are instructed to immediately comply with the local union by-laws relating to a recount request. The local union membership cannot set aside local union by-laws and deny a request for a recount as you indicate in your telegram.

Despite these telegraphed instructions, however, the election committee continued to refuse to grant permission for a recount. Its refusal was ratified by the local membership at a regular meeting on September 22. At the same meeting, Robert Shay was installed as president of the local. The chairman of the election committee wrote to Reuther the next day and told him what had transpired at the membership meeting. In the letter he also explained that the election committee believed they had followed their local by-laws and that Jones' petition for a recount had been unanimously rejected.

From the membership's ratification of the election committee's refusal to grant a recount, Jones appealed to the IEB. The case was heard by an IEB appeal committee on December 7. At that time the appeal committee directed that the ballot box be sealed and returned to the sheriff for safekeeping. Following its hearing, the appeal committee recommended that the IEB direct the local election committee to conduct a recount of the ballots cast for local president. The committee also recommended that the recount be supervised by the office of the International President. These recommendations were adopted by the IEB and the recount was conducted on December 29, under the supervision of the Administrative Assistant to the International President.

Before the ballot box was opened for the recount, it was first established that there should be 17 bundles of marked ballots in the box and, in addition, four or five bundles of unused ballots. It was also agreed that bundle #15 should be on top which, when the box was opened, it was. When the contents of the box were examined it was discovered that some of the unused ballots were loose; all other unused ballots were in bundles which had been taped completely around in two directions. The broken bundle had tape only on the bottom ballot. The tabulations as originally recorded and as corrected by recount were as follows:[2]

[2]No errors were discovered in bundles 16 and 17 which were from retirees and voters outside the main plant.

	Shay		Jones	
Bundle No.	Original Count	Recount	Original Count	Recount
1	47	43	52	56
2	55	49	44	50
3	53	47	46	52
4	31	31	58	58
5	51	46	49	54
6	51	45	47	53
7	47	47	52	52
8	45	45	55	55
9	41	41	59	59
10	57	57	44	44
11	46	46	52	52
12	62	62	38	38
13	43	43	57	57
14	58	58	40	40
15	52	53	46	45

When the figures from bundles 16 and 17 were added to the above, the recount showed that Jones had received 788 votes and Shay had received 775. On March 1, 1968, the IEB directed that Jones be installed in place of Shay as president of Local 1500.

Shay thereupon entered a formal protest with the IEB of his removal from office and the installation of Jones in his place. He was joined in his appeal by the Local 1500 election committee. They argued before the IEB tribunal that, since the ballot box had been left unguarded for three months between the election and the time the appeal committee ordered it sealed, it would have been possible to tamper with the ballot box. They claimed, moreover, it was clear from the physical condition of the ballot box that it had been tampered with and they suggested several tests to be made upon the ballots themselves which they maintained would conclusively show that the ballots had been altered or substitutions made. The IEB rejected their appeal, however, for the reason that they had offered no affirmative evidence of tampering with the ballot box. The IEB's opinion concluded: "The errors in the tally of voting, particularly the difference between the number of ballots cast on the first count and the number given to Brother Jones and Brother Shay on the second count can only be attributed to human errors occurring during the count of the ballots." Both Shay and the local election committee appealed this decision to the PRB.

In their presentation before the PRB, Shay and the election committee argued as follows:

1. The IEB improperly interfered in the affairs of the local by directing a recount when the local membership had approved the election committee's denial of Jones' request. The locals' action, they maintained, was in accordance with the procedures set forth in the UAW "Guide for Local Union Election Committee" which they claimed superseded their own by-laws (see Exhibit 1).

2. With respect to the results of the recount, the conclusion of the IEB that human error was responsible for the difference in the two counts was contrary to the overwhelming evidence. All the physical evidence available required the conclusion that the sanctity of the ballot box had been violated. For example, when the ballot box was re-opened, the seal around one of the bundles of unused ballots was broken. Furthermore, all of the errors, with but one exception, were discovered in the first six bundles and all these errors worked on recount to the advantage of Jones. Since all counting was done at the same time and under the same conditions, it seemed difficult to accept the idea that twenty-six errors could have occurred in the first six bundles and only one in the next eleven.

   At the time of the original count, all observers indicated their satisfaction with the accuracy of the tabulations. For this reason, the election committee felt it was unnecessary to continue to leave the ballot box with the sheriff.

Jones and the International Union argued in support of the IEB decision as follows:

1. Shay and the election committee had been unable to offer any affirmative evidence in support of their contentions that the results of the election were altered by means of tampering with the ballot box. At the time of the recount, several tests were made to determine whether the ballot box had been violated. In this way it was learned that (a) the proper bundle was on top when the box was opened; (b) no marked ballot was found that had not been folded at least once; and (c) the results of other contests were checked in one bundle where variance of six had occurred in the presidential vote without the same variance appearing in the totals of the other contestants.

2. The chairman of the election committee, who now claimed the ballot box must have been tampered with, at one time rejected the suggestion of Jones that the box be redeposited with the local sheriff pending the recount. At the time the chairman maintained that adequate measures had been taken to insure it would remain inviolate. Therefore, absent proof to the contrary, the position of the chairman of the election committee should be accepted as correct, and the resultant errors be attributed to human error rather than human misconduct.

Exhibit 1

UAW GUIDE FOR LOCAL UNION ELECTION COMMITTEE

Introduction

This booklet should help local unions to carry out the constitutional and legal provisions which regulate elections.

In some cases, the comments contained herein reflect constitutional language, or official interpretations of constitutional language. In most cases, however, the recommended details of election procedure can be varied by local unions without violating constitutional provisions or official interpretations so long as the basic thinking reflected in the recommendations is followed.

Section 2 - Procedure for Electing Local Union Executive Officers

Paragraph J - Recounts:

(1) Any candidate may request a recount from the election committee. The election committee in the exercise of sound judgment based primarily upon the closeness of the vote and the number of ballots cast, may grant or deny a recount. If the candidate who is requesting the recount is dissatisfied with the decision of the election committee, he has recourse by appealing to the local union membership meeting. Local unions should consider adopting a general rule whereby in any election where the difference between the candidate requesting a recount and the candidate receiving the highest number of votes is less than 1% of the total votes cast for that office, the election committee automatically grants such a recount upon request. Even if the local union should adopt such a rule, however, a candidate could request a recount, though the difference is more than 1%, in the normal way and if the election committee denies the candidate's request, the candidate could appeal the denial to the membership. In recounting the ballots, the same general procedure used in the original counting should be employed.

(2) The International Constitution provides that all ballots must be preserved for one year after the close of election and a notarized statement by the election committee shall be made with regard to the election results (i.e. the official canvass) and the disposition of the ballots before the ballots are destroyed. During this period the ballots should be kept in a safe place where they can be locked and sealed, and all challengers should be notified of the place of safekeeping and be entitled to be present when the ballots are originally locked and sealed and later when the seals are broken. While the Constitution specifies ballots must be preserved for a minimum of one year, if there is any question under consideration as to the validity or propriety of the election, or any appeal in progress growing out of the election, the local must continue to preserve the ballots indefinitely until any dispute or appeal is concluded.

SECTION V

Public Sector Relationships

PITTSTOWN POLICE DEPARTMENT (A)

On Tuesday afternoon, November 7, 1978, Robert Williams, Chief of Police of Pittstown, left his office at 4:00 in the afternoon and drove home. Around 11:15 that night he received a call from Police Captain Frank Bell. Bell reported that a majority of the eighteen patrolmen on the night shift had called in sick. Bell said, "It looks like the folks have really decided to take strong action, and this is it. What do you want me to do, Chief?" Williams said that he would come down to headquarters immediately and instructed Bell to call some of the off-duty police and ask them to report. This was not a mass coincidence in Williams' opinion; rather, it represented a concerted work stoppage by policemen in protest to the city's long delays in reaching a collective bargaining agreement with the Pittstown Police Officers Association (PPOA), the police union. Perhaps worse, the police of Pittstown might be in violation of the law!

As he drove to headquarters that night, Chief Williams pondered his next move. He enjoyed a close relationship with his force, formed during twenty-seven years of service to the Pittstown Police Department, where he started as a patrolman in 1951. He knew they were deeply dissatisfied with their level of pay, the age and condition of some of the patrol cars and, perhaps most important, they resented the manner in which city officials had dealt with their elected officials. Williams sympathized with the men and had taken a strong public stance on their behalf, but he was opposed to their use of concerted pressure tactics, especially when those tactics threatened to harm the image of the department. There had been a display of frustration by members of the force earlier in the year, in January and February, when the volume of traffic tickets dropped severely. But that was somewhat less serious, in Williams' opinion, than a mass "sick in" because failure to report to work could result in danger to public safety and security. Williams was torn. On the one hand he believed his men and women had legitimate gripes, but he knew that the City Manager and members of the City Council would hold him responsible for maintaining discipline. A mass work stoppage by members of the police force would be intolerable.

BACKGROUND

Pittstown was an industrial city of slightly over 100,000 located near a major midwestern metropolitan area. Workers in private industry in the area were heavily unionized, the major plants having been organized since the 1930s by large industrial unions.

The city operated on a calendar fiscal year, from January 1 to December 31. Its income each year, however, was not known until sometime during the summer when the state announced the "equalized valuation." As a result, changes in city employees' salaries, including police salaries, were determined during the late summer and early fall and made effective the first week in August. The tax structure of the city was set forth in its charter, and no changes in the type of taxes or rates could be made without amending the charter.

The Pittstown police force, excluding civilian personnel, consisted of 120 men and women. In addition to Chief Williams, the various ranks with the numbers employed in each and salaries in November 1978 were as follows:

Captains	4	$18,561
Lieutenants	6	16,403
Sergeants	14	15,237
Detectives	10	14,493
Policewomen	2	13,799
Patrolmen	83	13,477

For each rank there was a single salary except for rank of patrolman. The patrolman rate listed above was for persons who had four years or more of service. A newly hired policeman received a salary of $10,402 and moved up to the $13,477 by four automatic increases which were given at the end of the first six months, the first year, the second year, and the third year. The $13,477 figure was referred to as "patrolman's top-step salary." It was this salary which was frequently used when comparing rates between cities, and collective bargaining discussions usually centered around it.

All but a few of the officers including the captains, lieutenants and sergeants were members of both the Fraternal Order of Police (FOP) and the Pittstown Police Officers Association (PPOA). FOP was a part of a national organization with chapters throughout the country. The Association was originally a social and benefit organization, but had been certified as a collective bargaining organization in November of 1977.

PITTSTOWN POLICE OFFICERS ASSOCIATION

PPOA was organized in the late nineteen-sixties as a result of the feeling on the part of many of the officers, including Williams who was not chief at the time, that they needed an organization to represent them as a group in dealing with the city officials. PPOA was a purely local and independent organization. It had no ties in its early days with either the union movement or with other police organizations.

The objectives and purposes of PPOA were set forth in its Constitution as follows:

> Section 1. This Association shall be a non-political, non-sectarian, voluntary association not affiliated with any other union and composed of Police Officers in good standing in the Pittstown Police Department of the City of Pittstown for the purpose of promoting social fellowship and economic well-being, and towards this end to furnish a place where meetings may be held; of instilling in the members the spirit of cooperation and

of the high regard of our calling; of asserting a wholesome influence on the education of citizens of this City of Pittstown and visitors thereto, especially with the purpose of inculcating respect for law and order; to cooperate with Courts and Judges thereof and with the branches and departments of our Government, Federal, State and Municipal, of incorporating among the members a closer personal acquaintance and for the gathering, receiving and disseminating of such information that may be helpful to all our members in the pursuit of our calling and unified action with the administrative heads of the Department for the betterment of the Department.

Section-2. It is the intent of the members of this Association to remain free from any outside influence or domination.

Membership and dues were established in the By-laws as follows:

Section 1. A candidate for membership shall be a regular officer of the Pittstown Police Department, and shall have finished his/her probationary period.

Section 2. Candidates shall apply to the Secretary for application blanks and pay the initiation fee of $15.00.

Section 3. The yearly dues shall be $36.00, payable annually or by payroll deductions of $3.00 per month.

Section 4. The candidates may be accepted by a majority vote at any regular meeting.

Section 5. Resignation or dismissal of an officer from the Department shall automatically terminate his or her membership in the Association except when a dismissal is being appealed. In the latter case, the officer shall remain a dues-paying member until decision on the appeal.

Election of officers of the Association were provided as follows:

Section 1. Elective officers shall be elected and installed in office at the Annual Meeting in June, to serve for a term of two years, or until their successors are elected and qualified.

* * *

(b) No officer shall serve more than two consecutive terms in the same office, nor be eligible again for that office except after an interval of one year, with the exception of the three-year Director.

At first the city officials refused to recognize PPOA, but as time went on, this attitude changed and by the mid-1970s PPOA regularly represented members of the police force in discussions on salaries and other matters.

Prior to August 1977, the 1976-77 salary schedule had been in effect. Under this earlier schedule the patrolman top-step salary had been $12,806, and the salaries of the other ranks had also been lower than those shown on the 1977-78 schedule. As time for determining the new 1977-78 salary schedule approached in the summer of 1977, PPOA made two requests:

1. that the patrolman top-step salary be increased by 9.8 percent to $14,060.

2. that a system of longevity pay be installed whereby 3.25 percent would be added to a patrolman's pay for each five years of service up to 20 years.

In preparation for the salary discussion for the police and with other municipal employees the city hired a consulting organization to make a study of rates being paid for comparable jobs by communities in the general area of Pittstown. The consulting organization found that the patrolman top-step salary in twelve nearby communities averaged $13,089 (See Exhibit 1). It recommended that the salary in Pittstown be increased 5.2 percent to $13,477. The city accepted the consultants' recommendation and offered the 5.2 percent ($671 for patrolmen) increase to PPOA. Although recognizing that longevity pay was in effect as a reward for long service in a number of cities in the area, the Pittstown officials rejected this request, claiming the city did not have sufficient funds to meet the additional costs which such a plan would entail.

PPOA representatives indicated great disappointment in the city's offer. They argued that the consultant's survey was not fair because (1) it was made prior to the 1977 increases which had been or would be granted by the communities, and (2) it was heavily weighted with suburban communities where police work was not comparable to police work in an industrial city like Pittstown. They refused to accept the city's proposal and asked that the salary be increased at least 9.8 percent and that longevity pay be granted.

In reply the City Manager argued that the difference between the PPOA's demand and the city's offer, amounting to $583, could not be given to the police without providing a similar increase to the firemen and to all the other municipal employees at a total cost of $451,825. Likewise, he argued that to place a longevity plan such as proposed by PPOA into effect for all city employees would cost $438,000. The manager presented figures to show that the increase in salaries which had been offered already would cost $520,025 and would use up all the increased revenue which the city would have available. The city, he contended, clearly did not have the $889,825 which an additional $583 salary increase and 3.25 percent longevity pay would require.

As the discussions continued with no agreement in prospect

questions arose concerning the status of PPOA. The City Manager pointed out that PPOA had not been certified as a bargaining agent and, therefore, under the law the city did not have to bargain with PPOA but instead was free to make the proposed salary changes without reaching agreement with PPOA. On August 31 the city put into effect its proposed salary changes retroactive to August 1.

In September PPOA filed a petition with the State Labor Relations Commission signed by more than 30 percent of the police officers asking that PPOA be certified as the collective bargaining agent for all of the 120 Pittstown police officers except the Chief. On November 4 a secret election was held by the Commission in which all the officers except the Chief were given the opportunity to vote "yes" or "no" on the question "Do you desire to be represented by the PPOA as your exclusive representative for the purpose of collective bargaining?" The polls were open from 6:30 to 8:30 a.m. and from 2:30 to 5:30 p.m. Arrangements were also made to send mail ballots to officers on leave and on vacation and to members of the one shift who could not be present at the poll time. However, the voting during the poll periods was such that it was not necessary to count the mail ballots. The election results were as follows:

For the PPOA	83
For No Union	4
Void Ballots	0
Total Voting	87

On November 17, 1977 the State Labor Relations Commission certified PPOA as "exclusive representative of all the employees in the unit for the purposes of collective bargaining with respect to rates of pay, wages, hours of employment and other conditions of employment."

On November 25 the Secretary of PPOA addressed a letter to the City Manager asking for a meeting for bargaining "now that PPOA is recognized as the certified bargaining agent." "We wish," he wrote, "to negotiate a reasonable settlement on our wages and longevity plan."

A meeting was held on December 2. The city was represented by the City Manager, the Assistant City Manager and Chief Williams. PPOA was represented by a six-person wage committee composed entirely of police officers.

At the beginning of the meeting the City Manager stated that the city now recognized PPOA as the legal representative of the police officers and was prepared to bargain with it. The Chairman of the wage committee then indicated that PPOA still wanted the additional $583 for patrolmen and longevity pay and asked if the city was prepared to increase its original offer. The City Manager shook his head in the negative, whereupon the six members of the wage committee left the room, the chairman saying as he left that he guessed the officers would be forced to turn to other means.

On December 6, PPOA officers presented to Chief Williams a request on a regular department form for permission to use a sound truck throughout the city of Pittstown on Wednesday, December 7, from 8:00 a.m. to 9:00 p.m. for the purpose of informing the public of "a demonstration to promote PPOA in wage negotiations." Chief Williams granted permission. On December 7, in addition to using the sound truck, PPOA members in civilian clothes with their wives and children (about 75 to 100) engaged in peaceful picketing at the City Hall. The picket signs demanded higher salaries and longevity pay.

On December 8 the City Manager stated that he was willing as always to meet and negotiate with PPOA. The President of PPOA told the press that his reply to the City Manager would probably be favorable but that he wanted some time to research wages and fringe benefits before engaging in further negotiations. On December 16 the Wage Committee wrote to the City Manager saying that it was prepared to negotiate with him at his convenience.

Meetings were held on December 22, 1977 and January 3, 1978. However, no progress was made at either of these sessions, and on January 5 PPOA informed the Mayor that in its opinion further meetings with the City Manager would not be beneficial. PPOA suggested that the Mayor himself meet with them. Such a meeting was arranged, but it also failed to produce an agreement.

For some time a small group within PPOA had favored affiliation with one of the national trade unions as a means of increasing their bargaining power. The majority, however, had opposed such a move. In January 1978 the officers of PPOA decided to explore the advantages of such affiliation. They found the Pittstown local of the Teamsters union especially interested in discussing the possibility with them. A meeting was scheduled for January 12 by the Teamster officials and the PPOA officers to explore the matter. Chief Williams was informed of the meeting. He was aware that the sentiment in favor of affiliation had been growing in PPOA. He believed, however, that a large majority of the officers were still opposed to such action.

WORK SLOWDOWN

During the period from January 1 to January 12 of 1978 Chief Williams became suspicious that the patrolmen were staging a work slowdown as he noted a severe drop in traffic violation ticketing. By January 12 the Chief was convinced that this was a concerted job action. During the first twelve days of January 1977 they had written 4,885 tickets; for the same number of days in 1978 they had turned in less than half that number: 2,379. Nearly all of the policemen who were in positions to write tickets were turning in half or less than half of their usual number.

This sudden and severe drop in ticketing came as a surprise to Williams. Pittstown police officers had never before engaged in any form of job action. In addition, there had been a substantial drop during the same period in the number of burglaries reported by night officers—another indication of group pressure tactics.

After considerable thought Chief Williams came up with a plan to deal with the situation quickly and, for the time being at least, effectively. He was sympathetic to the officers' demands in bargaining, and he understood their frustration. But he was worried that any form of slowdown or job action would do great damage to the good public relations which the Pittstown Police Department enjoyed. As a result, the chances of getting salary increases and longevity pay might be hurt.

Williams thought he could convince the men that their action was neither desirable nor effective. However, in order to be successful he believed he would have to convince their leaders first. He prepared a statement of his position which he thought the members of the force would understand and had copies of it mimeographed for distribution. Before distributing it to them, however, he went over it with his captains, lieutenants, and sergeants. He believed that these leaders were convinced and were ready to help to convince the others. Williams' statement read as follows:

To: All Police Personnel

Certain areas of controversy have recently arisen in conjunction with current activity aimed at bettering police pay and associated fringe benefits. One such point of controversy originates from the mistaken premise that reductions in/or curtailment of police service will improve our bargaining position and thus increase our opportunity for being granted requested benefits. I cannot sufficiently emphasize the defectiveness and dangers in this type of faulty reasoning which in actuality could produce an effect strongly opposite from that desired. <u>Good police service builds</u> strong public support and <u>strong public support</u> produces <u>higher police pay, more generous fringe benefits,</u> and <u>better working conditions.</u> You may be assured that the reputation of our police department within the community will be established in direct relation to the quality of service that we render to the public. It would be foolhardy to assume that an organization charged with a serious public responsibility could expect to receive greater compensation for reduced or inferior service. Contrariwise it would be logical to assume that such an organization could reasonably expect to receive greater consideration for such things as higher pay, etc., by improving its service to the public.

The validity of this statement has been demonstrated in our city during the past eighteen months. The vastly improved police service made possible through each of your individual efforts during this period of time has elevated our image to the extent that public respect and support has been revived to a significant degree. Consequently, we have received or are about to receive substantial improvements in such important areas as pay, personnel increases, training budget and facilities, better equipment, and other items associated with better working conditions. If we feel that increases in pay and fringe benefits are not coming rapidly enough, then we should present a solid front in making the city admi-

> nistration and public aware of this condition. Likewise we should all pitch in and work even more diligently towards gaining support for our needs by continually upgrading our service to our community. May I assure each of you the complete sympathy and support of my office for any efforts directed towards improving the welfare of our personnel. It is my sincere desire that each of us may work in harmony during the accomplishment of this objective.
>
> Chief of Police

Williams followed his statement with discussions with individual members of the force and groups of them as opportunities arose. In February the ticketing increased, and by March it was close to normal. During the summer months of 1978 the ticketing actually exceeded by 40 percent the ticketing in the summer of 1977.

However, unrest among members of the police force did not subside. In February of 1978 PPOA filed a Prohibited Practice Complaint with the State Labor Relations Commission charging the city with failure to bargain in good faith.

PROHIBITED PRACTICE COMPLAINT

The complaint read as follows:

> Said public employer, through its offers and agents, has, since on or about August 1, 1977, unlawfully refused to bargain collectively in good faith with the undersigned collective representative of its Police Department employees in an appropriate unit in the following respects:
>
> (1) By unilaterally granting a general wage increase on or about August 31, 1977 and during the pendency of negotiations without prior negotiations and agreement with the union with respect thereto.
>
> (2) By assuming an adamant attitude after granting said wage increase, that no further increases in wage or other benefits could be granted because of lack of any available funds.
>
> (3) By failing and refusing to make a sincere and good faith effort to reach agreement with the undersigned representative on wages and other economic benefits prior to the deadline for submission of the 1978 budget.
>
> (4) By insisting that the undersigned representative follow the departmental chain of command required of individual employees who have complaints when requesting bargaining meetings and otherwise presenting grievances, although the subordinates in the chain of command are

without any authority to negotiate a binding agreement or settle grievances.

(5) By refusing to make any counter-proposals to the proposal made by the undersigned representative during negotiations and attempting to justify said refusal on the grounds that any benefits granted the employees represented by the undersigned must also be granted to other city employees.

(6) By assuming a hostile, adamant and arbitrary attitude toward the undersigned representative and its officers, all of which have evidenced a rejection of the collective bargaining process and a clear design and purpose from the beginning of negotiations to avoid reaching any agreement whatsoever with the undersigned representative.

By the foregoing acts, and other acts not herein specifically set forth, said employer has interfered with, restrained and coerced its employees in the exercise of their rights guaranteed in Section 2 of the Act.

The undersigned representative respectfully requests that this Board order said City of Pittstown and its Manager to forthwith cease and desist their unlawful refusal to bargain and to bargain with the undersigned representative in good faith as required by statute.

FIRE-POLICE PARITY

Over the years the city had attempted to maintain the same rates for comparable jobs in the Police and Fire Departments. In 1977 the jobs and rates were as follows:

Police Department	Fire Department	Salary
Chief	Chief	$22,960
Captain	Ass't Chief	18,561
Lieutenant	Captain	16,403
Sergeant	Lieutenant	15,237
Detective	Engineer	14,493
Patrolman	Pipeman	13,477

In the Fire Department a large number of men had been advanced from pipeman to engineer. As a result a considerably smaller percentage of the men in the Fire Department remained at the lowest pay level than was the case in the Police Department. The patrolmen were aware of this situation and had complained to Williams about it. Williams agreed and expressed the thought that the best way to meet the problem was to establish some sort of rank between patrolman and detective. He made such a proposal to the City Manager and found him receptive.

On February 9 of 1978 Williams sent the following letter to Joseph O'Donnell, President of PPOA:

> It is recommended that a new rank be established within the Police Department and designated as "Senior Patrolman." This position would be an intermediary rank situation between our current ranks of "Patrolman" and "Detective." A "Senior Patrolman" would be delegated supervisory responsibility over the rank of "Patrolman" and would be assigned an increased separate paygrade commensurate with the increase in responsibility.
>
> All officers holding the rank of "Patrolman" who have completed five (5) years of departmental police service and have maintained a satisfactory work record would qualify for the rank of "Senior Patrolman." This position would be assigned an annual salary of $13,799.

O'Donnell replied to Williams that the wage committee of PPOA would be happy to discuss his proposal regarding the establishment of a Senior Patrolman classification. Williams then arranged for the wage committee to meet with himself and the City Manager. On February 14 he sent the following note to the wage committee:

> At my request, a meeting has been scheduled with the City Manager in his office for 3:30 p.m. on Thursday, February 16, 1978 so that we may further discuss the "Senior Patrolman" plan and any associated subjects. Would you please plan on attending the meeting with me.

The meeting was held as scheduled on February 16, and agreement was reached to establish the Senior Patrolman classification with a salary of $13,799.

During March and April PPOA waited to see what would happen as a result of its prohibited practice complaint. As they waited, interest in affiliation with another union developed again among some of the members and officers. A committee was appointed to discuss possible affiliation with United Plant Guard Workers of America. UPGWA had been a part of the C.I.O. until 1947 when, under the terms of the amended National Labor Relations Act, it had been forced to disassociate itself from all other labor organizations. UPGWA had been successful in obtaining sizeable wage and benefit packages for its membership. Some of the PPOA members felt that the affiliation with UPGWA would provide many advantages without some of the disadvantages which were inherent in affiliation with the Teamsters or with one of the AFL-CIO unions.

Early in May the President of PPOA sent the following notice to the membership:

> To Members of the Pittstown Police Officers Association
>
> A Committee from the Pittstown Police Officers Association has met with Mr. John Blair, from the International Union, United Plant Guard Workers of America on two separate occasions. In these meetings we have discussed our problems in regard to obtaining a working Agreement with the City of Pittstown. In the

last meeting we made a rough draft of what we need and want in an Agreement and a chart of Organizational Rank within the Department.

Mr. Blair has checked with their International General Counsel for a legal opinion as to our being able to affiliate with Local 116, U.P.G.W.A. It is the opinion of their legal counsel that by holding a secret ballot election, we can vote to do so, and they in turn will petition the Commission to amend our certification.

At the PPOA meeting coming up on May 11th, 1978, at 8:00 p.m., Mr. Blair has indicated his desire to meet with all of you and to discuss the draft language in greater detail.

It is my opinion and the opinion of our Committee that we need outside help in our dealing with the city.

The above-mentioned union has many problems and working conditions similar to our own and has been handling these problems with large corporations for many years. Problems such as seven day operations, uniform and maintenance problems; continuous shifts, representation of enforcement type personnel, wage scales, grievance procedures, and many other working conditions.

The time for Police Officers to get ahead is NOW. We are the only department within the city without a contract. The Wage Committee has exhausted itself for our wants and needs as to pay and other necessities. If YOU as a member are interested in your job and in the welfare of your family, you <u>will</u> attend the meeting on May 11, 1978 and express <u>your</u> thoughts on this matter.

NOTE: On May 12, 1978 a Secret Ballot Election will be held in:

THE CONFERENCE ROOM on the 1st Floor
Pittstown Police Department
Time: From 6:00 a.m. until 11:00 p.m.

under the Supervision of the Pittstown Police Officers Association Election Committee.

The election was held as scheduled on May 12, and the members voted to remain independent. The vote was 42 - 35.

On May 18, 1978, a hearing was held on the prohibited practice complaint before an officer of the State Labor Relations Commission. PPOA was represented by its labor counsel. The city denied each of the charges. It claimed that it had been willing to bargain with and indeed had bargained with PPOA in good faith since it had been certified as the bargaining agent for the Pittstown police.

THE 1978-79 NEGOTIATIONS

In June 1978, Williams assigned one of his captains to make a survey of salaries and benefits being paid to police officers in other communities near Pittstown. The survey covered the 12 communities included in the study by a consultant for the city (see Exhibit 1) but added five other communities. The study concluded that the salary for each rank in the Pittstown department was below the average being paid in the area as follows:

Rank	Average Salary in Pittstown Area	Pittstown Salary	Below Average
Chief	$23,919	$22,960	$959
Captain	19,052	18,561	491
Lieutenant	16,756	16,403	353
Sergeant	15,604	15,237	367
Detective	14,984	14,493	491
Patrolman	13,918	13,477	441

The study also showed that all but three of the other 17 communities provided some sort of longevity pay. The data included in the study on patrolmen's salaries and longevity pay are set forth in Exhibit 2. In July, Williams sent copies of the survey to the City Manager and to Sergeant Joseph O'Donnell, President of PPOA.

On August 4, 1978, O'Donnell sent the following letter to the City Manager:

> The Pittstown Police Officers Association Wage Committee is prepared to meet with you. Our purpose is to discuss our request for a wage adjustment for 1978-79 fiscal year.
>
> During the past negotiations some of the City Commissioners stated their future policy would be to adjust our wages to the surrounding areas. The Wage Committee has surveyed these areas and finds we are once more far behind. In order to bring the Pittstown Police Department to an equitable wage level, we are requesting the following:
>
> 1. A blanket increase of $1,652 per year
>
> 2. Longevity
>   a. 3.25% base pay of patrolmen after five years
>   b. 6.5% after ten years
>   c. 9.75% after fifteen years
>   d. 13% after twenty years
>
> The Wage Committee, as the bargaining representative for the Police Department, requests a meeting with you prior to August 12, 1978 to formally present our request and discuss this matter.

On August 8, O'Donnell received a letter from Brian Sontag, the city Personnel Director, informing him that Sontag rather than the City Manager would represent the City in negotiations this year and suggesting that they meet on August 12.

On August 9 Williams sent the following letter to the City Manager and gave a copy of it to O'Donnell:

What do law violations cost the citizens of Pittstown annually? Traffic violations alone presented a bill to the taxpayers estimated at between 2½ million and 3 million dollars for the calendar year 1977. During the same period of time, stolen and maliciously destroyed property resulted in the loss of hundreds of thousands of dollars ($645,468).

This does not take into consideration the thousands of injuries, the loss of twenty-four (24) lives, nor the loss of peace of mind, neighborhood tranquility, or the deprivation of personal dignity. What is it worth to feel safe and secure in your home, in your car, on the streets, and in your business or place of employment? When you request police assistance, it is important that we respond immediately and in sufficient force to handle any emergency.

Our country is in the middle of a civil revolution which has compelled the police to play a difficult and almost untenable role that is fraught with hazards and danger. Serious crime has increased approximately 50 percent in the last six (6) years; traffic accidents have reached an all-time high; radical changes in court rulings have, to a large degree, reduced the effectiveness of our police and, simultaneously, afforded great protection to the criminal. In view of all this, the general public continues to either retreat or regard the situation with an attitude of no concern.

Assaults upon our police officers have increased sharply and, yet, in those instances where an officer utilizes force to protect himself or to effect a legal arrest, he must later bear the burden of proving himself to be innocent of the readily available and often used charge of "police brutality."

The police officer's role in our society has been greatly complicated, and personal dangers, aggravations and pressures continue to mount. Most police departments are undermanned, underpaid, undertrained, and suffer from a lack of modern equipment. Our city is no exception.

Our area economy is at its highest peak and continues to rise. Wages in private business and industry, as well as Federal and State Government, are experiencing great advances each year. Consumer prices are spiraling and the cost-of-living factor has subsequently increased. These conditions have created a tight labor market. These are the odds currently facing police administrators in their efforts to recruit qualified police personnel and to retain on a career basis those officers presently engaged in police service.

Of necessity, police officers must be generously endowed with intelligence, integrity, wisdom, courage and physical strength and, therefore, job qualifications must be maintained at a high level. How do you attract this caliber of person into the police profession with a starting salary of $13,900 when last year the average annual wage for the Pittstown area was over $16,000?

President Carter, U.S. Attorney General Bell, the Governor, and our state Attorney General have publicly expressed concern over the traffic toll and the rise in crime and lawlessness. Many newspaper, radio, and television editorials relating to this subject have also been published during the past year. Committees and panels of police experts and lay citizens alike have been appointed to study causative factors and to determine corrective measures. In each instance, one of the primary recommendations has been for a marked increase in police pay and associated benefits. Police officers are important to the safety and welfare of their communities and the communities must regard them with importance.

Police officers should not feel inferior because of sub-standard pay, but rather, they should be able to regard their chosen profession with an attitude of value and a feeling of pride. They must be able to maintain a mental state which will permit them to readily and willingly subject themselves to the dangers and aggravations which our modern day police officers must frequently face. They are entitled to be regarded at a fair and reasonable level and the express purpose of this communication is to so recommend. It is my honest and sincere evaluation of all pertinent factors that our police officers must receive no less than a fifteen hundred dollar annual increase at patrolman's level with corresponding increases at all ranks.

This would increase starting patrolmen's pay from $10,402 to $11,902 and top patrolmen's pay from $13,477 to $14,977. Police officers must also be provided with a long overdue longevity pay plan of a type that would be compatible to both the city and its employees. To my knowledge, Pittstown is the only major city in the metropolitan area that does not have a longevity program implemented.

The largest city in the area currently has a starting patrolman's pay of $13,520. Many of the major cities in the metropolitan area are now paying an annual top patrolman's wage of $15,250 or more and indications are such that this trend is spreading rapidly.

May I urge you to give my recommendation all possible consideration.

On August 12 the wage committee met with City Personnel Director Sontag. Sontag showed them a survey of police salaries and benefits which he had made in the area. The data were similar to those contained in the survey made by Williams (see Exhibit 2). Sontag stated that the city did not have the funds to grant anything like what PPOA was demanding. Additional meetings were held in August and in early September, but no progress was made in reaching an agreement. At one of these meetings Sontag said that the only way the city could possibly meet PPOA's salary and longevity demands would be by laying off 74 employees.

On September 8, O'Donnell addressed the following letter to the City Manager:

> During recent wage negotiation sessions between Mr. Brian Sontag, Personnel Director for the City of Pittstown, and the Pittstown Police Officers Wage Committee, serious wage inequities were presented on behalf of the police officers of the City of Pittstown by the Wage Committee.
>
> After considerable discussion, Mr. Sontag revealed the results of a survey conducted by the personnel office which further substantiated our position. Also, Mr. Sontag stated that should the City of Pittstown grant the increases proposed by the Pittstown Police Officers Association, it would necessitate the city laying off approximately 74 employees.
>
> We wish to advise you at this time that a regular meeting of the Police Association was held on September 7, 1978, and the aforementioned was discussed at some length. It was the unanimous opinion of those present that although the Pittstown Police Officers Association abhors the thought of 74 people being laid off and as a result causing a serious cutback in services to the community, this appears to be the only solution to the problem and, therefore, request that the City of Pittstown proceed as soon as possible to implement the requested wage increases for the Police Department and to subsequently take such further action regarding layoffs and as necessary to fully implement our requests.

The City Manager refused to consider cutting the number of city employees in order to provide funds for the increase demanded by PPOA.

On October 7, O'Donnell wrote the following letter to Sontag, the City Personnel Director:

> The Pittstown Police Officers Association has met with you on several occasions to discuss wage increases and a longevity plan. We presented our demands to you at one of these meetings. At that time we were advised by you that our demands would be studied and that you would then submit our demands, along with your recommendations to the City Manager, and to the City Commission. You also stated that you would then advise us as to your findings and the decision of the Commission.
>
> We have waited patiently for a reply to our wage and longevity demands and have not received such a reply.
>
> Please advise this Association, by letter, as to the decision of the Commission immediately. We will expect the letter on or before Monday, October 10, 1978.
>
> We will consider, if we do not receive a letter by

> October 10, 1978, that the city wil not grant a raise or a longevity plan and is not willing to discuss these issues further. If this is the situation this Association will take further and more drastic steps to obtain the benefits that we unquestionably deserve.

Sontag informed O'Donnell that no action on his proposal had been taken to date by the Commission.

On October 10 a membership meeting of PPOA was held at which time the wage committee reported the lack of progress to the membership. One of the members moved that the PPOA officers be given power to call a strike unless the city changed its approach. After long, serious and at times heated debate, the membership voted 45 to 10 in favor of strike action, if necessary.

O'Donnell communicated with the State Labor Relations Commission informing them that a strike was now a definite possibility. A Commission official responded by expressing great concern. He warned against such action, pointing out that it was illegal under the state labor law. He suggested strongly that O'Donnell seek advice of counsel and proposed mediation.[1]

After consulting with PPOA's legal advisor on labor matters O'Donnell requested the State Labor Relations Commission to assign a mediator to deal with the differences between the city and PPOA. The first mediation session was held on October 18. No progress was made at the meeting, however, and that same day O'Donnell addressed the following letter to the City Manager:

> Our members are deeply disturbed about the refusal of the city to bargain in good faith over wages and working conditions. The absolute negativism of the city negotiators at this morning's session has only heightened the concern of our members.
>
> As you know, they recently cast an overwhelming vote in favor of strike action to resolve our dispute. As officers of the Association, we believe all just and peaceful means should be exhausted to reach agreement. The safety and welfare of the citizens of our city demand no less. Accordingly, we have prevailed on our members to allow us to exhaust all possible avenues of settlement before any precipitous action is taken.
>
> The execution of the mandate of the membership is being deferred pending an indication from city officials that they too desire to exhaust all possible means of peaceful settlement.
>
> We believe our demands for a working agreement and increased wages are reasonable and just. We are willing to let an impartial panel of citizens be the judge; therefore, we make the following proposal as a means of resolving the dispute:

---

[1]Strikes by public employees were prohibited by the state's collective bargaining law. The law did provide for mediation, factfinding and last-best-offer interest arbitration as devices to deal with impasse situations.

> Our organization will select one member of the panel, and the city will select a member. These two members will mutually agree upon a third member. This panel of citizens shall be empowered to hear the issues in dispute and render findings, and a decision which will be final and binding on both parties.
>
> We would appreciate a reply no later than October 24, 1978, due to the urgency of the existing situation.

On October 20, the City Manager replied to O'Donnell's letter of October 18. He stated that it was his understanding that while they were in mediation the rules of procedure required that they should not make proposals directly to each other. As a result he was returning O'Donnell's letter.

O'Donnell then wrote to the City Manager informing him that he could consider mediation as having been terminated and requesting that they proceed to fact finding. On October 23 the City Manager replied as follows:

> It certainly comes as a surprise that you feel that you are out of mediation. Mr. Leonard Bennett, State Mediator, did not tell the city this, and until we receive specific information that mediation has been terminated, we have to assume it is continuing.
>
> Normal continuation of mediation is the fact finding process. Compulsory arbitration is a most unusual procedcure and, according to the state's Collective Bargaining Law, could only be considered after all legal procedures have been exhausted. At that time it would have to be analyzed very carefully, particularly from the legal aspects, before the city could even evaluate the merits of your suggestion. This can best be explained at a mediation session. If you wish to call one please contact the mediator.
>
> If you feel mediation is ready to be terminated, the next normal step is fact finding. I strongly urge that you take this step by filing the necessary request with the State Labor Relations Commission.
>
> It is sincerely hoped that the members of your organization will not take any action that would in itself create additional problems in this already difficult situation.

On October 15 PPOA published the following letter in the <u>Pittstown Daily Press</u>:

PITTSTOWN POLICE OFFICER'S ASSOCIATION

<u>OPEN LETTER TO THE CITIZENS OF PITTSTOWN</u>

> The members of the Pittstown Police Officers Association have been negotiating with the City of Pittstown for increased wages and longevity since August 1978. These negotiations have resulted in the usual

reply from the City Manager, "The City does not have the finances." The Police Association petitioned the State Labor Relations Commission for the presence of a State Mediator at our last session, which was held on October 18, 1978. At this time the City Manager admitted the City of Pittstown presently has a surplus of three-quarter million dollars and foresees a one-million dollar surplus for the Pittstown Police Department. The City Manager then stated that the Finance Department was presently undergoing a complete change, which would necessitate the hiring of several high-salaried personnel, and in order to hire these personnel, several police officers would be laid off.

Think now, these statements were made by the Chief Administrator of our city who was hired in 1976 and presently receives a salary of $39,000 per year. Is this good city administration? The lay-off of police personnel in a city where the crime rate has increased 11% during the first nine months of 1978, and already understaffed by 30 men according to accepted National Standards.

We, the officers of the Association, ask only one thing, that we be brought into the salary range of the Metropolitan area.

Our City Manager is one of the highest paid City Administrators in the State; our City Attorney and Personnel Director are also among the highest paid in their positions. The City Manager, at the last City Commission meeting, created a position that has not been filled in 39 years, that of Director of Public Works and Service, and elevated our City Engineer to this position at an increase of $3,500 per year. Now let us look at these salaries:

City Manager	$39,000
City Attorney	33,350
Director of Public Works	30,600

When our City Manager arrived in Pittstown in 1976, his salary was $37,000 per year, which was $4,500 more than the city paid its former Manager. The former Manager received this salary of $32,500 and fulfilled the duties of the present Personnel Director and the newly created post of Director of Public Works and Services. Now our Chief Administrator must have a Personnel Director to relieve him of his duties as negotiator with employee groups and a Director of Public Works and Services to relieve him of additional adminstrative duties and, on top of this, has had his salary increased $1,000 per year since his arrival in Pittstown.

The Mayor of Pittstown stated at an Open City Commission meeting in 1977 that it was his desire to keep the Pittstown Police Department reasonably close to the highest police wages in the area. This was brought to the Manager's attention at the October 18 meeting and he stated that neither the Mayor nor the City Commissioners had any right to make such a statement.

Now let's look at the facts. At the present time, the Pittstown Police Officers are grossly underpaid, and are the only officers in the state not receiving longevity pay. Longevity pay was recommended in the City Survey of 1977. The Pittstown Police Department ranks 31st among metopolitan areas according to a recent wage survey. The City Manager has adamantly refused our efforts to procure a working agreement between the City of Pittstown and its Police Officers.

As you know, the Police Officers for the City of Pittstown recently cast an overwhelming vote in favor of strike action to resolve our dispute. As Officers of the Association, we believe all just and peaceful means should be exhausted to reach agreement. The safety and welfare of the Citizens of our City deserve no less.

We would appreciate any comments, pro or con, from the citizens of Pittstown relative to this matter.

President
Pittstown Police Officers Association

NOVEMBER 7, 1978 EPIDEMIC

When Chief Williams arrived at police headquarters on November 7, it was five minutes before midnight. Captain Frank Bell, who had called Williams at home, told Williams that 16 of the 18 night patrolmen had reported by phone that they were too sick to work.

"The only men who have not reported off sick" said Bell, "are the two young probationers." Bell also reported that he had been unsuccessful in getting off-duty men to come in. "I had difficulty getting to most of them" he explained, "and in the cases where I did get them on the phone, they said they're too sick to work tonight. I guess we really got an epidemic on our hands, Chief."

Williams then instructed Bell to call the off-duty captains, lieutenants and sergeants and order them to report for night patrol duty. Bell was able to contact the men in this group without difficulty, and none of them claimed to be sick. Even Sergeant O'Donnell, President of the Pittstown Police Officers Association, accepted Bell's call and reported for night patrol duty. Before long Bell had a full crew ready for the night shift. It was an unusual night patrol, consisting of 16 captains, lieutenants and sergeants and two probationary patrolmen.

Williams had hoped that the "epidemic" would be limited to the night shift but as morning came sick calls began to come in rapidly from the day shift patrolmen. Only a few of them actually reported for duty at seven o'clock, all the others having called in sick.

Williams recognized now that he faced a very serious problem.

He split up the captains, lieutenants and sergeants into three groups and ordered each group to be prepared to work sixteen hours on and eight hours off until the emergency ended. Pittstown operated during the day shift of November 8 with a much reduced and very tired police force.

As the shift ended and the time for the afternoon shift approached the same process was repeated. All but a few of the patrolmen who were scheduled for afternoon duty called in sick. Pittstown faced a prospect of the three o'clock to eleven o'clock period also with a much reduced and very tired police force, made up almost entirely of captains, lieutenants, and sergeants.

As the "epidemic" continued, the pressure on Williams from the public and city officials to take drastic action increased. It was proposed that he issue a strong statement ordering every man back to work under penalty of dismissal from the force; send a police supervisor to visit each "sick" man and if he was found to be not really sick to order him back to work under penalty of dismissal; order all men who had called in sick to report immediately to headquarters for a medical examination.

Late on Wednesday afternoon (November 8), the City Manager asked Williams to come to his office. He told him that the city was going to bring charges against all the people who had not reported to work. Any person who was really sick would be excused if they reported to one of the city doctors and proved his or her illness. Otherwise they would be assumed to be striking against the city and would be dealt with accordingly.

Williams asked for time to see what he could do to get his people to come back to work. He inquired as to what the city was prepared to do regarding salaries and longevity pay if they should return. The City Manager said the city was prepared to accept immediate mediation and fact finding in accordance with provisions of the state's Labor Relations Act. The City Manager agreed to give Williams until 8:00 p.m. to get the police personnel back on the job, at which time he said that the city would take action if they had not returned.

Exhibit 1

SURVEY OF TOP-STEP SALARY OF PATROLMEN IN COMMUNITIES NEAR PITTSTOWN, SUMMER OF 1977*

Community		Population (1977 estimated)	Salary
1. Pittstown County		?	$12,750
2.	A	1,600,000	14,831
3.	B	202,000	13,860
4.	C	126,000	13,708
5.	D	111,000	14,156
6.	E	149,000	13,610
7.	F	90,000	14,157
8.	G	82,000	12,907
9.	H	80,000	12,078
10.	I	90,000	12,058
11.	J	57,000	11,638
12.	K	54,000	11,321
Average			$13,089
Pittstown		84,000	12,806

* Survey made by Consultant hired by the City of Pittstown.

Exhibit 2

TOP-STEP SALARIES AND LONGEVITY BONUSES PAID POLICE PATROLMEN IN 17 COMMUNITIES NEAR PITTSTOWN*

Community	Population (1977 est)	Top-Step Salary	Longevity Plan: Basic Amount	Longevity Plan: Service Required	Longevity Plan: Added Amount	Longevity Plan: Service Required
Pittstown County	?	$13,450	2%	- 7 yrs	2%	every 3 yrs
A	1,600,000	15,914	2%	-11 yrs	2%	every 3 yrs
B	202,000	13,607	None			
C	126,000	14,007	None			
D	111,000	13,516	**			
E	149,000	14,840	$25/yr	- 7 yrs	$25	every 1 yr
F	90,000	13,987	2%	-10 yrs	2%	every 10 yrs
G	82,000	14,534	$100	- 5 yrs	None	
H	80,000	12,588	5%	- ?	None	
I	90,000	13,737	2½%	- ?	None	
J	57,000	14,219	$100	- 5 yrs	$200	for 10 yrs
K	54,000	12,614	2%	- 5 yrs	2%	every 5 yrs
L	39,000	14,952	2%	- 7 yrs	2%	every 7 yrs
M	7,000	13,913	None			
N	86,000	13,176	$10/yr	-10 yrs	None	
O	32,000	14,447	None			
P	36,000	14,458	None			
Average		13,918				
Pittstown		13,477	None			

*Taken from a study made by one of the Police Captains for Chief Williams.
**$1.00 each month of service to 10 years, then $2.00 for each month.

WILMINGTON BUREAU OF FIRE (A)

Hon. Thomas Maloney, Mayor of Wilmington, Delaware was dedicated to the principle of fiscal responsibility in government. In the period 1967-1973 expenditures in Wilmington had risen at the rate of 16 per cent per year. However, the city's budget balanced in each of these years: partly as a result of new taxes, partly from federal grants.

Maloney's election campaign in 1972 had been based on promises to cut expenditures wherever possible while retaining most of the city's services - not an easy job in the face of rapidly-rising inflation and movement out of the city by citizens and businesses who contributed significantly to the tax base.

As a liberal Democrat, Tom Maloney owed a substantial part of his election success to organized labor and non-white minority citizens. Cost-cutting moves would most likely affect these groups most severely. Nevertheless Maloney, in his first term, made some important moves to fulfill his campaign promises, and doubts among his constituency were mounting. Most recently the city had reduced manpower in sanitation crews, and the Mayor had insisted that the city hold the line in negotiations with the sanitationmen's union - fomenting a city-wide strike. In order to help break the strike Maloney himself, accompanied by aides and a few other elected officials, initiated a "do-it-yourself" garbage pick-up campaign. He was picture in newspapers and on television hoisting garbage, much to the chagrin of local labor leaders. Since a substantial number of sanitation union members were minority citizens, the Mayor's moves were interpreted by some as anti-minority.

All this provides background for contract negotiations that were pending with firemen and policemen in Spring 1974. While Maloney did not participate directly in negotiations he maintained close contact with the negotiators and looked upon rising labor costs as among the most important causes of Wilmington's growing fiscal difficulties.

So it was, in March of 1974 that Tom Maloney received reports from the New York City Rand Institute and a City of Wilmington Project Team. These recommended the elimination of two fire engine companies in Wilmington at an estimated cost saving of $420,000 per year in manpower costs. According to the recommendations there would be no appreciable decline in response time if these moves were made. It was likely, however, that there would be strong opposition from the International Association of Firefighters, the firemen's union, and, possibly, from other unionized workers not directly affected by the negotiations. There was danger, too, that Maloney's contituency support would be further eroded if he supported implementation of the recommendations.

WILMINGTON, DELAWARE

As of March 1974 Wilmington, the county seat of New Castle County, Delaware, was the state's largest city. There were 15.77

square miles within its corporate limits. Population was close to 80,000, and about 44 per cent of the population was non-white. Beyond this, approximately 60,000 commuters came in to Wilmington each business day to work.

Between 1960 and 1970 the city's population had decreased by over 15,000 persons, while the county's population increased by over 93,000. The city's economic base had shifted substantially during that time from manufacturing to service industries and professional establishments.

Wilmington reflected the problems of many of the nation's urban centers. It had large concentrations of low income, aged, and minority persons, all with greater-than-average needs for city services, and a stagnant or declining tax base. The result was an increasing demand for city services coupled with a decreasing ability to pay for them.

Wilmington's government could be characterized as "strong mayor-council." Its City Council was composed of eight district councilmen, four councilmen at large, and a president elected at large. The city's operating budget for fiscal year 1974 was $32.2 million, which was a 9.5 per cent increase over the fiscal year 1973 budget.

THE WILMINGTON BUREAU OF FIRE

The Wilmington Bureau of Fire was administered by a chief who reported to the Public Safety Commissioner. The chief, who was appointed by the Mayor, was selected from the Bureau's ranks on the basis of merit, tenure and experience. Wilmington had the only paid fire department in Delaware. All of the communities surrounding the city were protected by volunteer companies. In fact, over half of the firemen employed in Wilmington commuted to the city each work day, and most of these men served on the voluntary departments during non-working hours in the places where they lived.

There were 13 fire companies in Wilmington located in eight firehouses. All the firehouses except one were old - the oldest having been built in 1873. Exhibit 1 shows the houses: their location, their ages and the number of companies operating from each.

Three types of companies comprised the 13: nine engine companies, three ladder companies and one rescue squad. All were employed on two shifts, providing stand-by service 24 hours a day. In total, the department employed 230 men. The city's budget authorized 245.

The authorized manpower complement is shown below:

AUTHORIZED MANPOWER OF WILMINGTON BUREAU OF FIRE

9 Engine Companies	1 Officer 3 Firefighters	=	36 Men
3 Ladder Companies	1 Officer 3 Firefighters	=	15 Men
1 Rescue Squard	2 Firefighters	=	2 Men
2 Batallion Chiefs & 2 Aids		=	4 Men
Vacation, Sick, Injury Replacements		=	8 Men
Allotted Day Replacements		=	11 Men
TOTAL per Platoon			76 Men
TOTAL Fire Suppression Personnel (3 Platoons)		=	228 Men
Administrative, Dispatchers		=	17 Men
TOTAL AUTHORIZED PERSONNEL		=	245 MEN

The Bureau of Fire's operating budget for 1974 was $3.4 Million. Of this, $3.2 Million was paid in wages and fringes. Ranks and pay rates for the 230 men on the rolls as of March 1974 are shown below:

RANKS AND PAY RATES - MARCH 1974

Rank	Step	Salary	# of Positions Funded
Firefighter	Probationary	$8,900	174
	Step 1	9,200	
	Step 2	9,500	
	Step 3	9,800	
	Step 4	10,100	
	Step 5	10,500	
	Step 6	11,000	
	Step 7	11,500	
Lieutenant:	Start	12,400	29
	Step 1	12,500	
	Step 2	12,700	
	Step 3	13,000	
Captain:		14,500	17
Battalion Chief:		15,600	7
Deputy Chief:		17,500	3

The average annual cost of manpower for one fire company was approximately $210,000. This covered wages and fringes (excluding pension contributions) of three firefighters and one officer on each of three platoons. In addition it was estimated that "house cost" which included maintenance, equipment, and debt service were about $30,000 per year, per company.

In order to make up the difference between the number of firemen on the rolls and the number authorized it had been regular practice to employ firefighters on overtime each week to meet minimum manning requirements.

In considering the various problems surrounding negotiations that were about to begin with the firemen's union, Mayor Maloney was aware that in recent years police and firefighter salaries had been equivalent. In fact negotiations for the two groups had typically taken place at the same time. In order to earn the same base salary, however, it was necessary for firemen to work 48 hours a week, while the policemen worked 40 hours.

Another factor that could become important concerned the "image" of firefighters. Almost universally these men were held in high esteem. Their work was admired by nearly everyone, and their presence was considered essential.

On a regular basis they were credited with heroic deeds - rescuing senior citizens from burning buildings, saving the lives of heart-attack victims, saving children from drowning, pulling pet cats down from telephone poles. Their shiny red trucks have always been objects for admiration of young boys, and the clanging bells and sirens are generally viewed as sounds of security. Firemen as a rule are well-trained, well-disciplined and enjoy high morale among themselves. They are unique among members of our work force.

THE NEW YORK CITY RAND INSTITUE

The Rand Corporation of Santa Monica, California had developed sophisticated mathematical models for study of corporate performance. After successful application in many private industries the company transferred its expertise to the study of urban problems. The New York City Rand Institute was formed during the regime of Mayor John Lindsay in New York and had done a great amount of work in the police, fire and sanitation departments there. Mayor Maloney in Wilmington was interested in their work, and was able to secure funding by the U.S. Department of Housing and Urban Development in order to employ Rand to study the applicability of its New York City approach to smaller cities like Wilmington.

In 1973, shortly after taking office, Maloney assigned a city project team, composed of the Department of Planning and Development, the Bureau of Fire, the Department of Public Safety, his chief labor negotiators, and staff from the Mayor's office to work with Rand personnel. By use of computers which analysed the pattern of past fires and the alternative deployment policies which could be used to fight those fires, the team determined that response times would change very little with two of the city's engine companies eliminated. There was concern that their analysis might not be readily understood by the public, editorial writers and union leaders; so the team compared Wilmington's firefighting statistics to similar statistics in 13 other cities. Their comparisons are shown in Exhibit 2. Among the factors in the comparative study which were most important, three stood out:

1. The per-capita budget for Wilmington for fire protection was significantly higher than that of the other 13 cities;

2. The minimum and average number of persons on duty at any given time was considerably higher in Wilmington than in the other 13;

3. The Wilmington fire department had two more engines than the median for the other 13 cities.

By eliminating two engine companies, Wilmington could realize savings of up to $420,000 per year in manpower cuts alone. Above this they could save $10,000 or so in "house costs" - not to mention costs avoided by not paying two companies whatever salary increase was ultimately negotiated. Therefore, the team had recommended a reduction of engine companies from nine to seven.

MALONEY'S PROBLEM

As Mayor Maloney pondered the situation he was impressed with the potential savings, especially in view of his campaign promises of 1973. Expenditures in the city were continuing to rise, and if drastic steps were not taken promptly his campaign promises were not likely to be fulfilled.

But there were serious problems involved. Maloney noticed that the per capita fire loss in Wilmington was well below the median for the other 13 cities - though the number of alarms were about equal to the median. Perhaps this figure was a reflection of Wilmington's greater number of men and equipment than the others.

Beyond the report itself, Maloney wondered whether these savings could ever be realized, because he was certain to encounter resistance from the Firefighters' Union. In the first place, they would oppose any manpower reductions - pointing out that the department already was below its authorized strength by 15 persons. In addition, they would point to the number of fire deaths in Wilmington. These were slightly above the median for the other 13 cities studied. Then too, they would be likely to question the accuracy of the comparison, pointing to all sorts of differences between Wilmington and the other cities that would make any attempts at comparison an exercise in futility.

If the union would ever agree to a reduction in manpower they would most likely do so only if the city raised the pay for firefighters who were asked to take on added responsibilities - because fewer men, travelling greater distances with less equipment would have to serve the same community needs.

Maloney felt some security in knowledge of the law. Chapter 13, Section 1312 of the Delaware Code expressly forbade public employees the right to strike. However, public employees did have the right to organize and to bargain over wages, hours and conditions of work, and less than six months earlier the Sanitationmen's Union had struck in defiance of the law.

Although the present contract with the firefighters union did not have a section on "Manning" it did include a provision for "Maintenance of Standards" (See Exhibit 3). Maloney's legal advisors felt that there was a legitimate question about whether manning issues would be covered by this section. Nevertheless it was clear that the subject would be bargainable.

Exhibit 1

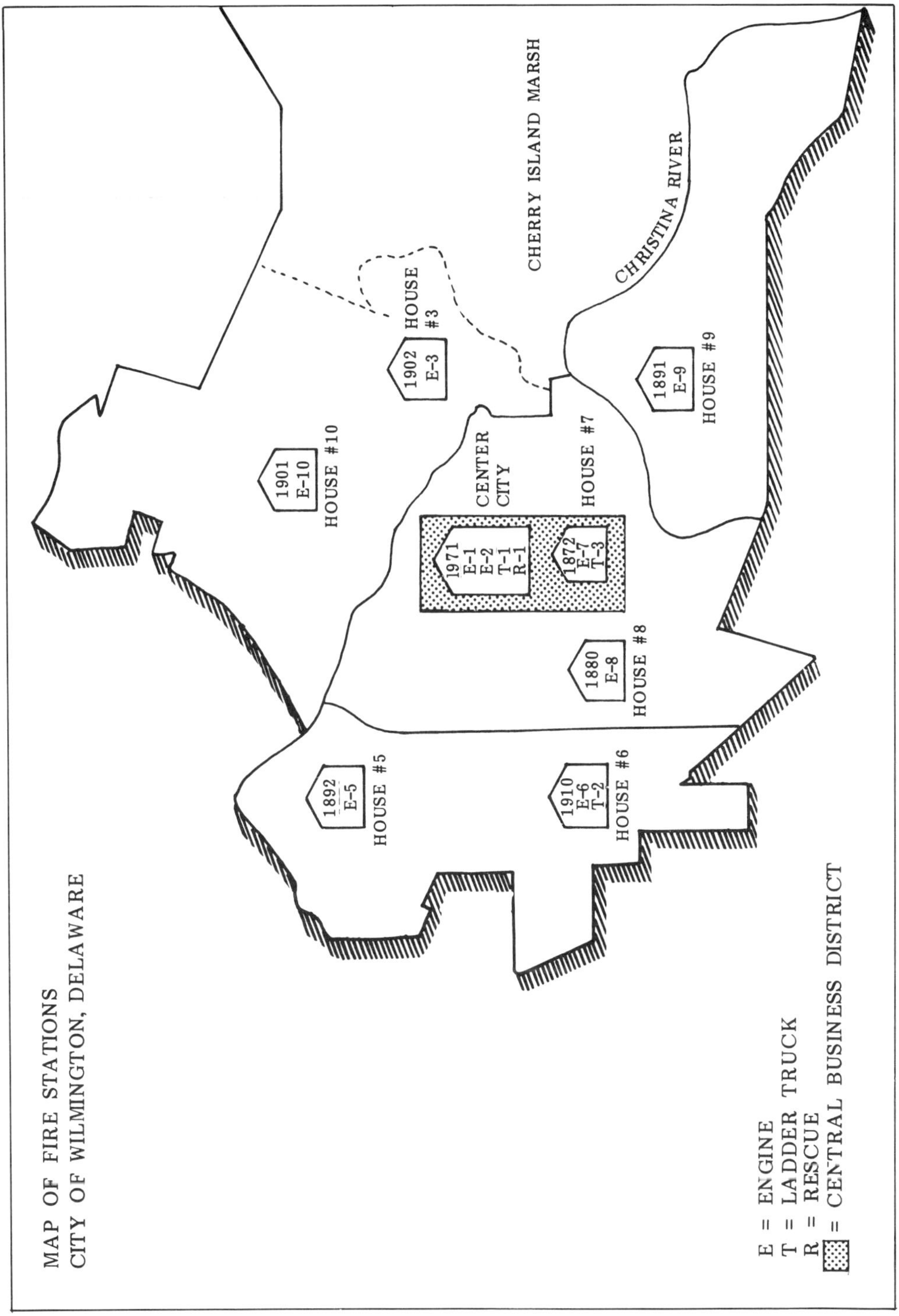
MAP OF FIRE STATIONS
CITY OF WILMINGTON, DELAWARE
CHERRY ISLAND MARSH
CHRISTINA RIVER
1902
E-3
HOUSE #3
1901
E-10
HOUSE #10
CENTER CITY
HOUSE #7
1971
E-1
E-2
T-1
R-1
1872
E-7
T-3
1891
E-9
HOUSE #9
1880
E-8
HOUSE #8
1892
E-5
HOUSE #5
1910
E-6
T-2
HOUSE #6
E = ENGINE
T = LADDER TRUCK
R = RESCUE
= CENTRAL BUSINESS DISTRICT

Exhibit 2

FIREFIGHTING STATISTICS - COMPARABLE CITIES

City	Population	1974 Fire Budget* per Capita	Hours per Work Week	1973 Alarms per Capita	1973 Alarms per Hour	1973 Alarms per Sq. Mile
Quincy, MA	87,966	38.26	42	.0419	0.42	229
Trenton, NJ	104,578	37.60	42	.0375	0.45	524
Medford, MA	64,409	36.56	42	.0478	0.35	386
Elizabeth, NJ	112,713	34.25	42	.0291	.037	280
Norwalk, CT	79,192	33.60	42	.0252	.023	91
Schenectady, NY	77,859	32.10	40	.0231	0.21	175
Camden, NJ	102,551	31.32	42	.0583	0.68	664
Clifton, NJ	82,437	29.21	42	.0226	0.21	158
Pawtucket, RI	76,992	26.95	42	.0234	0.21	205
Manchester, NH	87,754	25.96	48	.0314	0.31	86
New Britain, CT	83,441	25.48	42	.0270	0.26	170
Kalamazoo, MI	85,661	24.24	56	.0128	0.13	45
Bethlehem, PA	72,731	18.82	42	.0135	0.11	51
Medians	83,441	31.32	42	.0270	0.26	175
Wilmington	80,386	39.11	48	.0272	0.25	170

*Pensions and Debt Service Excluded

Exhibit 2
(continued)

FIREFIGHTING STATISTICS - COMPARABLE CITIES

City	1973 Fire Loss per Capita	'71-'73 Fire Deaths	Basic Response Policy*	Eng.	Lad.	Min. Men on Duty	Average Men on Duty
Quincy, MA	15.29	8	2-1	8	5	50	50
Trenton, NJ	14.05	10	2-1	9	4	52	56
Medford, MA	11.98	8	3-1	6	2	30	38
Elizabeth, NJ	19.71	19	3-1	9	3	52	56
Norwalk, CT			2-1	7	3	29	36
Schenectady, NY	8.50	1	2-1	7	2	30	33
Camden, NJ	5.18	11	2-1	9	3	37	56
Clifton, NJ	3.64	3	2-1	6	2	28	36
Pawtucket, RI	11.41	12	3-1	7	3	30	30
Manchester, NH	9.11	12	3-2	9	3	46	46
New Britain, CT			3-1	8	2	40	40
Kalamazoo, MI	3.90	5	2-1	7	4	42	50
Bethlehem, PA	3.26	3	2-1	7	3	29	32
Medians	9.11	8	2-1	7	3	37	40
Wilmington	6.90	9	2-1	9	3	56	58

*Engines - Ladders

Exhibit 3

MAINTENANCE OF STANDARDS

Provision of Existing Collective Agreement With Local 1590 International Association of Firefighters.

Section 1. The City agrees that all conditions of employment relating to wages, salaries, hours, insurance, vacations, sick leave, grievance procedures and all other terms and conditions of employment shall be maintained at not less than the highest standards in effect at the time of the signing of this Agreement and the same shall be improved wherever specific provisions for improvement are made elsewhere in this Agreement.

Exhibit 4

COMPARATIVE WAGE RATES*

WILMINGTON POLICE AND FIRE DEPARTMENTS

Fire Department:		Police Department:	
Firefighter:		Patrolmen:	
Probationary	$8,900	Probationary	$8,900
Step 1	9,200	Step 1	9,200
Step 2	9,500	Step 2	9,500
Step 3	9,800	Step 3	9,800
Step 4	10,100	Step 4	10,100
Step 5	10,500	Step 5	10,500
Step 6	11,000	Step 6	11,000
Step 7	11,500	Step 7	11,500
Lieutenant:		Sergeant	
Start	$12,400	Start	$12,400
Step 1	12,500	Step 1	12,500
Step 2	12,700	Step 2	12,700
Step 3	13,000	Step 3	13,000
Captain:	$14,500	Lieutenant	$14,500
Battalion Chief:	$15,600	Captain:	$15,600
Deputy Chief:	$17,500	Pol. Inspector:	$17,500

Exhibit 5

GLOSSARY OF FIRE TERMS

Number of Alarms:	The number of reports of fire or request for assistance by the fire department. In addition to actual fires, this number includes false alarms and miscellaneous requests for assistance which upon receipt cannot be distinguished from actual fires.
Company:	Used interchangeably with "fire company" to specify any fire department vehicle and its complement of firemen.
Engine Company:	A group of firemen who man a pumper and have the responsibility of connecting a hose to a fire hydrant and delivering water onto a fire.
Travel Time:	The time interval between departure of a fire company from its firehouse and its arrival at the scene.
Response Time:	The time interval between the report of a fire and the arrival of a fire company at the scene.
Fire House:	A building housing one or more fire companies. Used interchangeable with fire stations.
Truck Company:	A group of firemen who man a truck equiped with an aerial ladder. The truck also carries a large assortment of emergency tools, and the men are responsible for forcible entry, rescue, ventilations and salvage work. A truck company is often referred to as a ladder company.

NORWELL AIR FORCE BASE (A)

On June 1, 1979 Colonel Edward Thompson, Base Commander of Norwell Air Force Base, received a petition signed by more than 100 of the 400 civilian employees on the base in which they protested a change in their normal work hours. The petition had been circulated by the local officers of the National Federation of Government Employees (NFGE). This incident was the latest in a series of difficulties which the management of the base had experienced since the NFGE had begun to organize the civilian employees over two years earlier. Thompson was not sure what he should do about the petition.

NORWELL AFB - ORGANIZATION

Norwell Air Force Base was the home of three units under the command of the 337th Air Transport Wing. The principal unit included three squadrons under a Deputy Commander for Operations, which carried out the 337th's flying missions. The second unit was a support unit consisting of two maintenance squadrons and a supply squadron under a Deputy Commander for Material. A third unit, the Air Base Group under the Base Commander, had duties such as "housekeeping" and provided indirect support for the missions.

The Air Base Group consisted of four squadrons: Headquarters Squadron, responsible for personnel and administration; Security Police Squadron, responsible for security and law enforcement; Civil Engineering Squadron, responsible for construction and general maintenance; and Transportation Squadron, responsbile for most of the vehicles and the movement of personnel and materials. Colonel Thompson was in command of the Air Base Group.

THE WORK FORCE

Norwell Air Force Base was the largest single community in Paxton County. About 5,000 military personnel and dependents lived on the base and several thousand more lived in the surrounding area. In addition, civilian employees worked on the base which was by far the largest civilian employer in the area. Well over one half of the civilian employees were black.

The education level of the civilian work force was low, forty percent had not attended high school. A high percentage were veterans, many of whom had received training under the G.I. Bill. Seventy percent was comprised of blue collar workers: mechanics, truck drivers, building tradesmen, apprentices, helpers, and laborers. The white collar workers were mainly subprofessionals, clericals, and technicians. Both groups reported to civilian supervisors and Air Force officers.

Paxton County was classified as an economically depressed area with a high unemployment rate. There was on file at the base personnel office many more jobs applications than could be filled. Although approximately one-third of the military personnel was reassigned and departed the base each year the turnover of civilian employees was quite low.

NORWELL AIR FORCE BASE (A)

CIVIL SERVICE REFORM ACT OF 1978

Coverage. In October 1978, President Carter signed into law the Civil Service Reform Act. Title VII of the Act is The Federal Service Labor-Management Relations statute. Thus, for the first time in the history of the United States, federal labor-management relations activities were regulated by law. Prior to the enactment of the Civil Service Reform Act, federal labor-management relations activities were under the authority of a Presidential Executive Order orginally signed by President Kennedy as E.O. 10988 and subsequently revised by President Nixon as E.O. 11491. The primary elements of E.O. 11491 were carried forward into the new law. Title VII covers all agencies of the Federal Government except the GAO, FBI, CIA, NSA, TVA, Federal Labor Relations Authority, the Federal Service Impasses Panel, the U.S. Postal Service, AID, U.S. International Communications Agency, and Foreign Service Officers at the State Department.

Representation. Rights conferred by the federal labor-management relations policy, as stated in Title VII, included the following: (1) Employees have the right to form, join, or assist labor organization, or refrain from doing so, (2) employees are protected in exercise of this right, and (3) supervisors and other management officials must not participate in the management of or act as representative for a labor organization. The law requires a Federal agency to recognize and negotiate with a union which has been elected exclusive representative by the agency's civilian employees. To hold an election, a union must petition the Federal Labor Relations Authority (FLRA) through a Regional Office, and must demonstrate that a least 30 percent of the civilians it seeks to represent are interested in having the election. Local union membership is not a requirement to be counted within the 30 percent. Additional unions may participate in the election by submitting their own petitions with 10 percent showing of interest. The "no-union" option is automatically placed on every ballot.

The Regional Officer of the FLRA will review the showing of interest, the bargaining unit proposed by the union, the employees eligible to vote, and related matters specified in regulations. When all requirements are met, the Regional Officer will direct the activity to conduct a representation election, using a secret ballot.

If a union wins a simple majority of the valid votes cast in the election it becomes the exclusive representative of all the employees in the unit and must represent all of them in good faith, even those who are not union members. It then has the right to negotiate a labor contract, which must include a grievance system. The union also has the right to be represented at grievance proceedings between management and employees, at formal discussions between management and employees concerning any grievance or any personnel policy or practices or other general conditions of employment, and at any examination of an employee if the employee reasonably believes that the examination may result in disciplinary action and the employee requests union representation. Each agency is required to notify its employees annually concerning these rights.

Unfair Labor Practices. Both union officials and Federal managers are prohibited from certain behaviors in their dealings with each other and with the activity's employees. Those prohibitions are generally designed to protect employees in the exercise of their rights under Title VII, and to avoid coercion, or inducements to coercion, to prohibit dominance of a union by management; strikes by unions; management discrimination for union activites, to prohibit union discrimination for race, color, creed, sex, age, national origin, marital status or handicapping conditions, civil service status, or political affiliation. Title VII also seeks to insure that both unions and management bargain in good faith, and consult, confer or negotiate when required by the law and regulations. The FLRA is responsible for making determinations on charges of unfair labor practices. If any agency or labor organization is charged by any person with having engaged in an unfair labor practice, the General Counsel investigates the charges and may issue a complaint against the agency or labor organizaation. If a complaint is issued the General Counsel files and prosecutes the complaint before the FLRA. If the FLRA determines that an agency or labor organization has engaged in or is engaging in an unfair labor practice, the FLRA can, (1) issue a cease and desist order, (2) require the parties to renegotiate a collective bargaining agreement, (3) require reinstatement of an employee with backpay, or (4) any combination of the above actions.

Other Provisions. Employees, whether members or not, covered by a contract between their agency and a labor organization are bound by the terms of the contract and must use the grievance system negotiated in the contract except for grievances concerning EEO or adverse actions (discipline). In cases of this kind, an employee may use either the negotiated grievance system or the appellate procedures established by law, rule, or regulation. However, an employee may not use both systems for the same grievance. If an employee authorizes it, the agency must deduct union dues from the employee's pay and forward to the union without charging a fee for the service to either the employee or the union.

Any employee representing a labor organization in the negotiation of a collective bargaining agreement is authorized official time for such purposes. Any activities performed by any employee relating to the internal business of a labor organization (including the solicitation of membership, election of labor organization officials, and collection of dues) must be permformed on an employee's own time.

Scope of Bargaining. When a labor organization has been recognized as the exclusive representative of the employees, an agency must negotiate a collective bargaining agreement with that labor organization. Issues that are mandatory by law to be included in the scope of bargaining are: personnel policies and practices, and matters affecting working conditons so far as appropriate under applicable laws and regulations. Management may, at the election of the agency, negotiate matters with respect to numbers, types and grades of positions assigned to an organization unit, work project, or tour of duty; or the technology, methods and means of performing work. Management may not negotiate away its retained rights to hire, assign, direct, layoff, retain employees in the agency, suspend, remove, reduce in grade or pay, or to take other disciplinary action against employees; to assign work, contract out, and determine the personnel by which agency operations shall be conducted; to make selections for appointments; or to take whatever actions may be necessary to carry out the mission of the agency in emergencies.

UNIONIZATION AT NORWELL AFB

Paxton County, where Norwell AFB was located, was known as a non-union region. Outside the building trades, labor unions had not gained much of a foothold in the area. Thus, union organizing efforts could count on little or no outside community support in their campaigns.

On the Base, employee-management relations appeared to have been excellent. No formal complaint had ever been filed against any of the personnel policies, and only one grievance had been filed in the last five years. Pay, benefits, and continuty of employment at Norwell compared very favorably with other employers in the area. Moreover, rates of pay, benefit plans, and many other personnel policies and practices were determined by government directives and Air Force regulations and were not subject to collective bargaining under Executive Order 11491.

Although union organization of federal employees was authorized under E.O. 11491, Colonel Thompson's predecessor, Colonel James Richards, was convinced that he would not encounter union activity during his tour as Base Commander. Richards was finishing out a successful career in the Air Force and expected to retire in 1979. He had had no experience in dealing with labor unions prior to being assigned to Norwell, and was greatly surprised to learn, late in 1976, that the Association of Civilian Government Employees (ACGE), was carrying on a quiet membership drive at Norwell AFB.

ACGE was one of the largest unions of Federal government employees. It claimed a membership of 300,000 and, as a result of 1,770 recognitions, it represented over 650,000 federal employees. Sixty-five percent of its members were white collar workers. Much of its effort was placed at the national level, lobbying for legislation to replace E.O. 11491, improved wages and benefits, and for other matters affecting federal employees which were determined by legislation and directives. The military and civilian officials at the Base were of the opinion that they could develop a very good working relationship with ACGE leadership.

Early in 1977, just after the ACGE membership drive had come to light, representatives of the National Federation of Government Employees (NFGE), a rival union, began an organizing campaign on the base. NFGE was a smaller union. It claimed only 85,000 members and, as a result of 670 recognitions, it represented 139,000 federal employees. Sixty-five percent of its membership were from the blue collar workers. NFGE concentrated on achieving improvements and gains at the local level by means of political pressure and collective bargaining. From the very beginning it was clear that in both its organizing campaign and its relations with management NFGE would be more aggressive and militant than ACGE.

THE CIVILIAN PERSONNEL OFFICER

Jack Schafner, the Air Force's Civilian Personnel officer, served as management's key point of contact in its relations with the two unions. Schafner believed that the employees had joined the unions because "unions provide an umbrella for the workers — against what might happen. Some guys belong to both of the unions. That way no matter what they do they can count on protection."

Schafner, who had been in civilian personnel work for 28 years, 18 of which had been at Norwell, was concerned about the declining importance of the Personnel Officer. He said that employees no longer brought their problems to him to the extent that they had before the unions were recognized. Despite this, Schafner insisted that he bore no bitterness toward the unions. He believed instead that if properly dealt with they could be a real asset to management. They could serve, he said, as private inspection teams to alert management to problems before they got out of control. He believed, however, that it was necessary to be firm in his dealings with the unions. His job as he saw it was to protect the Commander - "to keep him out of trouble."

THE DRIVE FOR RECOGNITION

NFGE moved aggressively to increase its membership, campaigning on the pledge that with recognition it would be able to bring about important changes on the Base which would benefit the employees. Among other things it claimed that it would insist on a change in the attitude and make-up of the supervisory staff which it accused of being "arbitrary, domineering" and in many cases "completely unqualified."

John Reid, the National President of NFGE, spearheaded the drive. One of his first actions was to write a letter to the Labor Department, accusing management at the Base of certain "acts of foul play" against civilian employees and another to Air Force officials in Washington, claiming that there had been "thefts of government property" by some of the officials on the Base. He demanded an immediate investigation in each case. The Assistant Secretary of Labor's office responded to Reid by pointing out that under E.O. 11491, any charges of an unfair labor practice must first be submitted to the activity accussed of the practice for a joint investigation and attempts at informal settlement. An Air Force investigation of the alleged thefts was initiated but was dropped due to lack of evidence. Nevertheless, many employees were impressed by Reid's aggressiveness and his ability to make good on his promise to "get somebody down here from Washington to investigate this base."

On March 5, 1977 Julian Loper, a fuel distribution operator and Treasurer of the NFGE local, asked his supervisor, Staff Sergeant Wade, for permission to attend a meeting at the Base Commander's office. Wade refused the request and ordered Loper not to go to the Commander's office. Loper, however, did attend the meeting and later that day, Lt. Col. Colburn, Chief of Supply, sent to Loper an official letter of reprimand for disobeying orders. Loper answered Colburn's letter with a note stating that he intended to file an appeal. He was informed that he had the right to appeal but that it had to be submitted in writing to the Civilian Personnel Officer.

Loper never submitted a written appeal. Instead, Reid wrote to Richards asking that the letter of reprimand be removed from Loper's records explaining that "Loper had not taken time off from his official duties to attend the meeting since the meeting occurred during his lunch period, and no adverse action could be taken against an employee during a lunch period unless the employee had violated a statute or policy." Reid charged the party involved with discrimination against an active union member. Sergeant Wade claimed it was not discrimination because he had not known that Loper was in the union. He maintained that the reason he gave the order was because he thought Loper was violating the chain of command. The letter of reprimand was not withdrawn.

Several months passed and Richards thought that the issue had been dropped by the union when he was informed that Reid was attempting to have the Director of Civilian Personnel at Headquarters USAF intercede "to correct the inequity Loper had received." Reid had taken Loper and another employee who was also appealing an adverse action at that time to Washington. Both were impressed by the people Reid knew there.

The union eventually lost both cases. The UASF Director of Civilian Personnel ruled that no further action could be taken on Loper's case since he had not submitted an appeal within the ten days allowed by regulations. Before the other case was finally settled, however, a fact-finding group from Headquarters USAF visited Norwell. The word quickly spread among the workers that Reid had delivered a second time on his boast that he could pull people down from Washington to investigate.

NFGE's membership had continued to grow and in June 1977, Reid submitted a formal petition to the Labor Department, accompanied by the necessary 30 percent showing of interest, requesting a representation election among all eligible employees at Norwell AFB. ACGE quickly submitted its own petition, and collected the 10 percent showing of interest to qualify as an intervenor in the election. The Assistant Secretary of Labor for Labor-Management Relations (A/SLMR), through his Area Administrator ordered that a hearing be held to examine the unit for which NFGE was petitioning, and to insure that no management officials or supervisors would be considered eligible to vote. The A/SLMR reviewed the findings, approved them, and ordered an election at Norwell between NFGE, ACGE, and "No Union." The date for the election was set as September 11, 1977. The Base Commander decided not to do or say anything lest it be interpreted as unfair labor practice.

On September 10, just one day before the election, an event took place which the Civilian Personnel Officer, Schafner, believed swung the balance in favor of the NFGE. On that day two members of NFGE were killed in an automobile accident. As members of the union, both men were covered by an NFGE life insurance policy. Reid arranged to get the benefit checks delivered to him immediately and that same evening presented them personally to the widows.

The news of the event spread rapidly and apparently influenced many of the employees to vote for NFGE. In any event, the next day NFGE polled over 50 percent of the votes and as a result, achieved the status of exclusive recognition for all the 500 employees in the bargaining unit. Since E.O. 11491, as amended, provided exclusive recognition as the only form of reognition available to a union, ACGE had thereby lost any claim to represent employees at Norwell.

CONTRACT NEGOTIATIONS

As soon as NFGE had been given exclusive recognition Reid wrote to Richards asking that contract negotiations be undertaken. Under E.O. 11491, union and management representatives were obliged to negotiate in good faith with respect to personnel policies and practices and matters affecting working conditions, subject to applicable laws and regulations. Air Force regulations define working conditions to include safety, training, labor-management co-operation, employee service, grievance procedures, leave procedures, promotion plans, demotion practices, pay procedures, reductions-in force practices, and hours of work. Day-to-day operational procedures were not subject to negotiation. Agreements could relate only to matters within the discretion of the activity commander, could not be contrary to policy established by a higher echelon, and were only applicable to the unit for which negotiated.

Contract negotiations began in early October 1977 between a management team headed by Lt. Col. Jacobs, Base Staff Judge Advocate, and a union team led by Vincent Moore, President of NFGE Local #24. Neither Jacobs nor Moore had had previous experience in labor contract negotiations. Each proceeded very cautiously and frequently sought advice from their superiors. Progress was very slow during the first four months despite many meetings but the rate of settlements picked up in the late summer and fall, and at the meeting on February 2, 1978, Moore stated that he thought the negotiations were completed with the exception of a few small technical matters. After the meeting Jacobs reported to Richards that he believed they would have the agreement for signatures following the meeting which was scheduled for the next week.

On February 4, however, Reid called Richards and informed him that progress was not being made in the negotiations and suggested that an impasse be declared. Richards discussed the matter with Jacobs who then wrote to Moore indicating his surprise and asking for clarification of the union's position. He concluded his letter with the following paragraph:

> If you want to resume with a view toward completing a contract, I'm ready. But I think a meeting is unlikely to prove fruitful unless there is some change in your attitude that E.O. 11491 constitutes an open letter of credit permitting expenditures of funds in complete disregard of normal appropriation procedures. For example, your request for office space on the Base will cost money and the Commander must be able to justify the items in his budget that will be affected by this exception to this Air Force policy. . . .

During the next several weeks, Reid addressed a number of letters to officials in Washington. On February 12, 1978 he wrote to the Secretary of the Air Force alleging that the Base was using Airmen 2nd and 3rd Class (second and third ranks from the bottom in the enlisted rank structure) as supervisors over career civilian personnel. These airmen, he stated were untrained and unskilled and "they should not be acting as supervisors over skilled artisans because this tends to bring discredit upon journeymen and the Civilian Civil Service System." Reid claimed that this condition did not exist at Naval shipyards and Army installations and requested that the matter be looked into. He said he was bringing this to the Secretary's attention because the Base had denied the union's request for discontinuing this practice.

On Februay 17, 1978 Richards received a letter from Reid, copies of which had been sent to the two U.S. Senators representing the State, the Congressman repreesenting the local District (one of the highest ranking member in the House), both Chairmen of the Armed Services Committees, and both Chairman of the Post Office and Civil Service Committees. In his letter Reid expanded on the allegations that had been included in his letter to the Secretary of the Air Force and added the following points:

1. He criticized the Base for not providing safety shoes to employees where work required wearing them. He cited the example of a nearby base where, "due to contract negotiations, the Air Force now provides them." He stated that he was rebuffed in his efforts at Norwell in spite of a Secretary of the Air Force policy to the contrary.[1]

2. He cited at length the example of a nearby base where "I was invited to sit down with Air Force officials ... at management's request to go over any and all problems... and I can assure you there is mutual respect for one another at this installation. This respect, however, is not forthcoming from officials at Norwell AFB and... it makes one wonder about the caliber of Air Force officers this Base has been receiving over the past few years."

---

[1]On October 25, 1965 a message was dispatched by headquarters USAF to all major air commands advising that safety shoes could be issued to employees when required in their duty assignments.

3. On the subject of office space he stated, "although government agencies allow unions having exclusive recognition appropriate space for an office or file system, this request was denied at Norwell AFB even though there is a vast wilderness and acres of land and surplus buildings."

4. He concluded with the comment that he had been apprised of many serious unfair labor practices at Norwell over the past years and he intended to "exhaust every remedy at hand to prevent further violations."

The most severe pressure from the barrage of inquiries that followed was from the local Congressman. In addition to querying headquarters USAF he wired the Base Commander direct. He stated he "had known Mr. Reid for a number of years and respected him very much" and suggested that Richards see Reid and "discuss the allegations with him with a view to a harmonious adjustment." This message, along with an article containing Reid's letter and some of the high level comment evoked by it, was printed in the monthly union newspaper which was distributed to all civilian employees.

Richards was concerned about unfavorable employee reaction. He was worried that copies of the letter had been sent to a number of people whose good-will and support were important to the Air Force and particularly to his base. He wondered what he should do about the impasse and how he should answer the various charges. He felt that agreement with the Congressman's suggestions that he meet with Reid would weaken his position and "give cause for more letter writing." He realized that mediation could be used but he felt resumption of local negotiations would be the best solution with the initiative coming from the union. He decided it would be best to wait out the union. Before a final decision he discussed his proposed position with officials at Headquarters USAF. In general, they concurred and agreed to support him.

Richards' answer to Reid was a brief polite acknowledgement of his letter. He stated that all union proposals had been considered and had been disposed of either by a negotiated provision in the contract or were to be taken up by a consultation committee provided for in the proposed agreement. He reminded Reid of Jacobs' readiness to resume negotiations and said that he felt the negotiating committees were the appropriate ones to handle the details involved in negotiating the agreement.

In answering the inquiries, Richards took the position that he did not know what prompted Reid's letters or his suspension of the bargaining. He stated that Reid's comment on a union proposal regarding supervision of civilian employees by the military misrepresented the issue. The union proposal, which was turned down, was that no civilian employee should be required to accept orders of military supervisors of lower ranks. Richards explained that there were circumstances dictated by military necessity which would preclude this arrangement. In answering the criticism about not furnishing office space, he referred to Section 19(a)(3) of Executive Order 11491, which stated that such services were to be furnished only when consistent with the best interests of the agency as well as of its employees and the Union. Richards said that the union would be tempted to conduct union business during working hours if they held office space on the Base, and that the tightened appropriations generally available for office materials and equipment throughout the Air Force required that he refuse this request as an economy measure. Besides, Richards pointed out, NFGE already occupied office space directly across the street from the main gate into Norwell. Ricahrds commented also on the union's request that the time of union observers at grievance hearings be considered duty time and paid for by the Air Force. This item had been the subject of separate correspondence between Reid and the Civil Service Commission. The Commission had advised him that the Air Force may require this to be on the union representative's own time. The Base negotiating team had taken this position and Richards referred to the Civil Service Commission response in reply to Congressional inquiry on the matter.

He added that the remaining allegations and criticisms in the letters were general in nature and specific comment did not seem to be in order. Finally, he stated that "the Base Committee is ready to resume meaningful negotiations at any time convenient to the Union." The last of his replies was sent out March 1.

On March 10, Moore called Jacobs and informed him that the Union was ready to resume negotiations. The first of a series of weekly meetings was held on March 15. By April 30 a tentative settlement of all issues was reached by the two teams, subject to approval by the Union membership and the Director of Civilian Personnel, Headquarters USAF.

Air Transport Command Headquarters (ATC) reviewed the contract first and concluded that "although it could be much shorter and the language improved for the sake of clarity, the final product was excellent when compared to the original proposals." The main changes recommended pertained to the grievance procedure. NFGE had insisted on clauses which would have permitted the shop steward to represent employees at the first level of supervision. Air Force regulations did not explicitly prohibit representation at the first level, but since they defined a grievance as "a dissatisfication carried above the supervisory level" ATC decided that representation could be permitted only above the first level. ATC's recommendations, were forwarded with the contract to Headquarters USAF for review and approval.

After all the reviewing offices had been coordinated at Headquarters USAF and their remarks combined into one list, there were nine articles in the agreement which required modification in order to achieve regulatory compliance prior to approval. Additionally, there were thirteen articles on which clarification was requested or modification suggested for the sake of clarity.

The agreement was returned to the base for modification on May 25, 1978. There it was revised by the negotiating teams and sent up the command chain again. Despite the changes it was still considered unacceptable and was returned for more work by the teams. One of the most troublesome issues remaining was the grievance procedure. A clause had been written and approved by both parties which read:

> <u>Section 3.</u> A represntative of the Union shall, unless the employee objects, have the right to be present in an observer's status when an employee presents a grievance or appeal therefrom to an official of management at the first level of supervision and above and has not requested union assistance or representation. The union observer shall be given the opportunity to present the views of the union... however, the Union observer may not, in any way represent the employee when this discussion occurs at the first level of supervision in that the aggrieved employee is not entitled to Union representation at his first supervisory level under Air Force regulations.

The difficulty was in defining "first level of supervision." The teams had written a clause which ATC said did not apply in all cases. In its place they suggested a definition given in certain Air Force regulations which referred to the "full range of supervisory duties" as characterizing the first level. These duties were listed in the Civil Service Commission Supervisory Grade Evaluation Guide. The NFGE national headquarters expressed concern over the proposed definition. They said that the Base negotiators were taking the position that the first level supervisors were persons NFGE believed to be third or fourth level supervisors.

To relieve NFGE's concern Headquarters USAF asked the management team to give concrete examples of how the proposed definition would work. One of the examples used was the Base Fuel Section in which the levels of supervision were dispatcher, shift leader, noncommissioned officers in charge (NCOIC) of distribution and storage, and section officer in charge (OIC). The Union feared that the OIC would be the first level supervisor under the proposed definition. NFGE thought the shift leaders would be more appropriate but accepted management's position that these were merely "straw boss" positions. Management explained that in situations where an employee is changed from a crew he would work for a different work leader at different periods of times. The Union team finally accepted the NCOIC as the first level supervisor in this instance. Agreement was reached on all positions brought up by the Union and negotiations moved to other topics.

On July 10, 1978 the agreement was again sent to Headquarters USAF. On August 19, it was returned to the bargaining teams, this time with only four articles requiring revision prior to approval. Again the bargaining teams met and worked out new provisions which they hoped would meet the objections on the four issues. Then the contract was again submitted up the chain of command. Finally, on November 22, 1978, approval was received and the contract became effective. (All negotiated contracts in affect prior to January, 1979 the effective date of Title VII of the Civil Service Reform Act) were to remain in effect for the negotiated term of the contract.)

On February 15, 1979 Col. Richards was reassigned and Col. Edward Thompson replaced him as Base Commander. Thompson had recently returned from Korea where he had been the Operations

Officer of a combat wing. Up until now his experience had primarily been in the operations area as a pilot, squadron commander and as a wing operations officer. He looked forward to the many new challenges that a Base Commander's job offered. He knew the job was a "political" one; that getting along with all the various groups both on the base and in the community was important. He had been briefed by Col. Richards and Schafner about the union difficulties of the past. He was aware of how damaging unfavorable publicity could be to a base and to a base commander. Whether it was deserved or not seemed to make little difference. As a friend of his who had been a base commander, put it, "If you become a burden to higher command too often, regardless of the reason, before you know it you're gone." Thompson decided to maintain separation and to have Schafner handle all union matters.

UNFAIR LABOR PRACTICE CHARGE

Thompson had been on the Base only a short time when the first difficulty occurred with the Union. The situation developed out of a decision made jointly by both the Wing Commander and Thompson to change th Base's normal working hours. The decision was explained to the Union officials during the regular monthly union management relations meeting.

The meeting, the sixth in a continuing series, was held on March 1, 1979 in the Civilian Personnel Office. Representing NFGE Local #24 were Moore, Judge Advocate Phil Chapman and Chief Steward John Davis. Also attending the meeting were Schafner and Lt. Col. Gary Paulson, Executive Officer 337th Combat Group. The minutes of the meeting show that it was opened by Lt. Col. Paulson who stated that he was at the meeting on behalf of the Wing and Base Commanders to consult with the officers of the Union on a change of the normal tour of duty for the Base. Paulson quoted a portion of the agreement with the Union which stipulated that it was "agreed that before changing the normal work hours and/or established lunch period, the employer will consult with the Union." He stated that the Commander anticipated changing the starting time from 0730 to 0800 (7:30 to 8:00 a.m.) and the quitting time from 1630 to 1700 hours (4:30 to 5:00 p.m.). The discussion then proceeded as follows:

Paulson: The purpose of the change is to align the duty hours here with those of the next higher headquarters, Tenth Air Force. In the best interests of morale and to allow adjustments by families both for military and civilian employees, they will be given a two-week notice of the change.

Schafner: There will be a notice in the Daily Bulletin and other means of notification that are available.

Moore: Could this change again?

Paulson: Only if Tenth Air Force changes.

Davis: I'll be getting home late.

Paulson: By leaving the Base at 5:00 p.m. the traffic will be easier to cope with since people will arrive in places such as Benton after 5:30 thereby avoiding the traffic in Benton.

Davis: If we're going to do this I'd like to see a half-hour lunch period.

Paulson: The main idea of this change is to have the same hours as Tenth Air Force. If we had a half-hour lunch period, that would defeat the main purpose of the change. This change of time covers the Operation of Mission and not negotiable. Lunch is a negotiable time.

Moore: I'd like some time to consult the people of my organization.

Paulson: This will be done. We are trying to find a happy agreement. We are consulting. I am speaking for the Commander as employer. Mr. Moore is speaking for the people in the Union. We are not negotiating.

Moore: I would like to know why I haven't been consulted on this.

Paulson: Well, I'll take blame for that.

Moore: I will be getting too many phone calls on this as to why my Union wasn't notified.

Schafner: They're not supposed to be phoning you on Union business during working hours.

Moore: They can if it pertains to their jobs.

Paulson: You have no alternative. This is not negotiable and this is in keeping with your terms of agreement. This is mission-oriented. The Union has been consulted in accordance with the agreement and once again, this is not a negotiable item.

Mr. Moore then asked for a short recess during which the Union representatives could discuss the matter separately. After the recess Moore stated that since this had been discussed by the military and the change date determined by them the Union would have to agree to it.

Lt. Col. Paulson then departed the meeting. After he had left, the Union brought up problems pertaining to a new promotion plan, questions of interpretation involving overtime procedures, a complaint from an employee (WB-4) who claimed he was doing a WB-8 job, and a problem that had come up over an NCO who was alleged to be forcing substitute safety glasses on civilian employees. These matters were discussed in detail and in each issue either an agreement was reached or Schafner agreed to investigate the matter and report back at the next meeting. The Union was then advised on some changes in classification regulations, the latest on the Congressional pay raise, and given particulars on the flu shots schedule. The upcoming United Fund meeting was discussed and the meeting adjourned.

On March 13, Thompson received a call from Reid pertaining to the hours change. Thompson described the call as follows:

> Reid called me and after explaining his position made accusations concerning Mr. Schafner. He went on to say how cooperative the past Base Commander had been but that Schafner, my Civilian Personnel Officer, used forceful methods and had a habit of ramming things down Moore's throat. He asked, in reference to our change in duty hours, that I call Moore into my office and go over this and some other things. In general, the idea was for me to work with Moore and leave Schafner out of the picture. It was at this point that I explained to Reid, in a perfectly courteous manner, that Schafner was my representative in all dealings with the Union, that the Union members had been advised of the change in working hours, that Schafner was well qualified and there was no purpose to be served by my talking to the Union President. Reid's next comment was that he had hoped I would be as cooperative as the previous Base Commander. I then stated that everything would be fine as long as the union did not try to run the Base. It was at this time that Reid said, "I don't think we will get along worth a damn," and slammed down the telephone receiver.

In a letter to the Base Commander dated May 12, 1979 Reid stated that he was preparing to file unfair labor practice charges against the Base with the Federal Labor Relations Authority alleging that:

1. After the agreement had been approved it had been arbitrarily held up by the Base before finally being presented to the Union.
2. NFGE was not consulted on the changes in work hours as required by the agreement. Management had simply told the Union but had not consulted with it. The Union maintained that work-hour changes was a negotiable item.
3. Thompson violated the contract by indicating clearly to Reid during a telephone conservation that he would not discuss the matter with any Union official.
4. A situation of misutilization of personnel existed at Norwell AFB.

As a remedy Reid requested that the hours of work be returned to the original schedule; that the Base Commander "negotiate and consult" with the Union on such matters in the future; that negotiation be reopened to deal with the issue of personnel misutilization; and that the Base Commander "cease and desist" from interfering with promulgation of approved labor contracts at Norwell AFB.

In answering these charges, Thompson replied that he did not feel there had been an arbitrary delay in the contract since Moore had been immediately informed of its final approval and Moore had a carbon copy of it. There had been a delay, Thompson admitted, in the reproduction of the extra copies. With regard to the change in work hours, Thompson's position was that the item could only be negotiable at time of contract renewal and that the Union was consulted as required. Thompson believed the misutilization charge was there simply to cloud the issue. He refused to answer it unless the Union would be specific. However, NFGE refused to drop the charge. It claimed that it would furnish further evidence to the General Counsel when the formal complaint was filed. On May 20, Thompson wrote Moore that the working hours as set would not be changed. He suggested that any problem areas affecting the welfare and morale of the work force be brought to the attention of Schafner.

In the next union-management relations meeting, held June 1, 1979 Moore presented a petition pertaining to the changed duty hours. Moore commented:

> I have four pages of signatures protesting the change. This must have affected the morale of the people of the Base, or they would not have taken the time to sign their names. I would like this looked into. You can investigate the names, but I want these sheets back.
> There are over 100 signatures, and if this only affects 400 people, this is 25 percent.... In paragraph 6 of the Colonel's letter of 20 May 1979 that he mailed me it says "At that time a complete review of individual cases will be made." Will you notify me in writing or call me when you get the results of this investigation? Otherwise we will file a formal unfair labor practice complaint with the Federal Labor Relations Authority.

After the meeting, Schafner contacted Thompson and gave him the petition. Thompson had not expected this since he had done some private checking which had led him to believe that people were unhappy about the change in hours. He would have liked to ignore the petitions, but having invited the Union to bring cases to his attention he believed he had to do something. He suspected that many of the signatures had been obtained from workers who only wanted to support the Union and their fellow workers. An examination of the petitions and interviews with the petitioners could prove him right. If he showed too much interest, however, it might appear that he was afraid and was considering changing back the hours. He had to be careful not to make mistakes the Union could capitalize on. He was aware that a great deal of concern was being expressed at high levels that the situation at Norwell was getting out of hand. He wondered what he should do about the petitioners. What action could be taken on the complaints without weakening his overall position?

SECTION VI

Foreign Labor Relations

M-S LTD. (A)

BACKGROUND

M-S Ltd. which manufactured high qualilty electric switches and other electrical products was located in Bankdown, a medium sized community near Newcastle, England. In 1976 the company had 500 employees, 300 of whom were manual workers. From 1923 when it was founded by John Brewer who held the patents to its early products until 1965, it was a family concern. However in 1965 it was acquired by Imperial Electric Products Inc. Ltd. (IEP), one of Britains major electrical manufacturing companies. Following the acquisition Brewer retired. The management team which had served under him continued, but as time passed more and more of the executive group were appointees of IEP. The emphasis under the new management was on production and profitability. Employee relations which had been a special concern of Brewer were no longer given high priority.

Bankdown's primary industry was coal mining which accounted for 70% of its employment. It had a long history of militant left-wing unionism. It was not surprising, therefore, that a large majority of the manual workers at M-S joined unions early in the compay's history. For a number of years the manual workers were represented by several unions, including the foundry workers union and the Amalgamated Union of Engineering Workers (AUEW). However, in 1966 the foundry workers union was merged into AUEW at the national level and following that date all manual workers at M-S were represented only by the AUEW. Originally the company's designers and draftsmen were represented by a separate union, Draftsmen and Allied Technicians Association, but in 1971 it also was merged at the national level into AUEW becoming a separate negotiating unit, the Technical and Supervisory Section (TASS) of AUEW. Following the acquisition of the company by IEP in 1965 the clerical workers became represented by the Association of Professional Executive Clerical and Computer Staff (APEX) and the charge hands, foremen, supervisors, service engineers, sales engineers and laboratory staff became represented by the Association of Scientific, Technical and Managerial Staffs (ASTMS).

There were a number of intra-union and inter-union rivalries at M-S which caused serious difficulties. Despite the fact that the foundry workers union had been merged into AUEW nationally, the local foundry group retained its identity and there was continuous conflict between it and the engineering section of the union. Likewise TASS, although a part of AUEW, retained its separate identity and negotiated its own contracts both at the national level with the Federation and at the local level with M-S. After the office and staff employees became unionized disputes arose over lines of demarcation between TASS, APEX and ASTMS. A particularly bitter dispute had arisen recently between AUEW and ASTMS as a result of instructions from the national AUEW leadership to the M-S local that workers who became foremen should retain their membership in AUEW. ASTMS had always viewed foremen as within its jurisdiction and indeed had represented them at M-S for a number of years.

M-S was a member of the Engineering Employers Federation which represented 5,700 firms who employed over 2 million workers. The Federation negotiated national agreements with the major unions in the field, including AUEW, TASS, APEX and ASTMS. However, these national agreements covered only major issues including the basic wage structure. M-S and other member firms of the Federation negotiated local plant agreements with the union which supplemented the national agreements, including additions to the basic wages. The labor agreements were open ended. A union was free to raise a new demand at any time and after exhausting the settlement procedure of the agreement was free to strike.

THE 1975 STRIKES

Two strikes in 1975 were especially costly to the company. One strike involved demands of the foundry employees for higher pay and better working conditions. The company believed that the demands were extremely unreasonable. It was of the opinion that both wages and working conditions in its foundry were equal to or superior to those in other foundries in the area or in the industry. Moreover, it believed that to grant the foundry section's demands would create serious inequities within the plant, especially vis-a-vis the engineering section. Therefore, the company refused to grant the demand whereupon the AUEW, after having exhausted the settlement procedures of the agreement, called a strike of its 300 members which included both the foundry and the engineering sections. The strike lasted for 10 weeks at which time the company acceded to the foundry workers original demands.

Later in 1975 the engineers section of AUEW demanded an increase. The company was not opposed to granting an increase to the engineers but the foundry section insisted that any increase granted to the engineers must also be given to them. However, the engineers stated that if the increase was given also to the foundry, they, the engineers would strike. The company finally worked out a compromise which the AUEW agreed to. However, the foundry section breached the agreement and went on strike. This time the company stood its ground but the strike lasted for 10 weeks before the members finally voted to return to work on the terms agreed upon before the strike.

THE CLOSED SHOP ISSUE

A closed shop agreement is one in which the company and the union agree that an employee must be a paid-up member of the union in order to continue to work at the plant. Under the Industrial Relations Act of 1971 which was passed by a Conservative Government it was illegal for a company and a union to negotiate a closed shop. However, in 1974 the Labor Government repealed the 1971 Act and companies and unions were free to negotiate such clauses.

M-S LTD. (A)

In 1975 97% of the hourly-paid workers at M-S were dues-paying members of AUEW. From time to time friction had developed in the plant betweeen the members and the small group of non-members who were called "free riders". In December 1975 the AUEW indicated to the company that it wished to negotiate a closed shop for all hourly-paid employees. After a number of negotiating sessions during which the union leadership indicated a willingness to accept certain management proposals in return for the closed shop, the company agreed to a post-entry closed shop arrangement whereby management was free to hire union or non-union employees but after the probationary period the workers had to become and remain dues-paying members of the union. The agreement was reached on January 10, 1976 to become effective March 1, 1976.

Immediately following the signing by the company and AUEW of the closed-shop agreement for hourly-paid employees the three staff unions (TASS, APEX and ASTMS) notified management that they also wished to negotiate closed-shop provisions. The company indicated its willingness to negotiate such provisions provided an agreement could be reached first on the sphere of influence of each of the three unions. After a number of discussions the three unions were able to agree on clear lines of demarcation between their spheres which were satisfactory also to the company.

However, the sphere of influence of ASTMS remained unclear because of its dispute with AUEW over employees who were promoted to foremen. The company feared that negotiation of a closed shop with ASTMS under these conditions would provoke an extremely strong reaction from AUEW. On the other hand ASTMS, seeing its long term position threatened by the new AUEW attitude regarding foremen, aggressively pressed the company for a closed-shop agreement which would include the foremen.

The company, caught in the middle by the confict, called a conference of the two unions on February 3 for the purpose of trying to work out an arrangement. The conference was not successful. AUEW insisted on the right to retain in its membership workers who were promoted to foremen. ASTMS insisted that all foremen remain within its jurisdiction. Following the unsuccessful conference the company on February 5 addressed a letter to the unions which stated:

> The Company views with extreme concern the possible consequences of the present dispute, which they emphasize is essentially based on a conflict between the two Unions. They are accordingly not prepared to make any decision which implies acceptance of either Union's standpoint.
>
> The Company is willing to sign and implement the recognition and negotiating arrangements provided for in the draft agreement with ASTMS. The Company however is not prepared, in the absence of agreement between the two Unions, to sign the closed shop provisions of the draft agreement.

The Company urges the two Unions:

(a) to reconsider their positions, and

(b) to seek to utilize any available external machinery for resolving their differences, including discussions involving, as appropriate, the Executives of the Unions, the TUC[1] and the ACAS.[2]

The Company wishes it to be known that if the two Unions are prepared to refer the present dispute to arbitration, the Company will accept the findings of such arbitration.

WORK-TO-THE-RULE AND OVERTIME BAN

On February 10, 1976 the company received the following letter from the secretary of the ASTMS:

> A motion was passed at the Group Meeting this morning that the following action will be taken following the Management's decision to allow the AUEW a right of veto on an ASTMS agreement.
>
> 1. ASTMS will implement their Closed Shop Agreement.
>
> 2. ASTMS will implement an immediate work to the rule which will involve among other things production staff working a 40 hour week and non-production staff working a 37 hour week.
>
> This action has official backing from the ASTMS National Executive.

The "work-to-the-rule" action resulted in considerable inconvenience to the company. ASTMS members refused to answer telephones, refused to take orders from anyone except their immediate superior, and in other ways made life difficult for management. However the refusal to work overtime created a much more serious problem because of a flextime working schedule agreement which management had signed with the AUEW.

---

[1]The TUC referred to in the company's lettter is the Trades Union Congress. Both AUEW and ASTMS were members of TUC. In 1939 the TUC set up a Disputes Committee and established the Bridlington rules for settling demarcation disputes between member unions. The Committee hear about 60 or 70 cases each year. Its decisions have no force of law but are binding within TUC.

[2]The ACAS referred to in the company's letter is the Advisory Conciliation and Arbitration Service established by the Employment Protection Act of 1975 to offer industrial relations advice, provide concilitations service, and arrange for arbitration.

M-S LTD. (A)

THE FLEXTIME ISSUE

Under the flextime agreement hourly-paid employees worked a standard eight hour-day but were permitted to start work at any time between 7:00 and 9:00 a.m. which resulted in quitting times from 4:00 p.m. to 6 p.m. Because of safety requirements and also to allocate the work, supervisors had to be present at all times when manual workers were on the job. However, the supervisors were not on a flextime schedule but instead worked a regular 8 a.m. to 5 p.m. shift each day with one hour for lunch. Therefore, in order to have supervisors on hand from 7:00 a.m. to 6 p.m. the company had developed a rotating overtime system whereby a certain number of the supervisors worked overtime each day. The supervisors liked the system because they received more then 40 hour of pay each week and the additional hours were paid at time and one-half.

If the supervisors who were members of ASTMS refused to work overtime there would be no supervisions in the plant for the workers from 7 to 8 a.m. and from 5 to 6 p.m. The company decided, therefore, that if the supervisors were permitted to refuse overtime it could not continue to operate under the flextime schedule. However, the flextime schedule was a part of its written agreement with the AUEW.

The company recognized that it faced a very difficult dilemma. There were some in management who recommended a showdown with ASTMS. They argued that the ASTMS action constituted a breach of its contract and, therefore, the company had a legal right to suspend employees who followed the unions "work-to-the-rule" and overtime ban. Others argued that it would be better to tolerate the ASTMS action and simply discontinue the flextime schedule. The Managing Director was convinced finally that the latter approach was the wiser under all the circumstances. As a result, on Friday, February 13, the following notice was posted on the three plant bulletin boards.

Hours Of Work

Until further notice Supervision is only available during dayshift, from 8 a.m. - 5 p.m., and therefore, with immediate effect, flextime will be suspended and AUEW hours of work during dayshift will be confined to 8 a.m. - 5 p.m., Monday/Friday.

W.R. Embick
Plant Manager

A DISCIPLINE PROBLEM

A few hours after the notices were posted James Poppins, the AUEW senior steward, wrote in large letters across the bottom of each of these with a heavy black marker the following message:

FLEXTIME WILL OPERATE TOMORROW AS PER AUEW AGREEMENT WITH MANAGEMENT.

J. Poppins
Senior Steward

When the plant manager, William Embick, saw what Poppins had written he called him into his office and informed him that he was being suspended immediately for countermanding an order of management and that severe disciplinary action would be taken against him the next workday. Embick then attempted to get in touch with Brandon, the regional full-time representative of the union,[3] and when he was unable to do so had the following letter delivered to Brandon's office:

13.2.76

Dear Mr. Brandon,

Earlier today I tried unsuccessfully on several occasions to contact you on the telephone to advise you of a serious situation that has arisen. A Management written instruction has been countermanded in writing by Mr. J. Poppins (Shop steward of AUEW). On the basis of the facts available to us it is our intention to take severe disciplinary action and this we propose to do at 9 a.m. on Monday, 14 February 1976.

Yours Sincerely,

W.R. Embick

The following Monday a conference was held in the plant manager's office attended by Embick, the plant manager, the personnel director, Carl Brandon, the regional full time union representative, and Poppins. Embick stated that Poppins had openly countermanded his orders, which was a serious offense and that the company intended to discharge him. Brandon pleaded with the company not to take such drastic action pointing out that in his opinion the company itself had violated the agreement first by posting the notice. He said the men in the plant were in a very angry mood and that he could not guarantee that they would remain at work if Poppins were discharged. After the discussion the plant manager wrote Poppins the following letter with a copy to Brandon:

---

[3]The Industrial Relations Code of Practice which became effective February 28, 1972 provided that "no disciplinary action should be taken against a shop steward until the circumstances of the case have been discussed with a full-time official of the union concerned."

16.2.76

Dear Mr. Poppins,

I confirm, following our meeting this morning that, as a result of your countermanding a Management instruction last Friday, you have been dismissed from M-S for gross industrial misconduct.

Sincerely,

W.R. Embick
Plant Manger

The disciplinary procedure in effect at the company provided that an employee who was not satisfied with the decision of the plant manager had the right to appeal to the Managing Director.[4] Poppins exercised his right under this provision and immediately appealed. Three days later on February 19 the Managing Director, John Mahon, scheduled a hearing at 10:00 a.m. in his office which was attended by Embick, the plant manager, Carlson, the personnel director, Brandon, the regional union representative and Poppins. Embick and Carlson argued that Poppins' action in openly countermanding a management order clearly warranted discharge. Brandon argued that the company had breached its agreement with AUEW by posting the notice and that Poppins statement was in compliance with the agreement. Brandon warned again that the men in the plant were in a very angry mood and that he could not be responsible for their action if in his words "the company insists on sacking Poppins for doing his duty." After hearing both sides Mahon said he wished to have some time to think over the matter. He asked them to return to his office at 3:00 o'clock at which time he would give them his decision.

[4]The Industrial Relations Code of Practice (1972) stated that the disciplinary procedure should "provide for the right of appeal, wherever practicable, to a level of management not previously involved."

BOUCLIER COPPER (A)

Bouclier Copper Company's Grand Verger plant was located on the Adour river near Bayonne, France where it had the advantages of cheap water transportation of copper ore from Africa and South America and cheap electric power from the Pyrenees hydro stations. Grand Verger was fully integrated. It recieved the ore from the boats at its own unloading docks, smelted it, refined it electrolytically, and then rolled, cast, extruded or drew it into products which were sold both in France and abroad.

There were approximately 4,000 blue collar workers at Grand Verger when the plant was operating at capacity. These workers had a choice of four different metalworking unions which they could join. Each of these four unions was affliated in turn with one of the four big French labor federations: CGT, CFDT, OF and CFTC.[1] At Grand Verger CGT was the most important union followed by CFDT. The other two unions OF and CFTC, although they had some members, were not significant. However, workers were not required to be union members in order to hold their jobs[2] and as a result fewer than one fourth regularly paid dues in any of the unions.[3]

Some years ago Grand Verger had had a labor agreement which was signed by the leaders of all the unions. In recent years, however, CGT and CFDT which cooperated closely with each other both on a local and a national level had refused to sign an agreement. (Evidently they found it difficult to maintain interest and membership in the union once an agreement had been signed). CGT and CFDT jointly maintained a large list of demands. If some of these demands were met by the company, new demands were added. (For a list of the demands in effect on April 1, 1976, see

---

[1]CGT was the largest of the four French labor federations with approximately 2.3 million members. Its philosophy was based on the Marxist doctrine of class war. Its president and some of its other officers were active leaders in the Communist Party of France. CFDT was the second largest of the French labor federations with approximatley 700,000 members. Originally it was closely related with the Catholic Church and the Catholic Party but later acquired its complete independence and since 1970 had become left-wing socialist.

[2]In France there was a constitutional provision guaranteeing employees the right to join but also the right <u>not</u> to join the unions. Thus a closed shop agreement was illegal.

[3]The Act of April 1956 prohibited the check off of union dues. It stated "No employer shall deduct trade union dues from the wages of his workers or pay such dues on his behalf."

Exhibit 1.) As a result the unions were free to strike if their immediate demands were not met.[4]

The management at Grand Verger anticipated that the spring of 1976 might be a period of labor unrest at the plant. During 1974 and 1975 production at the plant had been low. The unions had hesitated to strike during that period knowing that the company was not in need of production. However, since the beginning of 1976 demand for the company's products had been increasing rapidly and as a result production by April 1 was close to capacity. Mangement was now anxious to avoid any losses in production as a result of strikes and the union leaders, therefore, were in a much stronger bargaining position. Morevoer, spring had always been the most troublesome time of the year in labor relations at Grand Verger. By that time, if work had been steady in January, February and March the workers would have paid off the debts they had contracted over the Christmas season. It was a good time, too, to spend some days working in the garden or taking a trip up in to the mountains to visit relatives and friends. Finally, the company recently had thoroughly revised the job classification system with the usual result that some groups of workers were dissatisfied with the evaluation of their jobs compared with other jobs.

One of the major operations at Grand Verger was smelting which was performed in a row of 12 furnaces in a separate building called the smelting plant. The copper ore and other materials were loaded into the furnaces by overhead cranes. The furnace men, the crane operators, and auxiliary workers were grouped together into the smelting department.

The 12 furnaces were lined with special firebricks which had to be replaced after a certain number of heats. The old bricks were removed by digging them out with a special machine which had been developed for that purpose. Then masons and their helpers were lowered down into the furnace and relined it with new firebricks. Management tried to arrange production so that only one or two furnaces were down for relining and other repairs at any one time. The employees who performed the work associated with relining, including the masons, were not part of the smelting department but instead were grouped into a separate refractories department. There were 48 manual workers in the refractories department.

Management was aware before Monday, April 5, that the refractory masons were not satisfied with the rate they were being paid under the new job classification system. For several months they had complained through the unions that the evaluation of their job was not accurate. They insisted that certain factors had been greatly underrated and claimed they were receiving about 10% less pay than they deserved. Management had carefully reexamined the evaluation and had concluded it was accurate and that the masons were being paid properly relative to other jobs in the

---

[4]The right to strike was written into the French constitution but strikes by certain groups such as police, prison officers and air traffic controllers were legally foridden.

plant. However, the union leaders had continued to support the masons' demand and had threatened action.

MONDAY, APRIL 5, 1976

On Monday morning, April 5, at 6:30 a.m. Jacques Raison, Manager of Grand Verger, received a telephone call at his home from the Director of Smelting Operations, Robert Bonjour. Bonjour informed Raison that the employees on the first shift in the refractories department were on strike. All of them had reported as usual at 6:00 a.m. and had remained in the plant but were refusing to do any work until their demands, including a 10% increase in pay for the masons, were satisfied by the company. The smelting department had not joined in the strike action, Bonjour reported, so production on the 10 operating furnaces was normal. Raison told Bonjour to call Francois Boulanger, Director of Labor Relations, and arrrange to have him meet with them in Raison's office at the plant in half an hour.

At Raison's office the following communication occurred:

Raison: Francois, the masons claim their rate is out of line. What about it?

Boulanger: We've checked it very carefully and we can't agree with them. The rate is very fair.

Bonjour: I agree with Francois. The rate is fair and if we increased it we'd have complaints from all the other men in the smelting plant who would then want an increase too.

Raison: There are two furnaces down now. What about the other ten?

Bonjour: Number 8 and Number 12 will probably have to be relined early next week but unless something unforeseen occurs we can operate 10 furnaces all this week.

Raison: Every day of strike by the masons will hurt us because we can use all the production we can get now but as long as the furance crews and the crane operators keep working we'll not be hurting too much if it doesn't last over a week.[5]

---

[5]Under French law the employer did not have the right to lock out employees. The burden was on the employer to show first that there was no work available for the specific employees before they could be laid off without pay.

Boulanger: I'm sure the unions will try to get the furnace men or crane operators or the electolytic plant to join the masons and then escalate the whole thing into a general negotiations involving Paris headquarters. That's what they'd really like to do if the men would support them.

Bonjour: When the furnace men walked out several years ago we had to close the whole plant down very soon because electrolytic had nothing to process and send through to rolling, casting and extruding. If the masons can prevent us from relining the same effect would occur here but it would take a lot longer. I don't think they'd be willing to do without pay that long. Moreover, the furnace men have special skills and there was no way to replace them. That's not true with the masons. There are lots of masons in the building industry in this area and any of them could do the relining job. As a matter of fact, J & M Construcion Company which is building the addition to the casting shop has a crew of masons who could do this job very well. Also our foremen would do it without any trouble.

Boulanger: Are you suggesting that we subcontract the work to J & M?

Bonjour: It's possible in this case. It would serve to show the masons that their job is not so skilled and that the company is not dependent on them.

Raison: I think we should make every effort to get masons to go back to work before we bring in outside masons. On the other hand, I agree, we can't let our masons get away with this kind of action. I suggest the two of you talk with the men and the union delegates again and if they continue to refuse to work we'll discuss the matter further at noon and decide then what action to take.

Bonjour and Boulanger went to the refactory area and had a long discussion with the union delegates and the striking employees. Boulanger indicated that the company would be willing to reconsider their demands if they returned to work. The delegates, supported by the employees, replied that the men would not return to their work until the company agreed to their demands including an increase of 10% for the masons.

At a meeting at noon Bonjour and Boulanger reported to Raison that the refractory employees had refused to return to work. After a discussion of the various possible alternatives it was decided to ask the J & M Company to do the relining. Arrangements were made to have the J & M masons begin work on the furnaces at 8:00 a.m. the next morning if the company's employees were still on strike at that time. The second shift refactory workers (2 p.m. to 10 p.m. and the third shift refactory workers (10 p.m. to 6 a.m.) joined the strike when they reported for work.

TUESDAY, APRIL 6, 1976

The next morning at 6 a.m. the first shift refactory workers returned to the plant but continued their strike action. At the shift change, Brandon, the CGT delegate, and Cassell, the CFDT delegate, addressed the smelting department employees, including the furances men and the crane operators, urging them in Brandon's words to "join the masons in this struggle to get some action on our demands." However, the first shift smelting department employees reported to their jobs and production got underway normally on the other ten furnaces and thoughout the rest of the plant.

At 8:00 a.m. the masons from J & M entered the smelting building and began to prepare the two furances for relining. At 10:30 the CGT delegate Brandon and 10 of the strikers who had been waiting in the change room went to the furances where the J & M men were working. They informed the J & M men that they were strikebreaking and urged them to leave. When the J & M men continued to work Brandon tried to block the elevator which was carrying the bricks up to where they were working. However, he was not successful and he and the strikers then left the building.

At 11:00 a.m. a meeting was held attended by Brandon and 3 of the grievants representing the employees and Bonjour and Boulanger representing the company. Boulanger stated that management was prepared to meet with the union leaders to negotiate on the refactory workers' demands on Monday, April 12, if the men would return to work today. At the change of shifts at 2:00 p.m. Brandon met with the first and second shift refractory workers and asked them it they wanted to accept the company's offer or continue to strike. The workers voted to continue the strike.

During the second shift (2 p.m. to 10 p.m.) CGT and CFDT delegates spoke through megaphones in various parts of the plant urging the workers in the words of one of them "to join the struggle with your comrades in the refractory department against the management and the strikebreakers and force Mr. Cabot (Bouclier's General Manager) to come down from Paris and negotiate with us." As a result, the maintenance mechanics in the smelting shop and all the employees in the casting shop joined the strike. However, the furnace men and the crane operators continued to run the furnaces and production in the smelting plant, the electrolytic plant and elsewhere, other than in the casting, shop continued to be normal

At 3:30 p.m. a group of strikers led by two union delegates blocked the entrance to the materials elevator which was being used to take firebrick up to the J & M masons. Bonjour went to the elevator and asked the delegates and the strikers to move aside but they refused to do so. Brandon said the strikers would stay in the plant "until Cabot agrees to sit down and settle with us the many serious grievances which the Grand Verger workers have placed before the company." Bonjour reported the blocking of the elevator to Raison and Boulanger. Since the J & M masons could not get firebricks they had to stop work.

At 4:00 p.m. Raison met with Bonjour, Boulanger and Jean Brun, the Plant Labor Lawyer, to discuss what action should be taken with respect to the elevator blockage. Brun informed Raison that the blockage was clearly illegal and recommended that the company have a sheriff witness it and then ask a court to take action against the union leaders who were involved. Raison followed Brun's advise. The sheriff arrived at 5:00 p.m. and observed "40 strikers blocking the elevator entrance." In the sheriff's presence Bonjour ordered the strikers to leave but they refused to do so and continued to block the elevator door. The sheriff later wrote and signed a report detailing what he had witnessed.

At 6:00 p.m. the J & M masons left the plant. On the third shift (10 p.m. to 6 a.m.) the refractory, casting and smelting maintenance mechanics continued the strike but production elsewhere was normal.

WEDNESDAY, APRIL 7, 1976

The next morning the casting employees returned to work. However the refractory employees and the smelting maintenance mechanics remained on strike and continued to block the materials elevator. The J & M masons waited in the parking lot to see if they could return to the furnace work. One of the CGT leaders addressed the company railroad workers urging them to join the strike. The railroad workers continued to operate the trains. The union leaders were more successful with the smelting plant electric maintenance men who stopped work at 7:30 a.m. At 11 a.m. the J & M masons were told that it would not be possible for them to work. They left the parking lot and returned to their homes.

At about 2 p.m. the sheriff again entered the refractory area and this time witnessed Bonjour order by name the two union delegates and 8 masons to stop blocking the elevator. They refused to move aside as did the other 15 strikers who were blocking the way.

Exhibit 1

CFDT and CGT List of Demands
April 1, 1976

1. A fifth crew and reduction of hours without reduction of pay where there is continuous operation.

2. A 40-hour week for others without loss of pay.

3. Complete revision of the job classification system.

4. An increase in the point value in the job classification system.

5. A general increase of 360 Francs to make up for salary losses.

6. A fifth week of paid vacation.

7. A general bonus to make up for the losses due to unemployment during the past 2 years.

8. One hour of trade union information per month.

9. No more cutting of the 6 month bonus because of strikes or sicknesses.*

10. A roof over the parking lot.

11. Free safety shoes for certain workers who do not now receive them.

12. A wage increase for the change house guards.

13. Production bonus for the change house guards.

14. Increase for the drivers and their replacements.

15. An additional truck at the smelting furnaces.

16. An increase for the masons and their helpers.

* Each employee received a bonus of one-half a month's salary every six months. However, the bonus was decreased by 1/150 for each day of absence and 1/20 for each day of strike.

PICKARDT-RHINE INTERNATIONAL A.G. (A)

One afternoon in March 1973, Klaus Muller stood at the window of his office overlooking Berlinerstrasse in Frankfurt. To Muller it seemed as if the weather that winter had been particularly cold, but from the tone of the telephone call he had just received things might be warming up a bit. Muller was Employee Affairs Manager for Pickardt-Rhine International A.G. (PRIAG), a wholly owned subsidiary of the Scott Food Company, a large American food processing and marketing company headquartered in Chicago, Illinois. Muller had just finished a 45 minute telephone conversation with Fritz Kringle, the Employee Relations Manager at PRIAG's vegetable canning plant in Krefeld near Dusseldorf in western Germany. Kringle had informed Muller that there were rumors of a "wild cat strike" circulating in the plant.

The chairman of the Krefeld Plant Works Council had met that morning with the Plant Manager and had demanded an immediate upward adjustment in the salaries of certain white collar employee groups. He had complained that the salaries of Krefeld white collar workers were not competitive with what was being paid in the other three food processing plants in the immediate area. After checking with his information sources in the plant, Kringle implied to Muller that a "wildcat strike was not out of question".

Muller knew that the present contract between PRIAG and the Union of Food, Stimulants, Hotel and Restaurant Employees (Gewerkschaft, Nahrung, Genuss, Gaststatten - NGG) still had three months to run. In fact, both the company and the union had only begun to outline their strategies for the annual contract negotiations due to begin in May. That such a demand should come so soon before the wage negotiations was unusual. Even more unusual, however, was the fact that the local Works Council had decided to involve itself in wage level discussions with the company. Under German law works councils had no authority to negotiate with the company over wages -- wage levels were a matter for the company and the union to decide. Nonetheless, the Works Council chairman had asked for an immediate increase of 12.6% for employees in certain job categories. Muller was even more disturbed, however, about the report that there might be a strike at a PRIAG plant — that would be unprecedented.

As he stood at the window Muller was pondering the steps he should take to handle this situation. He surmised that it would not be long before his boss, Hans Smoller-Halde, the Employee Relations Director, would be calling him for a recommendation. His thought pattern was broken by the buzzing of the telephone:

> "Yes, Herr Smoller-Halde. I don't know what to make of it either ... OK, I'll be right up, ... the Chairman's office ... OK."

PICKARDT-RHINE INTERNATIONAL A.G. (A)

THE COMPANY

PRIAG was a wholly-owned subsidiary of the Scott Food Company of Chicago. Scott Foods had purchased PRIAG from the Pickardt family in 1957. At the time of the acquisition PRIAG was involved only in the canning and processing of a limited number of fruits and vegetables. Although, the company's product line was small in size, the PRIAG brand name enjoyed an excellent reputation with German, Dutch and Belgian consumers. In fact, it was primarily the PRIAG brand image that Scott Foods was interested in acquiring. Once the acquisition was complete, the U.S. parent moved rapidly to expand the PRIAG product line. In the first 10 years after the acquisition, PRIAG introduced many new product lines, and as a result, PRIAG'S sales grew from DM 250 million in 1957 to just over DM 1.0 billion in 1967.

After 1967 the product expansion effort subsided somewhat, and PRIAG's top management began to concentrate on increasing the efficiency of their operations and the productivity of the workforce. One of the first steps taken in this regard was the launching of a major production modernization program. All of the company's older production facilities were either modernized or closed. Between 1968 and 1971 the company opened three new, highly automated food processing facilities. The plant at Krefeld was one of these new plants.

Throughout this period of modernization the company's growth in sales and earnings continued so that by 1972 year end sales stood at just over DM 1.5 billion with a pretax profit of DM 180 million. By 1973 PRIAG was one of the five largest food companies in Germany.

COMPANY ORGANIZATION

At the corporate level the company was organized along functional lines. The directors of the six functional departments (marketing, production, procurement, finance, research and personnel and social affairs) reported to the PRIAG General Manager. The six department heads and the General Manager formed the company's Management Board. See Exhibit 1 for the organizational chart of the Frankfurt headquarters.

The organization of PRIAG operating units was also along functional lines. The managers of all production units reported to the director of the production department, while managers of sales and distribution units reported to the head of the marketing department at Frankfurt. The staff departments (finance, procurement and personnel) had most of their personnel concentrated in Frankfurt. Staff in the operating units was kept to a minimum.

The seven processing and canning plants were also organized along functional lines with all functioanl managers reporting to the Plant Manager. (See Exhibit 2 for the organizational structure at the Krefeld Plant which is typical of other PRIAG plants.) When asked about the relationship between staff personnel in operating units and the staff at the headquarters, one company executive said that "an informal, dotted-line relationship exists", but he added that the local staff was always directly responsible to the local line manager.

PRIAG employed 7,600 people who were scattered among 15 locations in Germany. Approximately 65% of the 7600 employees were involved in production or production-related activities, 20% in marketing and distribution, and the remainder in staff organizations.

THE PRIAG BOARDS

At the highest level PRIAG had the two-tiered board system (i.e. a Management Board and a Supervisory Board) found throughout German industry. Under the provisions of the Works Constitution Act of 1952 employees in most German companies were given representation on their company's Supervisory Board. The employee representatives, who comprised one-third of the Board membership, were not selected by the union or the works council, but were elected directly by the employees in a secret ballot. PRIAG's Supervisory Board was made up of six members. In management's opinion, the two employee representatives had always been reasonable, intelligent individuals who discharged their reponsibilities in a diligent manner.[1]

One of the major tasks of the Supervisory Board was the selection of the company's Management Board which at PRIAG was made up of seven top managers (see Exhibit 1). Members of the Management

---

[1]A new law which became effective on July 1, 1976 provided for an increase in worker representation on supervisory boards. By June 30, 1978, the date set for implementation, all shareholding companies in Germany with more than 2,000 employees would have boards with 50% of the seats elected by the shareholders and 50% of the seats elected by the employees. While the equal split made it appear as if labor could effectively block any board action, the law provided that in cases where the board was deadlocked after two votes on any given issue, the board chairman was given a second vote. The selection of the chairman of the board was by a two-third majority vote of the board members. If the board was deadlocked on the election of a chairman, then the law provided that the shareholders representatives could select the chairman. If this occurred, then the employee representatives could select the vice-chairman.

To comply with the new law PRIAG would expand its Supervisory Board from six to twelve seats. Six seats would be filled by the stockholder (Scott Foods) and six seats were reserved for employee representatives. Although election of employee representatives to the Board was still by secret ballot, the new law gave certain groups of employees the right of representation. The trade union could nominate candidates for two "employee representatives". These two people did not have to be employees of the company, and so, it seemed likely that PRIAG would soon have two non-employee union leaders sitting on their Supervisory Board. The other four seats were to be filled by PRIAG employees. One seat was to be occupied by a "leading employee", in essence, a member of senior management; one seat by a white collar employee; and two seats by blue collar employees.

Board were elected by a majority vote of the Supervisory Board. Once elected to the Management Board, the new member was given a five year employment contract with the company. Under the terms of the joint-stock corporation law, the Supervisory Board could remove any member from the Management Board although this had never happened at PRIAG.

UNION AND EMPLOYEE RELATIONS

Unionized employees at PRIAG were represented by the Union of Food, Stimulants, Hotel and Restaurant Employees (Gewerkschaft Nahrung, Genuss Gaststatten - NGG). The NGG was one of the 16 unions in the Deutsche Gewerkschaftsbund (DGB), the trade union federation in Germany which represented 7 million German workers. Not all PRIAG employees were members of the NGG although PRIAG allowed all employees to enjoy the benefits the union was able to secure for its own members.

In the seven plants, union membership was very high with approximately 80% of all blue collar and approximatley 50% of all white collar employees being union members. The percentage of union members among PRIAG's white collar work force varied at the other operating locations, but was considerably less than the 50% represented by the union at the plants. Unionization of white collar employees was lowest at the Frankfurt headquarters where less then 1% of the employees were union members.

Unlike most German companies, PRIAG did not negotiate its labor agreements through an employer's association. Whereas many companies which belonged to these associations let the association negotiate a collective contract with the union, PRIAG negotiated its collective bargaining agreement directly with the NGG. Relations between the NGG and PRIAG's management had always been good. A company official spoke with some pride when he said,

> "We have never lost a day's work because of a strike. Relations with our employees have been characterized by cooperation, not confrontation. We have always tried very hard to maintain good communications with our workers, and we have always found the union and employee representatives to be reasonable in their dealings with the company.
>
> "Recently, the people at the Chicago office started a big Employee Relations Program. It's interesting to note that we found the things they suggested we had already been doing for more than five years."

Another company executive commented on the company's relationship with the head of the NGG by saying:

> "Herr Engles is an intelligent man who knows his business. He's been negotiating with this company for many years. He consistently drives a hard bargain for the workers in his union, but we have always found him to be reasonable in formulating the union's demands and in negotiating with the company."

The labor contract between PRIAG and the NGG was negotiated each year in May and was effective for 12 months beginning in June. Under the terms of the contract all jobs at PRIAG (both blue and white collar) below a certain level were placed in one of fifteen job categories. All jobs were assigned a category regardless of whether or not the employees in those jobs were union members. All blue collar employees in Job Categores 1-8 and all white collar employees in Job Categories A-F[2] had their minimum wages set by the terms of the contract.

For each job category the company and the union negotiated a "tariff minima" or minimum wage which the company was required to pay an employee in the category. The company was free to pay any employee at a rate above the established minimum, and in some cases did; however, like most companies which negotiated their contracts directly with the union, PRIAG tried to keep its payroll near the minimums set by the contract.

The question of fitting individual employees into specific job categories was not a matter for negotiation with the union. Placement of present employees in new categories or new employees in existing categories was a matter of "co-determination" between the company management and the works council of the operating unit involved. The actual salary paid any employee was a matter for management alone to decide as long as the salary met the prescribed minimum set by the contract for the job category to which the employee had been assigned.

Any salary increases for an individual or group of individuals were solely a management prerogative and was not a matter for co-determination with the works council. In fact, under the laws governing the management-works council relationship, the works council had no authority in the area of wage increases. Under German law, only the union could negotiate wage increase and then only increases in the tariff minima. This is not to say the German companies had not negotiated "across the board" or overall increases in all employees' actual wages, only that under the German labor law management was not forced to negotiate with either the union or the works council increases in the actual wages paid to company employees.

[2]Examples of personnel in Job Category F, the highest white collar Job Category covered by the Union contract, would be: a foreman of a workshop, a plant shift leader, or a junior sales representative (sales traineee). The company also had 3 white collar job categories above those covered by the contract and below the rank of "leading employee". Personnel in Job Categories G-I were not represented by the union, but by the company's works councils.

THE WORKS COUNCILS

Under German law any employer with more than 5 employees was required to have a works council. The works council was made up of company employees below the rank of "leading employees".[3] Members of the works council served a three year term and were elected by a secret ballot in which all employees above 18 years of age and below the rank of leading employee had one vote.

Management was required to consult with the works council on all matters which affected the well-being of employees. In many instances company policies and programs were matters for "co-determination", i.e. both the works concil and the management were required to reach agreement on the policy before it went into effect. If the parties were unable to reach an agreement then the matter could be referred to a conciliation commitee which had to be composed of an equal number of members appointed by the employer and the works council, plus an independent chairman acceptable to both parties. (If the parties were unable to agree on a chairman, one was appointed by the labor court.) A majority award of the conciliation committee had the same legal standing as an agreement between the parties.[4]

PRIAG operated from 15 locations in Germany, and so, the company had 15 local works councils representing its employees. In addition to these 15 local works councils there was also a Corporate Works Council which was composed of one or two representatives from each of the local works councils. The job of the Corporate Works Council was to represent the interests of all PRIAG employees on matters of corporate-wide policy.

Management officials at PRIAG were of the opinion that the works councils had proven to be a very valuable consultation device between mangement and the employees, providing an excellent avenue of communications both upward and downward in the organization. They were proud of the relationship which they had developed with the works wouncils and through them with the employees.

One company official referred to the manner in which a dispute over the pension plan had been handled as an indication of this good relationship:

> "We recently reached agreement with the Corporate Works Council on a rather important pension plan administration issue. As you know, in Germany pension plans (up to now) are not an area for bargaining with the union. The company is free to decide how much money will be set aside each year for pensions. The labor law does stipulate, however, that works councils have rights of

---

[3]Leading employees at PRIAG were considered to be white collar workers whose job category was above Category I. Leading employees were therefore usually members of senior management.

[4]See Exhibit A for a more detailed description of the functions and authority of the works council and a listing of subjects for co-determination.

co-determination in how the pension monies are administered and how they are to be distributed.

"We recently re-vamped the PRIAG pension plan and in our discussions with the Coporate Works Council we had a small problem over the definition of 'hardship cases'. The Works Council wanted hardship cases to be co-determinated between themselves and mangement. We asked, what if we can't agree on what should be done in some specific case? Well, the Works Council thought it over and came back to us with their solution. If agreement could not be reached between management and the Works Council on how to interpret the meaning of 'hardship case' as it applies in some particular context, rather than submit the dispute to the arbitration by a conciliation committee (as is required in the law), the Works Council would agree to leave the final decision up to the Management Board."

THE KREFELD PLANT

Situated in western Germany on the west bank of the Rhine, the Krefeld Plant was one of four food processing plants in the North Rhine area; Heins Food Products A.G. had a plant in Mulheim, Fischer Foods operated a facility near Oberhausen and Eurofoods had a plant near Koln.

When PRIAG began production at the Krefeld Platn in 1970, the company encountered some diffficulty in finding sufficient numbers of trained personnel in the local area. With three other food processors operating in the immediate area and with the German economy growing rapidly, labor was in short supply. To staff the facility at Krefeld, PRIAG was able to persuade certain key personnel to transfer from its plants elsewhere in Germany; however, the bulk of the 1,450 jobs at Krefeld were filled from the local labor pool. Many employees were obtained from other industries in the area, but PRIAG was able to induce many others away from Heins, Fischer and Eurofoods by offering wages at levels above those then prevailing in the local labor market.

Because the short labor supply required PRIAG to pay wages to its Krefeld employees which were well above wages paid in other parts of Germany, and because of other special circumstances surrounding the start-up of the plant, PRIAG negotiated a separate labor contract with the NGG. This special and separate labor contract was re-negotiated again in 1971, but after that the employees at Krefeld were covered under the nation wide collective bargaining agreement between PRIAG and NGG.[5]

---

5 Heins and Fischer negotiated a labor contract for all their workers directly with the NGG. Because the Eurofoods plant was the only operation the company had in Germany, Eurofoods negotiated their labor contract through an employers' association. Regardless of how these four contracts were negotiated they were all negotiated with the same union, the NGG.

In the years which immediately followed the start-up of the plant, the local labor market, indeed the labor market throughout Germany, tightened. In the early 1970s, unemployment in Germany was less than 1% and there were over 2 million foreign workers employed in German industry. Faced with these conditions, PRIAG was forced to continue paying the substantial wage premiums it had initially offered to Krefeld employees. In 1973, the average premium paid to employees at Krefeld was 20% above the tariff minima set forth in the PRIAG labor contract.

THE KREFELD WORKS COUNCIL

Over the years the PRIAG's management at the Frankfurt headquarters had come to believe that they had developed an efficient, loyal workforce at Krefeld. Relations between the plant management and the Krefeld Works Council appeard to be good. One company official stated:

> "Despite the fact that most of the employees at Krefeld were new to the company, they rapidly developed an esprit de corps. The plant in which they were working was one of the newest, most modern and efficient in the world. The workers at Krefeld were proud of their facility and I think they were proud to be working for PRIAG."

When asked to comment on the Works Council at Krefeld, another company official who manages the relationship between headquarters and all the PRIAG works councils said:

> "There have been some difficulties in getting the workers together at Krefeld. The workforce was drawn from workers in two provinces and traditionally people from these provinces have not worked together. You might say they were a little "provincial" in their outlook.
>
> The leadership of the Works Council has not always been the best. The chairman, Otto Schmidt, tries very hard to do a good job, but he's not what you would call a "natural leader", and he seems to have trouble getting all the workers together. He's a bit too emotional, not left wing or radical, just a little erratic at times. As a result, I sometimes think that the workforce is poorly informed on some issues. I don't mean to imply that the relationship between the company and the Krefeld Works Council is not good, just that things could be better."

THE 1973-74 CONTRACT NEGOTIATIONS

It was the custom in Germany for officials of the union and the employees they represent to meet several months prior to the expiration date of the labor contract to discuss the terms of the upcoming negotiations. As the representatives of the employees, union officials felt obliged to elicit from the employees their objectives for the coming year. The union leaders also believed that, having first consulted with the membership, their position was strengthened in the subsequent collective bargaining with the company.

Such a meeting between the leadership of the NGG and the union leaders in all of PRIAG's operations was held in mid March, 1973. The stated purpose of the meeting was for the union to learn what PRIAG employees wanted from their new labor contract which was due to be negotiated in May.

Apparently, the meeting started normally enough with the union soliciting the views of the delegations from the various plants. When discussion turned to the percentage increase in wages desired by the employees, the meeting took an unexpected turn. When asked what percentage increase in the negotiated tariff minima was desired, Otto Schmidt, the chairman of the Krefeld delegation, shouted: "28%." The chairman of the meeting, a NGG official, chuckled and asked if the Krefeld delegation was serious. However, members of the Krefeld delegation immediately supported their chairman's demand and the pace and intensity of the discussion subsequently quickened. Twenty eight percent was very much above the figure which the union leadership expected. Apparently, the members of the other delegations present were also taken aback. Everyone had been thinking in terms of a 8-10% increase in the tariff minima. The Krefeld group was very vocal in their demand even though there seemed to be little support elsewhere for such a high percentage.

Present at the meeting was the leader of the NGG, Herr Engles. As it would be Engles's task to negotiate the contract agreements with the company, he was asked for his opinion of the Krefeld delegation's remarks. Engles told the chairman of the Krefeld delegation that he was out-of-line. He said that he was not going to risk his personal reputation as a professional negotiator by asking for 28% and then having to settle for a more reasonable 8-10%. Furthermore, Herr Engles told the Krefeld delegation that he would not subject the NGG to the adverse publicity which would probably result from such a ridiculous demand.

At this point, Otto Schmidt apparently became very emotional. He complained that his people were being paid a lot less than workers at the other plants near Krefeld. He said that such an increase was necessary to close the gap which had developed in the wage rates. When he <u>insisted</u> that the union demand a 28% increase in the contract's tariff minima, Herr Engles walked out of the meeting.

THE WORKS COUNCIL'S DEMANDS TO THE PLANT MANAGER

News of what had occurred at the NGG Union meeting quickly spread around the plant. One morning several days after the meeting, Otto Schmidt walked into the office of the Plant Manager, Herr Dr. G. Heinemann, and in his capacity as the chairman of the Krefeld Works Council demanded that the company make an "on-the-spot correction in the area of wages and salaries" of employees in Job Categories B-F. The Works Council chairman said that these increases were warranted because PRIAG wages were not competitive with those of the other food companies in the area. The size of the increases demanded ranged from 12.6% for workers in job category B downward to 5.2% for workers in category F. In addition, the Works Council demanded that a new job classification plan be implemented. The Works Council's plan called for the four lowest white collar job categories to be replaced by 6 and that certain adjustments be made to the salaries in these job categories in addition to those requested for purposes of making PRIAG salaries more competitive with the neighboring food processing plants. Dr. Heinemann received the demand and told the Works Council chairman that he would think it over.

The Plant Manager then called to the office his Employee Relations Manager, Fritz Kringle, and asked him what was going on. Kringle explained to Dr. Heinemann what had transpired several days earlier at the union meeting and reminded him that the question of non-competitive wages had been an issue for some time. It had been a topic of discussion at several Works Council meetings over the past few years and, as Kringle reminded his boss, the topic had been discussed in many of the reports on Works Council meetings Kringle had submitted to him.

Dr. Heinemann responded:

> "Well, these demands are ridiculous - they always have been ridiculous. We are paying our people better than Heins, Fischer and Eurofoods and everyone knows it. Why does the Works Council insist on raising this issue? I'm tired of all this non-competitive nonsense. Call Muller in Frankfurt and see what he thinks. And tell Muller I'll be talking to his boss about this problem."

Kringle took the long way back to his office. He stopped several times to talk with employees in the plant and with several members of the Works Council. It was in these discussions that he got the feeling that the Works Council was serious about their demands and that they had informally been discussing what steps they would take if the management did not reply. No one mentioned the word "strike", but Fritz Kringle felt that a strike might have been one of the alternatives the Works Council had considered.

When he got back to his office he rang up Muller in Frankfurt to relate the events of the last few hours. Several times during the conversation Muller asked Kringle what he thought the company should do. He also asked for an assessment of how serious the situation really was.

Muller probed:

> "Is the Works Council really serious or is this just another case of Schmidt just letting off some steam. You know his pride may have been hurt by the way Engles treated him in that meeting. He may be doing this as a way of regaining some of his self-image as a leader of the Works Council."

Kringle replied:

> "I don't know, Herr Muller. It may be as you say, but from the people I've talked to around the plant, it appears as if Schmidt may have a stronger backing than you estimate. You know..."

Kringle hesitated a moment. He wondered if it would be proper to interject that in his opinion the problem had been brewing for quite some time, and that he had warned his boss about it on several occasions. Should he air the plant's "dirty linen" with the Employee Relations Manager at headquarters?

"I know what?" asked Muller.

Kringle decided that now was not the time to hold back:

> "Well, you must know that this issue has been simmering on the back burner for over a year now."

Surprised, Muller responded:

> "It has? I thought that the first time this dissatisfaction surfaced was at the union meeting several days ago. I have posed several questions about that meeting in a letter I mailed yesterday. All right, well, let's get all the facts out now, we have a decision to make."

Exhibit 1

Organizational Chart of Pickardt-Rhine International A.G.

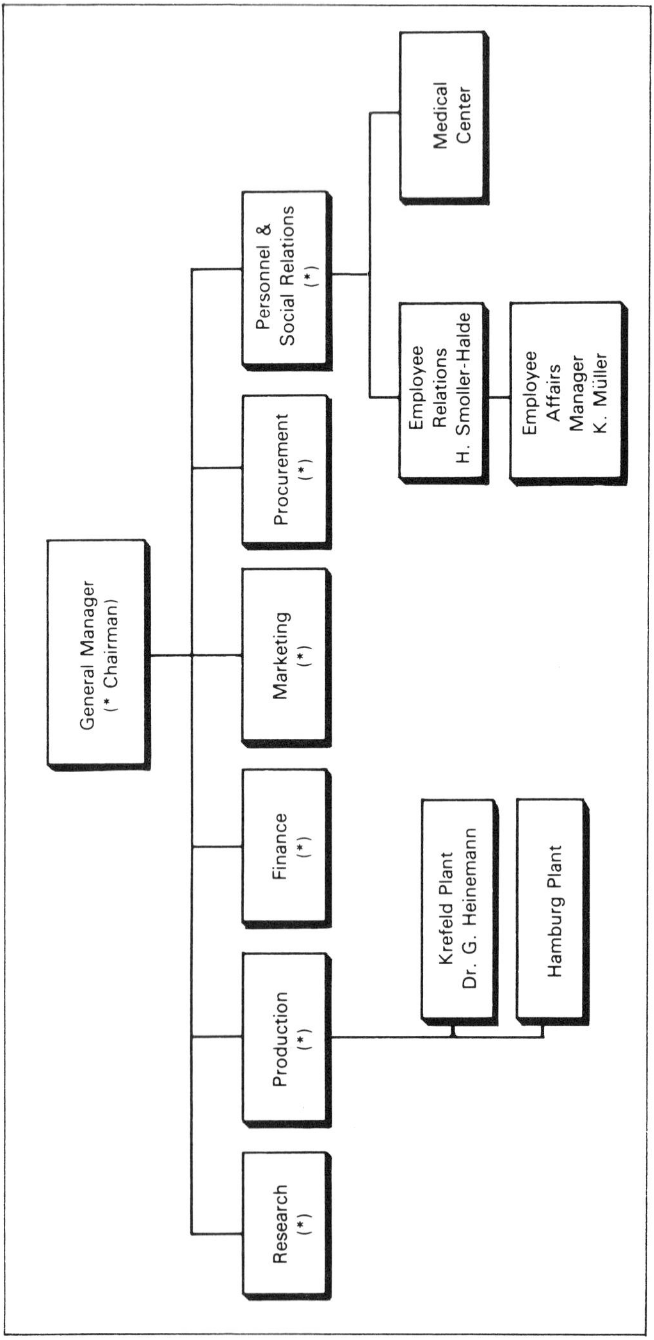

Note: * indicates members of the Management Board

Note: The Employee Relations Department maintained a "dotted line" relationship with Employee Relations Managers at all PRIAG plants.

Exhibit 2

Organizational Chart of Krefeld Plant

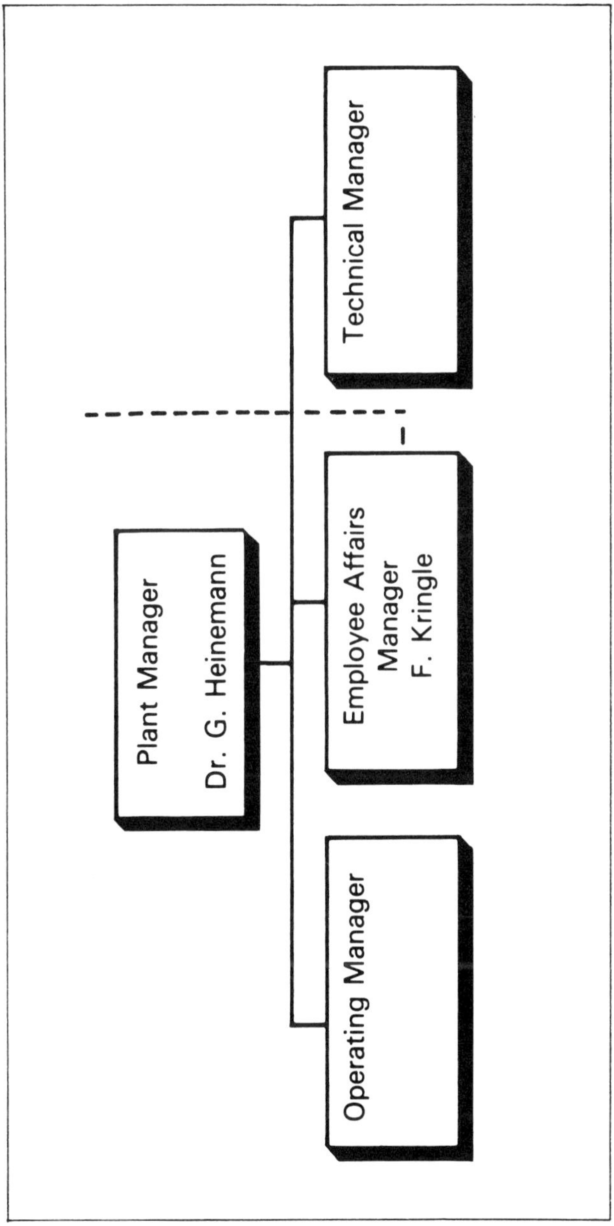

Note: (Dotted line relationship to Employee Relations Department at Frankfurt.)

Exhibit 3

FUNCTIONS AND AUTHORITY OF THE WORKS COUNCIL

Gerneral Duties

The Works Constitution Act of 1972 (Section 2) states, "The employer and the Works Council shall work together in spirit of mutual trust ... for the good of the employees and the establishment." Section 80 describes the general duties of the works council as follows:

1. see that effect is given to Acts, ordinances, safety regulations, collective agreements and works agreements for the benefit of the employees;

2. make recommendations to the employer for actions benefiting the establishment and the staff;

3. receive suggestions from employees and the youth delegation and to negotiate with the employer for their implementation;

4. promote the rehabilitation of disabled persons and others in particular need of assistance;

5, prepare and organise the election of a youth delegation and to collaborate closely with said delegation in promoting the interests of the young employees;

6. promote the employment of elderly workers;

7. promote the intergration of foreign workers in the establishment and to further understanding between them and their German colleagues.

Specific Areas of Co-Determination and Consultation

In addition to the general duties described in Section 80, the law sets forth the rights of the Works Council in five specific areas:

1. Social Matters (Section 87)

   The law specificallu provides the works council with "the right of co-determination" in the following matters:

Exhibit 3
(continued)

1. matters relating to the orderly operation of the establishment and the conduct of the employees in the stablishment;

2. the commencement and termination of the daily working hours including breaks and the distribution of working hours among the days of the week;

3. any temporary reduction or extension of the hours normally worked in the establishment;

4. the time and place for and the form of payment of remuneration;

5. the establishment of general principles for leave arrangements and the preparation of the leave schedule as well as fixing the time at which the leave is to be taken by individual employees, if no agreement is reached between the employer and the employees concerned;

6. the introduction and use of technical devices designed to monitor the behaviour or performance of the employees;

7. arrangements for the prevention of employment accidents and occupational diseases and for the protection of health on the basis of legislation or safety regulations;

8. the form, structuring and administration of social services where scope is limited to the establishment, company or combine;

9. the assignment of and notice to vacate accommodation that is rented to employees in view of their employment relationship as well as the general fixing of the conditions for the use of such accommodation;

10. questions related to remuneration arrangements in the establishment, including in particular the establishment of principles of remuneration and the introduction and application of new remuneration methods or modification of existing methods;

11. the fixing of job and bonus rates and comparable performance-related remuneration including cash coefficients (i.e. prices per time unit);

12. principles for suggestion schemes in the establishment.

Exhibit 3
(continued)

Where no agreement can be reached on any of the above 12 matters the conciliation committee may make an award which takes the place of an agreement by the parties.

2. Employees' Grievances (Section 85)

The law states that "the Works Council shall hear employee grievances and if they appear justified, induce the employer to remedy them." If the employer and the works council cannot agree whether the complaint is well founded the council may appeal to the conciliation committee. The award of the committee shall "take the place of an agreement" between the parties.

3. The Nature of Jobs and the Work Environment (Sections 90, 91)

Management is required to inform and consult with the works council of any plans it might have for the:

- construction, alteration or extension of the works, offices and other premises,

- modification of the technical plant, working process and operations, or

- modification of individual job design, or the way in which work is organized.

The law also requires that management take particular interest in the impact these changes may have on the nature of the work and demands the work places on employees. In cases where the changes envisioned by management are thought to have adverse effects on individual employees, the works council's rights are upgraded from consultation to co-determination.

Exhibit 3
(continued)

4. Personnel ("Staff") Matters (Sections 93-104)

Works Council rights in the formation of personnel policies are a mixture of rights to consultation and co-determination. In some areas only the right of consultation is guaranteed; in others, there is the implicit right of co-determination in that certain policy changes must be "approved" by the works council. If approval is not forthcoming then the matter is referred to a conciliation committee in the same way that disputes in areas governed by rights of co-determination are referred to the committee.

Specifically, the law provides:

- the works council be informed in all matters related to manpower planning,
- the works council may request that internal notification be made of all vacancies before they are filled,
- that guidelines for the recruitment, transfer, regrading and dismissal of employees shall require works council approval,
- that management consult with the works council in the development of vocational training programs,
- that the works council shall participate in the decision-making regarding the implementation of vocational training programs.

The law gives the works council clear rights of co-determination in the areas of individual personnel permanent or temporary transfer or movements, and in all cases involving the dismissal of employees.

In the case of dismissal of employees, the law states "any notice of dismissal that is given without consulting the works council shall be null and void". The law then goes on to state the grounds on which the works council can object to any dismissal notice and the procedures to be followed in cases where objections to management's actions are lodged. It is interesting to note that the law allows the works council to take the initiative and request that management dismiss employees who have in the works council's opinion "repeatedly caused serious trouble in the establishment." If management does not dismiss an employee that the works council has so designated, the works council may then directly petition the labor courts for a decision in the matter.

Exhibit 3
(continued)

5. Economic Matters (Sections 111-112)

The law gives the works councils certain rights when management decides that "alterations" to the company's business are required. The law defines "alterations" as being:

1. reduction of operations in or closure of the whole or important departments of the establishment;

2. transfer of the whole or important departments of the establishment;

3. amalgamation with other establishments;

4. important changes in the organization, purpose or plant of the establishment;

5. introduction of entirely new work methods and production processes.

Management is required to inform the works council of any proposed alterations which "may entail substantial prejudice to the staff or a large sector thereof..."

Where such alterations have a prejudicial effect on the interests of employees, management is required to work out an agreement with the works council as to how the alteration will proceed and how those affected by it will be compensated. Where no agreement can be reached, application can be made to the Land (State) employment office for mediation of the dispute. If no application for mediation is made or if efforts at mediation fail then the works council can request that the dispute be referred to the conciliation committee which will first attempt to mediate the differences. If the committee cannot resolve the differences, the committee itself will render an award which is then binding on both sides. If management fails to abide by the conciliation committee's award the employees who are affected by management's non-compliance can bring suit against the company in the labor court.

PICKARDT-RHINE INTERNATIONAL A.G. (B)

The evening of April 2, 1973, Klaus Muller, Employee Affairs Manager at the Frankfurt headquarters of Pickardt-Rhine International A.G. (PRIAG), had to run to catch the 18:45 intercity train from Dusseldorf to Frankfurt. As he settled into the seat in the first class section of the train, Muller began to reflect on the meetings he had held that day with the management and leaders of the Works Council at PRIAG's food processing plant at Krefeld. Muller had gone to Krefeld to investigate the background of a problem that had arisen concerning wages paid to white collar employees at the plant. Several days earlier, Muller had been informed by the Employee Relations Manager at Krefeld that there were rumors of a wild cat strike at the plant if certain demands of the Works Council were not met. In a subsequent meeting held in the Frankfurt office of PRIAG's Management Board Chairman, Muller had been charged with finding a solution to the problems at Krefeld.

As the train pulled out of the Koln Hauptbahnhof, Muller began writing his report of the day's events. The meeting at Krefeld was attended by Dr. G. Heinemann, Krefeld Plant Manager; Fritz Kringle, Employee Relations Manager at the plant; Otto Schmidt, Chairman of the Krefeld Works Council and Walter Bogden, Deputy Chairman of the Works Council. Muller was the sole representative of the Frankfurt headquarters. The meeting that morning started with Schmidt outlining what the Works Council saw as the basis for the problem. The Works Council believed that:

a) the minimum wages specified in the Krefeld labor contract (the tariff minima) were considerably below those paid at the three other food processing plants in the immediate area.

b) many new employees at Krefeld were being hired on at wage levels above those of employees who had been at Krefeld several years.

c) the tariff minima should be increased to the level of actual wages paid by the company.[1]

The Works Council chairman produced what he called "documented evidence" that what he said was true. Schmidt showed the management group copies of tariff schedules he had obtained from the Works Councils at Heins Food Company, Fischer Foods and Eurofoods A.G. As it was not clear to Muller how the Works Council based on this evidence had reached its conclusion, Muller said he would need some time to study the data the Works Council had compiled.

---

[1]Because of the short supply in the local labor market, PRIAG was forced to pay wages which averaged about 20% above the tariff minima specified in the labor contract.

Schmidt and Bogden went on to say that they had indications that certain white collar employees at Krefeld in lower job categories were being paid actual wages which were below those paid to PRIAG employees in similar jobs at other locations in Germany. The management group was led to believe that the cause of this problem was that these employees' job descriptions had been misclassified and, therefore, the Works Council was preparing a new plan for job categories for the whole plant which could be negotiated at the same time the tariff schedules were negotiated with the unions.

Management accepted Schmidt's arguments without substantive comment although on several occasions Muller was distressed by the way Dr. Heinemann reacted to certain of Schmidt's assertions. In three or four instances, Heinemann had interrupted Schmidt saying, "that's just not true" or "your facts are wrong." Muller had hoped that this meeting would help diffuse the situation by giving Schmidt and Bogden a chance to air their case. As the meeting adjourned for lunch, Muller thought that the Works Council representatives had had the opportunity to do just that, but Heinemann's interjections did not seem to help. Kringle had been silent during most of the morning; he seemed to defer his comments until he had an opportunity to see how Dr. Heinemann was reacting.

The management group lunched alone and in the privacy of an executive dining room they discussed individual reactions to the Works Council's presentation. Heinemann was incredulous about some of Schmidt's assertions. He knew that wages at Krefeld were at least on a par with those of other plants in the immediate area, and he just could not understand how Schmidt had reached some of the conclusions he had. Kringle reminded him of the "evidence" presented and said that there might be some basis for a misunderstanding.

Muller went on to say that because the processes and products of the other three plants were not identical to those at Krefeld, the other companies probably had organized the work of their employees in different manners. This would result in different job descriptions even though the titles used for specific jobs might be very similar to those used at Krefeld. If this was true, direct job-to-job comparisons of the tariff schedules could mislead the Works Council into believing that PRIAG wages were below those of the company's competitition.

About half-way through the main course Muller suggested that they begin to formulate a strategy for dealing with the Works Council's complaints. During the morning meeting Muller had told Schmidt and Bogden that he was sure they could work out something which would be acceptable to both sides. In less than an hour Muller and the other two managers would again be sitting across the table from the leadership of the Krefeld Works Council. If Muller was going to be successful in quickly defusing the situation at Krefeld, he would have to do it in the next several hours.

MEERT INTERNATIONAL

Upon his return from lunch on March 18, 1977 Paul Gemmil, Managing Director of Meert International, was informed by his secretary that Conrad Kopp, Secretary General of the International Electrical Workers Federation (IEWF), had telephoned from Geneva during his absence and had requested that he return the call. Gemmil was surprised because he knew of no significant labor dispute at any of Meert's subsidiaries. However, he had heard that IEWF might be interested in resuming discussions with Meert after a break of two and one-half years. If Kopp should request a meeting he wondered what his response should be.

THE COMPANY

Meert International with headquarters in Brussels was one of the world's leading producers of electrical and electronics equipment. From an original plant near Antwerp it had expanded its operations, frequently by acquisition, until in 1977 it had 58 plants in 22 countries and a total of over 100,000 employees including administration and staff.

Meert operated in a highly decentralized fashion. The central organization at Brussels made the major financial decisions regarding allocation of funds, methods of financing, dividends, etc., and the central staff also included experts in production, marketing, research, personnel and international law who were available to help local managers on request. However, the company was divided into a number of operating subsidiaries and within each subsidiary the Brussels management had delegated wide authority with little control from headquarters so long as the operation remained reasonably profitable. The system had worked well. Overhead headquarter costs were kept very low. Production and profits had expanded rapidly. Meert was proud of the quality of the managers it had developed.

THE INTERNATIONAL ELECTRICAL WORKERS FEDERATION

The International Electrical Workers Federation (IEWF) with headquarters in Geneva, Switzerland, was a loose confederation composed of national unions of electric and electronics workers. In 1977 it had 165 affiliated unions in 64 countries with aggregate membership of about 3 million. About 1/2 of the members were in Europe and 1/3 in North America.

IEWF was formed in 1902 by a number of the major European electrical workers unions. Originally it served primarily as a means of sharing information on wages, employee benefits, labor legislation, etc. However, from the very beginning it attempted to support new attempts at unionization and to gather funds for unions which faced financial difficulties because of strikes.

Although the basic authority of IEWF resided in its World Congress which met every four years, the actual work was carried out by the General Secretary, Conrad Kopp, and a small administrative staff which worked for him in Geneva. The national affiliated unions jealously guarded their autonomy and as a result IEWF had no control over their activities. It could not order them to strike or take any other action. It could only urge them to offer support to affiliates in need and suggest such action as might be appropriate.

In recent years as a result of the growth of multinational companies the affiliated unions had shown much greater interest in and support of IEWF than had been true earlier in its history. General Secretary Kopp had been successful in developing ongoing wage and financial studies of a number of the major companies in the industry. According to the companies the studies were well done and increasingly sophisticated. They provided the national electrical unions throughout the world with valuable financial, wage, and employee benefit information in each of the companies and between companies. These data were used effectively in contract bargaining.

Under Kopp's leadership IEWF had also established company councils which were made up of affiliated unions throughout the world which bargained with a particular company. The council members traded information and offered advice and support to each other. Kopp hoped that through the company councils IEWF would be able to meet and talk with the multinational companies regarding the labor problems in their various subsidiaries. However, to date, only one company had agreed to such meetings.

RELATIONS BETWEEN MEERT AND IEWF

Before 1969 IEWF made no direct contact with Meert management. In that year a strike occurred at one of the company's French plants. During the strike Kopp sent a telex to Paul Gemmil, Meert's Managing Director, stating that the French subsidiary was not dealing reasonably with the French unions and suggesting that "it might be desirous for us to consult together in order to bring about a mutually satisfactory settlement." However, the strike in France was settled by the French management and the French unions the next day and no further action was taken on Kopp's proposal by the company or IEWF.

During the succeeding three years, IEWF undertook an active program to enable it and its affiliates to deal more effectively with the large multinational electric and electronics companies, including Meert. With the help of its affiliates it gathered financial, wage, employee benefit, labor contract terms, and other information concerning Meert and its numerous subsidiaries. In 1972 this information was printed in a "confidential report" which IEWF sent to all of its members. The report was purely factual and contained no criticisms of Meert. The company was impressed with the extant of the information and its accuracy.

Further organizational effort on the part of IEWF resulted in the convening of a "Meert World Conference" in Amsterdam in April 1974 attended by 54 delegates from 19 countries. In addition to pledging the exchange of information and financial and other support to each other, the conference: created the "Meert World Council" consisting of 13 professional unionists to carry forward the Conference's objectives; established a confidential information bulletin to be issued periodically; and drew up the following list of specific demands which was sent to Paul Gemmil, Managing Director of Meert, along with a request for a meeting to discuss them and other matters of common interest.

IEWF Meert 1974 World Conference Demands For Meert Employees in Every Country

1. Full recognition and respect of trade union rights.
2. Advance information to unions on mergers, transfers, closings, rationalizations, layoffs, expansions, new plants, investments, dividends, etc.
3. Elimination of unfair wage policies
   a) no discrimination between unionized and non-unionized employees.
   b) no differentials due to age, sex, race or nationality.
4. Job security guarantees.
5. Consultation with trade unions before specific decisions affecting work forces of different countries.

Following receipt of the communication Gemmil called together his top management group to discuss the Conference's request for a meeting with him. Although all agreed that labor matters should be reserved for local negotiations, some were of the opinion that, if a sufficiently narrow agenda could be agreed upon in advance, such a meeting could do no harm and might result in better relations with the individual unions which made up the Conference. They pointed out that a few other multinational companies had held such meetings with representatives of International Trade Secretariats (ITSs) with apparently no undesirable results. Others on the management team opposed such a meeting, arguing that it was the opening wedge which IEWF would try to use to eventually achieve multinational bargaining which the nature of the demands clearly indicated was its ultimate goal. They pointed out that, although a few companies had acceded to such requests by their ITSs, most companies had politely refused to do so. It was simpler and easier to draw the line at this point, they contended, than to prevent a gradual movement toward multinational negotiations once discussions were undertaken.

After careful consideration Gemmil decided that the long term interest of the company would be served by agreeing to meet with the IEWF. A meeting was arranged for May 21, 1974 at the company's headquarters in Brussels. On that date Kopp accompanied by three other members of the Meert World Council met with Gemmil and three other members of the Meert management.

Gemmil opened the meeting by welcoming Kopp and the other IEWF representatives. He then stated that:

1. Meert was in favor of unions except where they followed political objectives opposed to free enterprise;

2. the decentralized structure of Meert did not allow headquarters to deal with working conditions of employees in the affiliated companies.

Kopp replied that IEWF was not trying to do the job of local unions or interfere with local negotiations but instead wanted only to deal with the central management of the company on certain general principles. He said the Meert Council was of the opinion that in the past the company had not made it clear to its subsidiaries that it did expect them to respect union rights and that it hoped the company would do so in the future. Gemmil replied that he was prepared to make appropriate recommendations to affiliates if this matter should become an issue.

Kopp said the Meert Council was also of the opinion that the comapny had not kept the union properly informed in advance on such matters as investment programs, plant closures, transfers, mergers and other company actions that would affect employees. Gemmil replied that the company could not give IEWF and the unions any more information than it provided to its stockholders. He said he would be happy to review the matter with a view to providing such information as could reasonably be given without harming the company. The meeting ended on a friendly note and Gemmil was of the opinion that the company's best interest had been served by developing this open relationship with the IEWF representatives.

THE SPANISH INCIDENT

In August 1974, three months after the meeting with the IEWF delegates at headquarters, Meert management announced its decision to construct a plant in Spain in collaboration with a Spanish company. Immediately following the announcement Gemmil received a letter from Kopp which read in part as follows:

> Through the press we have learned of your intention to build a plant in Spain. According to the news article this plant will make it possible for you to discontinue importing certain Meert products into Spain.
>
> Will you please inform us which Meert plants now export to Spain and will, therefore, be affected by this new plant and what steps will be taken to protect the workers in those plants.
>
> We want to inform you also that IEWF and the entire world labor movement is opposed to the Spanish dictatorship and its attitude toward unions. The legitimate Spanish leaders are either in jail or in exile. We strongly urge that Meert reconsider its decision to invest in this fascist country and instead use its capital to increase production by free workers represented by free unions.

Gemmil replied to the IEWF letter in part as follows:

> Your information is correct. Meert is planning to construct a plant in Spain. The present plants which will be affected significantly are the Belgian plant at Antwerp and the French plant at Bayonne. The company will take the necessary steps to see that employees in those plants who may be affected will be treated fairly in every way.
>
> The opening of a Spanish plant is something which the company has been forced to do to retain its share of the market in that country. We would have preferred to have continued to supply it from our French and Belgian plants where we already have ample capacity. However, we had no choice. Had we not agreed to build the new plant we would have lost the market to other companies who were willing and anxious to do so.
>
> Since we have had no plant in Spain we have had no actual experience on the social questions in that country. We are, of course, aware of the political regime which exists there. However, as you know, it has always been our policy not to become involved in the political problems of any country where we operate.

THE KOREAN INCIDENT

Meert had a plant in South Korea which supplied not only that country but produced sizeable quantities for export. The employees in the Korean plant were represented by the Korean Electrical Workers Union. In the fall of 1974 the company and the union were not able to reach agreement on a new labor contract and a strike resulted. However, after one week an agreement was reached and work was resumed. The union then demanded that the strikers be paid for the period they had been on strike, claiming discrimination because non-striking workers had been paid. When the management refused, the union workers stopped production and occupied the plant. The management appealed to the government which declared the strike illegal but the employees disregarded the order and continued to occupy the plant.

The Korean union then appealed to the IEWF which sent a telex to the Meert management at Brussels urging it to order the Korean subsidiary to "discontinue its discrimination against the union members." IEWF also urged its affiliates around the world to appeal to the Meert headquarters and to send financial help to the Korean union. To provide immediate on the spot help IEWF sent its General Secretary for Asia, Mr. Kisaka of Japan, to Korea.

In Korea Mr. Kisaka requested a meeting with the managing director of the Korean company. A meeting was arranged. However, the managing director refused to negotiate with Kisaka although indicating a willingness to talk with the local union leaders. Kisaka then went to the plant and spoke to the striking workers promising them support and financial aid. The managing director informed the government of Kisaka's actions, whereupon he was expelled from the country. The strike continued for another week at which time an agreement was reached whereby the employees returned to work but the company did not pay for any time that they had spent on strike.

IEWF was greatly disturbed by the treatment of its Asian General Secretary. It insisted that Meert central management was responsible. Telexes were sent to the Brussels headquarters not only by IEWF but by many of its affiliates throughout the world protesting "the company's action in having a legitimate union leader expelled from the country." The company denied any responsibility for the expelling of Kisaka, claiming it was entirely an action of the Korean government which the company had neither suggested nor approved. It stated, however, that management at the Korean plant had its support in refusing to negotiate with Kisaka but instead insisting on local negotiations. It reiterated its position that all labor matters should be negotiated by the local managers and the local unions without interference from either central company management or international union organizations.

Following the Korean incident IEWF adopted a very belligerent attitude toward Meert. No more meetings were requested. IEWF studies, publications and news releases used every opportunity to criticize the company and its activities. Management was of the opinion that any goodwill that may have been generated as a result of the meeting with IEWF representatives in May had been destroyed by the events in the fall in Korea. IEWF was now engaged in a "cold war" against the company.

THE U.S. INCIDENT

In 1952 Meert had purchased a small electronics company in United States, the Gener Corporation, with a plant at Waltham, Massachusetts. At time of purchase Gener had only 300 employees, 85 of whom were white collared including 55 engineers and technicians. The 160 hourly paid employees were represented by the Amalgamated Electrical Workers union (AEW) which had won a certification election at the plant in 1948.

Following the purchase by Meert production facilities at Waltham were rapidly expanded and by 1977 the plant had 1,500 employees, including 1,300 production workers. Relations between the company and AEW were excellent. There had never been a work stoppage of any kind and only two grievances had gone to arbitration. In 1966 Gener had agreed to a union shop clause with the AEW.

In 1968 Meert opened two new U.S. plants, one near Dayton, Ohio and one near San Francisco. Soon after the plants were opened the AEW won bargaining rights at each of them. In the first negotiations at each plant the company agreed to a union shop in return for certain concesssions made by the union. Union relations at both of these plants were very good. There had been no strikes or work stoppages.

In 1975 Meert purchased Carolina-Southern Electronics Inc. (CSE). CSE operated 4 plants in small towns in the southeastern area of U.S., two in South Carolina, one in Georgia and one in Mississippi. From its beginning in 1955 CSE had been a non-union operation and, despite active organizing campaigns by AEW during the 70s, it remained non-union. The union's activity had resulted in elections at one of the South Carolina plants and at the Georgia plant but in each case considerably less than one-half of the ballots had been for AEW (33% in South Carolina, 22% in Georgia).

During the organizing campaigns CSE management rigorously opposed unionization. It sent letters to the employees' homes, held meetings in the plants addressed by the president and other officers, and trained its supervisors to deal with questions regarding the union. Under American law the company had the right to oppose unionization so long as it did not discriminate, or threaten the employees, or promise them advantages for not joining the union. Throughout the campaign the company was careful to stay strictly within the law. Following each of its election defeats the union filed unfair labor practice charges against the company but in each case they were dismissed by the National Labor Relations Board.

After the purchase of CSE by Meert the union appealed to the IEWF for help in organizing CSE. IEWF responded by asking its affiliated unions to inform Meert of their opposition to CSE's action. As a result the company received 42 communications from unions asking it to order the local CSE management to discontinue its anti-union activities and to recognize and bargain with AEW. From its Geneva office IEWF sent a telex to the Managing Director of Meert which read in part:

> The local CSE management in U.S. continues to display extreme hostility to AEW union efforts to represent its employees. This is clearly in violation of what you have informed us is the policy of meert. We urge you to now implement your policy by ordering the CSE management to discontinue its anti-union activities and to accept the AEW as the representative of its employees.

IEWF then issued several press releases which condemned the "anti-union action of Meert in its southern U.S. plants." The President and the Secretary General of IEWF also telephoned the company headquarters and requested management to take action.

To all of these communications by IEWF and its affiliates the company replied that it was its firm policy and practice that labor relations should be dealt with at the local level by the associated or allied companies who alone had the necessary elements for evaluating the situations. The company refused to intervene in the CSE-AEW dispute.

MANAGEMENT REASSESSES ITS POSITION

During the winter of 1976-77 under Gemmil's guidance Meert management gave considerable thought as to how it should meet IEWF's new belligerent approach. IEWF was now issuing a "confidential information bulletin" every month. Whereas the early bulletins, which were published less frequently, were not highly critical of Meert's activities such was not the case with recent issues. The recent bulletins dealt not only with labor matters but with other aspects of the business and generally painted the company in a very unfavorable light. Meert management was continually subject to accusations of malintentions which were completely untrue. Gemmil wondered if management should disregard the bulletins or respond to them, perhaps by issuing bulletins of its own to its local managers or even to its employees.

IEWF was now supplying sophisticated information regarding wages, employee benefits, and other personnel information on all Meert subsidiaries to all of its union affiliates throughout the world. It was also advising local union leaders on how to bargain more effectively with local managers. Finally, the local union leaders knew that IEWF was prepared to launch strong campaigns of financial and other support for any union which became involved in a strike with a Meert subsidiary. Gemmil wondered if the company should be making an effort to train its local managers in labor relations and also to supply experts to advise them during negotiations.

At times some local managers had taken action in labor relations matters which had been embarrasssing to the Meert central management. Although Gemmil was very desirous of preserving local autonomy in labor relations, he wondered if headquarters should be exerting more leadership and guidance, at least with respect to general policies in the area.

As the management proceeded to discuss the above matters during the early months of 1977, it received copies of IEWF's January and February "Meert Confidential Bulletins." It was surprised to see that they were much less critical of the management than earlier bulletins. Gemmil also was informed by some friends in Geneva that Kopp had indicated to them that he would not be adverse to meeting with Meert management with the hope of improving relations. Gemmil had decided not to take the initiative but he wondered what his answer should be if Kopp should propose such a meeting.

SECTION VII

Negotiation Simulations

FERITE TOOL COMPANY

The 1977 collective bargaining agreement between the Ferite Tool Corporation and Local 1776 of the United Auto Workers expired on Friday, April 18, 1980. That agreement was the third contract negotiated by the parties since Ferite Tool had been acquired by Sembro-Rhodes, Inc., a multi-million dollar conglomerate. Ferite's plant was located in Gainswell, Indiana, some 15 to 20 miles from one of the centers of the mobile home industry and about 50 miles from several highly industrialized urban areas.

COMPANY HISTORY

-Early Years-

Ferite Tool Corporation was founded in 1930 in a suburb of East Chicago, Indiana. The company began as a relatively small, specialized machine shop operation for the production of metal cutting tools. The company's founder and sole owner was a hard-nosed German-Scot named Frederich Dietrich. As head of the company, Dietrich ruled with an iron hand. Only he gave orders, and he demanded that they be carried out quickly and without argument. He kept a close and constant watch on all operations. While his management style was strict, he was also a fair man and was not unreasonable in his demands.

Ferite began operating with about a dozen employees. Through Fred Dietrich's leadership, the company grew to a size of about 35-40 employees and remained at that level throughout the war years. Mr. Dietrich expressed little interest in tremendous growth, in fact he preferred a company that could provide him and his family with a comfortable living, but one that he could manage himself.

Shortly after the end of World War II, Fred Dietrich moved his company from the metropolitan East Chicago area some 50 miles away to the rural community of Gainswell. At the time of the move, practically all of the local inhabitants worked on farms in the area. As a result, there was a relative scarcity of skilled or even semi-skilled labor needed by a cutting tool company such as Ferite. Recognizing this, Mr. Dietrich brought five key personnel with him from East Chicago to Gainswell. These men were knowledgeable in the technology of the business. They could perform the required setup operations and, equally important, they trained the labor force in the skills necessary to operate efficiently. These men continued for quite some time to perform the more complex functions of the company, leaving the more routine operations to the new employees. This organization was maintained as a foundation for efficient operations for many years.

Fred Dietrich was very satisfied with his company's progress after the move. By the mid fifties Ferite had grown to approximately 120 employees, and had annual sales around $750,000. In

1956, however, Fred Dietrich became seriously ill and died. The major share of ownership of Ferite fell to his only son, Lester Dietrich.

-New Management-

Lester Dietrich, a graduate of Purdue University's engineering program, assumed the presidency of Ferite Tool Corporation in 1956. Les continued his father's policy of concentrating Ferite's energies on the production of high-speed cutting tools primarily used for thread cutting. Ferite produced only the perishable cutting tools, while many competitors produced tool holders as well as cutting tools. Competing firms specialized in one of five major types of tool holders and produced cutting tools compatible only with their particular holder. Ferite's product line included tools for use in any of the five distinct holders.

Ferite's success, attributable to a competitive price advantage and a wider product line than its competitors, had been realized without a formal marketing plan. However, for several years after Les took over the firm sales remained constant. In 1959, Mr. Robert Evans, a man familiar with Ferite and the industry, prevailed upon Les Dietrich to hire him as national sales manager. As a result of Mr. Evans' efforts, a national marketing plan was developed.

During the following years, Bob Evans gained some control over the business by assuming partial ownership as a result of provisions of his employment contract. Throughout the 1960s, Bob Evans was probably the individual most responsible for the company's growth. Sales by the end of the decade had increased substantially.

-New Ownership-

Early in 1970, Lester Dietrich sold the company to a large, diversified conglomerate. He notified employees of this change in ownership through the following notice which he had posted on the bulletin board.

> It is my pleasure to formally announce that Ferite Tool Corporation is now a division of Pembroke Tool Company, a subsidiary of Sembro-Rhodes, Inc. Ferite will continue to operate under its present management, manufacturing metal cutting tools as we do now. General future plans are for expansion of production facilities in this plant.
>
> This association holds a lot of promise for a bigger and brighter future for Ferite and all its employees. Sembro-Rhodes, Inc., our parent company, is a diversified manufacturer, providing products and services for the transportation, housing, education, and service industries.

Association with the multi-million dollar conglomerate, Sembro-Rhodes, held benefits for all. Les and other minor shareholders received shares of stock in the conglomerate; the plant benefited through investment by the parent company in machinery and inventory; employees were now part of a multi-million dollar enterprise.

The management team was retained to operate Ferite Tool. During this period, Sembro invested in new machinery and expansion of both plant and inventory. Employees' attention was drawn to the capital investments made by Sembro-Rhodes and such attention had an impact upon 1971 negotiations. The company's labor relations are described in the section below.

Les Dietrich's interest in the day-to-day management of Ferite Tool slacked off during the second year of the merger. As 1971 drew to a close, Les withdrew from active management and Bob Evans was appointed President of Ferite Tool by the Group Manager of Sembro-Rhodes Machine Tool Division.

LABOR-MANAGEMENT RELATIONS

During the formative years of the 1930s and throughout World War II, Ferite remained non-unionized. Much of the surrounding industry was being organized by the newly formed CIO labor organizations. In 1946, Ferite faced the prospect of itself becoming unionized for the first time. The UAW and Steelworkers had successfully organized the major auto and steel manufacturers and, following World War II, had begun to focus their attention on organizing smaller plants located near the major industrial centers. Before a serious attempt to organize Ferite could materialize, Fred Dietrich padlocked the door of the plant one Monday morning and announced that the plant was closed and would not reopen. In that same year (1946) he moved the entire operation to Gainswell, a small farming community about 50 miles from East Chicago. Mr. Dietrich found the rural setting much to his liking. The threat of unionization was as remote in these new surroundings as it was ever-present at the company's prior location. The new setting enabled Mr. Dietrich to raise horses and to live the life of a country gentleman. The plant site he selected included a small horse track which he used in pursuit of his hobby. To this day, the track is still found next to the company's plant.

Fred Dietrich substantially reduced the complement of employees when he reopened operations in the new plant. From 1946 until the mid 1950s, the company grew to about 120 employees, three times the level it had been prior to the relocation.

In this new location, Fred Dietrich treated his employees and the towns-people well. He advanced employees money for emergencies, provided loans for down payments, was generous at the holiday season, and made his facilities available for local functions (the horse track doubled as a fairgrounds). Mr. Dietrich's personal relationships with his employees, while paternalistic, were good, attested to, in part, by the complete absence of any attempt to organize during this period.

Following the father's death in 1956 and assumption of leadership by his son, Les, things began to change at Ferite. Les lacked much of the personal interest in the company that his father had had before him. His interests as an engineer were concentrated in the technical side of the business. He began a program of "modernization" designed to make operations faster and cheaper, while producing a better quality product. He expended large sums of money on new tooling. Most of his time was spent at the drawing board, and he virtually refused to become involved in the day-to-day operations of the company. His relationship to Ferite and to the employees was not at all like that of his father. Whereas Fred had been most generous to the employees, if Les were asked for a loan, he would graciously point the way to the local bank. He dictated policy, but found it nearly impossible to relate to those implementing his orders. Management of the shop was left to two individuals who had moved with his father from East Chicago. Lacking the strong guiding hand of the founder, however, shop management began to play favorites; raises and promotions became a largely personal process. Performance mattered little when raises were given - who you played poker with was much more important. Management-employee relations became strained in the late 1950s.

Throughout the decade of the '50s, the mobile home industry had been growing up in nearby Elkhart and in the '60s was successfully unionized by the UAW. The union established a local in the vicinity and a drive to organize the smaller businesses in the area was undertaken. Les Dietrich hired a new plant manager for Ferite to try to alleviate some of the employee problems. This man's tenure was short lived, increasing rather than easing tension. He was succeeded by several others, who remained on the job for comparable lengths of time.

In 1960, Bob Evans, who was becoming more influential in the operations of the company, prevailed upon Les to hire his (Bob's) father, R.T. Evans, Sr., as plant manager. RT, as he was known in the plant, did much to increase worker morale, including the establishment of a rationalized wage structure, relating wages more to duties than to friendships. Largely as a result of his efforts, a representation election that took place in 1963 resulted in defeat of the UAW. At that time, however, RT was forced to take a leave of absence from Ferite because of family illness in the East. When he left, Les Dietrich once more assumed the role of plant manager. Again, morale began to deteriorate.

During this same period, Ferite Tool experienced a new wave of growing pains. Due to the effots of Bob Evans, sales began to rise significantly with concurrent increases in employment. Together with the personnel situation at the company, the employees felt they no longer could afford to stand still. In 1964, there was another union election and Local 1776 of the UAW became the bargaining agent for Ferite employees. Les Dietrich felt that this was the beginning of the end, something his father never would have accepted. Mr. Evans saw this development as an inevitable one, and felt that Ferite had to learn to live with the union on a cooperative basis.

The parties' first agreement was negotiated for a period of one year and expired on April 23, 1965. Reaching agreement on the second contract which covered a three-year period presented few difficulties. Negotiations were carried out on a relatively informal basis, taking into account local conditions and values. For example, working hours were arranged so that employees would have sufficient time to tend to necessary chores on their farms. The parties negotiated their third contract in 1968, again covering a three-year period. While the agreement was ratified, the employees did not return to work until after a work stoppage lasting approximately one week.

The 1971 negotiations took on a much different character. Ferite Tool had become part of Sembro-Rhodes, Inc., a multi-million dollar conglomerate. Employees could not help but notice the differential between Ferite's rates and those negotiated in the fall of 1970 at Pembroke Tool Company, another Sembro-Rhodes company. Investment in inventory and new machinery at Ferite was also visible to bargaining unit members. At the same time, the machine tool and metal cutting tool industry began to experience severe problems. Negotiations started in early 1971 in anticipation of major problems. The parties remained far apart as the April 23rd expiration date approached. They agreed to a statement regarding retroactivity and a two-week extension with day-to-day extensions beyond the two-week period. Negotiations and contract extensions continued through Memorial Day but shortly thereafter the employees struck at Ferite. The strike was finally settled in the first week of August, just prior to the wage-price freeze imposed by President Nixon. Company and union representatives executed a three-year agreement expiring April 22, 1974.

Relations were a bit strained after the lengthy strike. Bob Evans assumed the reins at Ferite in late 1971 and initiated what he believed to be a realistic approach to management-union-employee relations. Negotiation of the parties' sixth agreement was accomplished without a strike and resulted in a contract covering the three-year period April 22, 1974 - April 22, 1977. Pembroke Tool Company, whose contract with UAW Local 162 expired April 7, 1974, was out on strike at the time the Ferite agreement was executed. Again, in 1977, the parties agreed to a new three-year contract without a strike.

On February 15, 1980, Local 1776 sent notice to the company in accordance with Article XVI of their agreement. In March, Bob Evans and his management team were preparing for the upcoming negotiations. He knew the President of Local 1776, Ray Haskell, well. May Bauman and LeRoy McSweeney had also been officers of the local and members of the union negotiating committee since the initial contract. Two new members of the union, not known by Bob, had been elected to the committee. He reflected on prior negotiations and wondered how this one would come out.

OAKLAND MANUFACTURING CORPORATION

In February of 1981 Local 421 of the United Auto Workers (UAW) notified Oakland Manufacturing Corporation (OMC) that the local wished to renegotiate the parties' collective bargaining agreement which was due to expire on Friday, April 24, 1981. The company's Personnel Manager, Mr. Robert Hills, was hired in late 1978, a few months after that agreement had been negotiated. Although he had delt with the union President, J. J. Shaver, during the last two years over grievances and other labor-management problems, the renegotiation of the agreement would constitute their first encounter across the bargaining table. They each set about preparing with their respective bargaining committees for these important negotiations.

I. COMPANY HISTORY

Oakland Manufacturing Corporation was founded in 1915 in Battle Creek, Michigan to machine parts for various industries including the young automotive industry. OMC was acquired by Precision Motor Parts in 1927 after which it began to specialize in machining camshafts. A midwestern company purchased OMC in 1931 and continued ownership until 1952 when the firm was bought by an individual investor, Mr. R. J. Phillips, who took over as President of the firm.

During the early 1960s Oakland purchased some other, unrelated businesses in an attempt to emulate the successful conglomorates of the day. These moves soon proved financially disasteous. Bankruptcy proceedings began in 1965 and continued until a plan for reorganization was approved four years later. Hayworth-Clarke, a Connecticut-based corporation which had been OMC's principle supplier, accepted its bankruptcy settlement in the form of OMC stock. It acquired, through the settlement, a one-third interest in Oakland. The remaining two-thirds was purchased by a syndicate comprised of local businessmen headed by Mr. Phillips. In 1973 local interests decided to liquidate their holdings and Hayworth-Clarke made a tender offer for the available shares. The tender offer was accepted and Hayworth-Clarke assumed full ownership.

After Hayworth-Clarke took over the management of Oakland in 1973, Mr. Paul Richardson was appointed Vice-President and General Manager. R. J. Phillips continued to hold the position of President but he did not participate in the day-to-day management of the firm. He retired fully in 1980. That same year Paul Richardson was promoted to head up Hayworth-Clarke's entire midwest operations. This new position required Paul to spend more and more time at other locations and Jerry Sadat, Plant Manager, assumed responsibility for many of the daily operations at OMC. However, all major decisions continued to be made by Hayworth-Clarke through Mr. Richardson.

Oakland Manufacturing Corporation was one of the larger employers in the Battle Creek area, where many of the major companies were controlled by outside organizations. OMC's production facilities and product lines have been subject to some changes over the years. In 1971 OMC opened its second plant three miles away from its original Battle Creek location. At the time the original plant was over sixty years old and in poor condition. The second plant, Plant #2, was expanded in 1978 and in 1979 all operations were consolidated in Plant #2. In November 1980 Oakland introduced a new, numerically-controlled machine tool to its production facilities and announced its intention to introduce additional machines begining in the summer of 1981.

Prior to World War II, OMC had specialized in machining camshafts for the automobile industry. Automobile production ceased during the war and OMC shifted to the machining of parts for military engines and industrial diesel engines. Following the war, Oakland returned to the machining of camshafts, primarily for desiel engine manufacturers in the automotive and heavy-duty vehicle industries. Sales of OMC products were made to approximately six major customers with giant Turbo-Diesel by far its largest customer. Management was quick to point out that, in addition to foreign competition, their customers were potentially their biggest competitors. If Oakland's price became prohibitive, delivery poor, or quality unacceptable, the firm's customers could embark upon camshaft machining themselves.

II. LABOR-MANAGEMENT RELATIONS

Oakland Manufacturing had been engaged in collective bargaining for many years. Local 421 of the United Auto Workers was certified by the National Labor Relations Board in the early 1940s. Although the only contract negotiation strike against Oakland occurred over twenty years ago and lasted only four days, it would be remiss to assume that relationships have been overly cozy. Mr. Phillips used to characterize the parties relationship as one of "mutual respect and competition with a degree of cordiality."

Initially the union's leadership was composed of older employees. However, over the years younger workers have moved into leadership positions. Local 421's President, J. J. Shaver, at 350 pounds, has carried much weight withih the company. Shaver, 41 years old and the son of an OMC retiree, was initially hired as an employee in 1960. He has been the union President since 1971, and was a member of the union's bargaining team for the last three negotiations.

J. J. Shaver has been a great soapbox orator, embellishing his speaches with earthy analogies. He also has been an astute politician. His political savvy has been demonstrated by his scheduling of union elections to coincide with contract negotiations. He has pointed out to the membership, on more than one occasion, that it would be unwise to change the union's helmsman in the midst of a negotiating storm. JJ has fought hard for members of his local, including those who have already retired. Almost all grievances have been processed vigorously.

He has spent a good deal of time cultivating rank and file support, devoting much of his workday to union business. Oakland management has acknowledged, if reluctantly, that no member of management understands the contract as well as JJ.

During the late 1960s Battle Creek, like many American cities with a black population, experienced some racial unrest. OMC was not immune to the racial tension of the city. One racial incident actually resulted in the closing of the plant to allow a cooling off period of a few days. The last decade has benefited from an improvement in race relations within the city and Oakland's has established an affirmative action program. This has resulted in a slight decrease in the number of family relationships among bargaining unit members. However, close to fifty percent of the unit remain related, by either blood or marriage, to at least one other member of the workforce. Three years ago union members elected, for the first time, a black member to serve as Vice President.

Wages at OMC had been quite low prior to Hayworth-Clarke assuming control. This had contributed to the "country club" atmosphere which prevailed prior to the 1975 negotiations. Management's lack of control over the operartion was due to a number of factors. The company was not able to attract and retain the best workers due to the low wages. Union members often refused to follow orders, with no disciplinary action taken by management. Management had developed a defeatest attitude which contributed to the problem. They felt overwhelmed by the strength of the union and did not know how to respond. A past practices clause in the contract helped to perpetuate the "country club" environment.

Faced with this situation when it took control of OMC in 1973, Hayworth-Clarke established three management objectives:

> To regain managerial control of the plants.
>
> To tie increased wages to increased productivity.
>
> To establish a solid no-strike clause.

III. 1975 - A CHANGE IN DIRECTION

Two years after taking control of OMC, Hayworth-Clarke was at the bargaining table negotiating a contract with Local 421. In an effort to attain the goals it had established, Hayworth-Clarke brought in a tean of industrial engineers from one of their other operations to negotiate their first agreement with the UAW. The company traded higher wages for increased management rights in an attempt to end the lax working conditions. Oakland gave the employees a substantial wage increase, although some employees may have disagreed as to the amount of the increase. In return, OMC instituted an incentive plan, the Engineered Work Standards Plan; obtained a clause prohibiting strikes on almost all issues; eliminated the past practices clause; and acquired generally stronger management rights. Negotiation of the 1975 contract had not been an easy matter, there had been many, many negotiating sessions and the agreement was rejected on the first vote of the union membership.

Increased productivity and the end of a temporary peak in production resulted in the layoff of over two hundred hourly employees in 1975 and early 1976. Anticipation of these layoffs may have accounted for the initial rejection of the parties' tentative agreement. As a result of the layoffs the work force had dropped from about 650 to 420 employees.

Approximately half of the hourly-rated employees were covered by Engineered Work Standards. The standards had been developed for individual jobs, for a group of jobs or for part of an entire production line. Industrial engineering methods, as set out in the Engineered Work Standards Manual, were used to determine the time it took a qualified operator to perform a specific operation or operations. While the incentive system resulted in higher earnings, employees did not realize the substantial earnings expected in the first year or so due to certain changes in the diesel industry. By 1977 OMC had started to get a handle on the problems resulting from these changes and many incentive employees began to earn large pay checks for their increased efforts.

IV. THE 1978 NEGOTIATIONS

The 1978 OMC-Local 421 negotiations proved less than satisfactory to both sides for a number of reasons. The company did not have the benefit of the experience and skill of those who had played a major role in the 1975 negotiations. The company's entire negotiating team had been killed in the unfortunate crash of the Hayworth-Clarke company plane shortly after conclusion of the 1975 negotiations. OMC's new Personnel Manager, Mr. James Smithe, headed the 1978 negotiating team. Although a qualified individual, this was Jim's first experience in contract negotiations. He and JJ had many heated exchanges during the course of negotiations, some because of their strong personalities, others because of the firm positions taken by each side on certain issues.

Throughout negotiations Local 421 took the position that any multi-year contract had to contain annual wage increases and an unlimited cost of living allowance (COLA). Management was equally adamant in its opposition to including an increase each year together with an expensive, unlimited COLA. Smithe insisted that any COLA clause had to include a cap. The union did not even wish to discuss the possibility of a cap on their COLA. While the parties differed on many other issues, including more flexible use of skilled workers, extent of incentive coverage, pension improvements and a past practices clause, wage protection and the length of the contract remained at the center of their dispute.

The company was steadfast in its refusal to discuss pension improvements. In 1975 the parties had agreed to a six-year pension agreement which was to span two contract negotiations, 1975 through 1981. The union attempted to obtain some improvements in 1978 but management would not discuss the matter because of the six-year pension agreement. The union finally dropped their demand for improvements in 1978.

The wage issue was finally resolved when, realizing that JJ and the other union representatives would not agree to a multi-year contract which included a cap on COLA, management agreed to drop its insistence on a cap. In exchange management obtained the union's agreement to update the consumer price index used in the calculation of the quarterly COLA adjustments. This breakthrough, together with some other improvements in wages and benefits, resulted in the union representatives agreeing to take management's offer to the rank and file for a vote. The union recommended neither acceptance nor rejection. The company also announced at this time the expansion of the more modern Plant #2. The union membership accepted management's offer by a slim margin on the afternoon of April 21, 1978, thereby averting a strike.

V. THE 1981 NEGOTIATIONS

In the fall of 1979 management closed the old plant, Plant #1, and consolidated all production and office operations in the expanded Plant #2. This resulted in some layoffs of junior, low skilled employees. Additional layoffs were caused during the term of the 1978 agreement due to a slight downturn in business. Management was somewhat concerned with foreign competition. Imported camshafts of a quality superior to OMC's products were being purchased by some of OMC's customers. Management was convinced quality had to be improved.

In order to improve quality and become more competitive, Oakland embarked upon a Capital Equipment Program. The first new, numerically controlled milling machine was introduced into the plant in November 1980. The company had a number of meetings, not only with union officials but with the employees as well, and explained their plan to modernize production machines and equipment. The program would have its major impact during the term of the next agreement.

In early 1980 OMC instituted a Point System to control absenteeism. The system involved the accumulation of points for unexcused absences or tardiness in reporting for work. The accumulation of nine (9) points by an employee resulted in an automatic suspension, whereas twelve (12) points resulted in discharge. Without doubt the Point System has been as effective in reducing absenteeism as it has been in generating the animosity of employees. When it installed the program management contended that the Point System was a management policy and not subject to negotiation under the National Labor Relations Act. Management was also aware that the union had received numerous demands for the elimination of what the members viewed as a draconic, oppressive system.

Jim Smithe had resigned from OMC in 1979 in order to join his family's business. Robert Hills had been hired to replace Jim and it was Hills who would head the company's negotiating team for the 1981 negotiations. Bob Hills was 34 years old, had been trained as an engineer but had moved into labor relations with his former employer. Bob had participated in two rounds of negotiations as a member of the negotiating committee of a Fortune 500 company. The UAW had also represented those employees. The 1981 negotiations would be Bob's first negotiations as Oakland's chief spokesman.

Bob was a bit concerned with the recent increase in grievances. Traditionally the grievance rate had been fairly low but constant. However, in recent weeks he sensed a spurt in the number filed and it seemed that the union was more reluctant than ever to settle pending disputes. On Tuesday, March 17th, he was faced with a more pressing problem. The entire second shift walked off the job in a wildcat strike in order to press a demand for a full-time nurse on the second shift. While each employee who participated in the walkout received a one day suspension (paper penalty) the company did hire a nurse for the second shift.

Bob reviewed the union's sixty day notice which indicated that it wished to renegotiate the 1978 agreement. He was aware that the union membership had passed a resolution of No Contract - No Work. Bob also knew JJ was under pressure from certain groups within the local. He also wondered what effect the elimination of the government's wage-price program would have on this round of negotiations.

In starting to prepare for the 1981 contract negotiations, each side attempted to evaluate those they would soon face across the bargaining table. They also began to get to know their own team members and to research the demands they intended to put on the bargaining agenda.

ALPHABETICAL LISTING OF CASES